Redressing Rape in War

Redressing Rape in War

A Medico-Legal Approach to Sexual Violence

SUNNEVA GILMORE

OXFORD
UNIVERSITY PRESS

OXFORD
UNIVERSITY PRESS

Great Clarendon Street, Oxford, OX2 6DP,
United Kingdom

Oxford University Press is a department of the University of Oxford.
It furthers the University's objective of excellence in research, scholarship,
and education by publishing worldwide. Oxford is a registered trade mark of
Oxford University Press in the UK and in certain other countries.

Published in the United States of America by Oxford University Press
198 Madison Avenue, New York, NY 10016, United States of America.

British Library Cataloguing in Publication Data
Data available

Library of Congress Control Number: 2025948265

ISBN 9780198919704

DOI: 10.1093/9780198919735.001.0001

Printed and bound by
CPI Group (UK) Ltd., Croydon, CR0 4YY

MIX
Paper | Supporting
responsible forestry
FSC® C013604

The manufacturer's authorised representative in the EU for product safety is
Oxford University Press España S.A. of Parque Empresarial San Fernando de Henares,
Avenida de Castilla, 2–28830 Madrid (www.oup.es/en or product.safety@oup.com).
OUP España S.A. also acts as importer into Spain of products made by the manufacturer.

For Leif & Hugo

Acknowledgements

This book has been a long project punctuated by COVID-19 as well as other life and work commitments. Drawing inspiration from my PhD research on reparations for conflict-related sexual violence (CRSV) and my experiences as a medical practitioner, I aimed to create a book that reflects the complex realities of CRSV while offering hope and innovative ideas for reparations. My goal was to present reparations not just as a means of justice, but as one pathway towards meaningful repair and measures to prevent recurrence. Throughout the writing process, I was mindful of the growing global focus on CRSV. While acknowledging this attention, I sought to challenge the often sensationalist narratives around CRSV and reparations and to propose thoughtful, forward-looking approaches. I also hope this book serves as a tribute to the many inspirational individuals who quietly navigate complex challenges, often away from the spotlight, and deserve recognition and appreciation.

Since completing my PhD, I have been fortunate to work on reparations at both international and national levels while continuing to enhance my expertise in sexual and reproductive health. I am deeply grateful for the opportunities to contribute to the International Criminal Court's work on the *Ntaganda* case and to the Victims' Payments Board in Northern Ireland. These experiences have offered invaluable insights into the multifaceted frameworks required to deliver reparations and assistance to victims and survivors of mass crimes including sexual violence. They have also allowed me to refine my medico-legal approach by bridging theoretical concepts with the practicalities of designing, claiming, and implementing reparations. Anything stated in this book is my personal view and does not reflect any of the institutions I have worked for or currently work for.

I hope this book proves useful and accessible to everyone committed to delivering meaningful justice to victims of grave violations, especially those affected by conflict-related sexual violence. Whether you are a victim, healthcare practitioner, work in transitional justice, or a member of the public, I trust you will find relevance in these pages.

I am thankful to my two PhD supervisors Kieran McEvoy and Rachel Killean for their guidance and support. Thanks also to Amrei Muller, who provided secondary supervision for part of the PhD, as well as Kevin Brown, Clare Patton, Amanda Kramer, and Brian Jack who read over extracts of my work and provided helpful feedback. My PhD was kindly funded by the Department for the Economy and some of my travel was supported by the Emily Sarah Montgomery Travel Scholarship. I was fortunate to work alongside members of the Reparations,

Responsibility and Victimhood in Transitional Societies project team; conversations with Clara Sandoval, Cheryl Lawther, Luke Moffett, James Gallen, and Peter Dixon were enriching to this project. I am particularly grateful for being able to work closely with Clara Sandoval and Julie Guillerot, who also helped support my fieldwork in Colombia and Peru and encouraged me to develop my own perspective on reparations. I am also indebted to Susan Burton in the School of Law for her administrative insights and support during my PhD. In addition, thanks to Heather Kinning for her assistance in the School of Law.

Many thanks to my interviewees who took the time to talk to me about reparations and sexual violence. In Uganda, thanks to John Ogony, Women's Advocacy Network, AYIRA, and AYINET for facilitating interviews and focus groups. I would also like to thank Melissa Wong Oviedo for translation and the Peruvian Coordinadora Nacional de Derechos Humanos for facilitating and providing space for my fieldwork in Peru. In Colombia, many thanks to Alejandra Muñoz Solano who facilitated numerous interviews in Colombia. I am especially thankful to Red de Mujeres Victimsas y Profesionales and in particular Angela Maria Escobar Vuisquez as well as Women's Link, Sisma Mujer, Pilar Reuda, and Tatiana Olarte. I have also been fortunate to have had many productive interactions with the team at Physicians for Human Rights and in particular I extend my thanks to Susannah Sirkin and Karen Naimer. I am also thankful for all the enriching discussions with my colleagues on the Walter and Patricia Rodney Commission on Reparations.

My heartfelt gratitude to the victims and survivors who spoke to me during my fieldwork. I have been lucky enough to meet some of them subsequently and continue our conversations and collaboration. Their courage and resilience continue to inspire me. I am also deeply appreciative of the victims and survivors I have had the privilege to care for in my medical practice; their bravery is manifested in countless ways.

The book would not have been possible without the steadfast encouragement of Mary Murnaghan who supported my research interests and believed in my proposed interdisciplinary focus of reparations many years ago, despite falling outside the typical medical career pathway. I am grateful to the School of Obstetrics and Gynaecology in Northern Ireland for granting me the flexibility to pursue research and work in law. I am appreciative of the Professional Support Unit at Northern Ireland Medical and Dental Training Agency, especially Camille Harron, for her open-mindedness and conversations about alternative medical career paths.

I owe a heartfelt thanks to Diarmuid O'Donovan who has provided continuous encouragement and support for my research and work on global health throughout the years. The greatest thanks to Maria Lohan who warmly welcomed me back into academia after a hiatus, seeing value in my ideas and always making time. I am equally grateful to Mike Clarke for his thoughtful advice and guidance in refining my research proposals, as well as to Fionnuala Ní Aoláin for her insightful mentorship in the development of my research. I also extend my thanks to

Queen's University Faculty of Medicine, Health, and Life Sciences for supporting my interdisciplinary work.

Special thanks go to the Daphne Jackson Trust, especially Katie Perry and my advisor Sally Bolton, whose patience and progressive support for researchers balancing multiple responsibilities have been both refreshing and inspiring. My deepest appreciation extends to the team at Oxford University Press, including Lindsay Glick, Robert Cavooris, and Rizwaan Ahmad, for their dedication and professionalism throughout the editing process.

I am particularly thankful to Olive Buckley for her lifelong dedication to providing holistic, victim-centred care for those affected by sexual violence. Her advocacy for victims and her gentle support and nurturing for colleagues remain a constant source of inspiration. I also deeply value the training and experience I received at Northern Ireland's Sexual Assault Regional Centre and the support of the health and social care trust where I work. My thanks to Caroline Hunter for her invaluable training and mentorship in psychosexual medicine. To my sexual and reproductive health colleagues in Northern Ireland, I am grateful for your contribution in ensuring sexual and reproductive health rights are not only realized but fulfilled. A special mention to Siobhan Kirk and Hans Nagar, who, early in my career, saw the potential in my unconventional approach which places sexual and reproductive health at the heart of all my endeavours, whether clinical or academic. I also extend thanks to everyone who has contributed to my growth in obstetrics and gynaecology, sexual and reproductive healthcare, and law.

Several ideas and outputs related to this book were presented at conferences, including the Law and Society Association, Historical Dialogues, Justice and Memory Network, the Lancet, Colombia's Ministry of Health, and QUB Human Rights Centre. I also presented at workshops with the United Nations OHCHR and IOM and would like to acknowledge the work of Igor and Sandra. I am appreciative to all those who listened and provided comments. I would like to express my thanks to Jelke Boesten and Carla Ferstman who provided support to myself and other researchers at an early careers workshop.

Special thanks to Susan, Heather, Thomas, Sonya, Donna, Oonagh, Frida, and Michele for their support, which enabled my time on this book to be productive and fulfilling. I am thankful to Mary Espie for her consistent support and engaging chats. I appreciate the compassionate care I received from Laura Doherty and the team. My gratitude also goes to Dave Chatoor for his invaluable support in navigating physical challenges and for creating innovative paths that allow me to continue my work.

My heartfelt thanks to Thierry Marteaux for his words of wisdom and advice throughout the writing of this book. I would like to thank my PhD examiners Brandon Hamber and Eithne Dowds for such a robust engagement with my work and an enriching viva.

Finally, I am deeply appreciative of the unwavering support of my family and closest friends who kept me fuelled with coffee, treats, and emotional care during this demanding journey. To my parents, Carmel and Colm—thank you for your enduring love and encouragement. Thanks to my siblings, especially Aisling, for your interest in my work and your commitment to advancing girls' education. I am forever grateful to Maria and Joe for their care and guidance as I grew up, and to Valerie and Stanley for their steadfast support.

In particular, I want to acknowledge and deeply thank Luke, my companion through life's journey, whose belief in my work, unwavering faith, and constant encouragement have been vital. This book would not have been possible without him.

I dedicate this book to Leif and Hugo; our two brilliant and joyous children. They remind me daily of all the wondrous and beautiful chaos in this world. They are responsible for instilling a fierce tenderness in me and for driving me forward on issues that are close to my heart.

Contents

1

Introduction: Redressing Sexual Violence in Conflict

Sexual violence has long been considered an integral feature of war and political violence.[1] It remains pervasive in a range of ongoing conflicts in Sudan,[2] Colombia,[3] the Democratic Republic of Congo,[4] Syria,[5] and Ukraine.[6] Over the past decade there have been increased efforts to tackle conflict-related sexual violence (CRSV) and its consequences. These have included the establishment of a special representative of the United Nations (UN) Secretary General on this issue, a range of resolutions from different elements of the UN including the Security Council, and several prominent prosecutions at different international tribunals including the International Criminal Court (ICC). Notwithstanding these efforts, rape and other sexual and reproductive violence continue unabated.

Despite the historic prevalence of sexual violence during wartime, until relatively recently the issue did not significantly feature in post-conflict reparations programmes. For example, the Nepalese reparations programme established after the peace agreement in 2006 has been widely condemned for failing to address the issue and a similar omission was only addressed in Kosovo following significant international pressure and demands from victims.[7] As explored in this book, there is a growing body of literature on reparations for conflict-related sexual violence.[8]

[1] Maria Eriksson Baaz and Maria Stern, *Sexual Violence as a Weapon of War? Perceptions, Prescriptions, Problems in the Congo and Beyond*, Zed Books (2013) p1; and Conflict-related Sexual Violence, Report of the UN Secretary General, S/2019/280, 29 March 2019, para 2.

[2] Fred Harter, Women in Sudan Facing a 'Tragedy' of Sexual Violence as Rape Cases Rise, *The Guardian*, 29 August 2023.

[3] There were 668 CRSV incidents reported in 2023, see Conflict-Related Sexual Violence Report of the Secretary-General, S/2024/292, April 2024, p20.

[4] There were 733 cases of CRSV reported in the Democratic Republic of Congo in 2023, ibid, para 32

[5] At least 30 women and girls were raped by one armed group at a detention facility in February 2020, see Report of the Independent International Commission of Inquiry on the Syrian Arab Republic, A/HRC/45/31, 14 August 2020, para 61.

[6] Ivana Kottasová and Olga Voitovych, Survivors Say Russia is Waging a War of Sexual Violence in Occupied Areas of Ukraine. Men are Often the Victims, CNN, 30 May 2024.

[7] Victims of CRSV were not recognized as a specific category under the 2011 law (No 04/L-054). The 2014 amendment adds them as a specific victim category (Law No 04/L-172). See Across the Lines: The Impact of Nepal's Conflict on Women, Advocacy Forum and International Center for Transitional Justice, 2010. UN Women, The Conflict did not bring us Flowers: The Need for Comprehensive Reparations for Survivors of Conflict-Related Sexual Violence in Kosovo, United Nations Entity for Gender Equality and the Empowerment of Women, 2016.

[8] See Ruth Rubio-Marín, *The Gender of Reparations: Unsettling Sexual Hierarchies*, CUP (2009); Fionnuala Ní Aoláin, Catherine O'Rourke, and Aisling Swaine, Transforming Reparations for Conflict-Related Sexual Violence: Principles and Practice, *Harvard Human Rights Journal* 28(1) (2015) 95–144;

Redressing Rape in War. Sunneva Gilmore, Oxford University Press. © Sunneva Gilmore 2026.
DOI: 10.1093/9780198919735.003.0001

However, I argue that such analysis remains siloed in relevant fields. There is too little crossover between the social science and medical understandings of harm and legal developments on reparation for victims of CRSV. In particular, I draw upon my own experience as a medical practitioner and seek to marry it with a socio-legal understanding of both harm and reparations in this area.

The book is informed by semi-structured interviews in three sites (Colombia, Peru, and Uganda) with victims of CRSV, transitional justice practitioners, and medical professionals as well as practice as a forensic and sexual and reproductive health doctor, in addition to my role in reparations processes at the international and domestic level. I argue that a more transdisciplinary approach is needed that draws from different disciplines and practical expertise to fully understand the harm and the means to remedy CRSV. Taking this approach provides a more detailed analysis of the consequences of sexual violence and encourages a more nuanced understanding of what contribution reparations make in redressing CRSV. Before diving into the substance of my discussion it is worth setting out some parameters of CRSV that frame the issue of redressing rape in war, prior to discussing my approach and the layout of this book.

1.1 Conflict-Related Sexual Violence

Understandably, considerable international attention is paid to CRSV and 'rape as a weapon of war'. Sexual violence can be part of a strategy to attack the 'enemy' community,[9] upset conjugal or communal norms,[10] or achieve other strategic goals.[11] It can also be used to build social cohesion amongst combatants,[12] reflect a social construction of masculinities,[13] be tolerated due to social interactions,[14]

Ruth Rubio-Marín and Clara Sandoval, Engendering the Reparations Jurisprudence of the Inter-American Court of Human Rights: The Promise of the Cotton Field Judgment, *Human Rights Quarterly* 33 (2011) 1062–1091; and Philipp Schulz, *Male Survivors of Wartime Sexual Violence, Perspectives from Northern Uganda*, California University Press (2020).

[9] Shana Swiss and Joan Giller, Rape as a Crime of War: A Medical Perspective, *Journal of the American Medical Association* 270(5) (1993) 612–615, p613.

[10] Megan H MacKenzie, *Female Soldiers in Sierra Leone: Sex, Security and Post-Conflict Development*, New York University Press (2012) p100.

[11] Elisabeth Jean Wood, Variation in Sexual Violence during War, *Politics and Society* 34(3) (2006) 307–342.

[12] Dara Kay Cohen, The Ties That bind: How Armed Groups Use Violence to Socialize Fighters, *Journal of Peace Research* 54(5) (2017) 701–714.

[13] Chris Coulter, *Bush Wives and Girl Soldiers: Women's Lives through War and Peace in Sierra Leone*, Cornell University Press (2009) pp133–134; and Sara Meger, Rape of the Congo: Understanding Sexual Violence in the Conflict in the Democratic Republic of Congo, *Journal of Contemporary African Studies*, 28(2) (2010) 119–135.

[14] Elisabeth Jean Wood, Conflict-Related Sexual Violence and the Policy Implications of Recent Research, *International Review of the Red Cross* 96(894) (2014) 457–478, p471.

function as entertainment, individual or group pleasure, or be used to resolve community disputes.[15] In addition, political conflict can also lead to opportunistic sexual and gender-based violence by intimate partners or family members.[16] Feminist scholarship in international relations and law has for a long time underscored gender-based and sexual violence that is committed not only during wartime by arms-carriers, but also within homes during a breakdown in law and order, transitions to peace, and fragile transitional environments.[17] So, to speak of 'conflict-related' sexual violence is a concept with fuzzy parameters. For the purposes of this book, sexual violence is 'conflict-related' due to it occurring during a period of armed conflict, whether by armed-carriers or civilians, who use violence or exploit the insecure environment to carry out violations of a sexual nature.

Much of the analysis of conflict-related sexual violence concentrates on women and girls. Although work is ongoing to improve awareness of sexual violence to men, boys, and other gender identities, common themes in the literature include the importance of 'power and dominance'[18] and the construction of violent masculine identities[19] as well as sexuality, sexual gratification, and opportunism.[20] While this book is primarily concerned with the consequences rather than the aetiology of CRSV, all of these themes permeate the discussion below. Given my own background in obstetrics and gynaecology, I framed my research on the impact of CRSV mostly on women and girls, but I do make reference to male victims at times through this book.

With regard to terminology, the World Health Organization defines sexual violence as:

> any sexual act, attempt to obtain a sexual act, unwanted sexual comments or advances, or acts to traffic, or otherwise directed, against a person's sexuality using coercion, by any person regardless of their relationship to the victim, in any setting, including but not limited to home and work.[21]

[15] Jelke Boesten, Analyzing Rape Regimes at the Interface of War and Peace in Peru, *International Journal of Transitional Justice* 4(1) (2010) 110–129, p127; and Sexual Violence Patterns, Causes, and Possible Solutions: An Interview with Julienne Lusenge, Solidarité Féminine pour la Paix Intégral (SOFEPADI), Democratic Republic of Congo, in Doris Buss, Joanne Lebert, Blair Rutherford, Donna Sharkey and Obijio Aginam (eds) *Sexual Violence in Conflict and Post-Conflict Societies: International Agendas and African Contexts*, Routledge (2014) 58–65, p58.

[16] See Doris Buss, The Curious Visibility of Wartime Rape: Gender and Ethnicity in International Criminal Law, *Windsor Yearbook of Access to Justice* 25(1) (2007) 3–22; and Boesten, n 15.

[17] Ní Aoláin, O'Rourke, and Swaine, n 8, p127.

[18] Sandesh Sivakumaran, Sexual Violence Against Men in Armed Conflict, *The European Journal of International Law* 18(2) (2007) 253–276, p267.

[19] Philipp Schulz, Displacement from Gendered Personhood: Sexual Violence and Masculinities in Northern Uganda, *International Affairs* 94(5) (2018) 1101–1115.

[20] Philipp Schulz and Heleen Touquet, Queering Explanatory Frameworks for Wartime Sexual Violence Against Men, *International Affairs* 96(5) (2020) 1169–1187, p1177.

[21] WHO, World Report on Violence and Health, 2002, p149.

This book adopts a similarly broad interpretation of sexual violence.[22] The discussion below is also informed by the ways in which CRSV is legally framed. Reparation programmes often focus resources on acts of sexual violence that amount to violations of international humanitarian law or human rights law.[23] International criminal law concentrates on a narrow range of sexual violence which includes 'rape, sexual slavery, enforced prostitution, forced pregnancy, enforced sterilization, or any other form of sexual violence of comparable gravity' as crimes against humanity and war crimes.[24] More recently, some have suggested an additional area of inquiry through the rubric of 'conflict-related reproductive violence'.[25] Duggan and Jacobsen point out that reproductive violence, which involves physical or psychological violence that impedes individuals' 'biological ability to reproduce or effectively parent', often 'accompanies and intensifies the effects of sexual violence'.[26] Perpetrators and their supporters can also inflict further psychological, social, and cultural damage on the victims of sexual violence by impugning their reputation, perpetuating 'rape myths',[27] and stigmatizing any children born of such sexual violence.[28] I address all these issues in more detail in Chapter 3 when considering the harms associated with CRSV.

As is discussed further below, the issue of CRSV is inevitably highly politicized. The increased prominence of the issue is highlighted by the 2018 Nobel Peace Prize being awarded to gynaecologist Denis Mukwege, who treats victims of CRSV, and Yazidi victim-advocate Nadia Murad, a former ISIS sex slave. However, for some commentators the political profile of the issue is not without controversy. For example, the 'iconic image' of the 'brown woman rape victim' often appears in campaign literature, civil society annual reports, and other campaigning tools, but the 'real world' marginalization of such women in reparation processes—inevitably

[22] Marie Keenan and Estelle Zinsstag, Restorative Justice and Sexual Offenses: Can 'Changing Lenses' Be Appropriate in This Case Too? *De Gruyter* 97(1) (2014) 93–106, p97.

[23] See Law 1448/2011, Article 3, Colombia; in Kosovo it refers to 'sexual abuse and rape' Article 4(6), Law No 04/L-172 (2014); and the Croatia scheme defines sexual violence more in line with the Rome Statute, but also includes domestic criminal offences that were 'directly related to the aggression against the Republic of Croatia in the Homeland War'—Article 2(1), Law on the Rights of Victims of Sexual Violence during the Armed Aggression against the Republic of Croatia in the Homeland War 2015 NN64/15, 98/19.

[24] Articles 7(1)(g), 8(2)(b)(xxii) and 8(2)(e)(vi) Rome Statute.

[25] See Tanja Altunjan, *Reproductive Violence and International Criminal Law*, Asser Press (2021).

[26] Colleen Duggan and Ruth Jacobson, Reparation of Sexual and Reproductive Violence: Moving from Codification to Implementation, in Rubio-Marín, n 8, 121–161, p125.

[27] Rachel Killean, Eithne Dowds, and Anne-Marie McAlinden, Sexual Offence Trials in Northern Ireland: The Cultural and Legal Dimensions, in Rachel Killean, Eithne Dowds, and Anne-Marie McAlinden (eds), *Sexual Violence on Trial Local and Comparative Perspectives*, Routledge (2021) 3–21, p11.

[28] Paul Kirby, How is Rape a Weapon of War? Feminist International Relations, Modes of Critical Explanation and the Study of Wartime Sexual Violence, *European Journal of International Relations* 19(4) (2012) 797–821, p810; Rangira Béa Gallimore, Militarism, Ethnicity, and Sexual Violence in the Rwandan Genocide, *Feminist Africa* 10(1) (2008) 9–30, p24; and Todd Salzman, Rape Camps as a Means of Ethnic Cleansing: Religious, Cultural, and Ethical Responses to Rape Victims in the Former Yugoslavia, *Human Rights Quarterly* 20(2) (1998) 348–378, p364.

mediated through not only race, but illiteracy, poverty, and gender—continues unabated.[29] Some commentators argue that international and local civil society organizations seek to 'cash in' on the issue or use it to justify their own existence, with little money or support actually reaching victims.[30] This may also reflect the fact that donors are more likely to respond to calls to help 'ideal victims' of violations— such as by contributing to the ICC Trust Fund for Victims[31]—rather than to address broader cultural or structural inequalities, which are inevitably more abstract.[32] As Schwöbel-Patel argues, this is part of the 'global victim industry' that commodifies victims' suffering, homogenizing and repackaging their needs to legitimize international institutions.[33] Such criticisms resonate with broader critiques of human rights and transitional justice as being top-down and driven by the norms of the Global North that reduce those in the Global South to 'savages' and victims to vindicate those in the North as saviours.[34] With regards to CRSV, such distinctions matter. While attention is paid to sexual violence committed by rebel groups against women, male sexual violence or sexual exploitation by missionaries, humanitarian agencies or peacekeepers is less of a cause célèbre, where concerns over negative publicity may affect funding and the contribution of the troops to peacekeeping missions trumps redressing victims' suffering.[35] Nevertheless, these victims may experience similar harms and barriers, such as stigma.

While this book focuses on addressing the harm caused by sexual violence, the full extent of CRSV remains insufficiently recognized. Nevertheless, the systematic collection and analysis of data play a crucial role in identifying patterns and informing effective humanitarian responses and reparation measures. Several datasets now track CRSV, though they often acknowledge the persistent challenges associated with underreporting and documentation.[36] In addition, some data may

[29] Chiseche Salome Mibenge, *Sex and International Tribunals: The Erasure of Gender from the War Narrative*, University of Pennsylvania Press (2013) pp158 and 164.

[30] Luke Moffett, International Reparation Initiative for Conflict-Related Sexual Violence: Four Challenges, *Opinio Juris*, 28 March 2019 www.opiniojuris.org/2019/03/28/international-reparation-initiative-for-conflict-related-sexual-violence-four-challenges/, accessed 17 November 2025.

[31] The ICC Trust Fund for Victims provides assistance to victims in situations before the Court, as well as implements reparations to victims in cases where criminal proceedings against a convicted person have been completed.

[32] Christine Schwöbel-Patel, *Marketing Global Justice: The Political Economy of International Criminal Law*, CUP (2021) p145.

[33] ibid pp143–146.

[34] See Makau Mutua, Savages, Victims, and Saviors: The Metaphor of Human Rights, *Harvard International Law Journal* 42 (2001) 201–245.

[35] Carla Ferstman, Reparation for Sexual Exploitation and Abuse in the (Post) Conflict Context: The Need to Address Abuses by Peacekeepers and Humanitarian Aid Workers, in Carla Ferstman and Mariana Goetz (eds), *Reparations for Victims of Genocide, War Crimes and Crimes Against Humanity: Systems in Place and Systems in the Making*, Brill (2020) 271–297.

[36] For instance, Conflict-Related Sexual Violence Data, Humanitarian Data Exchange, https://data.humdata.org/dataset/conflict-related-sexual-violence?force_layout=desktop, accessed 14 November 2025; Sexual Violence in Armed Conflict (SVAC), dataset available at http://www.sexualviolencedata.org/dataset/, accessed 17 November 2025; The Armed Conflict Location and Event Data Project (ACLED), data available at https://acleddata.com/2019/04/23/sexual-violence-in-the-acled-dataset/, accessed 4 April 2025.

not be accessible to databases, such as information related to healthcare that is protected by confidentiality. Therefore, providing estimates of true prevalence in conflict situations is shrouded in difficulty. In addition, 'zero' reporting or the absence of evidence in databases does not mean that CRSV is absent, given the silence that pervades communities.[37] There is a pressing need for qualitative data and analysis capable of uncovering subtle, coded references to sexual violence that may otherwise remain obscured—a necessity highlighted by the empirical research underpinning this book. There too remains a concern about isolating CRSV without considering its connection to intimate partner or domestic violence, as well as sexual violence that occurs after conflicts.[38] However, the Sexual Violence in Armed Conflict (SVAC) database attempts to better represent the continuum of violence that succeeds conflict by collecting data from the years of active conflict as well as the first five post-conflict years.[39]

Although my primary focus in this book is on harms and how reparations can address them, I want to stress from the outset that I am well aware of the broader dynamics of measurement and the politics surrounding CRSV. Cognizant of that broader context, I will argue that there is added value in a book such as this, which draws upon fieldwork, medical practice, and evidence-based medicine to shed more light on the issue of appropriate reparations for victims of CRSV. As noted above, I will, for example, highlight the importance of reparations for reproductive and sexual harms, which are often missed or obscured given their 'messy' overlap with bodily functions.[40] My background in obstetrics and gynaecology offers insights on female anatomy and medical interventions which can usefully augment socio-legal understandings of harm from the perspective of law and transitional justice.

1.2 Approach

This book emerged from my PhD thesis and has been informed by my subsequent work on reparation initiatives as well as my ongoing medical practice in forensic medicine and sexual and reproductive healthcare. It draws from desktop research of relevant literature in law, medicine, political science, history, sociology, and

[37] C Hangwook Ju, Determinants of Conflict-Related Sexual Violence: A Meta-Reanalysis Distinguishing Two Classes of Zero Observations, *International Studies Quarterly* 67(3) (2023) http://doi.org/10.1093/isq/sqad044.

[38] The ACLED dataset from 2018 collected data on sexual violence related to war or political instability perpetrated by an armed actor. Despite overlaps it excludes domestic, interpersonal, or intimate partner violence.

[39] Sexual Violence in Armed Conflict (SVAC), dataset available at http://www.sexualviolencedata.org/dataset/, accessed 17 November 2025.

[40] Janine Natalya Clark, 'Leaky' Bodies, Connectivity and Embodied Transitional Justice, *International Journal of Transitional Justice* 13 (2019) 268–289.

criminology to map out the current discussions on reparations for CRSV. It also examines some of the relevant laws, regulations, protocols, and policies on reparations in Colombia, Peru, and Uganda in relation to sexual violence. I also conducted semi-structured interviews and focus groups across these three case sites as well as drawing upon some secondary quantitative data sources.[41] The three case sites were chosen because they depict different stages of transition from conflict,[42] as well as to reflect on a diversity of harms, the effect of time on the evolution of consequences and a range of reparative responses to conflict-related sexual violence.

The three case studies represent a range of experience in terms of the contexts for their conflicts and their practice in implementing some or all forms of reparations. In Uganda, the colonial period was marked by a number of rebellions that were ruthlessly put down, and dozens of conflicts have erupted since independence that often included rape by government soldiers and civilians.[43] My research in Uganda focuses on the conflict in the northern part of the country where, since 1986, an armed rebellion by what came to be known as the Lord's Resistance Army (LRA) fought against government forces, leading to mass displacement and violence until peace talks in 2006.[44] While those talks collapsed in 2008 before a final peace agreement was signed, the LRA has been kept outside of the borders of Uganda. Nevertheless the group was responsible for abducting tens of thousands of adults and children, and many women and children were subjected to sexual enslavement, forced marriage, and rape—some of whom were interviewed—and such harms are of relevance for this book.[45] At the same time, government forces carried out a brutal counterinsurgency campaign and collective punishment against the Acholi people that used sexual violence against males,[46] and used rape as a punishment for women and girls who left displaced persons' camps to forage for food or collect water.[47] Some 35 years on from the conflict's origin, Uganda

[41] The research methodology adhered to the Belmont Principles and Beauchamp and Childress's Principles of Biomedical Ethics by ensuring informed consent, minimizing harm, and promoting justice through trauma-informed and participatory practices tailored to victims of CRSV—see Tom L Beauchamp and James F Childress, Principles of Biomedical Ethics, 7th Edition, OUP (2013); National Commission for the Protection of Human Subjects of Biomedical and Behavioral Research, The Belmont Report: Ethical Principles and Guidelines for the Protection of Human Subjects of Research, US Department of Health and Human Services, 1979.

[42] Uganda is at the initial policy development stage; Colombia is currently in the middle of a transitional justice process, with a number of reparation policies and programmes; and Peru has effectively completed its reparations programme.

[43] Annelieke van de Wiel et al, *Compendium of Conflicts in Uganda*, Refugee Law Project, 2014, p45.

[44] See Adam Branch, *Displacing Human Rights: War and Intervention in Northern Uganda*, OUP (2011).

[45] See Phuong Pham, Patrick Vinck, and Eric Stover, *Abducted: The Lord's Resistance Army and Forced Conscription in Northern Uganda*, Berkeley-Tulane Initiative on Vulnerable Populations, June 2007.

[46] See Schulz, n 8, p56.

[47] See Breaking the Circle: Protecting Human Rights in the Northern War Zone, Amnesty International, 1999, pp47–53; and Between Two Fires: The Human Rights Situation in 'Protected Camps' in Gulu District, Human Rights Focus (HURIFO), 2002, pp52–54.

has yet to establish a reparation programme and faces political indifference from the state to confront violations by all actors.[48] The Ugandan government has instead created a number of general assistance and reconstruction programmes.[49] The proposed National Transitional Justice Policy states that reparations will be comprehensive to facilitate victims' reintegration into society, with attention to the gender-challenges the conflict created, such as children born of war, but this has not yet been implemented.[50] As a case study, Uganda was chosen given the protracted conflict, the range of sexual violence, and efforts of medical professionals to remedy the harm caused through private and public health institutions in the absence of a reparation programme.

In Colombia, there have been a series of periods of violence over the past sixty years, which deteriorated in the 1980s and early 2000s with confrontations between guerrilla groups, such as the Revolutionary Armed Forces of Colombia (FARC) and the National Liberation Army (ELN), and the state and paramilitary groups.[51] Sexual violence was often carried out by paramilitary groups to punish communities,[52] against men,[53] Afro-Colombians, and indigenous groups,[54] as well as targeting members of the LGBTI+ community.[55] Guerrilla groups also imposed forced abortions and contraception on female members.[56] The 2011 Victims and Land Restitution Law, which mainly governs reparations, aims to ensure comprehensive or integral reparations that satisfy victims' rights and to achieve 'reconciliation and lasting and sustainable peace'.[57] Reparation measures include 'restitution,

[48] See Jeremy Sarkin, Providing Reparations in Uganda: Substantive Recommendations for Implementing Reparations in the Aftermath of the Conflict that Occurred over the Last Few Decades, *African Human Rights Law Journal* 14(2) (2014) 526–552.

[49] See Stephen Oola and Luke Moffett, *'Cul Pi Bal' Reparations for the Northern Uganda Conflict*, Reparations, Responsibility and Victimhood in Transitional Societies (RRV) 2020, pp13–23.

[50] JLOS, National Transitional Justice Policy, Ministry of Internal Affairs, 2019, pp20–21.

[51] Fabio Andrés Díaz Pabón, Conflict and Peace in the Making: Colombia From 1948–2010, in Fabio Díaz Pabón (ed), *Truth, Justice and Reconciliation in Colombia: Transitioning from Violence*, Routledge (2018) 15–33.

[52] See Natalia Suarez Bonilla, Rape, Blaming the Victim and Social Control in Paramilitary Enclaves: An Approach to the Case of Colombia, in R Branche and F Virgili (eds), *Rape in Wartime*, Palgrave (2012) 79–89.

[53] Isabella Flisi, Engendering the Understanding of Wartime Sexual Violence in Colombia: Hyper-Masculinities and Sexual Violence against Men, in S Danielsson (ed), *War and Sexual Violence: New Perspectives in a New Era*, Brill (2019) 243–275.

[54] See Julie Goldscheid, Gender Violence Against Afro-Colombian Women: Making the Promise of International Human Rights Law Real, *Columbia Human Rights Law Review Online* 4 (2020) 249–267; and Mónica Acosta et al, The Colombian Transitional Process: Comparative Perspectives on Violence against Indigenous Women, *International Journal of Transitional Justice* 12(1) (2018) 108–125.

[55] This included sexual violence as well as the killing of over 540 LGBTI+ individuals between 2014 and 2019. See Jennifer Bates, The Violence of Norms: Resisting Repertoires of Gender Violence in Post-Conflict Colombia, *Journal of Gender Studies* 31(2) (2022) 153–164.

[56] Along with being traumatic it also had a detrimental effect on the morale and retention of female fighters, see Francisco Gutiérrez Sanín and Francy Carranza Franco, Organizing Women for Combat: The Experience of the FARC in the Colombian War, *Journal of Agrarian Change* 17(4) (2017) 770–778, p775.

[57] Article 8, Law 1448/2011.

compensation, rehabilitation, satisfaction and guarantees of non-repetition, in their individual, collective, material, moral and symbolic dimensions'.[58] These measures are to be delivered to victims alongside assistance support.[59] Since 2017 there has been a dedicated stream for service provision to victims of CRSV, including training for medical professionals who come into contact with such victims. Under the scheme, victims of sexual violence have special protection and face less onerous evidential requirements.[60] More broadly, the 2016 peace agreement between the FARC and the Colombian government also established a truth commission and a domestic court for international crimes (the Special Jurisdiction for Peace), which will address, in part, sexual violence.[61] For this book, the Colombian case study represents a complex experience of sexual violence in a protracted conflict, with ongoing violence, but despite this, efforts continue to redress such violations through a national reparation programme.

Peru experienced an armed conflict from 1980 until the mid-1990s, between government forces and guerrilla groups such as the Shining Path and Túpac Amaru Revolutionary Movement (MRTA).[62] Over 70,000 people were killed or disappeared, and thousands of women and girls were raped. During this time, the government under President Fujimori became more authoritarian, and public policies such as forced sterilization of poor, indigenous women and men also were carried out.[63] Peru has a comprehensive reparations programme similar to that of Colombia, which came about as a result of the recommendation by the Truth and Reconciliation Commission (Comisión de la Verdad y Reconciliación (CVR)) to 'repair and compensate for the violation of human rights as well as the social, moral and material losses or damages suffered by the victims as a result of the internal armed conflict'.[64] Victims of rape have been included in the reparation programme from the outset,[65] reflecting the attention given to sexual violence by the CVR.[66] However, it excludes other forms of sexual violence, such as forced pregnancy,

[58] Articles 25 and 69, which also states: 'Each of these measures will be implemented in favor of the victim depending on the violation of their rights and the characteristics of the victimizing act.'

[59] Article 21, Law 1448/2011.

[60] Articles 38,41, 42, 137(2), and 181(3), Law 1448/2011.

[61] There have already been some efforts before the JEP to receive reports from victims and Case 007 on child soldiers is covering sexual enslavement, see Rocío Quintero, *Colombia: The Special Jurisdiction for Peace, Analysis One Year and a Half After its Entry into Operation*, International Commission of Jurists, 2019, pp67 and 81. In November 2023 the Special Jurisdiction for Peace opened a macro case on sexual, gender, and reproductive violence committed during the conflict.

[62] See Hatun Willakuy, abbreviated version of the Final Report of the Truth and Reconciliation Commission (2003); and Rebecca K. Root, *Transitional Justice in Peru*, Palgrave (2012).

[63] See Jelke Boesten, Free Choice or Poverty Alleviation? Population Politics in Peru under Alberto Fujimori, *Revista Europea de Estudios Latinoamericanos y del Caribe* 82(1) (2007) 3–20.

[64] Comisión de la Verdad y Reconciliación (CVR), Final Report, vol IX (2003) p154; Article 1, Law 28592, 29 July 2005; and Julie Guillerot, *Reparations in Peru: 15 Years of Delivering Redress*, RRV (2019) p12.

[65] See Guillerot, n 64.

[66] Article 6, Law 28592. Some 6,820 victims have been registered and benefited from the reparation programme, see Guillerot, n 64, p31.

mutilation, and abortion that were documented in the CVR's report. The Peru case study exhibits the intersection of sexual and reproductive violations as well as the long-term effects of reparations to victims.

The empirical research of this book can be described as interdisciplinary. As such, it offers a space in which to transcend some of the theoretical and methodological restrictions of one discipline.[67] This involved integrating the skills, knowledge, and experience of medicine and law to formulate an approach to understanding the harms of CRSV and potential repairs.[68] In particular, I take a medico-legal approach that draws from my background in medicine to better appreciate the extent of harms and the positionality of the medical profession in relation to victims of sexual violence and reparations. A socio-legal approach recognizes the limitations of the law and the role of the social context in shaping institutions, policies, and regulations.[69] Such an approach analyses the role of actors, policies, and institutions by being critically reflexive of the values and established knowledge that is often relied upon in law, but is also tested and continually reassessed in medicine.[70] At the same time, I interrogate the role of medical practitioners in reparation programmes and in my fieldwork have explored the understanding of concepts, such as reparations, with such individuals, as well as their own biases and contribution to victimization.

Much of the literature on CRSV takes an avowedly feminist perspective, drawing important attention to gender and power dynamics and this informs my deliberations throughout.[71] However, some commentators have argued that the hyper-focus on rape and sexual violence as a war tactic risks overlooking ordinary violence, sexual violence against other gender identities, and complex victimhood, including forced contraception amongst female combatants within armed groups.[72] This book builds on this complementary work by looking at the role of medical professionals in deciphering and producing harms, devising repairs, and in perpetuating sexual violence or rape scripts/narratives. I argue against a reductionist interpretation of the experience of sexual violence as merely a series

[67] Reza Banakar and Max Travers, *Law, Sociology and Method*, Hart (2005).
[68] ibid p6.
[69] Naomi Creutzfeldt, Marc Mason, and Kirsten McConnachie, *Routledge Handbook of Socio-Legal Theory and Methods*, Routledge (2021) p4–5.
[70] Banakar and Travers, n 67, p6.
[71] See Nicola Henry, The Fixation on Wartime Rape: Feminist Critique and International Criminal Law, *Social and Legal Studies* 23(1) (2014) 93–111; Karen Engle, Feminism and Its (DIS)contents: Criminalizing Wartime Rape in Bosnia and Herzegovina, *American Journal of International Law* 99(4) (2005) 778–816; and Susan Harris Rimmer, Sexing the Subject of Transitional Justice, *The Australian Feminist Law Journal* 32(1) (2010) 123–162.
[72] Jelke Boesten, Revisiting Methodologies and Approaches in Researching Sexual Violence in Conflict, *Social Politics: International Studies in Gender, State & Society* 25(4) (2018) 457–468, p460; and Henry, n 71, pp97–98. The identification of victim and survivor is discussed further in Chapter 4.

of medical (physical and psychological) harms to assert that it is also experienced politically, socially, and culturally.[73]

This study uses qualitative methods to complement existing quantitative data (including medical data) on the consequences of sexual violence in conflict and non-conflict settings, as well as the gap in understanding the harms of CRSV in transitional justice literature. I adopted a qualitative approach to this research as a way of best capturing the lived experiences of CRSV as well as examining the extent to which reparations delivered on promises to victims and survivors.[74] While quantitative data can provide a useful baseline for examining patterns and trends of harms and the operation of reparations programmes, it is hampered by barriers to reporting and risks diminishing the complexities of CRSV.[75] Boesten offers a persuasive critique of the methodology of some of the CRSV literature as too focused on quantitative political science. In Boesten's view this reflects governance demands for quantitative evidence to inform interventions, overlooking the difficulties associated with collecting such evidence, its reliability, and the impact of heightened global attention on the implementation of such data in policy.[76]

I conducted in-depth semi-structured interviews and focus groups across the three case countries from July 2018 to May 2020.[77] A total of 92 participants were interviewed or participated in one of five focus groups: 34 persons in Colombia; 31 persons in Peru, and 23 persons in Uganda. In addition, four interviews were conducted through secure virtual platforms with actors with experience in one or more of the case countries and at the preference of the actor. In total, there were five focus groups involving 40 people and 43 interviews with 52 persons across the three case sites. The self-identified gender of these participants consisted of 75 women and 17 men.[78] While men were interviewed in each country, most men were from Uganda (n = 10).[79]

[73] Holly Porter, Rape Without Bodies? Reimagining the Phenomenon We Call 'Rape', *Social Politics: International Studies in Gender, State & Society* 25(4) (2018) 589–612, pp590 and 592; and Anette B Houge and Kjersti Lohne, End impunity! Reducing Conflict-Related Sexual Violence to a Problem of Law, *Law and Society Review* 51(4) (2017) 755–789, p778.

[74] Melissa DeJonckheere and Lisa M Vaughn, Semi-Structured Interviewing in Primary Care Research: A Balance of Relationship and Rigour, *BMJ Family Medicine and Community Health* 7(2) (2019), doi:10.1136/fmch-2018-000057, p2.

[75] Inger Skjelsbæk, Silence Breakers in War and Peace: Research on Gender and Violence with an Ethics of Engagement, *Social Politics: International Studies in Gender, State & Society* 25(4) (2018) 496–520, pp505–506; and Houge and Lohne, n 73, p777.

[76] Jelke Boesten, Revisiting Methodologies and Approaches in Researching Sexual Violence in Conflict, *Social Politics* 25(4) (2018) 457–468, pp458–459.

[77] Research was conducted at intervals in Colombia, with the researcher making two visits to carry out fieldwork, which also had the added benefit of building trust with victims and victim groups. A third visit in March 2020 also allowed dissemination of some of the thesis findings with respondents and a training session for medical practitioners.

[78] As the primary focus of this thesis was on women, most of the victim participants were women who had directly suffered CRSV, with the exception of two men who were indirect victims.

[79] Most of the data collected and all participants identified as cisgender.

Semi-structured interviews were chosen for their flexibility in questioning and the space they provide to explore participant ideas and delve into sensitive subjects while also allowing some comparison of issues between interviews.[80] Focus groups provided the opportunity to distinctly observe the interactions between participants, their conversation, and dynamics with regard to certain questions and issues.[81] Most focus groups were comprised of victims and were organized by victims. This had the advantage of enabling victims to choose their preferred method of participation. As an added benefit, participants were already comfortable with each other because of their prior dealings and relationships. In contrast to group interviews (comprised of no more than two people), through which individual views were sought, the focus groups allowed for the analysis of silences, debates, and relations within the group. Typically, a full day was allocated to each focus group, which could last from two to seven hours with breaks and opportunities for separate conversations with those who preferred not to disclose certain information in front of the group. One-to-one interviews were normally one to two hours in duration. Feedback was welcomed from participants after each interview and focus group, and a public roundtable on preliminary findings, inviting views from the public and all participant groups, occurred in March 2020, alongside a discussion on a linked policy report.

Participants were categorized according to one of three actor groups: victims of CRSV; transitional justice actors (TJAs) involved in advocating, litigating, designing, or implementing reparations; and healthcare professionals (HCPs) who provide care to victims of CRSV. Transitional justice actors included a range of practitioners who worked in civil society or government on issues related to reparations and former members of armed groups. The HCP group was equally diverse, including doctors (physicians and surgeons) in forensics, general/family medicine, psychiatry, and obstetrics and gynaecology; nurses; midwives; community health workers; clinical psychologists; counsellors; and medical coordinators. Two individuals identified as both victims and transitional justice actors, given their role in advocating for redress for themselves and their group.

The most obvious ethical challenge for this research was to ensure that research with often traumatized victim interviewees was performed in a respectful and sensitive fashion which did not lead to retraumatization. Towards this end, I spent considerable time reviewing the relevant methodological literature on conducting research with victims of sexual violence in general and victims of sexual violence in conflict in particular.[82] A trauma-informed approach was applied throughout

[80] DeJonckheere and Vaughn, n 74.

[81] Jenny Kitzinger, The Methodology of Focus Groups: The Importance of Interaction between Research Participants, *Sociology of Health & Illness* 16(1) (1994) 103–121, p105.

[82] eg WHO, Ethical and Safety Recommendations for Researching, Documenting and Monitoring Sexual Violence in Emergencies, 2007; Jelke Boesten and Marsha Henry, Between Fatigue and Silence: The Challenges of Conducting Research on Sexual Violence in Conflict, *Social Politics: International Studies in Gender, State & Society* 25(4) (2018) 568–588; and Kirsten Campbell,

the stages of research, with particular attention to the interviewing process of participant groups which fully supported choice and control of interviewees.[83] I also discussed the ways in which the work should be done at length with my supervisory team. In these circumstances, I drew upon my own medical training and practice in patient empathy, reading body language, and observation, as well as my experience in treating and managing victims of sexual violence. I received training from a number of professional and victim organizations, including in my medical practice, before embarking on research. By approaching each interviewee with sensitivity and empathy, I was able to have a conversation with them about more present and forward-looking issues related to reparations, rather than concentrating on the violation. In light of the risk of vicarious trauma, I was, if needed, able to avail myself of a mentor who had considerable experience in researching sexual violence.

The other aspect of the fieldwork to which I gave particular attention was my own background as a medic with professional knowledge of obstetrics and gynaecology as well as sexual and reproductive health. Undoubtedly this background enabled healthcare professionals to speak at more length about specific physical and psychological health issues and the treatment options they use in their practice. However, I was also conscious that, particularly with victim interviewees, my position as a doctor could complicate how they perceived me and what expectations that might evoke. Victims who have had bad experiences with medical professionals in the past can be distrustful, viewing them as extensions of the state or as medical authority figures to whom they *must* answer. To accommodate such issues, I repeatedly explained that while I had a background as a medic, for the purposes of this research I was a researcher and they were completely free to tell me (or not) what they wished about their experiences. Although I had been worried about these factors before commencing the fieldwork, in practice, my background as a doctor appeared to encourage interviewees to speak openly, and no obvious concerns about power-relations emerged during the fieldwork. I also received psychological training to recognize if trauma was impinging on the interaction and how this could be positively navigated in our encounter. In the event of retraumatization or an urgent medical issue, I had compiled a network of trusted organizations I could refer an interviewee to if they felt this would be beneficial and I received training in psychodynamic psychotherapy. This also served to counteract my limitations as a researcher and not a care provider.

Producing Knowledge in the Field of Sexual Violence in Armed Conflict Research: Objects, Methods, Politics, and Gender Justice Methodology, *Social Politics: International Studies in Gender, State & Society* 25(4) (2018) 469–495.

[83] Rebecca Campbell, Rachael Goodman-Williams, and McKenzie Javorka, A Trauma-Informed Approach to Sexual Violence Research Ethics and Open Science, Journal of Interpersonal Violence 34(23–24) (2019) 4765–4793.

My own fieldwork in Peru, Uganda, and Colombia is used to add a qualitative and original contribution to better understand the harm suffered by CRSV victims. The harms caused by sexual violence are contextualized by incorporating the empirical research from the case studies, as well as drawing from other comparative research in the literature. Although I do not argue that the experiences of these sites can be mechanistically transposed to other transitional contexts, I will suggest that there are themes which are of broader relevance concerning the experience of suffering and harm caused by sexual violence related to conflict.

1.3 Book Outline

This book is comprised of six further chapters and a conclusion. These chapters unpack some of the conceptual and practical issues regarding reparations for conflict-related sexual violence. Chapter 2 examines some of the theoretical foundations in the broader practice of transitional justice and restorative justice that are often used to rationalize reparations as a means of addressing past harms, in particular sexual violence. Of particular relevance to both areas of scholarship are their frequent invocation of healing and rehabilitation, which I argue resonates strongly with the traditional emphasis within medical research on the same theme. This section introduces the concept of a medico-legal approach by exploring key intersectional areas and demonstrating how they can be developed and applied to reparations for CRSV, a theme that is woven throughout each chapter. I argue that by fusing several elements of the medical literature with socio-legal approaches to reparations, we can provide a 'thicker' understanding of the utility of reparations to address the harms created by CRSV.

Chapter 3 explores in some detail the consequences and suffering experienced by victims of CRSV, and introduces some of the experiences of the victims interviewed by the author as well as insights from medical practitioners and civil society actors working with victims and reparations. The chapter critically examines the range and depth of harm suffered by CRSV victims, which will inform later chapters on appropriate and effective reparations. The types of harms examined include psychological, physical, reproductive, transgenerational, identity-based, iatrogenic (related to medical assessment or treatment), and communal or social. I also detail the role of forensics in documenting harm and the scope of 'repairs' that are required to address them.

Chapter 4 analyses the variety of identities that can be attached to those who suffer conflict-related sexual violence. Three prevalent identities of victim, survivor, and patient are discussed. I argue that identity is often neglected in the literature and practice of reparations, yet it has important implications for how individuals claiming such measures see themselves and are perceived by others. This is particularly apparent in relation to sexual violence, where accessing or claiming redress is differentiated through the identities of victim, survivor, or patient. I argue that a more nuanced understanding of the political and social consequences of these overlapping identities illustrates the ways that different terms and language are used in medicine and law to address the same subject, albeit but from different disciplinary perspectives. This analysis also aims to draw out the nuances between legal claims making and medical access to service delivery based on need. It examines how the human body intersects with and reflects different variants of identity, which I argue has important implications for understanding reparations and finding appropriate forms of redress that are shaped by an individual's self-perception and relationship to their body in the aftermath of sexual violence.

Chapter 5 outlines the historical and theoretical justifications for reparations of sexual violence and how these have been operationalized through different legal and political principles. The chapter considers the historical practice of reparations for sexual violence, noting that it is only over the past fifteen years that such reparations have become more prevalent, through developments in international criminal justice, truth commissions, bottom-up efforts from civil society, and human rights jurisprudence. The chapter then examines the conceptual development of reparations, with reference to the gender-orientated approach and transformative justice. It critically interrogates the predominant notion of transformative reparations as being the solution to the difficulties of transitional justice effectively dealing with sexual violence, around the emphasis of the benefits of process over outcome, and victims' individual lived experience.

Chapter 6 outlines some of the contemporary practice and guidance on the five forms of reparations (restitution, compensation, rehabilitation, measures of satisfaction, and guarantees of non-repetition) for CRSV drawing upon transitional justice practice and jurisprudence from human rights and international criminal fora. This analysis of reparation practice identifies deficiencies in comprehending and responding to CRSV across administrative and judicial bodies. This chapter brings into focus interdisciplinary perspectives on rehabilitation as reparation for sexual violence and examines how the role of the human body may be better integrated into reparations. It prepares a new space in which to conceptualize rehabilitation alongside vulnerability for victims of sexual violence, which will be explored further in Chapter 7.

Chapter 7 discusses what a medico-legal approach to reparation for CRSV might entail through the specific lenses of vulnerability and resilience. I argue for a broader understanding of vulnerability beyond age and gender and argue that in some instances reparation policies can compound the vulnerability of victims of CRSV. In addition, this chapter discusses how victims can address their own vulnerability, manage harm, and even engage in self-repair to navigate the daily consequences of such violations through the notion of resilience. I argue that a more nuanced understanding of both concepts can make reparations more attuned and effective in remedying their harm.

The book concludes by outlining three original contributions of the book, namely the need to focus more on the harm caused by CRSV to more effectively and appropriately remedy the harm caused; efforts to redress CRSV require creative solutions around stigma, in particular the biases that medical professional and society can have that can inhibit victims coming forward for support; and the role of identity, vulnerability, and resilience in shaping victims' experience of living with the consequences of CRSV that necessitates considering the short, medium, and long-term impact of such violations on individuals, families, and communities. This final part of the book also makes some tentative recommendations for the future evolution of the field of reparations for conflict-related sexual violence.

2

A Medico-Legal Approach to Justice, Restoration, and Reparations

Reparations are measures intended to remedy harm. Legally speaking this involves some sort of violation or breach of obligation that requires a remedy. Remedy is synonymous with notions of repair, redress, even to heal, which resonates with medicine and healthcare in treating and diagnosing ailments, disease, and trauma. This chapter explores the theoretical intersections of law and medicine, in particular around dealing with mass atrocities under the rubric of transitional justice. Given my medical background and legal research, in particular working on a number of reparations initiatives, a transdisciplinary approach can broach these two fields that are instructive for reparations. Reparations themselves are an interdisciplinary, even multi-disciplinary, endeavour that requires more than lawyers to make them operational—beyond just transferring money to victims—and to fully appreciate the harm caused by mass atrocities.

Reparations can be considered along a 'justice continuum of repair', which reflects the different perspectives and expectations of reparations in redressing violations.[1] Such a continuum includes notions of redress, restoration, and transformation that a medico-legal approach can shed further light on the effectiveness of reparative measures, especially in responding to harm to a person's integrity and wellbeing that is often evident with gross violations like conflict-related sexual violence (CRSV). Reparations are one of the five central pillars of transitional justice recognized by the United Nations as necessary in redressing atrocities.[2] Despite this and the increased attention to conflict-related sexual violence in recent years, there remains a lack of substantive attention to adequately and effectively remedy such violations—attention that requires going beyond money or compensation to consider how we treat the trauma to the body and mind.

Any sort of official, legal, and medical response to mass violence will always be inhibited by scarce resources. However the way in which violence and justice

[1] See Lisa J Laplante, Just Repair, *Cornell International Law Journal* 48 (2015) 513–578.

[2] Guidance Note of the Secretary-General: United Nations Approach to Transitional Justice, DPA/UNSG/2010-00904 (10 March 2010); Wendy Lambourne, What Are the Pillars of Transition Justice: The United Nations, Civil Society and the Justice Cascade in Burundi, *Macquarie Law Journal* 13 (2014) 41–60, p43; and Kora Andrieu, Political Liberalism after Mass Violence: John Rawls and a 'Theory' of Transitional Justice, in S Buckey-Zistel et al (eds), *Transitional Justice Theories*, Routledge (2014) 85–104, p95.

Redressing Rape in War. Sunneva Gilmore, Oxford University Press.
DOI: 10.1093/9780198919735.003.0002

responses are framed can also inhibit effective redress of such violations. Boesten argues that where transitional justice does address sexual violence it tends to narrow the focus to rape as a weapon of war, which can in turn limit the recognition of other forms of sexual violence, as well as forcing victims to 'fit the story' regarding such a script.[3] Reparations in transitional justice often take an individualized approach that ineffectually responds to the lived experience of victims of conflict-related sexual violence where violence is marked by 'discontinuity' of the enormity of terror and 'social ruin' of their lives.[4] Where reparations are made for sexual violence it often entails trauma being dealt with rather superficially—such as focusing on only quantifying certain physical harms—rather than understanding the victims' broader range of needs associated with both physical and psychological harms, as well as other complexities linked to gender, community, society, and other variables.[5] This is why moving beyond a legal/policy perspective to consider a medical understanding of the consequences of sexual violence are critical in ensuring that reparations for such violations is effective and comprehensive in effectively remedying such harm.

This chapter begins by outlining what a medico-legal approach entails before turning to its implications for sexual violence. The second section of this chapter discuss the field of transitional justice and its intersection with key elements of the medical literature, including the sociology of medicine and how this can inform the role of medical professionals in transitional justice, in particular their response to sexual violence through reparations.

2.1 A Medico-Legal Approach to Conflict-Related Sexual Violence—An Expanded Framework

The medico-legal approach is a complex and dynamic field that transcends the mere convergence of medicine and law in areas of shared interest. It represents a deep and multifaceted relationship where medical expertise and legal frameworks exert a strong reciprocal influence. Medical expertise plays a critical role in legal contexts, contributing to capacity assessments, the interpretation of forensic evidence, and the determination of factual causation in cases involving acts or omissions. Conversely, legal frameworks significantly shape medical practice—safeguarding patients' rights, regulating healthcare providers, enforcing

[3] Jelke Boesten, Analyzing Rape Regimes at the Interface of War and Peace in Peru, *International Journal of Transitional Justice* 4(1) (2010) 110–129, p127.

[4] Margaret Urban Walker, Gender and Violence in Focus: A Background for Gender Justice in Reparations, in Ruth Rubio-Marín (ed), *The Gender of Reparations Unsettling Sexual Hierarchies while Redressing Human Rights Violations*, CUP (2009) 18–62, p29.

[5] Magdalena Zolkos, Redressive Politics and the Nexus of Trauma, Transitional Justice and Reconciliation, in Buckley-Zistel et al, n 2, 163–183, p177.

data protection, and guiding public health policy.[6] Law has shaped the evolution of medical ethics, especially around cases on consent such as *Gillick* and *Montgomery*.[7] The interdependence of medicine and law becomes especially pronounced in contexts involving grave violations, such as CRSV.

Sexual violence underscores the critical need for a coordinated and integrated approach that addresses the medical and legal dimensions. Professional regulatory bodies play a vital role in defining medico-legal practice. In the UK, the General Medical Council (GMC) provides essential guidance on the core principles and responsibilities of doctors in medico-legal contexts.[8] These guidelines emphasize patient confidentiality and maintaining public trust in the medical profession.[9] However, they also acknowledge circumstances where legal or ethical obligations may necessitate breaching confidentiality without the person's informed consent, such as when it is in the public interest (a risk of serious harm) or when the law requires it.

Mandatory reporting laws in some countries illustrate this tension, requiring healthcare professionals to report instances of sexual and domestic violence to authorities. This legal obligation can conflict with patient confidentiality but is often justified by the need to protect victims and prevent further violence. Medical confidentiality and privacy are particularly important for CRSV victims, significantly influencing their decision to seek healthcare. Contrary to medical ethics such as 'do no harm', mandatory reporting can delay or obstruct medical care such as preventative medication for HIV transmission.[10] Chapter 3 considers ways in which healthcare professionals navigate the potential harms when there are limits on confidentiality while ensuring therapeutic needs are met. This requires balancing the victim's privacy with legal obligations and medical ethics.

On the international stage, there has been a significant increase in guidelines aimed at preventing and responding to CRSV in recent years, with the goal of establishing consistent standards across healthcare, humanitarian, and peacekeeping sectors. The World Health Organization's (WHO) clinical protocol provides detailed instructions on delivering ethical, evidence-based care to victims and

[6] Shafeek Sandy Sanbar, *Legal Medicine*, 8th Edition, Elsevier (2024) p1–10.

[7] *Gillick v West Norfolk and Wisbech Area Health Authority* (1986) AC 112; *Montgomery v Lanarkshire Health Board (Scotland)* (2015) UKSC 11, UKSC/2013/0136.

[8] General Medical Council (GMC), Confidentiality: Good Practice in Handling Patient Information, updated 2024; GMC, Good Medical Practice, 2024; GMC, Providing Witness Statements or Expert Evidence as Part of Legal Proceedings, 2024. GMC guidance extends to doctors as well as physician associates and anaesthesia associates.

[9] Other healthcare professionals are regulated by professional bodies and have their own codes of ethics and standards of practice that are tailored to their respective roles, for instance, in the UK, the Nursing and Midwifery Council (NMC), or the United States of America, the American Nursing Association (ANA).

[10] ICRC, Revictimised: The Humanitarian Consequences of Mandatory Reporting of Sexual Violence, 2019, 9

survivors,[11] while the UN Handbook (2020) offers a practical framework for UN missions, promoting coordinated responses and early warning systems.[12] In addition, medico-legal guidelines have been developed to ensure the accurate documentation and use of evidence to support legal accountability.[13] These national and international frameworks collectively underscore the deeply interconnected roles of medicine and law in responding to CRSV. However, they do not adequately conceptualize a comprehensive medico-legal framework for reparations.

A medico-legal approach holds particular significance in cases of sexual violence, as it sits at the critical intersection of medical care and legal obligations. This includes the responsibility to document and, in some cases, report incidents of sexual violence (eg mandatory reporting), as well as the collection and preservation of forensic evidence, such as biological samples. In addition, it encompasses the provision of therapeutic care, including emergency and preventative interventions like contraception and treatment for injuries or infections.[14] International humanitarian organizations such as Médecins Sans Frontières (MSF) and International Committee of the Red Cross (ICRC), emphasize the critical importance of providing prompt and comprehensive care, shedding light on how CRSV is a pressing healthcare issue.[15] Most healthcare providers will deliver care to victims, and document their story and their injuries.[16] However, enhanced evidence collection and documentation are not typically conducted by general healthcare practitioners, but are instead carried out by specially trained doctors and nurses,[17] who operate under a multilayered framework involving professional bodies, legal standards, and organizational policies.[18] Their specialized training ensures compliance with legal standards while prioritizing the dignity, autonomy, and care of

[11] WHO, Clinical Management of Rape and Intimate Partner Violence Survivors, Developing Protocols for Use in Humanitarian Settings, 2020.

[12] United Nations, UN Handbook for United Nations Field Missions on Preventing and Responding to Conflict-Related Violence, 2020.

[13] International Protocol on the Documentation and Investigation of Sexual Violence in Conflict, Best Practice on the Documentation of Sexual Violence as a Crime or Violation of International Law, Second Edition, 2017; Global Code of Conduct for Gathering and Using Information about Systematic and Conflict-Related Sexual Violence, 13 April 2022.

[14] WHO, Guidelines for Medico-Legal Care of Victims of Sexual Violence, 2003, p19.

[15] Médecins Sans Frontières, Medical Activities, Sexual Violence, https://www.msf.org/sexual-violence, accessed 10 April 2025. Note the ICRC adopts reverse burden of proof for sexual violence and assumes it occurs unless proven otherwise. Thus, proactively considering what responses and services are needed, see ICRC Strategy on Addressing Sexual Violence 2018–2024, p4, https://www.icrc.org/sites/default/files/topic/file_plus_list/icrc_strategy_on_sexual_violence_2018-2024_eng_layout_0.pdf, accessed 1 August 2025.

[16] WHO, Strengthening the Medico-Legal Response to Sexual Violence, 2016, p29; WHO, Guidelines for Medico-Legal Care of Victims of Sexual Violence, 2003, p19.

[17] There are variations in the titles but some that exist include: forensic medical officers, physicians, nurses, and examiners.

[18] WHO, Guidelines for Medico-Legal Care of Victims of Sexual Violence, 2003, p98. For instance, in the UK, regulatory bodies include the GMC and the Faculty of Forensic & Legal Medicine (FFLM) of the Royal College of Physicians. Legal standards include mandatory reporting of certain crimes (eg child abuse) and laws on the collection and handling of evidence. There is also organizational governance with clinical guidelines and policies.

victims.[19] The professional international organization, the Chartered Society of Forensic Sciences, supports forensic practice through accredited courses as well as sets quality standards for practitioners and scientists.[20]

In humanitarian action and efforts to end impunity for sexual violence, a medico-legal approach is seen as a crucial 'intersection of medical and judicial services' that requires coordination between a range of actors and sectors ranging from healthcare providers, investigators, social workers, judges, and forensic laboratory services.[21] The medico-legal system reflects 'the set of principles, regulations and procedures for the investigation of crimes against life and personal integrity by different public entities that belong to the judiciary, law enforcement and forensic services'.[22] The role of medical practitioners in such a system is to 'support the administration of justice' through their expertise and analysis of relevant evidence.[23] The required competencies of such medico-legal practitioners should range from understanding the relevant laws and policies on sexual violence, adhering to ethical standards, understanding the medico-legal system, respecting a victim's choices, following principles of confidentiality and data protection, and training in how to communicate and interact with victims of sexual violence.[24]

In situations of ongoing conflict or a lack of local justice infrastructure, medico-legal services can be disrupted preventing the coordination, expertise, and resources being brought to bear by such a system that is needed to document and treat sexual violence. That said non-governmental organizations (NGOs) and international organizations with staff trained in providing such forensic examinations and documentation can mitigate some of these gaps. For instance medico-legal certificates, which doctors complete on examination and treatment of a victim, can be important evidence in the future.[25] MSF recall that the collection of medico-legal certificates in Congo-Brazzaville were used years later and admitted as evidence by a judge.[26] However, non-forensically trained staff can be hesitant to sign certificates if it means they have to be put through an onerous judicial process

[19] See Chapter 3 for more information on forensic quality standards relating to sexual offence medicine (SOM). For instance, in the UK, the FFLM of the Royal College of Physicians training provides tailored educational programmes, qualifications, as well as guidance and standards for those working in key areas of forensic medicine, eg sexual offence medicine and police custody medicine—see the FFLM of the Royal College of Physicians, https://fflm.ac.uk/, accessed 5 May 2025).

[20] An example of an internationally recognized professional organization is the Chartered Society of Forensic Sciences; see https://www.csofs.org/, accessed 5 May 2025.

[21] WHO, Strengthening the Medico-Legal Response to Sexual Violence, 2016.

[22] Maria Dolores Morcillo Mendez, Strengthening the Medicolegal System: Fulfilling International Law Obligations During Conflicts and Disasters to Prevent and Resolve Issues of Humanitarian Concern, *International Review of the Red Cross* 106 (926) (2024) 795–822, p797.

[23] ibid p798.

[24] WHO, Strengthening the Medico-Legal Response to Sexual Violence, 2016, pp13–14.

[25] The sexual violence medical certificate includes a patient's account of the sexual violence, findings on medical examination, and related treatment.

[26] Françoise Duroch and Catrin Schulte-Hillen, Care for Victims of Sexual Violence, An Organization Pushed to its Limits: The Case of Médecins Sans Frontières, *International Review of the Red Cross* 96 (894) (2014) 601–624, p621.

as well as subjected to threats from warring parties given the political dimension to CRSV.[27] That said, other medical records can also be used as medico-legal documentation, as many reparation programmes recognize the reluctance and stigma of victims of CRSV appearing before a medical professional and the general lack of evidence.

Healthcare professionals need to have an astute understanding of domestic law, but greater emphasis on international law and avenues for reparations, is typically not part of education, unless specific attention is given to this. Medical actors providing care to victims of CRSV do so with their own professional objectives, and it is important to appreciate how they are navigating practical and legal issues without causing further burdens to their role. A medico-legal approach to reparations appreciates the potential and limitations of forensic evidence for CRSV (as explored in Chapter 3), but also enriches our understanding of harm as well as considers how it intersects with legal processes to dismantle common misconceptions of what injuries may or may not ensue. A medico-legal approach presented in this book considers how forensic medicine may be employed more effectively in reparations, from identifying key patterns of violence, providing evidence to fulfil eligibility for reparations, to demonstrating the needs of certain population groups, without necessarily going through criminal justice procedures.

A medico-legal approach conceptualizes the mind and body as a whole. Thus, a key component of a medico-legal approach is interdisciplinary medicine, considering how multiple medical specialties may complement our understanding of harm. It too reflects on what might be the appropriate responses intended to mitigate harm, as well as how to maximize medicine's potential to repair while limiting its ability to cause further harm. In considering reparations for CRSV, it draws on obstetrics and gynaecology, forensic medicine, public health, urology, community sexual and reproductive healthcare, psychiatry, and genito-urinary medicine, among others. While this book does not intend to address every possible consequence, a wider lens appreciates the cascading health impacts that could otherwise be missed by focusing on only the well-known consequences of CRSV, or from the perspective of siloed specialties. In turn, this book urges us to adopt a holistic approach that emphasizes the biopsychosocial(legal) model. By doing so, it interrogates the sexual and reproductive health nexus of CRSV, how justice measures influence health, and challenges assumptions on what is deemed to be 'sexual violence' or what could be an appropriate legal right to repair.

In theory, a medico-legal approach should opt for a more inclusive perspective on diverse victim groups. While such research is valuable, generalizations should be avoided, and the diversity of experiences recognized.[28] It also requires

[27] ibid p620

[28] Kirsten Campbell, Producing Knowledge in the Field of Sexual Violence in Armed Conflict Research: Objects, Methods, Politics, and Gender Justice Methodology, *Social politics* 25 (2018) 469–495.

us to recognize that inclusion without nuance risks obscuring the particularities of each group's experiences. Gender identity, age, disability status, ethnicity, and socio-economic background all shape how CRSV is perpetrated, experienced, and understood. A medico-legal approach thus demands that we interrogate not only who is counted as a victim but also how power dynamics—within medicine, law, and society—structure opportunities for acknowledgement, care, and redress. The identities attached to persons who suffer sexual violence may shape their experiences of claiming redress, as explored in Chapter 4.

This book appreciates how research conducted into the consequences of sexual violence shapes which harms are made visible and which victims are prioritized. There are challenges to collecting epidemiological data on CRSV and health outcomes owing to practical, definitional, and ethical reasons. The known impact of CRSV is shaped by population selection including country choice and concerns around feasibility of conducting research in conflict affected countries or displaced populations. It is important to critically consider why some conflict situations have been researched to a greater degree than others; at the expense of representing a complex problem as a simple one.[29] In medical research, two systematic reviews on the negative consequences of CRSV included only civilian victims, missing opportunities to understand harms to victims of CRSV within armed groups.[30] In essence, medicine is also at risk of hierarchizing victims when it fails to take a holistic approach and embody its own principles of non-discrimination. A medico-legal approach recognizes that many victims of conflict-related sexual violence will not have any visible physical injuries but can be left with significant psycho-social impairments. It also acknowledges that harm to transgender persons may be missed if they are not recognized as a legal identity in their home or host country.

A medico-legal approach dissects what counts as adequate and meaningful repair by aligning the articulation of harm with the articulated needs of survivors. Therefore, it encourages us to consider why transitional justice measures are assumed to be intrinsically 'therapeutic' and by what metrics such therapeutic value is assessed. Crucially, it visibilizes the intricacies of gathering quality data on CRSV—ethical challenges in consent, the stigma that suppresses disclosure, and the definitional ambiguities that complicate prevalence estimates. A medico-legal perspective urges us to scrutinize how data on harm is produced—who collects

[29] Chloé Lewis, The Making and Re-Making of the 'Rape Capital of the World': On Colonial Durabilities and the Politics of Sexual Violence Statistics in DRC, *Critical African Studies* (14) (2022) 50–72

[30] Elena Rubini et al, Negative Consequences of Conflict-Related Sexual Violence on Survivors: A Systematic Review of Qualitative Evidence, *International journal for Equity in Health* 22(1) (2023) 227. Ines Ba and Raj S Bhopal, Physical, Mental and Social Consequences in Civilians who have Experienced War-Related Sexual Violence: A Systematic Review (1981–2014), *Public health* 142 (2017) 121–35.

it, under what conditions, and with what research questions—and how that data subsequently informs reparation measures. It calls for conscious deliberation on the epistemic frameworks we employ, and how these shape the forms of reparation deemed appropriate.

As societies are affected by conflict on multiple levels—physical infrastructure, social cohesion, cultural memory—a medico-legal approach dissects the vulnerabilities inherent in reparations aimed at restoring health. It compels us to consider quality of life including when profound disability results from sexual violence, to weigh psychological trauma against physical injury, and to appreciate the interplay between community-based support and individualized clinical care. Reparations must therefore be calibrated to need, responsive to intersectional vulnerabilities, and grounded in international humanitarian law's protections for the most at-risk populations.

Finally, this approach calls for continuous learning and training to keep apace with evolving understandings of medical conditions and therapeutic care. It recognizes that insights from non-conflict sexual offence medicine—suited to forensic assessment, trauma-informed therapy, and long-term rehabilitation—can enrich reparative frameworks for CRSV. By expanding conceptualizations of rehabilitation as reparation, we move beyond narrow legalistic compensation to embrace ethics of care, in which every clinical encounter becomes an opportunity to restore agency, foster dignity, and generate positive ripples of trust within fractured communities. In doing so, the medico-legal model positions both individual healing and collective restoration at the heart of transitional justice—a holistic nexus where medicine, law, and human rights converge.

In summary, by fostering a deeper theoretical comprehension of the interplay between medicine and law, the medico-legal approach aims to enhance the quality of healthcare, protect patient welfare, and uphold the integrity of the medical profession—factors that are instrumental in identifying and contributing towards repair. When healthcare professionals have greater legal literacy, in particular on justice mechanisms such as reparations for victims of CRSV, then they can better navigate public and private healthcare systems and avenues of redress such as reparation. Therefore, integrating medical expertise with legal principles, the medico-legal approach ensures that reparations are not only responsive to the individual needs of victims but also illuminate structural determinants of health and contribute to systemic changes that promote justice and accountability. Providing victims with medical and psychological care may provide more opportunities for victims to articulate other aims and objectives needed for transformative reparations and other justice measures. Thus, a medico-legal approach can reveal what vehicles are needed to assist with repairing the harm in a holistic manner. As a final issue, I want to briefly discuss quality of life and how it relates to approaching harm for CRSV.

2.1.1 Quality of life

The incorporation of quality of life can help illuminate the multidimensional nature of harm from CRSV that moves beyond viewing such violence as only a violation of bodily integrity. It can also assist in formulating responses and monitoring their effectiveness. The WHO defines quality of life (QoL) as an, 'individual's perception of their position in life in the context of the culture and value systems in which they live and in relation to their goals, expectations, standards and concerns'.[31] Thus it is both a concept and an attempt to produce a measurement scale outside of biomedical or clinical outcomes.[32] The dynamic nature of QoL appreciates that it will evolve over time and depend on biological, social, psychological, and *legal* factors.

While QoL is an imperfect and contested tool, it encourages reparation processes to consider alternative, victim-centred outcomes for measuring success, and serves as a valuable form of complementary analysis. Although the subjective nature of QoL evaluation—particularly when based on victims' self-assessment—has drawn criticism, it importantly centres the victim in the process, incorporating what they personally value and consider meaningful. Thus, QoL should incorporate whether there are real opportunities for victims to achieve the life they wish to live.[33] For instance, a medical intervention might be deemed clinically successful, yet the resulting side effects could still impair the individual's ability to pursue valued life goals. Similarly, a person may receive an educational opportunity, but prevailing harmful social norms might prevent them from exercising their skills or fulfilling their vocational aspirations. It is important to consider the adaptation of QoL measurement scales to ensure their relevance and applicability within reparations frameworks.

It is also important to recognize that individuals living with severe illness or injury sometimes report QoL levels equal to or higher than those without such conditions.[34] This highlights the importance of focusing not only on physical recovery, but also on whether victims have real, substantive opportunities to pursue the lives they wish to lead and whether the way in which care is delivered makes a difference, for example with compassion and in partnership. What constitutes a meaningful life varies between individuals and can evolve over time, particularly as a result of psychological adaptation or therapeutic interventions—a phenomenon known as response shift where one's internal standards, values, or conceptualization of

[31] WHOQOL User Manual, Programme on Mental Health, 2012, WHO/HIS/HIS Rev 2012.

[32] A plethora of measurement tools have been devised. See Jasneth Mullings, Sage Arbor, and Medhane Cumbay, *Health-Related Quality of Life Measurement Tools, Predictors and Modifiers*, IntechOpen (2022) p1.

[33] Amartya Sen, *Development as Freedom*, OUP (1999) 5 and 87.

[34] Jamie O'Hara et al, Evidence of a Disability Paradox in Patient-Reported Outcomes in Haemophilia, *Haemophilia: The Official Journal of the World Federation of Hemophilia* 27(2) (2021) 245–252.

QoL change.[35] Nevertheless, victims should be able to access reparative measures without needing to internally adjust their expectations of what quality of life means to them. To adequately capture this complexity, reparations programmes should incorporate semi-structured and participatory methods for understanding harm and evaluating outcomes. These might include free-text survey responses, narrative interviews, or other qualitative approaches that allow victims to articulate their own conceptions of wellbeing, capability, and redress.

Ultimately, reparations that meaningfully integrate quality of life principles acknowledge that addressing CRSV is not solely about remedying past harms. It is also about enabling victims to determine their futures, live with dignity, and exercise agency in their lives. This approach must also account for the structural and institutional barriers that may limit individual capabilities or goals—underscoring the need to contextualize QoL within broader socio-political environments. In some contexts, it may be necessary to measure functional and rehabilitative outcomes alongside QoL, given the inherent challenges in assessing whether personal goals are due to choices or constraints in post-conflict settings.[36] By embedding quality of life considerations into reparative frameworks, responses to conflict-related sexual violence can move beyond symbolic redress to foster conditions in which victims are genuinely supported to rebuild meaningful, self-directed lives.

2.2 Transitional Justice

Transitional justice involves a range of processes and mechanisms (eg trials, truth commissions, amnesties, reparations, and vetting) to facilitate a society's transition from authoritarianism, post-conflict situations, or colonialism towards democracy or independence.[37] Over the past four decades, transitional justice has expanded its scope to keep pace with the global human rights discourse, social victim movements, and the proliferation of truth commissions, reparation programmes, and international criminal justice mechanisms.[38] The transitional justice 'field' has become enriched by legal and non-legal disciplines that emphasize a transformative aspiration to address the social, cultural, and economic inequalities which potentially contribute to conflicts and post-conflict tensions.[39] The normative justification for transitional justice is that the past must be dealt with to address harms for

[35] Lena Ring, Quality of Life, in K Petrie and L Reynolds, *Cambridge Handbook of Psychology, Health and Medicine*, Second Edition, CUP, (2007) 178–182.

[36] Sabina Alkire, Why the Capability Approach?, *Journal of Human Development*, 6(1) (2007) 115–135.

[37] S/2004/616, para 8.

[38] See Ruti Teitel, Transitional Justice Genealogy, *Harvard Human Rights Journal* 16(1) (2003) 69–94.

[39] Christine Bell, Transitional Justice, Interdisciplinarity and the State of the 'Field' or 'Non-Field', *International Journal of Transitional Justice* 3(1) (2009) 5–27.

individual victims, but also to improve social cohesion, consolidate democracy, and prevent future violence.[40]

Transitional justice emerged as a field from the campaigns of human rights activists and victim associations—most notably families of citizens disappeared under Latin American authoritarian regimes in the 1970s and 1980s—as well as political, legal, and cultural actors attempting to change the way in which their societies were governed.[41] Arthur notes that the term 'transitional justice' did not come into common usage until the mid-1990s.[42] It has now evolved into a global discourse seen as a preferred response to the needs of societies emerging from authoritarianism or conflict,[43] as well as in settled democracies in confronting historical abuse,[44] such as the Canadian Truth and Reconciliation Commission on the residential schools for First Nation children.[45] In many instances, transitional justice developments in one jurisdiction have been cross-pollinated and adapted by others with appropriate tweaks for their own local contexts.[46]

Given the emphasis upon the 'rule of law' as a key tenet of democracy, remedying civil and political rights violations has often been prioritized in transitions.[47] The origins of transitional justice are usually traced to the International Military Tribunal at Nuremberg, where proceedings focused on criminalizing the acts of individual Nazi leaders and those deemed most responsible for the Second World War.[48] Accountability for past human rights violations has since often been framed primarily in legal terms of prosecutions. However, it is also a fact that many conflicts or periods of authoritarianism have also been followed by amnesties since the Second World War which suggests that the drive for accountability has been coterminous with pragmatic accommodations with past human rights violators as part of the transition from the violence of the past.[49] At the same time reparations

[40] Paige Arthur, How 'Transitions' Reshaped Human Rights: A Conceptual History of Transitional Justice, *Human Rights Quarterly* 31(2) (2009) 321–367, p325.

[41] Teitel, n 37, refers to this as the second phase of transitional justice.

[42] Arthur, n 40, p330.

[43] Simon Robins and Erik Wilson, Participatory Methodologies with Victims: An Emancipatory Approach to Transitional Justice Research, *Canadian Journal of Law and Society* 30(2) (2015) 219–236, p220.

[44] Anne-Marie McAlinden, An Inconvenient Truth: Barriers to Truth Recovery in the Aftermath of Institutional Child Abuse in Ireland, *Legal Studies* 33(2) (2013) 189–214, p192; and James Gallen, Jesus Wept: The Roman Catholic Church, Child Sexual Abuse and Transitional Justice, *International Journal of Transitional Justice*, 10(2) (2016) 332–349.

[45] See Joanne Quinn, The Development of Transitional Justice, in C Lawther, L Moffett, and D Jacobs (eds), *Research Handbook on Transitional Justice*, Elgar (2017) 11–33.

[46] See Kieran McEvoy and Louise Mallinder, Politics, Theory and Praxis: The 'Respectabilisation' of Transitional Justice, in Kieran McEvoy and Louise Mallinder (eds), *Transitional Justice: Critical Concepts in Law* (2017) 1–25.

[47] Paul Gready, *The Era of Transitional Justice: The Aftermath of the Truth and Reconciliation Commission in South Africa and Beyond*, Routledge (2010) p233.

[48] Padraig McAuliffe, *Transformative Transitional Justice and the Malleability of Post-Conflict States*, Elgar (2017) p38; and Teitel, n 37, p72.

[49] See Louise Mallinder, *Amnesty, Human Rights and Political Transitions: Bridging the Peace and Justice Divide*, Hart (2008).

programmes and truth commissions have been adopted by dozens of states to provide redress to victims, as well as to uncover the patterns, causes, and consequences of violations to prevent their repetition. However, such mechanisms can sometimes require compromises and trade-offs on accountability—leading to the charge that transitional justice is a byword for 'compromised justice'.[50]

In light of these shortcomings, in recent years there has been increased attention in transitional justice towards a more transformative vision of the field.[51] This transformative approach to transitional justice has been articulated as a means to counter such social exclusion in transitional moments by paying attention to a participatory process over outcomes, as well as challenging unequal power relations.[52] McAuliffe considers that transitional justice can be politically transformative, but its narrow focus on punishing a few perpetrators limits that transformative potential.[53] For others, the emphasis on transformation including societal inequalities and the structural roots of violence risks conflating transitional justice with peacebuilding.[54] A transformative perspective on transitional justice as a means to not only hold perpetrators accountable, but also address the needs of victims and simultaneously challenge broader complicity and cultures of patriarchy that are often the root cause of such violations is important to keep in mind when tackling sexual violence. A transformative approach to sexual violence is discussed in more depth in Chapter 5—for now its value is in visiblilizing the diverse range of sexual violence that occurs before, during, and after conflict that are rooted in society but also require individual, familial, and communal transformation to prevent their recurrence.

In line with this more transformative vision of transitional justice, over the past 15 years there has also been a sustained critique of the dominance of legalism in the field.[55] Legalism can 'side-line' victims in satisfying their needs, by concentrating more on establishing and reforming institutions and laws as well as serving the interests of lawyers and legal institutions.[56] Sociologists, anthropologists, psychologists, and indeed self-aware lawyers have increasingly engaged in moving 'beyond legalism' in transitional justice.[57] As McEvoy and Bell suggest, there is a

[50] Bronwyn Anne Leebaw, The Irreconcilable Goals of Transitional Justice, *Human Rights Quarterly* 30(1) (2008) 95–118, p97.

[51] Paul Gready and Simon Robins, From Transitional to Transformative Justice: A New Agenda for Practice, *International Journal of Transitional Justice* 8(3) (2014) 339–361.

[52] ibid.

[53] McAuliffe, n 48, p39.

[54] Lars Waldorf, Anticipating the Past: Transitional Justice and Socio-Economic Wrongs, *Social & Legal Studies* 21(2) (2012) 171–186, pp179–180.

[55] Bell, n 39, p22.

[56] Vincent Druliolle and Roddy Brett, Introduction: Understanding the Construction of Victimhood and the Evolving Role of Victims in Transitional Justice and Peacebuilding, in V Druliolle and R Brett (eds), *The Politics of Victimhood in Post-conflict Societies: Comparative and Analytical Perspectives*, Palgrave (2018) 1–22, p3.

[57] Kieran McEvoy, Beyond Legalism: Towards a Thicker Understanding of Transitional Justice, *Journal of Law and Society*, 34(4) (2007) 411–440, p411.

willingness, even amongst lawyers drawn from other disciplines, to inform the approaches and effectiveness of transitional justice contributing to the 'thickening' of the field.[58]

The anti-legalistic critique of transitional justice is also linked to calls to 'decolonize law's hold on the discourse' and recognize the political and practical projects involved in transitions after mass atrocities.[59] For example, de Grieff has called for a shift from this broadly legalistic and normative focus of transitional justice towards a greater emphasis on explanatory approaches as to how transitional mechanisms can be practically implemented.[60] In line with this argument, a medical perspective on harm and treatment can be instructors in how we move beyond theory and normative concepts of justice to adequately and effectively remedy CRSV. This requires an analogous grasp of the empirical scale of CRSV, the range of psychological and physical complications that can emerge as a result of such harms, and the potential therapeutic medical treatments that may contribute to more effective reparations.[61]

An anti-legalist, even anti-conformist/state-centric approach to justice also requires appreciating that mass atrocities are not simply committed by individuals, but through systems and cultures of practice. In turn, conflict or authoritarianism can warp professional practice, whether through the system or context it finds itself in,[62] such as the complicity of the medical profession in Peru in forced sterilizations or doctors involved in torture in Guantanamo Bay or the Occupied Territories in Israel/Palestine.[63] In periods of conflict or transition, issues of justice may not always be at the forefront of medical professionals' minds. Instead, those affected and responsible for atrocities often come before them as patients or next of kin. Yet periods of conflict and transition are politically charged environments that inevitably shape professional fields such as medicine, whatever their claims to the primacy of professional ethics and neutrality, which can become stressed by direct or indirect attacks on their facilities and personnel. Later in this book I examine the notion of 'ordinary' medicine in such contexts and how the medical profession and its work respond to the harms wrought by sexual violence.

[58] ibid; Bell, n 39, p23.

[59] Bell, n 39, p21; and Pascha Bueno-Hansen, Decolonial Feminism, Gender, and Transitional Justice in Latin America, in Fionnuala Ní Aoláin et al, *The Oxford Handbook of Gender and Conflict*, OUP (2018) 456–467.

[60] Pablo de Greiff, Bridging the Research-Practice Gap: Applied Transitional Justice Research, lecture at Oxford University, 30 June 2017.

[61] Irving Kenneth Zola, Medicine as an Institution of Social Control, *The Sociological Review* 20(4) (1972) 487–504.

[62] Such as the culture of quietism amongst lawyers during the Troubles/conflict in Northern Ireland, see Kieran McEvoy, What Did the Lawyers Do During the 'War'? Neutrality, Conflict and the Culture of Quietism, *The Modern Law Review* 74(3) (2011) 350–384.

[63] Sunneva Gilmore and Luke Moffett, Redressing Forced Sterilisation: The Role of the Medical Profession, *BJOG* 127(8) (2020) 923–926; and Steven J Hoffman, Ending Medical Complicity in State-Sponsored Torture, *The Lancet* 378 (9802) (2011) 1535–1537.

2.2.1 Transitional justice and sexual violence

Historically transitional justice has been more concerned with prosecuting and punishing perpetrators rather than being driven by addressing the needs of victims, which has been particularly acute for victims of CRSV.[64] Ní Aoláin notes that gender violations and violence against women has traditionally been 'under-enforced' or deprioritized due to the focus on killings, torture, and repression that marked authoritarian states, as well as women often being excluded from peace agreements and transition negotiations.[65] The issue of sexual violence was largely neglected in the Nuremberg and Tokyo tribunals after the Second World War.[66]

Since the 1990s, with the creation of the ad hoc tribunals for the former Yugoslavia and Rwanda, as well as in truth commissions in Guatemala and South Africa, there has been greater attention to the experience and patterns of sexual violence in transitional contexts. Yet even victim-centred transitional justice measures that organically developed within states, such as truth commissions and reparation bodies, have often neglected sexual violence or failed to sufficiently include women in their design and delivery.[67] Transitional justice's apparent neutrality and normative basis can hide gender biases and the distinct impact of individual or group violence and conflict on women.[68] Bell has queried the extent to which transitional justice can effectively respond to CRSV and sufficiently protect such victims in transitional mechanisms.[69] For instance, in a number of transitional societies there is evidence that some women may not come forward to participate in truth commissions or other bodies for fear of their partners or community finding out they were victims of sexual violence.[70]

This is particularly acute with criminal trials. While sexual violence was prosecuted in a number of cases before the International Criminal Tribunal for the former Yugoslavia, International Criminal Tribunal for Rwanda (ICTR), and Special Court for Sierra Leone (SCSL),[71] the extent to which these provided

[64] Ruth Rubio-Marín, The Gender of Reparations: Setting the Agenda, in Ruth Rubio-Marín (ed), *What Happened to the Women? Gender and Reparations for Human Rights Violations*, ICTJ (2006) 20–47, p22.

[65] Fionnuala Ní Aoláin, Gendered Under-Enforcement in the Transitional Justice Context, in S Buckley-Zistel and R Stanley (eds), *Gender in Transitional Justice*, Springer (2012) 59–87, pp64–65.

[66] Kelly D Askin, Prosecuting Wartime Rape and Other Gender Related Crimes under International Law: Extraordinary Advances, Enduring Obstacles, *Berkeley Journal of International Law* 21(2) (2003) 288–349, p288.

[67] See Ruth Rubio-Marín, The Gender of Reparations, in Rubio-Marín (ed), n 4, 63–120.

[68] Fionnuala Ní Aoláin, Catherine O'Rourke, and Aisling Swaine, Transforming Reparations for Conflict-Related Sexual Violence: Principles and Practice, *Harvard Human Rights Journal* 28 (2015) 97–146, p115.

[69] Bell, n 39, p7.

[70] Lisa J Laplante, From Theory to Practice: Implementing Reparations in Post-Truth Commission Peru, *Waging War, Making Peace: Reparations and Human Rights*, Left Coast Press (2009) 75–93, p84.

[71] See Rosemary Grey, Sexual Violence against Child Soldiers: The Limits and Potential of International Criminal Law, *International Feminist Journal of Politics* 16(4) (2014) 601–621.

justice to victims or indeed assisted in the personal healing of such victims has been questioned.[72] This neglect has also been acutely felt in the first few cases at the International Criminal Court (ICC) where the failure to charge defendants with sexual violence in the *Lubanga* and *Katanga* cases resulted in victims being unable to claim reparations for these crimes before the Court.[73] While the subsequent cases of *Kenyatta, Gbagbo, Bemba,* and *Al Hassan* involving rape and forced marriage resulted in the cases collapsing or acquittal of those charges, more recent cases have resulted in convictions for a range of sexual violence including rape and sexual slavery in the *Ntaganda* case and forced pregnancy and forced marriage in the *Ongwen* case, but not male sexual violence.[74] Those successes apart, challenges in convicting individuals of rape that can lead to reparations are illustrated by the appeals judgment in the *Hissène Habré* case at the Extraordinary African Chambers in Senegal, which acquitted the defendant of personally committing rape against a victim, but upheld other sexual violence charges.[75] As Chappell points out, a gender-orientated approach 'must be identified and articulated from the outset or they will be overridden by the biases that lurk under the surface of formal rules.'[76] In Chapter 7 we will return to examine this in more detail with regards to reparations.

A gender perspective on transitional justice has been important in highlighting the disproportionate violence that women and girls suffer during authoritarian regimes and conflicts.[77] Analysis of the types of violations committed in periods of violence or authoritarianism, in particular CRSV, expose a wide spectrum of sexual violence during conflict, including rape, gang rape, enslavement, and related offences.[78] There are also increasing reports on the misuse of non-medical

[72] See Binaifer Nowrojee, 'Your Justice is Too Slow': Will the International Criminal Tribunal for Rwanda Fail Rwanda's Rape Victims? in D Pankhurst (ed), *Gendered Peace: Women's Struggles for Post-War Justice and Reconciliation*, Routledge (2007) 107–136; and Nicola Henry, Witness to Rape: The Limits and Potential of International War Crimes Trials for Victims of Wartime Sexual Violence, *International Journal of Transitional Justice* 3(1) (2009) 114–134.

[73] Luke Moffett, Transitional Justice and Reparations: Remedying the Past? in C Lawther, L Moffett, and D Jacobs (eds), *Research Handbook on Transitional Justice*, Elgar (2017) 377–400, p378.

[74] See Rosemary Grey, *Prosecuting Sexual and Gender-Based Crimes at the International Criminal Court Practice, Progress and Potential*, CUP (2019) p253 and 258. See also *Prosecutor v Bosco Ntaganda*, Judgment, ICC-01/04-02/06-2359, 8 July 2019; and *Prosecutor v Dominic Ongwen*, Trial Judgment, ICC-02/04-01/15-1762, 4 January 2021, paras 2717–2729. See further Sunneva Gilmore, Better Later, Than Never: Reparations for Sexual Violence before the International Criminal Court, *Journal of Human Trafficking, Enslavement and Conflict-Related Sexual Violence*, 2(1) (2021) 27–47.

[75] See Christoph Sperfeldt, The Trial against Hissène Habré: Networked Justice and Reparations at the Extraordinary African Chambers, *International Journal of Human Rights* 21(9) (2017) 1243–1260, p1249.

[76] Louise Chappell, The Gender Injustice Cascade: 'Transformative' Reparations for Victims of Sexual and Gender-Based Crimes in the Lubanga Case at the International Criminal Court, *International Journal of Human Rights* 21(9) (2017) 1223–1242, p1235.

[77] See Catherine O'Rourke, Transitional Justice and Gender, in C Lawther, L Moffett, and D Jacobs (eds), *Research Handbook of Transitional Justice*, Elgar (2017) 117–141, p118; Ní Aoláin et al, n 68, p115.

[78] See Elisabeth Jean Wood, Conflict-Related Sexual Violence and the Policy Implications of Recent Research, *International Review of the Red Cross* 96 (894) (2014) 457–478.

and medical technologies to destroy, control, or prevent reproductive capacity (such as forced sterilization),[79] in some instances designed as instruments of genocide, or at the very least as part of broader 'gender-control' strategies,[80] such as forced contraception used by state and non-state armed groups, such as FARC and ISIS.[81] Structural inequalities can exacerbate the suffering of certain groups such as women, minorities, the disabled, and the elderly during conflicts. In this respect, the predominant type of harm and intended result are beyond 'ordinary'—that is, familiar to settled democracies[82]—but exacerbated in scale and severity by the underlying structural contexts of conflict and authoritarianism and requiring scaled-up transitional justice responses.

Uncovering the scale of sexual violence before, during, and after conflict, in order to inform justice and medical responses, is also inherently difficult. CRSV documentation can be misleading, due to definitional and methodological variances,[83] and (as noted above) the confidence of victims in presenting themselves before legal mechanisms or institutions during or after conflict. Aside from documentation obstacles in conflict, many types of CRSV may not be routinely collected or detected by researchers, such as the indirect impact of witnessing family members being raped or mutilated. It is difficult to assume how exceptional CRSV is when it is not adequately captured in data collection, or where a multidimensional view of harm is not considered.[84] Underreporting of sexual violence is a problem in 'ordinary' settled democracies, as it has a cost for victims in terms of stigma and the unlikelihood of the perpetrator being convicted.[85] However, in times of war such dynamics are exacerbated by the lack of local criminal justice or policing capacity (or willingness) to investigate and prosecute such crimes, fear or lack of trust in official institutions to report sexual violence, the reality of social and medical services disrupted or destroyed by fighting, fractured social and political relationships, and victims who are often subjected to multiple violations by perpetrators who enjoy impunity to commit such violations—all of which aggravates

[79] Jocelyn Getgen, Untold Truths: The Exclusion of Enforced Sterilizations from the Peruvian Truth Commission's Final Report, *Boston College Third World Law Journal* 29(1) (2009) 1–34.

[80] Jennifer Klein, Recent Developments in Health Law: Compensating Victims of Forced Sterilization, *Journal of Law, Medicine & Ethics* 40(2) (2012) 422–426; Amnesty International, *Crimes of Hate, Conspiracy of Silence: Torture and Ill Treatment Based on Sexual Identity*, 2001; and Luz E Nagle, Giving Shelter From the Storm: Colombians Fleeing Persecution Based on Sexual Orientation, *Tulsa Law Review* 48(1) (2012) 1–26.

[81] See Daniela Suárez Vargas, The Subversive Victim: Victimhood and Sexual and Gender-Based Violence Inside Non-State Armed Groups in Colombia, PhD Thesis, (2024); and Aldo Borda, Putting Reproductive Violence on the Agenda: A Case Study of the Yazidis, *Journal of Genocide Research* 26(1) (2022) 94–114, p108.

[82] Eric Posner and Adrian Vermeule, Reparations for Slavery and Other Historical Injustices, *Columbia Law Review* 103(3) (2003) 689–774.

[83] Linda Saltzman, Definitional and Methodological Issues Related to Transnational Research on Intimate Partner Violence, *Violence against Women* 10(7) (2014) 812–830.

[84] L Shanks, et al, Responding to Rape, *The Lancet* 357 (9252) (2001) 304.

[85] W David Allen, The Reporting and Underreporting of Rape, *Southern Economic Journal* 73(3) (2007) 623–641.

victims' suffering.[86] As discussed above, CRSV in such contexts has tended to focus on women and girls, neglecting similar violence against men, transgender and non-binary individuals, as well as other gender-based harms.[87]

As is discussed further in later chapters, civil society can play a particularly important role in ensuring that gender-sensitive approaches to transitional justice are encouraged—approaches that facilitate grassroots engagement or 'safe spaces' for victims' narratives, and help them navigate through the legal thicket.[88] Such an approach can help ensure that the design and delivery of transitional justice mechanisms is premised on the inclusion of women as well as sexual orientation and gender minorities.[89] Of course not all local grassroots activities may deliver a victim-centred, sensitive, or restorative approach.[90] Victims of CRSV can choose to remain silent for a number of reasons, but bottom-up approaches do not guarantee that the stigma of CRSV will be overcome, particularly in light of frequent proximity to victims and affected communities.[91] Local approaches to justice may also replicate cultural norms of discrimination of certain groups such as women.[92] As Guillerot points out, in Peru women played the leading role in struggling for justice and against violence, despite many of them only speaking Quechua and lacking basic education.[93] Nonetheless, with all such caveats taken as a given, I argue that such initiatives may indeed have a role to play in maximizing gender-sensitive reparations for sexual violence.

2.2.2 Transitional justice and medicine

Transitional justice and medicine share some conceptual common ground in responding to post-conflict situations. Medicine can be defined as the provision of investigations, examinations, and assessments to determine the type and extent of a disease, together with the range of medical and surgical interventions which are

[86] Shana Swiss and Joan Giller, Rape as a Crime of War: A Medical Perspective, *Journal of the American Medical Association* 270(5) (1993) 612–615, p613.

[87] Rosemary Nagy, Transitional Justice as Global Project: critical reflections, *Third World Quarterly* 29(2) (2008) 275–289, p287; and Sandesh Sivakumaran, Sexual Violence Against Men in Armed Conflict, *The European Journal of International Law* 18(2) (2007) 253–276, p255.

[88] See Elisabeth Porter, Gendered Narratives: Stories and Silences in Transitional Justice, *Human Rights Review* 17(1) (2016) 35–50.

[89] Wendy Lambourne and Vivianna Rodriguez Carreon, Engendering Transitional Justice: A Transformative Approach to Building Peace and Attaining Human Rights for Women, *Human Rights Review* 17(1) (2016) 71–93.

[90] See Lars Waldorf, Mass Justice for Mass Atrocity: Rethinking Local Justice as Transitional Justice, *Temple Law Review* 79(1) (2006) 1–87; and Simon Robins, Challenging the Therapeutic Ethic: A Victim-Centred Evaluation of Transitional Justice Process in Timor-Leste, *International Journal of Transitional Justice* 6(1) (2006) 1–23.

[91] Porter, n 88, pp44–46.

[92] Gready and Robins, n 51.

[93] Julie Guillerot, Linking Gender and Reparations in Peru: A Failed Opportunity, in Rubio-Marín, n 64, 136–194, p143.

designed to improve a patient's health.[94] The sociology of medicine takes a wider perspective, encompassing the intersection between medicine, medical practice, and broader society. As Friedson has suggested, such an approach explores '... how signs or symptoms get to be labelled or diagnosed as an illness in the first place, how an individual gets to be labelled sick, and how social behaviour is moulded by the process of diagnosis and treatment'.[95] It also interrogates how medicine and medical knowledge and treatment is framed as 'neutral' and 'objective', informed only by science.[96]

The sociology of medicine has evolved into a field that also examines the socialization and education of medical professionals, including their professional organization, role relationships, bureaucracy, rituals, value systems, cultures and practices.[97] Such analysis examines medical professionals' autonomy, over-attachment, and cynicism; paternalism; and their economic and political dominion over patients.[98] More critical accounts have also tried to unpick medicine's 'monopoly' of the experience of illness.[99] Constructivist accounts have considered the process of medicalization as a broader effort of the 'specialization of knowledge', in which technical solutions are advanced to tackle social problems risking 'alienation from genuine social and political debate'.[100] Cassell also draws attention to the role of medical professionals in relieving human suffering but also in making it worse.[101]

The social construction of 'medicine' may be best construed within a 'metamedical' framework in which the culture and context, including conflict, will shape ideas and responses to illness.[102] Indeed, normative values around issues such as termination of pregnancy may allow 'continuity of medical care'. Yet such care is vague enough to enable personal biases to 'deeply influence the health-related behaviours or choices of their patient'.[103] Trust in healthcare professionals

[94] David Mechanic, The Sociology of Medicine: Viewpoints and Perspectives, *Journal of Health and Human Behavior* 7(4) (1966) 237–248.

[95] Eliot Freidson, *Profession of Medicine: A Study of the Sociology of Applied Knowledge*, Dodd, Mead and Company (1970) p212

[96] ibid p214.

[97] Robert Straus, The Nature and Status of Medical Sociology, *American Sociological Review* 22(2) (1957) 200–204; and Renee C Fox, Reflections and Opportunities in the Sociology of Medicine, *Journal of Health and Social Behavior* 26(1) (1985) 6–14, p7.

[98] Fox, n 97.

[99] Paul Berger and Thomas Luckmann, *The Social Construction of Reality*, Penguin (1967) pp103 and 128; and Ivan Illich, *Medical Nemesis: The Expropriation of Health*, Patheon Books (1976).

[100] M R Bury, Social Constructionism and the Development of Medical Sociology, *Sociology of Health and Illness* 8(2) (1986) 137–169, p144.

[101] Eric J Cassell, The Nature of Suffering and the Goals of Medicine, *New England Journal of Medicine* 306 (11) (1982) 639–645.

[102] Note 'Western' medicine has its origins in non-Western advances yet the latter contains ethnocentric connotations. Some scholars favour the less frequently used term 'cosmopolitan' medicine. Peter Worsley, Non-Western Medical Systems, *Annual Review of Anthropology* 11 (1982) 315–342.

[103] Paul Bouvier, Sexual Violence, Health and Humanitarian Ethics: Towards a Holistic, Person-Centred Approach, *International Review of the Red Cross* 96 (894) (2014) 565–584, p580.

can be undermined in times of conflict or authoritarianism where healthcare practitioners are perceived as biased toward one side or involved in violations. Indeed, the complicity of healthcare professionals in violations and discrimination during conflicts has been highlighted by the South African Truth and Reconciliation Commission and evidenced in the German reparation programme.[104] As discussed in Chapter 7, this was also apparent in my own fieldwork where some medical professionals continued biases towards female and male victims of sexual violence. In turn, this has the potential to affect reparations such as the quality of care or eligibility for medical rehabilitation for these victims.

Transitional justice has also been critiqued as being a predominantly 'top-down' way of addressing the past, which often neglects the voices of victims and traditionally marginalized groups in decision-making processes.[105] The medical profession has of course been similarly criticized for its tendency towards an elitist approach in its use of scientific knowledge and administration that exerts 'technical and cognitive power' over patients.[106] While there have been efforts in recent years to increase patients' voices in medical decision-making, medicine has broadly continued to struggle with deeply engrained professional cultures of superiority and uneven power dynamics.[107] Again such dynamics mirror some of the privilege of transitional justice experts (or entrepreneurs)[108] in the application of their 'scientific' knowledge and experience—often applied to communities of colour by white experts, and in some cases without the same level of developed ethical, peer, or legal frameworks for oversight.[109] In the following chapters I explore these dynamics amongst both transitional justice and medical practitioners on victimhood, voice, and agency in the design and delivery of reparations to victims of sexual violence.

Within transitional settings more generally, there is an emerging critical analysis of medicine's monopoly of harm and trauma. In Colombia, Gamboa and Cian have critiqued the medicalization of suffering as a means of bureaucraticizing,

[104] Glenda Wildschut and Pat Mayers, Conflict, Complicity, and Challenges: Reflections on the South African Truth and Reconciliation Commission Health Sector Hearing. *Journal of Nursing Scholarship* 51(3) (2019) 299–307; and Christian Pross, *Paying for the Past: The Struggle over Reparations for Surviving Victims of the Nazi Terror*, translated by Belinda Cooper, John Hopkins University Press (1998).

[105] Patricia Lundy and Mark McGovern, Whose Justice? Rethinking Transitional Justice from the Bottom Up, *Journal of Law and Society* 35(2) (2008) 265–292.

[106] Frederic W Hafferty and Donald W Light, Professional Dynamics and the Changing Nature of Medical Work, *Journal of Health and Social Behavior* (1995) 132–153, p138.

[107] Alison O'Shea, Annette L Boaz, and Mary Chambers, A Hierarchy of Power: The Place of Patient and Public Involvement in Healthcare Service Development, *Frontiers in Sociology* 4 (2019); See also generally Michel Foucault, *The Birth of the Clinic: An Archaeology of Medical Perception*, Routledge (2003).

[108] Tshepo Madlingozi, On Transitional Justice Entrepreneurs and the Production of Victims, *Journal of Human Rights Practice* 2(2) (2010) 208–228, p210.

[109] Kieran McEvoy, Travel, Dilemmas and Nonrecurrence: Observations on the 'Respectabilisation' of Transitional Justice, *International Journal of Transitional Justice* 12(2) (2018) 185–193, p189.

homogenizing, and depoliticizing victims as well as delegitimizing indigenous knowledge sources of remedying harm.[110] Bowyer, drawing from his research on victims in Peru, underscores that the nature of suffering is not linear and that reparations as a bureaucratized process can neglect victims' lived experience and have a 'deadening effect on the survivor's intellectual, mental and emotional life'.[111] Such a perspective is shared by Lykes and Mersky who argue that, in some such contexts, there is a tendency to universalize, pathologize, and psychologize victims' suffering in highly medicalized discourses which in turn divorce such suffering from subjective, intergenerational, political, economic, and social phenomena.[112] That said, transitional justice has emerged as a legal field, and while in the past two decades it has become more interdisciplinary through engagement by scholars from the humanities and arts, there is still a notable absence of healthcare practitioners, with only some engagement by those working on trauma and mental health.[113]

Transitional justice is even promoted for its supposed therapeutic effects, with some suggesting that it can have 'salutary direct and/or indirect health benefits' on victims and affected communities, even if it is just to mitigate the scale of violence in situations of armed conflict.[114] This moves transitional justice beyond a normative or legal exercise to also suggest that it can benefit an individual's or a community's wellbeing and health. Yet attacks on healthcare facilities and medical personnel are often a feature of conflict and can in turn compound harms for victims and affected communities that can substantially degrade health outcomes and service provision for years, even decades, for a local population.[115] Medical ethics stipulate respect for patient autonomy where potentially fatal or harmful choices are made by victims.[116] Gradually, health actors (international or national branches) have been incorporating a human rights-based approach to their operations, and this may increasingly bring their seemingly objective world into conflict with political and social forces, such as with the termination of pregnancy or contraceptive provision.[117] Such contests may bring into sharp relief the realities

[110] Angélica Franco Gamboa y Laura Franco Cian, Managing Suffering in War-Affected Pluricultural Contexts: Reflections on the Assistance to Victims in Colombia, *Revista de Estudios Sociales* 73(1) (2020) 109–121, pp115–117.

[111] Timothy James Bowyer, *Beyond Suffering and Reparation: The Aftermath of Political Violence in the Peruvian Andes*, Springer (2019) pp15 and 148.

[112] M Brinton Lykes and Marcie Mersky, Reparations and Mental Health: Psychosocial Interventions Towards Healing, Human Agency, and Rethreading Social Realities, in Pablo de Greiff (ed), *Handbook of Reparations*, OUP (2006) 589–622, pp595–596.

[113] See Brandon Hamber, Transitional Justice, Mental Health and Psychosocial Support, UN (2023).

[114] Phuong Ngoc Pham, Patrick Vinck, and Harvey M Weinstein, Human Rights, Transitional Justice, Public Health and Social Reconstruction, *Social Science and Medicine* 70 (2010) 98–105, p99.

[115] Sunneva Gilmore, Expert Report on Reparations for Victims of Rape, Sexual Slavery and Attacks on Healthcare, *The Prosecutor v Bosco Ntaganda*, International Criminal Court, 28 October 2020, Public Redacted Version, ICC-01/04-02/06-2623-Anx2-Red2, para 99.

[116] Patrick Davey et al (eds), *Medical Ethics, Law and Communication*, Wiley (2017) p6.

[117] This began in January 2017 to cut funding for international organizations working on family and reproductive health that was followed by the dilution of the Women and Peace Security resolution in April 2019 after threats of the US to veto the UNSC resolution if it included reference to sexual and

of illness and medical treatment that are 'racialized, gendered and market driven', including for victims of sexual violence.[118]

It is apparent that transitional justice and medicine have some conceptual and practical overlaps. As will be discussed below, the sociology of medicine can shed further light into the practice of the profession in transitional societies emerging from conflict, in particular around their role in treating victims and their own biases they may perpetuate, which can cause further harm. Such considerations are relevant to reparations and sexual violence where medical professions are responsible for the initial treatment of injuries, but also providing documentary and forensic evidence that may be used for accountability processes or to support victims' claims for redress, as well as rehabilitation as reparation measures. Reparations as a means to remedy, and even, as some suggest, as a way to 'heal' victims,[119] reflects some of the goals of medicine and so the medical/reparations interaction in transitional justice regarding redress for conflict-related sexual violence is a very common relationship. It is worth turning now to discuss the place of reparations in transitional justice and its efforts to remedy CRSV.

2.2.3 Transitional justice and reparations for sexual violence

Reparations aim to remedy the harm caused to victims of gross violations of human rights as well as serious breaches of international humanitarian law. In international law the legal basis for reparations is usually traced to the *Chorzow Factory* case in which it was held that such measures are intended to 'as far as possible, wipe-out all the consequences of the illegal act and re-establish the situation' before the violation.[120] The UN Principles (2005) on reparations state that their purpose is 'intended to promote justice by redressing' gross violations of human rights and grave breaches of international humanitarian law.[121] In addition, such reparations should be 'appropriate and proportional to the gravity of the violation and the circumstances of each case, be provided with full and effective reparation'.[122] The Principles outline five main measures of reparations: restitution (eg

reproductive healthcare. See Stacy Banwell, Gender, North–South Relations: Reviewing the Global Gag Rule and the Defunding of UNFPA under President Trump, *Third World Quarterly* 41(1) (2020) 1–19.

[118] Sara E Davies and Sophie Harman, Securing Reproductive Health: A Matter of International Peace and Security, *International Studies Quarterly* 64 (2020) 277–284, p278.

[119] Jo-Anne Wemmers, The Healing Role of Reparation, in J M Wemmers (ed), *Reparation for Victims of Crimes against Humanity: The Healing Role of Reparation*, Routledge (2014) 221–233, p228.

[120] *Germany v Poland*, The Factory at Chorzow (Merits), PCIJ, Docket XIV:I Judgment No 13, 13 September 1928, para 125

[121] Principle 15, UN Basic Principles and Guidelines on the Right to a Remedy and Reparation for Victims of Gross Violations of International Human Rights Law and Serious Violations of International Humanitarian Law A/RES/60/147, 16 December 2005.

[122] Principle 18.

property and rights); compensation; rehabilitation (eg medical and socio-legal); measures of satisfaction (eg apologies and memorials); and guarantees of non-repetition (eg institutional reforms), examined in more depth in Chapter 6.

There have been a range of reparation programmes established between states (eg reparations paid by Germany to Israel for the Holocaust),[123] by international bodies (eg the UN Claims Commission for Iraq's invasion and occupation of Kuwait), and domestically (eg in Peru)[124] to respond to mass violence. Reparations are seen as more victim-centred measures for addressing their suffering compared to trials. As such, reparations have become a key pillar of transitional justice.[125] De Greiff notes that given the challenges of mass victimization and the inadequacy of quantifying the irreparable harm caused to individuals, reparations in transitional societies instead reaffirm victims' status as citizens, acknowledging their harm and alleviating the consequences of that harm.[126] He also argues that they are intended to contribute to wider transitional goals of building civic trust, rule of law, and societal recognition of the consequences of violence to prevent its repetition.[127]

Sceptics of transitional justice sometimes argue that reparations are a substitute for a state's inability to hold individuals responsible to account—sometimes referred to as 'blood money'.[128] Certainly the investment in reparations has been underwhelming compared to trials in international or hybrid courts. The Special Court for Sierra Leone convicted nine individuals (including former Liberian president Charles Taylor) costing $300 million USD, yet only $3 million USD was donated for reparations under the UN Peacebuilding Fund.[129] More recently, however, as is discussed below, Colombia and Peru have seen substantive expenditure in reparations.[130]

There are also broader debates about the relationship between reparations in transitional justice and individual or societal healing. For some, reparations are

[123] Gideon Taylor, Greg Schneider, and Saul Kagan, The Claims Conference and the Historic Jewish Efforts for Holocaust-Related Compensation and Restitution, in Ferstman et al (eds), *Reparations for Victims of Genocide, War Crimes and Crimes against Humanity*, Brill (2009) 103–114.

[124] See Cristián Correa, Reparations in Peru from Recommendations to Implementation (ICTJ) June 2013.

[125] Olsen et al note that only 14 out of 84 have implemented reparation programmes. Tricia D Olsen, Leigh A Payne, and Andrew G Reiter, *Transitional Justice in Balance Comparing Processes, Weighing Efficacy*, USIP (2010) p53.

[126] Pablo de Greiff, Justice and Reparations, in Pablo de Greiff, n 112, 451–477, pp457–461.

[127] ibid.

[128] Brandon Hamber, Repairing the Irreparable: Dealing with the Double-Binds of Making Reparations for Crimes of the Past, *Ethnicity and Health* 5 (3–4) (2000) 215–226, p220.

[129] Edward Conteh and Maria Berghs, *'Mi At Don Poil': A Report on Reparations in Sierra Leone for Amputee and War Wounded People*, Amputee and War-Wounded Association (2014) p7.

[130] Over $26 million USD was paid out in compensation to victims in Peru, with over $100 million USD spent on collective projects, see Julie Guillerot, *Reparations in Peru—15 Years of Delivering Redress*, RRV (2019) p36; and Cristian Correa, *Reparations in Peru From Recommendations to Implementation*, ICTJ (2013) p12. In Colombia over $31.4 million USD ($118 billion COL pesos) has been spent on reparations to victims, but will require a further $94 million USD by 2030 to meet the number of victims registered (over 9.1 million)—see Séptimo Informe sobre la implementación de la Ley de Víctimas y Restitución de Tierras al Congreso de la Repúblic 2019-2020, 20 Agosto 2020, p7.

part of a broader process of publicly acknowledging and remedying the continuing consequences of violations, a means for victims to obtain 'cognitive recovery' from their experience and a further component of society recognizing the truth of what happened to them while vindicating their dignity.[131] Some question the extent reparations can be tied to notions of recovery or a 'once and for all' notion of healing, and argue that they should instead be viewed as an element of an ongoing, even intergenerational process of self-repair after atrocities.[132] These issues are explored more in Chapter 7.

Over the past two decades, there has been increasing attention to reparations in transitional justice to address sexual violence in particular. The 2007 Nairobi Declaration, driven by civil society and survivors of CRSV, has further focused attention on the issue.[133] The Declaration states that:

> reparation must drive post-conflict transformation of socio-cultural injustices, and political and structural inequalities that shape the lives of women and girls; that reintegration and restitution by themselves are not sufficient goals of reparation, since the origins of violations of women's and girls' human rights predate the conflict situation.[134]

However, in many instances, states still appear to be reluctant to remedy and acknowledge CRSV.[135] Reparation programmes can be contentious as they speak to notions of who is viewed as a deserving victim and who is deemed responsible for past wrongs.[136] As noted, victims of CRSV in particular may be stigmatized from publicly coming forward due to cultural sensitivities, ostracism, patriarchal discourses, continuing intimidation by those responsible, or ongoing immunity for perpetrators.[137] Victimhood can be further complicated by victims of CRSV sometimes cohabitating or marrying their former abusers and having a family together or experiencing forced abortions, which some detractors of reparations may use to argue for their exclusion.[138] Alternatively, victims of CRSV can be

[131] Yael Danieli, Massive Trauma and the Healing Role of Reparative Justice: An Update, in C. Ferstman and M. Goetz (eds), *Reparations for Victims of Genocide, War Crimes and Crimes Against Humanity: Systems in Place and Systems in the Making*, Brill (2020) 38–85, p54–56.

[132] Brinton Lykes and Mersky, n 112, Reparations and Mental Health: Psychosocial Interventions Towards Healing, Human Agency, and Rethreading Social Realities, in Pablo de Greiff, n 112, 589–622, p615.

[133] Nairobi Declaration on Women's and Girls' Right to a Remedy and Reparation 2007, https://www.fidh.org/IMG/pdf/NAIROBI_DECLARATIONeng.pdf, accessed 1 August 2025.

[134] ibid para 3.

[135] See CREHPA and ICTJ, 'To Walk Freely with a Wide Heart' A Study of the Needs and Aspirations for Reparative Justice of Victims of Conflict-Related Abuses in Nepal, September 2014.

[136] See Moffett, n 73.

[137] de Greiff, n 112, p458.

[138] Nissa Dossa et al, Fistula and Other Adverse Reproductive Health Outcomes among Women Victims of Conflict-Related Sexual Violence: A Population-Based Cross-Sectional Study, *Birth* 14(1) (2014) 5–13.

instrumentalized to advance certain narratives of the past and the responsibility of certain groups, emphasizing these victims' 'innocence' and creating a hierarchy of victimhood.[139] This is apparent in Iraq, where the 2021 Yazidi [Female] Survivor Law concentrates on women and girls' experiences of sexual and reproductive violence at the hands of ISIS. While the law also includes three other minority groups (Christian, Shabak, and Turkmen) who suffered similar violations, Sunni women, children born as a result of rape, and others killed by ISIS are excluded from the range of benefits, including compensation, housing, and psychological support, under the law.

Most CRSV reparation measures are framed as compensation or psychological rehabilitation. While these can meet some victims' needs, they may not have access to treatment for the physical complications that could improve their quality of life, even with compensation.[140] CRSV victims can suffer a range of physical complications including severe genital lacerations, pelvic floor injuries, fistulas, chronic pelvic pain, and genital mutilation or other conditions that require appropriate treatment and reparations.[141] This brings into question the extent and effectiveness of reparations as repair, given that the timing of such measures are often years or decades later. This often results in such physical and/or psychological harm becoming aggravated over time, creating further complications, such as adhesions, infertility, and even death. Under the Yazidi [Female] Survivor Law, for those survivors of sexual enslavement who died before their application was approved, their family will not be able to benefit, and if they died during receipt of the monthly pensions, the benefit to their family, including children born as a result of rape, will cease. As later chapters will discuss, time is crucial in remedying the consequences of CRSV. In the case of Ukraine, the 'interim' reparation measures that have been trialled since 2024 are aimed at mitigating the long-term impact of sexual violence. Yet even these efforts during armed conflict are only aimed at providing a one-off payment of compensation to some 500 eligible victims,[142] rather than specialist care. This reflects the difficulties of delivering such specialist care during conflicts and the reparative-legal frame of responding to such harm, which translates redress into money to acknowledge suffering, but not necessarily medically 'treat' the scope of harm.

[139] Kieran McEvoy and Kirsten McConnachie, Victimology in Transitional Justice: Victimhood, Innocence and Hierarchy, *European Journal of Criminology* 9(5) (2012) 527–538, p532.

[140] Cristián Correa, Getting to Full Restitution: Guidelines for Court-Ordered Reparations in Cases Involving Sexual Violence Committed during Armed Conflict, Political Violence, or State Repression, ICTJ (2017).

[141] E Dartnall and R Jewkes, Sexual Violence against Women: The Scope of the Problem, *Best Practice & Research Clinical Obstetrics and Gynaecology* 27 (2013) 3–13; and A Gisladottir et al, Obstetric Outcomes of Mothers Previously Exposed to Sexual Violence, *PLoS ONE* 11(3) (2016).

[142] Law on Legal and Social Protection of the Rights of Victims of Sexual Violence Related to the Aggression of the Russian Federation against Ukraine, and Urgent Interim Reparations (No 10132). Weronika Strzyżyńska, Reparations to be Paid to Survivors of Wartime Sexual Violence in Ukraine, *The Guardian*, 26 April 2024.

Scholars have increasingly been paying attention to the role of transformative reparations to better respond to sexual violence.[143] Simply using reparations to restore the victim back to the position they were in before the violation fails to dismantle the structural violence and unravel patriarchal social norms that contributed to the commission of sexual violence.[144] Beyond structural reform, specialist rehabilitation measures being accessible to the most marginalized groups subject to cultural and/or physical barriers may itself amount to transformative justice. For example, the leading Inter-American Court of Human Rights case on sexual violence and disappearances concerning the women of Cuidad Juárez ordered the state to provide transformative and remedial reparations, including medical and psychological care, alongside compensation, measures of satisfaction, and non-repetition to prevent recurrence.[145] Thus, the transformative turn within transitional justice has resonated particularly strongly with regard to CRSV and reparations, particularly in tackling the causes, structures, and responses to sexual violence.[146] Transformative justice can be a versatile concept that 'emphasizes local agency and resources, the prioritisation of process rather than preconceived outcomes and the challenging of unequal and intersecting power relationships and structures of exclusion at both the local and the global level'.[147] Transformative justice can also aim to address disparities of material goods, as well as the residual psychological impact of the community.[148] Sankey goes so far as envisioning transitional justice as a transformative means to redress subsistence harms (ie to self-supporting livelihoods), including those related to gender and poverty.[149] These two attributes are often interlinked given socio-economic obstacles arising from the caregiver role and lack of economic and educational opportunities many women face in certain communities. In terms of health, subsistence may amount to selective access to health services based on male 'guardianship', or inaccessibility to an acceptable level of care for human life. A medico-legal approach to such issues would also consider health as a measurable set of indicators as to whether elements of a reparations programme are actually working.[150] This is explored more in Chapters 6 and 7.

143 See Ní Aoláin et al, n 68.
144 Rubio-Marín, n 64.
145 *Gonzáles et al v Mexico* (Preliminary Objections, Merits, Reparations, and Costs) IACtHR Series C No 205 (16 November 2009) 50, 471, and 549.
146 Rubio-Marín, n 64; Ní Aoláin et al, n 68.
147 Gready and Robins, n 51.
148 Anu Pillay, Violence against Women in the Aftermath, in S Meintjes, A Illay, and M Turshen, *The Aftermath: Women in Post-Conflict Transformation*, Zed Books (2001) 35–45; and Rama Mani, *Beyond Retribution: Seeking Justice in the Shadows of War*, CUP (2002) p42.
149 McAuliffe n 48, p43; and Diana Sankey, Towards Recognition of Subsistence Harms: Reassessing Approaches to Socioeconomic Forms of Violence in Transitional Justice, *International Journal of Transitional Justice* 8(1) (2014) 121–140.
150 Phuong Pham, Patrick Vinck, and Harvey Weinstein, Human Rights, Transitional Justice, Public Health and Social Reconstruction, *Social Science and Medicine* 70(1) (2009) 98–105.

2.3 Justice, Restoration, and Medicine

Restorative justice has also been extended to transitional justice contexts. For example, the South African Truth and Reconciliation Commission explicitly framed its participatory process with victims as a restorative one, drawing in particular on the indigenous tradition of Ubuntu and emphasizing the interconnection between truth and healing as restorative justice.[151] Restorative justice has also been deployed in transitional justice work in Northern Ireland, Colombia, Uganda, Indonesia, and a range of other post-conflict contexts.[152] According to the UN Vienna Declaration on Crime and Justice, in order to satisfy 'restorative justice,' an invention must encompass all its core principles.[153] These principles can be synthesized to restoration being centred around voluntary participation of victims and perpetrators, accessibility at all stages, and sensitivity to potential power imbalances such as age or gender.[154] Perceptiveness to gender and the unique nature of sexual crimes has been praised as a particularly suitable form of redress and justice.[155] If restorative practices are not feasible, whether due to lack of resources, consensus on the programme, or 'restorative agreement', then the offender can be encouraged to make reparations to the victim(s).[156]

While there is a broader critique of criminal trials in restorative justice, there is also a heightened awareness of the inadequacies of retributive justice in addressing the harm caused by sexual violence for individual victims and in assisting offender reintegration into the community.[157] Sexual violence is unique in that it often leads to victim-blaming across cultures where victims themselves may feel almost put on trial for their behaviour, past sexual history, or other variables by which they are deemed 'responsible' in some way for their own victimization.[158]

Many cases of domestic and sexual violence will never be subject to criminal proceedings for a multitude of reasons. These may include: failure to meet the

[151] South African Truth and Reconciliation Commission (SATRC), (1998) Vol 5, Chapter 1, para 19; Naomi Roht-Arriaza and Javier Mariecurrenza, *Transitional Justice in the Twenty-First Century: Beyond Truth Versus Justice*, CUP (2006) p3.

[152] See Kerry Clamp, *Restorative Justice in Transitional Justice Settings*, Routledge (2016).

[153] Tenth United Nations Congress on the Prevention of Crime and the Treatment of Offenders Vienna, 10–17 April 2000; Vienna Declaration on Crime and Justice: Meeting the Challenges of the Twenty-first Century (2010) p10.

[154] Niamh Joyce-Wojtas and Marie Keenan, Is Restorative Justice for Sexual Crime Compatible with Various Criminal Justice Systems?, *Contemporary Justice Review* 19(1) (2016) 43–68, p59–60.

[155] Susan L Miller, M Kristen Hefner, and LeeAnn Iovanni, Practitioners' Perspectives on Using Restorative Justice with Crimes of Gendered Violence, *Contemporary Justice Review* 23(1) (2020) 65–90, pp81–82.

[156] UN Handbook, n 12, p10.

[157] See Anne-Marie McAlinden, Restorative Justice as a Response to Sexual Offending: Addressing the Failings of Current Punitive Approaches, *Sexual Offender Treatment* 3(1) (2008) 1–12.

[158] Rachel Killean, Eithne Dowds, and Anne-Marie McAlinden, Sexual Offence Trials in Northern Ireland: The Cultural and Legal Dimensions, in Rachel Killean, Eithne Dowds, and Anne-Marie McAlinden (eds), *Sexual Violence on Trial Local and Comparative Perspectives*, Routledge (2021) 3–21, p12.

threshold of evidentiary standards; victim unwillingness to participate in such legal processes due to stigma or fear of reprisal from perpetrators who may live in the same community; or children who may not be aware of the gravity of abuse.[159] In addition, even for victims who overcome these obstacles and who do go to trial, there are risks of secondary or retraumatization from sexually insensitive criminal proceedings or where a defendant is found not guilty.[160] In turn, as word spreads, poorly handled legal proceedings may have a chill factor on other victims coming forward.

In terms of a restorative response to sexual violence, there have been proposals to insert such frameworks into criminal justice proceedings, such as reparations.[161] Yet less attention has been paid to the practical implementation and exploration of 'lived' harm. Clamp proposes steering away from notions of 'crime', towards comprehensions of 'harm'.[162] Hence, responsibility and punishment is exchanged for an emphasis on remedying harm rather than crime per se. This harm-based approach chimes well with the purpose of reparations and its attention to acknowledging and alleviating victims' harm, which although not on the scale of transitional justice, is seen as a key component in requiring offenders to make amends to victims and to recognize their harm.[163]

Victims and perpetrators are likely to live in the same community or geographical area where they may come across each other. In situations of protracted conflict, such as in Colombia, victims were subjected to repeated violations. In Uganda, those returning from the bush as former sex slaves faced stigma and discrimination from their families and communities. In Peru, sexual violence was carried out by armed actors, which coincided with reproductive violations through forced sterilization as a public health policy of marginalized groups. These are explored in more depth in subsequent chapters. In such situations, a restorative approach that involves perpetrators, victims, and the community may overlook the broader range of responsible actors in war and peace, and may fail to provide effective redress when confined to individual relationships between perpetrators and victims. Jülich and Thorburn suggest that a restorative approach can facilitate substantive equality of the parties through ensuring a fair outcome for those involved in sexual violence.[164] Yet this optimism should be tempered as the practice

[159] ibid.

[160] Francesca Marsh and Nadia Wager, Restorative Justice in Cases of Sexual Violence: Exploring the Views of the Public and Survivors, *Probation Journal* 62(4) (2015) 336–356, p338.

[161] John Braithwaite, Principles of Restorative Justice, in Andrew von Hirsch et al (eds), *Restorative Justice and Criminal Justice: Competing or Reconcilable Paradigms?*, Hart (2003) 1–20; and Jim Dignan, Restorative Justice and the Law: The Case for an Integrated, Systemic Approach, in L Walgrave (ed), *Restorative Justice and the Law*, Willan (2002) 168–190.

[162] Clamp, n 152, p30.

[163] Lucia Zedner, Reparation and Retribution: Are They Reconcilable? *The Modern Law Review* 57(2) (1994) 228–250, p234.

[164] Shirley Jülich and Natalie Thorburn, Sexual Violence and Substantive Equality: Can Restorative Justice Deliver? *Journal of Human Rights and Social Work* 2(1) (2017) 34–44.

of restorative justice may not overcome the power dynamics in conflict or post-conflict environments.

Restorative justice as a response to CRSV resonates with the medical impulse to repair. After a violent crime, such as sexual violence, the first person a victim may come into contact with is a healthcare professional.[165] While such victims may not wish to formally report the crime, in the safe and confidential space of patient–doctor consultations, they may be more willing to open up to a healthcare practitioner. Such medical practitioners can ensure victims are at least offered a number of ameliorative interventions and are referred to other non-medical services that can treat and manage their harm, such as emergency contraception and sexually transmitted infection or psychosexual clinics. The resonance between medicine and restoration leads to important questions as to what *is* exactly being restored and what *should* ideally be restored.

First, a key focus for medical practitioners is the restoration of 'the person' in terms of physical, mental, and emotional integrity. In the context of sexual violence, rape, sexual slavery, forced sterilization, and other CRSV-related harms, in addition to physical injuries requiring treatment, a person's sexuality and sexual identity may be fractured or damaged. Socially constructed norms of what is 'masculine' and 'feminine' can rest on reproductive organs, therefore any violation or harm to these structures can distort their self-image and gendered or sexual identities.

Second, treating a patient is different to how victims are often dealt with through reparations. A patient may have to regularly attend medical appointments for investigations, treatment, or to forensically document their harm. Reparations often involve a one-off assessment of a person's eligibility based on their evidence and harm they have suffered in the past. Medical treatment is often looking at the patient's past history and present symptoms, involving a detailed family and personal medical history, as well as subsequently treating them. This has a relational aspect between the patient and the medical practitioner where rapport and trust can be built up over time.

Third, is the relationship between the victim and perpetrator 'restored' via superficial or deep 'acceptance and accountability' of the perpetrator?[166] In relation to sexual violence, it is questionable whether the restoration of relationships is desirable or beneficial to all, especially in the case of mass crimes where there may be no original relationship between the perpetrators and victims. More broadly, communities may benefit from transitional justice sexual health educational programmes, but the impact of these should not be over-sold. Medical treatment of a

[165] WHO, Health Care for Women Subjected to Intimate Partner or Sexual Violence: A Clinical Handbook, UN Women and UNFPA, WHO/RHR/14.26, 2014, p1.

[166] Mary P Koss, The RESTORE Program of Restorative Justice for Sex Crimes: Vision, Process and Outcomes, *Journal of Interpersonal Violence* 29(9) (2014) 1623–1660.

person harmed by CRSV, similar to a restorative justice encounter, has only limited capacity to transform structural or socio-economic inequalities and its contribution to sexual violence whether in settled democracies or post-conflict societies.[167]

2.4 Conclusion

Reparations are considered a key mechanism for achieving the goals of transitional and restorative justice. Both fields have struggled to address sexual violence, and only recently in the past few years have they engaged with a thicker understanding of what reparations should look like in such contexts. Nevertheless, there remain conceptual and practical benefits, as well as tensions, in introducing medicine to both fields in reparations for sexual violence. This is particularly evident when considering sexual violence as a systematic and widespread problem in societies transitioning from conflict; the role and bias of practitioners in treating or remedying victims' harm; the need to engage with a transformative approach to confront the causes, structures, and responses to sexual violence; the need to identify and remedy the harm; and the role of those responsible in making amends for their wrongdoing to help alleviate stigma and relational harm caused by sexual violence. A medico-legal approach in connecting the relationship between transitional justice, restoration, and medicine in the specific area of reparations for CRSV is the key focus of this book.

[167] Sarah Williams and Jasmine Opdam, The Unrealized Potential for Transformative Reparations for Sexual and Gender-Based Violence in Sierra Leone, *International Journal of Human Rights* 21(9) (2017) 1281–1301.

3

Harm and Consequences Caused by Conflict-Related Sexual Violence

Sexual violence can have a profound effect on a person's integrity, dignity, and quality of life. Much of what is written on sexual violence during conflict rudimentally sets out that such violations cause physical and psychological harm, in particular stigma.[1] However, it does not detail the extent of such consequences on a person's bodily integrity and dignity. This chapter addresses some of those gaps by examining the consequences and suffering experienced by victims of conflict-related sexual violence. An examination of harm is important in understanding the impact of sexual violence and to develop appropriate reparations to remedy them as far as possible. Indeed, Rubio-Marín highlights that 'reparations must give primordial attention to the notions of harm' so as to 'duly recognize victims and help them cope with the effective of violence to move forward properly'.[2] Focusing on the harm rather than the crime takes a more medico-legal approach to responding to conflict-related sexual violence (CRSV).

The first section begins by briefly discussing the concept of harm, followed by an outline of the different types of harm through a health lens. These include physical (including forensic documentation), mental health/psychological, reproductive, transgenerational, identity-based, iatrogenic (related to medical assessment or treatment), and communal or social that reparations need to remedy. This chapter critically examines the harms caused by sexual violence and explains how conditions arising from such acts may cause physical and other impairments, which have the potential to be detrimental to the victim's quality of life. The final subsection spends some time unpacking the harm of stigma, given its prevalence and experience amongst victims of CRSV. It considers the relational harms of CRSV, such

[1] See Preamble, Nairobi Declaration; African Commission on Human and Peoples' Rights, Resolution on the Right to a Remedy and Reparation for Women and Girls Victims of Sexual Violence, ACHPR/Res111(XXXXII) 07, 2007; Guidance Note of the UN Secretary-General: Reparations for Conflict-Related Sexual Violence, 2014, p4. In contrast see Fionnuala Ní Aoláin who challenges the limited recognition in international law of the experience of sexual violence in Rethinking the Concept of Harm and Legal Categorizations of Sexual Violence during War, *Theoretical Inquiries in Law* 1(2) (2000) 307–340.

[2] Ruth Rubio-Marín, Reparations for Conflict-Related Sexual and Reproductive Violence: A Decalogue, *William and Mary Journal of Women and the Law* 19(1) (2012–2013) 69–104, p74.

Redressing Rape in War. Sunneva Gilmore, Oxford University Press.
DOI: 10.1093/9780198919735.003.0003

as to victims' relationships with themselves, with others (eg family), and their communities.[3] As such, this chapter will explore gaps in the understanding of harms and the benefits of a medico-legal approach. This has corresponding effects on the scope of appropriate and effective 'repairs' that will be explored in later chapters to address the harms identified, as well as what this means for transformative reparations. I argue that discussions on other acts of violence that can be sexual in nature (and their harms) tend to be overlooked in court-ordered and administrative reparation programmes. The final section of the chapter underscores the impact of conflict on health and the positionality of medical practitioners in treating victims of CRSV as well as assessing them for the purposes of reparations that can cause secondary victimization.

3.1 The Concept of Harm

Harm is a central element to victimhood and harm from wrongdoing often stems from the wrong itself.[4] Harm can be understood as 'evil (physical or otherwise) as done to or suffered by some person or thing; hurt, injury, damage, mischief'.[5] The World Health Organization (WHO) defines harm as an 'impairment of structure or function of the body and/or any deleterious effect arising there from. Harm includes disease, injury, suffering, disability and death.'[6] Harm for the purposes of this book follows a broad definition of suffering, impairment, or injury to better appreciate the lived experience and impact on health that sexual violence causes. However, in medical practice harm is not normally used as a term, instead medical professionals are more concerned with understanding injury, the extent of the medical condition, in light of the patient's symptoms, history, examination, and outcome of investigations.[7] Where harm does arise it can be due to the impact of medical interventions (secondary harm/iatrogenic), or as an issue of safeguarding.[8] Iatrogenic harm can encompass complications or risks of medical treatment and interventions, or as a result of some negligence or malfeasance on

[3] Sarah Clark Miller, Moral Injury and Relational Harm: Analyzing Rape in Darfur, *Journal of Social Philosophy* 40(4) (2009) 504–523.

[4] Trudy Govier, *Victims and Victimhood*, Broadview Press (2015) pp26–28.

[5] *Oxford English Dictionary*. https://www.oed.com/dictionary/harm_n?tl=true, accessed 5 December 2020.

[6] WHO, Definitions of Key Concepts from the WHO Patient Safety Curriculum Guide, 2011, para 27.

[7] 'Medical condition' is a broad term typically referring to abnormal anatomical or physiological states which may amount to a disorder, syndrome, or disease, as well as non-pathological conditions such as pregnancy.

[8] Billy Boland, Jamima Burnage, and Adrian Scott, Protecting Against Harm: Safeguarding Adults in General Medicine, *Clinical Medicine* 14(4) (2014) 345–348.

the part of a medical professional.[9] Indeed, the ethical obligation to 'do no harm' denotes not only medical practitioners refraining from engaging in harm to patients, but also reflects their relationship of healing and care in ensuring that medical interventions benefit the patient's health.[10] This approach contrasts with transitional justice and law, which aims to categorize harm and delimit what can and cannot be claimed, due to finite resources and other priorities.[11]

International law recognizes harm in a broad sense. The UN Basic Principles on the Right to Remedy and Reparations define harm as 'physical or mental injury, emotional suffering, economic loss or substantial impairment of [victims'] fundamental rights'.[12] At the International Criminal Court (ICC) in relation to reparations and participation, harm can either be direct or indirect as long as it is personal in nature to the victim.[13] In other words, the harm must be proximate to the person to the extent that it negatively affects their life. As cases for reparations often only occur years after the crime (if at all), personal harm allows for the evolution of harm over time to be considered. Yet a common criticism of reparations in transitional justice is that focusing on personal harm makes reparations individualistic and does not tackle the social drivers of such violence.[14] In contrast, restorative justice considers harm beyond the material, physical, and psychological consequences, to also include the social and emotional harm or communication breakdown caused by crimes that impacts communal 'shared values, understanding, and relationships'.[15] This approach is relevant for discussions later in this chapter, given the impact of sexual violence with regards to stigma and relationships. Institutions, such as the Inter-American Court of Human Rights and some domestic reparation programmes, have been attuned to these issues, including collective reparations alongside individual measures to devise an appropriate remedy for the harm caused. While such measures may aim to respond to the collective

[9] Discussed further in Chapter 7. Virginia A Sharpe and Alan I Faden, Introduction, in Virginia A Sharpe and Alan I Faden (eds), *Medical Harm: Historical, Conceptual and Ethical Dimensions of Iatrogenic Illness*, CUP (2008) p1–2.

[10] Virginia A Sharpe, Why 'Do No Harm'?, *Theoretical Medicine* 18 (1997) 197–215, pp203–204.

[11] Rosemary Nagy, Transitional Justice as Global Project: Critical Reflections, *Third World Quarterly* 29(2) (2008) 275–289, p276.

[12] Principle 8. Replicating Principle 1 of the UN Declaration of Basic Principles of Justice for Victims of Crime and Abuse of Power, A/RES/40/34, 1985.

[13] *Bosco Ntaganda*, Reparations Order, ICC-01/04-02/06-2659, 8 March 2020, para 33; *Lubanga*, Amended Reparations Order, ICC-01/04-01/06-3129-AnxA, para 6; *Al Mahdi*, Reparations Order, ICC-01/12-01/15-236, para 40; *Lubanga*, Judgment on the appeals of the Prosecutor and the Defence against Trial Chamber I's Decision on Victims' Participation of 18 January 2008, 11 July 2008, ICC-01/04-01/06-1432, para 32; and *Katanga*, Reparations Order, ICC-01/04-01/07-3728, para 39.

[14] Aurélien Pradier, Maxine Rubin, and Hugo van der Merwe, Between Transitional Justice and Politics: Reparations in South Africa, *South African Journal of International Affairs* 25(3) (2018) 301–321, p306.

[15] Heather Strang and Lawrence W Sherman, Repairing the Harm: Victims and Restorative Justice, *Utah Law Review* 1 (2003) 15–42, p22; and Simon Green, Gerry Johnstone, and Craig Lambert, What Harm, Whose Justice?: Excavating the Restorative Movement, *Contemporary Justice Review* 16(4) (2013) 445–460, p455.

nature of harm, as well as to broaden the effects of repair, contribute to repairing relationships, and express shared values, they also risk being conflated with wider social harms experienced by non-victims, such as poverty and lack of access to adequate healthcare.[16]

Focusing on all the consequences flowing from the violence that are personal to victims can cause some tensions in practice regarding the labelling of suffering and the passage of time. For instance, pregnancy as a result of rape can cause a number of secondary harms that may be obscured by the victim to try to maintain normality or to avoid unwanted attention. The use of vocabulary may not be intended to be covert in meaning and can be culturally appropriate, but it may not map onto explicit harm headings for the purpose of reparations. However, across the sites where I conducted my fieldwork, interviews with victims suggest that alternative terms can also be used as a way of reducing the discomfort and pain when conversing about the circumstances of a pregnancy.[17] These references were also used to protect the direct victim of rape as well as younger family members in deciphering what happened. In terms of the passage of time Correa argues that responding to the short-term consequences only is not appropriate as these harms may not necessarily affect victims' lives at the time of reparations many years or decades later.[18] Instead, appropriate reparations are supposed to consider the needs of the victims while not losing the threshold of causality to the violation.[19] For medical care and in particular rehabilitation, it may be difficult to restrict care to only the consequences arising from sexual violence years after the violation occurred. Furthermore, rehabilitation in such narrow terms can be counterintuitive to rehabilitative goals of restoring function as much as possible. The ICC adopts the 'but/for' relationship between the crime and the harm, applying the standard of 'proximate cause' described in the *Lubanga* principles.[20] Some domestic reparation programmes more broadly require harm to be established as a 'probable cause' between the violation and damage to the victims' health.[21] However there can be several challenges in deciphering and assessing the harm, particularly when the crime occurred a number of years prior and there have been intervening acts of sexual violence or protracted conflict.

Harm as a result of violence substantially reduces individuals' wellbeing.[22] In other words, a harmful act 'is what makes life worse than it would have been before

[16] Elisabeth Bunselmeyer, *Truth, Reparations and Social Cohesion: Transitional Justice Lessons from Peru*, Routledge (2020) p201.

[17] P6, Lima, Peru, May 2019.

[18] Cristián Correa, Operationalising the Right of Victims to Reparation, in Anne Peters and Christian Marxsen (eds), *Reparations for Victims of Armed Conflict*, CUP (2021) 92–178, p148.

[19] ibid.

[20] ICC-01/04-01/06-2904, para 249; followed in *Katanga*, Judgment on Reparations Order, ICC-01/04-01/07-3778-Red, para 75; *Ntaganda*, Reparations Order, ICC-01/04-02/06-2659, para 132; and Ongwen Reparations Order, para 193.

[21] Such as in Germany, see Marilyn Henry, *Confronting the Perpetrators: A History of the Claims Conference*, Vallentine Mitchell (2007) p36.

[22] Govier , n 4, p26.

otherwise, if that action or event had not occurred, or if that condition was not present'.[23] Thus, harm can be understood temporally or counterfactually.[24] The notion of harm can also be contested and subjective, as a harmed person (such as a person born with a physical disability) can perceive their wellbeing as high, and reject ableist norms that consider disabled persons to be of lower value than non-disabled persons.[25] This understanding is replicated in the victimological literature whereby victimization is understood as how an individual and/or groups suffer harm as a 'violation of rights, or significant disruption of their well-being'.[26] Restorative justice advocates have long pointed out that crime violates relationships between humans and social wellbeing.[27] Therefore, harm is not necessarily linked with biological normality, but rather rests on whether it deprives the person from carrying out their desired activities. Harm as a concept has developed to encompass economic, social, and cultural forms, all of which can be interlinked. This is particularly apparent when the effects of harm go beyond individuals to have a disintegrative effect in breaking social bonds in communities and society, which diminish the normal support structures that would help victims cope with their suffering.[28]

Specifically, there remain significant gaps in the understanding of the harm caused by sexual violence related to war. Most of the literature focuses on a heteronormative understanding of harms to women and girls. Ní Aoláin considers the legal vocabulary used to uncover the harms to women including that of sexual violence during the Second World War as insufficient.[29] Furthermore, there is a tendency to refer to the crime of sexual violence as harm in itself, without considering the varying consequences arising from different acts or circumstances.[30] Despite some advances on what constitutes sexual violence, international and domestic bodies have paid inadequate attention to the harms to be remedied in reparation measures. For instance, forced sterilization is not necessarily interpreted as causing sexual harm, but instead labelled as reproductive harm, and as such is

[23] Guy Kahane and Julian Savulescu, The Concept of Harm and the Significance of Normality, *Journal of Applied Philosophy* 29(4) (2012) 318–332, p319.

[24] ibid pp318–319.

[25] Fiona K Campbell, Refusing Able(ness): A Preliminary Conversation about Ableism. *M/C Journal* 11(3) (2008), https://doi.org/10.5204/mcj.46, accessed 10 February 2025; and Fiona Campbell, Exploring Internalized Ableism Using Critical Race Theory, *Disability & Society* 23(2) (2008) 151–162, p153–154.

[26] Jo-Anne Wemmers and Anne-Marie de Brouwer, Globalization and Victims' Rights at the International Criminal Court, in Rianne Letschert and Jan van Dijk (eds), *The New Faces of Victimhood: Studies in Global Justice*, Springer (2011), 279–300, p282.

[27] Howard Zehr, *Changing Lenses: A New Focus for Crime and Justice,* Herald Press (1990), p181.

[28] Luke Moffett, *Justice for Victims before the International Criminal Court,* Routledge (2014), p19; and Wemmers and de Brouwer, n 26, p287.

[29] Fionnuala Ní Aoláin, Rethinking the Concept of Harm and Legal Categorizations of Sexual Violence during War, Faculty of Law, Hebrew University (2000), p339.

[30] Letizia Paoli and Victoria A Greenfield, Harm: A Neglected Concept in Criminology, a Necessary Benchmark for Crime-Control Policy, *European Journal of Crime, Criminal Law and Criminal Justice* 21 (2013) 359–377, p360.

not deemed as having sufficient gravity or conflict-related causality to be dealt with in reparation programmes.[31] Likewise, shaving a person's hair is not usually included within reparation programmes, even though, in the case of the Cham in Cambodia, it was used to destroy women's natural long hair as a symbol of their morality and purity.[32] In Ireland, shaving women's heads was a punishment for consorting with members of the British security forces, and to symbolize their betrayal of the community.[33]

The recent cases at the ICC on sexual violence have demonstrated that there remain missed opportunities to fully understand harms arising from sexual slavery and rape. In the *Al Hassan* case, the majority found that the defendant's armed group had committed persecution against women and girls in Timbuktu through use of sexual slavery and forced marriage, but that the defendant was not criminally responsible for such acts as gender persecution, only religious persecution against the whole community due to duress.[34] Unless this finding of duress is appealed, victims of sexual slavery in Timbuktu will not be eligible for reparations. The Court's lack of recognition of CRSV harm is also shown by the limited information collected from victims through their application forms in the *Ntaganda* trial.[35] In turn, this has contributed to delays in reparations including the preparation of a representative sample of potential beneficiaries so as to determine the harms and needs of victims and inform the Trial Chamber's reparation order.[36] It can be helpful to update information on harm when designing appropriate reparations. However, as the *Ntaganda* case illustrates, it is difficult to collect such information in contexts of insecurity and infectious disease pandemics. Thus, as a minimum, harms should be included at the initial engagement with courts that have judicial avenues for reparation. It is worth examining in more depth the nature of harm caused by sexual violence and its impact on health.

[31] The creation of a list of harms, and in particular harms arising from what is interpreted as sexual violence, can also restrict interpretation on what constitutes a harm. See Ni Aoilain, n 29, pp320 and 328. In Peru, the CVR received a large number of testimonies (538) of sexual violence including violations beyond rape including humiliation, forced abortion, sexual slavery, and forced prostitution; see Rebecca Root, *Transitional Justice in Peru*, Palgrave (2012) p90.

[32] See Rachel Killean et al, *Cham: Culture and History Story of Cambodia*, Documentation Center of Cambodia (2018) p28.

[33] Mary McAuliffe, The Homefront as Battlefront: Women, Violence and the Domestic Space during War in Ireland, 1919–1921, in L Connolly (ed), *Women and the Irish Revolution: Feminism, Activism, Violence*, Irish Academic Press (2020) 164-182, p174.

[34] Trial Judgment, ICC-01/12-01/18-2594-Red, 26 June 2024, paras1566 –1574.

[35] The two expert reports in *Ntaganda* explained the limited case information on harm that had been collected throughout the case; see ICC-01/04-02/06-2623-Anx2-Red2.

[36] *Bosco Ntaganda*, First Decision on Reparation Process, 26 June 2020, ICC-01/04-02/06-2547, para 37. A new combined form for both participation and reparation is being introduced in the ICC with one specific question on personal harm and another question on reparation. These are intended to be used in any future cases in the reparation phase. The application forms are not publicly available, and so it is unclear the extent to which these questions adequately address the issue of harm. See the reference to the new application form in Independent Expert Review of the International Criminal Court and the Rome Statute, Final Report, 30 September 2020, para 902.

3.1.1 Harm and health

Victims of sexual violence can suffer a range of physical and mental health harms as well as socio-economic consequences as a result of such crimes.[37] These consequences do not distinguish between civilians and combatants, with both groups and in particular child soldiers, being subjected to protracted and repeated violations, especially in cases of sexual slavery.[38] This chapter considers the consequences of sexual violence through a medico-legal lens, which takes a comprehensive perspective to the concept of health similar to the definition adopted by the WHO as 'a state of complete physical, mental and social well-being and not merely the absence of disease or infirmity'.[39] Equally, the presence of disease is not incompatible with health.[40] The determinants of health have since expanded,[41] and what is meant by 'good health' varies across cultures and amongst different communities in society.[42] As a result, the addition of economic and spiritual wellbeing is added to ensure that intercultural understandings on health are not lost. Health as a state free from disease and associated with a biostatistical ability to perform typical functions efficiently has been superseded by a deeper understanding of the lived experience of health beyond what is physiologically within normal parameters.[43] This book identifies with Bluhm's perspective—that a person with an illness can be healthy through adaption of goals in line with their abilities.[44] Chapter 7 explores vulnerability in relation to CRSV and reparations in terms of repairing, as far as possible, harms that maximize a person's abilities and providing opportunity to determine their own meaningful goals under the rubric of quality of life.

[37] See Ed Gibney, Rebuilding the Harm Principle: Using an Evolutionary Perspective to Provide a New Foundation for Justice, *International Journal for Crime, Justice and Social Democracy* 9(3) (2020) 100–115.

[38] Civilians and former combatants refer to adults and children of all gender identities. Civilian infants and neonates (within the first month of life) can also be victims.

[39] WHO, Constitution of the World Health Organization, in Basic Documents, Forty-ninth edition, 2020, p1, https://apps.who.int/gb/bd/pdf_files/BD_49th-en.pdf#page = 7, accessed 1 August 2025.

[40] Robert Bluhm, Vulnerability, Health and Illness, *International Journal of Feminist Approaches to Bioethics* (2012) 5(2) 147–161, p154.

[41] Social Determinants of Health in Countries in Conflict: A Perspective from the Eastern Mediterranean Region, World Health Organization and WHO Regional Office for the Eastern Mediterranean, 2008, pp11–13.

[42] Estefanía Bautista-Valarezo et al, Towards an Indigenous Definition of Health: An Explorative Study to Understand the Indigenous Ecuadorian People's Health and Illness Concepts, *International Journal for Equity in Health* 19(1) (2020), doi: 10.1186/s12939-020-1142-8; George Khushf, An Agenda for Future Debate on Concepts of Health and Disease, *Medicine, Health Care and Philosophy* 10(1) (2007) 19–27.

[43] Christopher Boorse, Health as a Theoretical Concept, *Philosophy of Science*, 44(4) (1977) 542–573, p546. For a phenomenological perspective on the lived experience of health and illness see Havi Carel, *Illness: The Cry of the Flesh*, Revised Edition, Routledge (2014) pp24–26. For a discussion on the various theoretical positions of health that depart from Boorse's notion of statistical normality see Bluhm, n 40, p159.

[44] Bluhm, n 40, p154.

One exacerbating factor concerning the harm done by sexual violence to health is the passage of time, discussed further in Chapter 7. The time elapsed between a crime or violation being committed and victims' receipt of reparations will have an impact on their health. For example, in one case which emerged from the Kurdish conflict in Turkey, the European Court of Human Rights held that rape 'leaves deep psychological scars on the victim which do not respond to the passage of time as quickly as other forms of physical and mental violence'.[45] The UN Human Rights Committee has found that time is a factor in an effective remedy that can aggravate harm, as such 'in certain circumstances' it requires states to 'endeavour to repair at the earliest possible opportunity any harm that may have been caused by such violations'.[46] Prompt, adequate medical care is also critical to treat and/or prevent a number of further harms. It is worth noting that while it may be difficult to ascertain statistics, many victims of conflict-related sexual violence do not receive much medical assistance, particularly in the days after the event, which is a key window for certain medical interventions.[47] This may be partly attributed to the victims' distance from major hospitals or health posts necessitating travel, perhaps not by road and in the midst of hostilities, as well as health facilities that can be poorly equipped.[48] Humanitarian healthcare programmes may not be sufficiently funded to follow up on victims or identify and grant access to those who remain 'hidden' in the community.[49] Attacks on healthcare and the lack of short-term medical assistance in a conflict zone have a number of serious implications for victims, including injuries, infections, and other complications that can become chronic and life-threatening.[50]

Sexual violence may cause long-term physical and psychological harms that can persist over a person's lifetime, reflecting its pervasive effects.[51] The Inter-American Court has recognized that sexual violence,

> in addition to affecting the physical, psychological, and moral integrity of the victim, breaking her dignity, rape invades one of the most intimate spheres of

[45] *Aydin v Turkey*, App no 57/1996/676/866, European Court of Human Rights, 25 September 1997, para 83.

[46] General Comment No 31, The Nature of the General Legal Obligation Imposed on States Parties to the Covenant, CCPR/C/21/Rev.1/Add. 13, 26 May 2004, para 19.

[47] Sunneva Gilmore, Expert Report on Reparations for Victims of Rape, Sexual Slavery and Attacks on Healthcare, *The Prosecutor v Ntaganda*, International Criminal Court, 28 October 2020, Public Redacted Version, ICC-01/04-02/06-2623-Anx2-Red2.

[48] Enrico Pavignani et al, Making Sense of Apparent Chaos: Health-Care Provision in Six Country Case Studies, *International Review of the Red Cross* 95(889) (2013) 41–60, p49 and p52.

[49] Lebeza Alemu Tenaw et al, Medical and Psychological Consequences of Rape Among Survivors During Armed Conflicts in Northeast Ethiopia, *American Journal of Obstetrics & Gynecology* 175(2) (2022) 320–325

[50] Françoise Duroch, Melissa McRae, and Rebecca Grais, Description and Consequences of Sexual violence in Ituri Province, Democratic Republic of Congo, *BMC International Health and Human Rights* 11(5) (2011) 1–8, p4.

[51] Govier, n 4, pp26–27.

an individual's life, invading her physical and sexual space, and taking away her ability to make autonomous decisions concerning her own body.[52]

Visible harm is generally easier to comprehend by the victims and others, yet unseen physical or psychological harms can be poorly understood and difficult to discuss due to their sensitive and intimate nature. The analysis of harm from a medico-legal perspective addresses some of these deficiencies in the understanding of harms from sexual violence. As suffering is the conscious awareness of pain or discomfort from harm and cannot be adequately captured by statistics,[53] then the harms depicted in this chapter will be experienced in various ways by different individuals and groups as well as over generations. The following subsection begins by outlining the common harms suffered as a result of sexual violence such as rape, including the physical, mental, and socio-economic harm caused by sexual violence to male and female victims. As such, it is not intended to analyse all the potential consequences arising from each type of sexual violence.[54] Instead, it details the quantum of harm caused by conflict-related sexual violence to provoke a more transparent discussion of what reparations may be feasible or desired by victims in subsequent chapters.

3.2 Physical Harm

Sexual violence is often associated with rape, and indeed most of the victims interviewed as part of this book spoke of suffering this violation and were repeatedly raped. Some victims identified that such rape was part of sexual slavery, others spoke of different power dynamics, such as fighting off their attacker or being physically subdued, which caused further physical harm. One victim in Peru, Maria,[55] was only 12 years old when a government soldier dragged her into a room, beat her, and then raped her with a gun to her head, and she said 'at that moment all I could think of was someone please help me, save me, I wanted to become a stone'. After the rape she begged for her life with the soldiers, but managed to distract them, though while escaping, they shot at her causing her to fall, hit her head, and

[52] *Fernández Ortega et al v Mexico*, Judgment, Inter-American Court of Human Rights, 15 April 2010, para 91.

[53] Govier, n 4, p27; and Paul Farmer, *Pathologies of Power*, University of California Press (2005) p31.

[54] For instance to take a comprehensive approach to what amounts to sexual violence, see the Hague Principles which consists of three parts: The Civil Society Declaration on Sexual Violence which aims to shed light on what violence may be perceived as sexual; Key Principles for Policy Makers on Sexual Violence including legislative and judicial strategies; and International Criminal Law (ICL) Guidelines. The latter attempts to explain when acts of sexual violence amount to international crimes. See The Hague Principles on Sexual Violence, 2019, https://4genderjustice.org/wp-content/uploads/2020/02/MASTER-DOC-The-Hague-Principles-on-Sexual-Violence.pdf, accessed 1 August 2025.

[55] These are pseudonyms for the victims, which do not reference their interview code to protect their identities.

lose consciousness, leaving her for dead. Her grandmother found her and brought her to their village, but it was attacked the next day by the army and they only survived the massacre by hiding. This left Maria with several visible scars as well as genital physical pain from the rape.

In Colombia, Luisa was gang-raped by three members of a paramilitary group, who then threatened her and her family, resulting in her being forcibly displaced and having to turn to prostitution to support her children. In Uganda, Jane was abducted at 11 years old by the Lord's Resistance Army, repeatedly beaten, and forced to be the wife of a senior commander and give birth to his children. She identified several physical complications, one from living in the bush and having a bullet left in her abdomen; the others related to captivity as,

> one of the things is related to it is a fistula because if you're abducted as a young girl and then you've been forced into having sex and also giving birth at an early age ... The other problem is that in captivity we are giving birth, but there wasn't any qualified medical person to do that. The girls were giving birth and there was no one to really give us special attention, like what is currently happening when they returned home from hospital. That is why we have developed complications."

These experiences touch on some of the complex physical harms victims of sexual violence suffer that is not simply captured by a single instance of rape.[56]

Physical harms depend on various factors such as the *type of sexual violence* committed (eg the aggressiveness of the act,[57] rape, sexual slavery, sexual assault, or use of a weapon); *individual factors* (eg pre-existing health conditions, age, sex, disability, pubertal and menopausal state of the victim, prior sexual activity,[58] and intoxication by drugs or alcohol[59]) and *external factors* (eg the availability of healthcare,[60] ongoing stressors, the social and cultural environment,[61] and poor sanitation and hygiene). Thus, victims of CRSV are likely to have pre-existing and

[56] Other physical injuries sustained during the sexual assault may include head trauma, intracranial haemorrhage, venous thromboembolism from long bone fractures, and self-neglect from depression.

[57] Interpretation of genital findings, P370-1, in Jonathan Wyatt et al, *Oxford Handbook of Forensic Medicine*, OUP (2011).

[58] ibid.

[59] eg the victim may be on regular blood thinning medication, such as anticoagulants, which increases bleeding risk, see Ian Wall, The Examination: Injuries, in M Dalton (ed), *Forensic Gynaecology*, CUP (2015) pp55–59.

[60] For further information on post sexual violence care see sections 6-13, British Association for Sexual Health and HIV (BASHH) National Guidelines for the Management of Individuals Disclosing Sexual Violence in Sexual Health Services, 2022. Other resources include: Beata Cybulska, Immediate Medical Care after Sexual Assault: Best Practice & Research, *Clinical Obstetrics & Gynaecology* 27(1) (2013) 141–149.

[61] Sarah McIvor Murray et al, Stigma Among Survivors of Sexual Violence in Congo: Scale Development and Psychometrics, *Journal of Interpersonal Violence* 33(3) (2015) 491–514; and JT Kelly et al, Experiences of Female Survivors of Sexual Violence in Eastern Democratic Republic of the Congo: A Mixed Methods Study, *Conflict and Health* 5(25) (2011).

new vulnerabilities related to the conflict that can create cumulative harm.[62] Some victims will not have physical injuries,[63] but the risks of it occurring increase with further incidents. As a result of data collection difficulties, we do not know what proportion of victims of sexual violence sustain physical injuries in conflict.[64] This chapter explores the value of forensic medicine in assisting reparation claims by providing an understanding on the mechanism and visibility of some injuries in sexual violence. The rest of this section concentrates on three common areas of physical harm caused by sexual violence: infectious diseases; pregnancy; and gynaecological and other physical complications including breast trauma.

3.2.1 Injuries: a forensic medicine perspective

Forensic medicine is defined as 'incorporating those areas of medicine that interact with the law or legal process'.[65] Forensic medicine applies medical knowledge or expertise when interpreting legal issues including related to crime.[66] However, this definition is wide ranging and could encompass mental capacity assessments, medical negligence, clinical forensic medicine (which investigates trauma to a living person), and forensic pathology (which examines trauma of a deceased person and cause of death);[67] this is broader than our focus here. In comparison, forensic science is the connected scientific discipline that applies scientific methods and techniques[68] on a case (or multi-case) basis to trace past activities and assist in investigations and other legal or public interest matters.[69] It is an evolving area encompassing many disciplines such as toxicology, odontology,[70] biology, and DNA.[71] The collection of forensic specimens ('sampling') is

[62] Jane Hunt, Rachel Witkin, and Cornelium Katona, Identifying Human Trafficking in Adults, *BMJ* 371 (2020) 1–6.

[63] Jack Crane, Interpretation of Non-Genital Injuries in Sexual Assault, *Best Practice & Research Clinical Obstetrics & Gynaecology* 27(1) (2013) 103–111.

[64] WHO, Strengthening the Medico-Legal Response to Sexual Violence, 2016, p5.

[65] Jonathan Wyatt et al, n 57, p2.

[66] Roy G Beran, What is Legal Medicine—Are Legal and Forensic Medicine the Same? *Journal of forensic and legal medicine* 1(3) (2010), 137–139.

[67] Forensic pathology is concerned with the cause and mechanism of injuries or death. See Suzanne Bell, *A Dictionary of Forensic Medicine*, OUP (2012)

[68] Neeti Kapoor et al, *Introduction to Forensic Science*, in P Shrivastava et al (eds), *Textbook of Forensic Science*, Springer (2023) 41–44, p42

[69] The Sydney Declaration states: 'Forensic science is a case-based (or multi case-based) research-oriented, science-based endeavour to study traces – the remnants of past activities (such as an individual's presence and actions) – through their detection, recognition, recovery, examination and interpretation to understand anomalous events of public interest (e.g., crimes, security incidents).' See Claude Roux et al, The Sydney Declaration—Revisiting the Essence of Forensic Science through Its Fundamental Principles, *Forensic Science International* 332 (2022) 111182–111182.

[70] Odontology refers to the scientific study of the structure and diseases of teeth, this is useful in the interpretation of bite marks and identity confirmation. See the *Oxford English Dictionary*.

[71] DNA is the abbreviation for deoxyrubonucleac acid, which is a molecule containing the genetic material or code of living organisms. For specialties see National Library of Medicine, Forensic

influenced by the rapidly changing area of forensic science which aims to preserve and analyse relevant material. Professional bodies issue regular guidance and best practice techniques on sampling.[72]

This section does not intend to delve into the complexities of forensics, but rather provides an overview of how documented injuries in living victims falling under the definition of harm can assist in claims for reparations.[73] While this is an extensive area, this book focuses on crimes of a sexual nature related to conflict. For medico-legal purposes, a standard classification of injuries can be helpful for forensic documentation and understanding possible causation.[74] The area of clinical forensic medicine of most relevance is sexual offence medicine (SOM). The forensic medical examination (FME) for victims of sexual offences entails: documentation of the relevant history of the incident; a medical history; a limited or systematic physical examination ('top to toe', anogenital if relevant); a description of any injury with or without sampling of forensic material known as 'specimens' (eg for DNA, to trace foreign material or infection).[75] The collection of relevant material depends on the type of sexual violence, other violence encountered, pubertal status, and time lapsed from the incident.[76] Locard's exchange principle in forensic science states that when two objects come into contact with each other, there is an exchange of material, that is, 'every contact leaves a trace',[77] therefore potentially connecting a victim with a suspect or a crime scene. Injury description may be accompanied by photography or videography.[78] A sexual violence or

Specialties Chart, https://www.nlm.nih.gov/exhibition/visibleproofs/exhibition/III_A_109.pdf , accessed 1 August 2025.

[72] There can also be other considerations, such as if the victim has not been able to wash then some evidence may still be preserved. Forensic specimens are just one consideration when undertaking a forensic medical examination. See the Faculty of Forensic & Legal Medicine (FFLM) of the Royal College of Physicians, https://fflm.ac.uk/, accessed 1 August 2025.

[73] Guidance exists on: history-taking (relevant to incident and general medical); how to document injuries (absence and presence); and common types of injuries in general forensic medicine (GFM) and sexual offence medicine (SOM). See Recommendations for the Documentation of Injuries, FFLM, September 2024, https://fflm.ac.uk/wp-content/uploads/2024/09/Recommendations-for-the-documentation-of-injuries_Sep24.pdf, accessed 1 August 2025.

[74] Wall, n 59, p56. Death can ensue from injuries, but this is beyond the scope of this section.

[75] Professional guidance can help medical centres to devise mobile or in-house kits for use in health centres by clinicians. They may comprise paperwork, such as proformas, body charts, and digital evidence (photographs, recordings), as well as sampling kits. For instance, Recommended Equipment for Obtaining Forensic Samples From Complainants and Suspects, FFLM of the Royal College of Physicians, January 2025, https://fflm.ac.uk/resources/publications/recommended-equipment-for-obtaining-forensic-samples-from-complainants-and-suspects/, accessed 1 August 2025.

[76] Timescales are based on studies on the persistence of material, but forensic strategy is case specific. Examples of exceptions include if the victim has not washed or is confined to bed.

[77] Ewelina Mistek et al, Toward Locard's Exchange Principle: Recent Developments in Forensic Trace Evidence Analysis, *Analytical Chemistry* 91(1) (2019) 637–654; and Wyatt et al, n 57, p502.

[78] Renjulal Yesodharan et al, Looking Through the Lens of a Sexual Assault Examiner: Novel Trends and Approaches in Forensic Photography, *Egyptian Journal of Forensic Sciences* (2021) 11(27) doi.org/10.1186/s41935-021-00241-7; P Smith et al, An Evaluation of Injury Photography Practices in Sexual Assault Referral Centres (SARC), *Journal of Forensic and Legal Medicine* 91 (2022) 102429–102429.

assault kit refers to a standardized package of components to assist in a thorough examination and sampling procedure according to best practice.[79]

An FME should only be performed with informed consent, which includes ensuring the victim understands the procedure and any reporting laws.[80] The clinician should obtain continuous consent throughout the FME, communicating that consent can be withdrawn at any time, or consent can be given by the victim for only parts of the FME; thereby reinforcing a trauma-informed approach and that victims are in control of the examination. It is important to ensure guidance and domestic laws on capacity to consent are understood by the forensic clinician. That said, other documentation can be used in medico-legal cases, such as hospital medical notes or intraoperative notes when an examination under anaesthetic or surgical repair is required. Where sexual violence occurs in a humanitarian crisis (such as a conflict) and services are organized differently, every clinical examination could be considered as a prospective forensic analysis and form part of legal investigations.[81]

Injuries from sexual violence can be anogenital and non-anogenital. Forensic medical expertise is required to document injuries from sexual violence in adults and children. Depending on the type of sexual violence involved, non-anogenital injuries may involve anatomical structures such as the lips and oral cavity (eg penile–oral penetration) and breasts.[82] A forensic examination for non-acute physical and psychological consequences can be undertaken even if sampling for forensic specimens in the acute period has lapsed. If there are positive findings on FME, injuries are described using standardized terms for medico-legal purposes as some types of injuries can imply mechanism of causation.[83] For instance, bruises

[79] If forensic samples are obtained, then forensic DNA-grade (FDG) kits are used. It is also important to consider the order of anogenital sampling and attempt to minimize contamination, Recommendations on the Order of Ano-Genital Sampling When Obtaining Forensic Specimens From Complainants and Suspects of Sexual Offences, FFLM, July 2024.

[80] Generally, where there is concern that an adult may lack the capacity to consent then there needs to be efforts to support that person, and ultimately the decision to proceed with an FME (or parts of it) is in that person's best interests. For children, there is specific guidance, and consent may be obtained from those with parental responsibility, potentially the child if they have sufficient understanding, or legal entity (eg court order or care order). Forensic Science Regulator, Forensic Medical Examination of Sexual Offence Complainants, March 2025; see paras 5.4.4–5.4.14, https://www.gov.uk/government/publications/forensic-medical-examination-of-sexual-offence-complainants/forensic-medical-examination-of-sexual-offence-complainants-accessible, accessed 1 August 2025; General Medical Council, Decision Making and Consent, updated 13 December 2024, https://www.gmc-uk.org/professional-standards/the-professional-standards/decision-making-and-consent, accessed 1 August 2025.

[81] Ioannis Ketsekioulafis et al, Humanitarian Forensic Medicine: A Systematic Review, *International Journal of Legal Medicine* 139 (2025) 139, 747–761; Debra Komar et al, A Comparison of the International Protocols for the Forensic Assessment of Conflict Related Sexual Violence Victims, *Journal of Forensic Sciences* 66 (2021) 1520–1523.

[82] Emmeline Brew-Graves and Louise Morgan, Injuries and Allegations of Oral Rape: A Retrospective Review of Patients Presenting to a London Sexual Assault Referral Centre, *Journal of Forensic and Legal Medicine* 34 (2015) 155–158

[83] A consistent approach to terminology by trained forensic clinicians is recommended to avoid any confusion or misinterpretation. This book does not go through every term.

and lacerations are caused by blunt force trauma, whereas lacerations are caused by sharp force trauma.[84] Injuries are also described according to anatomical location and whether there is any clinical evidence of underlying functional damage. It is not within the remit of this work to address the forensic intricacies of anatomical injuries in sexual violence; however, some salient elements are laid out, given the implications for understanding the harm as well as reparation claims.

Not all injuries may be straightforward to document. Some anogenital injuries in the acute period, especially involving superficial structures, can heal well without noticeable signs of trauma by the time examination is conducted.[85] Healing is a complex process, but many injuries leave no residual defect, unless complicated by infection or repeated trauma to the wound.[86] Unfortunately, victims interviewed for this research experienced such complications including infection and sepsis, and some spoke of how they had felt disfigured.[87] However, some forms of sexual violence do not result in physical injury,[88] yet they can cause significant psychological distress. Physical injuries, where present, are more likely to be detected when examined close to the time of trauma. A history of genital bleeding following sexual violence makes finding an anogenital injury more likely.[89] It is also important to consider differentials for injuries or symptoms (eg genital bleeding).[90] To illustrate, a scar or a healing injury could be the result of a skin condition such as lichen scleroses or normal variants in anatomy.[91] Despite this, the presence of anogenital injuries can influence decisions in domestic criminal justice systems,[92] and generally there is a call for forensic evidence (physical and digital) to be used more in international courts.[93]

[84] Christine Bassindale and Amrin Rahuf, The Genital Examination, in Dalton, n 59, p56; Forensic Pathology of Physical Injury, in Wyatt et al, n 57, p115–143.

[85] Bassindale and Rahuf, n 84, p61.

[86] Carol Berkowitz, Healing of Genital Injuries, *Journal of Child Sexual Abuse* 20(5) (2011) 537–547; and Catherine White, Genital Injuries in Adults: Best Practice and Research *Clinical Obstetrics & Gynaecology* 27(1) (2013) 113–130.

[87] Sepsis is defined as a life-threatening organ dysfunction due to the body's dysregulated response to an infection. See BMJ Best Practice, Sepsis in Adults, 2024, https://bestpractice.bmj.com/topics/en-gb/3000098, accessed 1 August 2025. U6, Lira, Uganda, July 2019; U4, FG1, Gulu, Uganda, July 2018.

[88] The Extent of Anogenital Injuries at Examination (Chapter 7), in *The Physical Signs of Child Sexual Abuse*, RCPCH, 3rd Edition, 2024, pp17–18.

[89] ibid.

[90] There can also be accidental injuries. Anogenital Signs of Accidental Injuries in Girls and Boys (Chapter 8), in RCPCH, n 88.

[91] Healing of Anogenital Injuries (Chapter 9), in *The Physical Signs of Child Sexual Abuse*, 2nd Edition, RCPCH, 2015, pp 172–192. Lichen scleroses is a chronic inflammatory skin condition which can affect the skin of the vulva and around the anus. See, British Association of Dermatologists, Lichen Sclerosus in Females, Patient Information Leaflet, 2022, https://www.bad.org.uk/pils/lichen-sclerosus-in-females/, accessed 1 August 2025.

[92] Marilyn Sawyer Sommers, Bonnie Fisher, and Heather Karjane, Using Colposcopy in the Rape Exam: Health Care, Forensic, and Criminal Justice Issues, *Journal of Forensic Nursing* 1 (2005) 28–35.

[93] Marie-Helen Maras and Michelle D Miranda, Overlooking Forensic Evidence? A Review of the 2014 International Protocol on the Documentation and Investigation of Sexual Violence in Conflict, *Global Security: Health, Science and Policy* 2(1) (2017) 10–21, p12. There are special considerations for prosecuting international crimes. However, international crimes can be prosecuted in domestic courts

There is variability of positive physical examination findings among clinicians from different professions and specialties, settings (including conflict), and countries.[94] Nevertheless, there should be clear language when interpretating a physical finding's probable relationship to possible sexual abuse using the Istanbul Protocol.[95] This allows a clear standardization and gives clinicians confidence when presenting signs and writing medico-legal reports. It is also important to highlight that acute and non-acute findings will differ, with many victims unable to access an FME until further down the line when they have been able to reach safety. While non-specialists can conduct FMEs with guidance and support, specialized training and mentorship, as well as auditing of standards, is ideal given the rigour required for this sensitive area of clinical work: an undertaking that can be more difficult in settings impacted by conflict and destruction of infrastructure.

Forensic assessments may help in claiming reparations, which carry a lower burden of proof compared to criminal procedures. They provide a documented trail of events, potentially physical signs of sexual violence, and may help provide other evidence (STI transmission) alongside therapeutic care. The latter should always take priority. FMEs can point to the needs of certain groups who may be targeted, such as children or the transgender population. Importantly, the absence of apparent injuries or no injuries in the acute or non-acute setting in adults or children does not negate that sexual violence has occurred.[96] This cannot be overstated. A finding of 'no injuries' is a neutral finding—it does not mean that sexual violence did not occur. Injuries can also occur with consensual sexual activity.[97] Furthermore, some harms may only be revealed after the immediate aftermath by other specialists (eg a gynaecologist or psychiatrist), and documentation by healthcare professionals may not adequately recognize the moral harm incurred. It is worth discussing forensic issues in relation to CRSV in more depth that may be useful for practitioners in this area.

Forensic considerations in children affected by CRSV

There are important distinctions in possible presentations of sexual violence in children compared to adults,[98] and it is best practice to conduct a Paediatric

and therefore admissibility criteria of medical evidence need to be fulfilled by professionals conducting forensic work.

[94] Nancy D Kellogg, Karen J Farst, and Joyce A Adams, Interpretation of Medical Findings in Suspected Child Sexual Abuse: An Update for 2023, *Child Abuse & Neglect* 145 (2023) 106283.

[95] Istanbul Protocol: Manual on the Effective Investigation and Documentation of Torture and Other Cruel, Inhuman or Degrading Treatment or Punishment (2022 Edition), Professional Training Series No 8/Rev 2, United Nations Human Rights, Office of the High Commissioner, 29 June 2022, p89, https://www.ohchr.org/sites/default/files/documents/publications/2022-06-29/Istanbul-Protocol_Rev2_EN.pdf, accessed 1 August 2025.

[96] Wall, n 59, p55.

[97] Interpretation of Genital Findings, Wyatt et al, n 57, pp370–371.

[98] Jean Price and Catherine Golding, Child Sexual Abuse, in Dalton, n 59, pp117–135.

Forensic Medical Examination with appropriate expertise when sexual violence is suspected or witnessed.[99] The purpose is to identify and treat any trauma or medical conditions (eg STIs); collect corroborating evidence of sexual abuse if such signs are present; and carry out a holistic assessment on growth, development, and other health needs. However, this type of FME entails specific child protection procedures to mitigate and prevent further exposure to harm. In conflict or post-conflict settings where caregivers may have suffered violence or are deceased, supporting children through their trauma when their sense of safety has shifted may require extra considerations to reduce harm.[100] There also remain challenges in establishing whether a child has suffered sexual violence as well as interpreting the significance of anogenital findings.[101] There is no gold standard 'test' to confirm whether child sexual abuse has occurred, but there are signs and injuries that can indicate an increased probability.[102] This needs to be accounted for in claims for reparations where a flexible approach to evidence should be taken. A child may communicate or 'tell' about the sexual violence (eg through drawings or play), or 'show' it through behavioural indicators.[103] For instance, in the *Ntaganda* case before the ICC, male former child soldiers spoke about their role as 'cot', which was assumed to be a porter role within the armed group but actually indicated that they were used as sex slaves.[104] Symptomology as well as examination techniques can vary according to a child's sex, developmental stage, and pubertal status.[105]

In the UK, an evidence-based review and guidance is issued periodically on best practice by a number of professional stakeholder organizations with multidisciplinary board oversight on anogenital signs of sexual abuse in those less than 18 years as well as on other related issues such as sexually transmitted infections and accidental injuries.[106] This is distinct from the Adams Classification, as the Royal College of Paediatrics and Child Health (RCPCH and partners) review evidence separately and look specifically at findings for standard examination given variation in examination practices. There are clinical signs in the context of an allegation of sexual abuse that would support it to varying degrees. Nonetheless, there

[99] Paediatric clinicians with a minimum amount of experience should be involved in order to carry out child protection medical assessments. It is also important to be familiar with anogenital signs of accidental injury and non-traumatic causes of genital bleeding. For more information on child protection see FFLM & RCPCH, Quality Standards for Clinicians undertaking Paediatric Sexual Offence Medicine (PSOM), https://fflm.ac.uk/wp-content/uploads/2024/08/Quality-Standards-for-Clinicians-undertaking-Paediatric-Sexual-Offence-Medicine-PSOM-Jun24.pdf, accessed 1 August 2025.

[100] UN Convention on the Rights of the Child (UNCRC), 1989.

[101] ibid; and Introduction, in RCPCH, n 88, pp1–5. For instance, the clinician must be familiar with female genital anatomy and the appearance of the pre-pubertal hymen. This includes variations of normal clinical findings of the hymen as well as acute and healed injuries.

[102] Research Priorities, in RCPCH, n 88.

[103] Good Practice (Chapter 12), in RCPCH, n 88.

[104] Gilmore, n 47, ICC-01/04-02/06-2623-Anx2-Red2, p21.

[105] Price and Golding, n 98, p128; RCPCH, n 88.

[106] See Introduction (Chapter 1) and Methodology (Chapter 2), in RCPCH, n 88; and Dr Jo Gifford, RCPCH Webinar, October 2024.

are also non-specific signs, and the absence of anogenital signs is considered neutral with regards to child sexual violence.[107] In other words, the absence of signs does not mean the sexual violence did not happen. Furthermore, certain sexually transmitted infections diagnosed in children, where vertical transmission[108] or voluntary sexual transmission is not deemed clinically likely, are suggestive or indicative (more precise) of sexual violence.[109] This significant harm should be considered in reparation claims.

Other classifications of injuries exist but are not universally used. For instance, Dr Mukwege developed a classification of injuries (four types) in children who suffered sexual violence which is based on the depth of injury and structures involved.[110] While this can be helpful for demonstrating the extent of injury, it is important to consider circumstances in which injuries are not apparent but the child has still suffered significant harm. In situations of armed conflict, it may be easier to have a simpler classification of injury to allow wider training and consistent documentation. The next section considers the feasibility of capturing injuries and other harms through FMEs for conflict-related sexual violence.

Feasibility of forensic medical examinations for CRSV

FMEs are typically performed for possible future criminal investigations, and in areas of conflict, to identify patterns of violence that may assist in evidencing war crimes and crimes against humanity.[111] When viewed with the correct data protections in place, it may also be able to help plan public health responses. To assist with relevant data collection and to prompt all clinicians who may be conducting any medical assessment to document key information, regional guidance could be situated within international protocols on documentation that have accountability for violations of international law in mind.[112] Unfortunately, research on FMEs after CRSV (whether in-country or elsewhere) is lacking, despite the number of victims affected.[113] Aside from experience and training, the identification of

[107] The Extent of Anogenital Injuries at Examination (Chapter 7), in RCPCH, n 88, p17.

[108] Vertical transmission refers to infections transmitted between the mother or pregnant person and their baby. For example, HIV, Herpes Simplex Virus (HSV), rubella, and syphilis.

[109] It is important to consider sexual abuse in a child diagnosed with Neisseria gonorrhoea, chlamydia trachomatis, syphilis, or anogenital warts (caused by the Human Papilloma Virus). RCPCH, n 88, pp2–3; and Sexually Transmitted Infections (Chapter 10), in ibid.

[110] Denis Mukwege, Classification of Gender-Based Genitourinary and Rectovaginal Trauma in Girls Under Five Years of Age, *International Journal Gynaecology & Obstetrics* 124(1) (2014) 97–98.

[111] Physicians for Human Rights, MediCapt Factsheet, https://phr.org/wp-content/uploads/2022/11/PHR-MediCapt-Fact-Sheet-FINAL.pdf, accessed 1 August 2025.

[112] International Protocol on the Documentation and Investigation of Sexual Violence in Conflict, Best Practice on the Documentation of Sexual Violence as a Crime or Violation of International Law, Second Edition, March 2017.

[113] Elena Rubini et al, Forensic Medical Examination After Conflict-Related Sexual Violence: A Scoping Review of the Literature, *Journal of Legal and Forensic Medicine* 106 (2024) 102736; and Lisa Smith, Heather Flowe, and Wangu Kanja, Achieving More With Less: A Critical Review of Protocols for Forensic Investigation of Sexual Violence in Low-Resource Environments, *Forensic Science International Synergy* 1 (2019) 108–113.

injuries may also depend on the method of examination, as an instrument called a colposcope may allow for better imaging.[114] This may not always be affordable or feasible. It is also important to consider the potentially retraumatizing effect of 'micro-visualization technologies' such as colposcopy.[115] Where CRSV has been reported, there is an attempt to capture all relevant information in one sitting to minimize retraumatization, however some in humanitarian forensics caution against excluding a second supplementing history or examination due to such fears.[116] It may not be practical or appropriate to complete a thorough FME in a single session and trauma-informed techniques may help mitigate further trauma.

Training can be given to non-specialist clinicians to carry out some degree of forensic examination where capacity for forensic clinicians is limited.[117] This allows for evidence capture before healing without residual defect occurs. However, two main issues call for consideration. First, there needs to be clarity on intimate examination techniques in appropriate dignified settings of care, which was a concern of victims in interviews.[118] Second, if there are collection and analysis of forensic samples, basic scientific principles are required to ensure integrity and the best possible results. A forensically secure setting with adequate cleaning protocols as well as the availability of complementary kits to help clinicians may be limited in ongoing conflict settings. There is also the issue of which laboratory tests are available, as well as the storage required to inhibit deterioration of samples until analysis can be carried out. These resources may simply not be available to victims or clinicians. Victims of CRSV are also less likely to report the incident of sexual violence before receiving care,[119] thus potentially losing a forensic opportunity to collect specimens even if they present within appropriate timeframes for sampling, as there may be significant contamination.

The challenge of securely gathering forensic data in conflict zones was not lost on Physicians for Human Rights who designed a digital mobile application called 'MediCapt' that supports clinicians in their forensic documentation (including photography) of sexual violence while helping to identify patterns of violence.[120] Ultimately, it aims to help with prosecutions of CRSV as war crimes and crimes against humanity and potentially support verification of reparations claims. A review of the application's effectiveness revealed it did improve the standard of

[114] Interpretation of Genital Findings, in Wyatt, n 57, p370.

[115] White, n 86, p114.

[116] Ketsekioulafis et al, n 81.

[117] Karen Naimer, Muriel Volpellier, and Denis Mukwege, The Case of Kavumu: A Model of Medicolegal Collaboration, *The Lancet* 29(393)v(2019) 2651–2654, p2653.

[118] Interpretation could be assisted by more experienced clinicians.

[119] Ariadna Capasso et al, Factors Associated with Experiencing Sexual Violence Among Female Gender-Based Violence Survivors in Conflict-Afflicted Eastern Ukraine, *BMC Public Health* 789 (2021) doi.org/10.1186/s12889-021-10830-9.

[120] MediCapt was developed as part of the Program on Sexual Violence in Conflict at Physicians for Human Rights, see Physicians for Human Rights, MediCapt Factsheet, https://phr.org/wp-content/uploads/2022/11/PHR-MediCapt-Fact-Sheet-FINAL.pdf, accessed 1 August 2025.

forensic documentation, but time is needed to learn and navigate the system as well as grapple with difficulties in technology or WiFi connections.[121] Financial and technical support as well as clinician capacity is needed to operationalize innovative systems, but use of forensic photography on smartphones has been used outside conflict settings with better identification of injuries.[122] There are also technical considerations and digital safeguards needed to identify trends as well as perpetrators (eg an armed group in a certain region).[123] Photo documentation is generally a welcome addition to SOM, but a working group on photography in custody or sexual assault centres has issued guidance for clinicians, and recommends specific training to reduce medico-legal issues or concerns regarding quality.[124] These considerations can play a role in considering how best to raise standards for CRSV documentation. Similar to all other forensic evidence, it also must be interpreted in light of other evidence presented.

Consequences from forensic medical examinations

The high level of impunity can prevent victims from engaging in a forensic assessment and a potentially intimate examination. Forensic evidence is an additional layer that complements justice claims for reparations, without necessarily needing to go through criminal procedures, where there is a higher evidential standard. Reparations can be awarded through administrative programmes or as part of a criminal trial. By way of example, clinicians in the *Kavumu* case captured key forensic evidence which helped to secure a conviction of 11 men who were found guilty by the High Military Court of the Democratic Republic of Congo (DRC) in 2018 of crimes against humanity for the rape of dozens of children in the Democratic Republic of Congo.[125] Reparations have been awarded in this case[126] but not yet implemented.[127] A medico-legal report based on interviews and physical findings (including photographs) of the children complemented adult witness testimonies.[128] However, forensic evidence is not immune to misuse or misinterpretation. Wright explains how FMEs were misused during the Francoist legal

[121] Suzanne Kidenda et al, 'Evaluating the Effectiveness of a Mobile Application to Improve the Quality, Collection, and Usability of Forensic Documentation of Sexual Violence, *PLoS ONE* 17(12) (2022) e0278312. https://doi.org/10.1371/journal.pone.0278312.

[122] Anousha Victoire et al, Smartphone Digital Photography in Sexual Assault Forensic Examination in Regional New South Wales, *Pathology* 57 (2025) S12–S12.

[123] For more information on the use of digitized forensic evidence, see International Protocol on the Documentation and Investigation of Sexual Violence in Conflict, Best Practice on the Documentation of Sexual Violence as a Crime or Violation of International Law, n 122. See Part V: Documentation in Practice (pp160–260) and Part VI: Analysing Evidence and Information.

[124] PICS Working Group Guidelines on photography, FFLM, January 2024.

[125] Naimer et al, n 117.

[126] ibid.

[127] The victims of the Kavumu case faced barriers attaining reparations, despite being awarded them. See, Global Survivors Fund, Global Reparations Study, Executive Summary Report of Preliminary Findings, 27 September 2021, p8.

[128] Naimer et al, n 117.

system of the 1970s to counter any justice or reparation efforts.[129] Instead medical evidence was used to reinforce harmful patriarchal norms in order to 'fit' who was a legitimate 'victim' or 'perpetrator' under the illusion of forensic legitimacy. Police and laboratory staff are also influenced by stereotypes of who is considered a deserving victim, which can in turn affect which kits are processed by the laboratory.[130] The role of medical forensics in the criminal justice system can still be misunderstood, and the veracity of a claim should not lie with forensics. This can similarly be a problem for reparation programmes, which may use FMEs or past documentation to verify CRSV claims, but claimants may be unable to meet the evidential standard of proof for historic violations.

McMillan and colleagues warn about the oversimplification of the FME as medical or scientific evidence. They consider it potentially onerous on the victim as they 'must actively negotiate—not just passively endure—to claim and maintain credibility',[131] giving rise to other possible harms on their social and moral standing. In essence, FMEs are an additional tool that can help us understand the harms of sexual violence, including when conducted on a mass scale or in a systematic manner, but they cannot fully address what is a complex social problem particularly when relating to conflict. Victims should be informed of the optional nature of FMEs and be clear that it is not contingent on access to treatment so they feel no element of coercion.[132] The FME can be a difficult experience for victims, but Du Mont and colleagues found that where compassionate care is performed by clinicians who also prioritize women's health concerns, it can be empowering and represent a physical step in a 'sense of doing something';[133] taking back some control. One positive consequence that arose in interviews was that a forensic examination can also be restorative, providing reassurance about a victim's anatomy,[134] as well as help them to psychologically move forward.[135] In relation to child sexual abuse, FMEs can reassure the child and their parents or caregivers, alleviating

[129] Stephanie Wright, 'Facts That Are Declared Proven': Sexual Violence, Forensic Medicine, and the Courtroom in Early Francoist Spain, *Women's History Review* 32(7) (2023) p939-959.

[130] Rebecca Campbell and Giannina Fehler-Cabral, 'Just Bring Us the Real Ones': The Role of Forensic Crime Laboratories in Guarding the Gateway to Justice for Sexual Assault Victims, *Journal of Interpersonal Violence* 37 (7–8) (2022), https://doi.org/10.1177/08862605209513; Mary Carr et al, Debunking Three Rape Myths, *Journal of Forensic Nursing* 10(4) (2014) 217–225,| doi:10.1097/JFN.0000000000000044.

[131] Lesley McMillan et al, Compliance and Credibility: A Critique of the Sexual Assault Forensic Examination From International Perspectives, *Gender and Justice* 1(1) (2025) 119–139; C9, Bogotá Colombia, September 2018.

[132] Janice Du Mont, Deborah White, and Margaret J McGregor, Investigating the Medical Forensic examination From the Perspectives of Sexually Assaulted Women, *Social Science & Medicine* 68(4) (1982), 2009-02, 774–780. In some legal jurisdictions, there may be exceptions. In Colombia, until 2022, there was specific restrictive criteria for legal abortion, including rape.

[133] ibid.

[134] C3, Bogotá, Colombia, September 2018; C13, Bogotá, Colombia, March 2019.

[135] Rachael Goodman-Williams, Jessica Volz, and Kathryn Fishwick, Reasons for Not Reporting Among Sexual Assault Survivors Who Seek Medical Forensic Exams: A Qualitative Analysis, *Journal of Interpersonal Violence* 39(9–10) (2024) 1905–1925, p1906.

anxiety about abnormality.[136] It can also present an opportunity to carry out health promotion that may have been missed due to conflict factors, such as arranging the HPV vaccine and cervical screening.[137] It is worth considering how to integrate specialized clinics for sexual and reproductive health, or maternity care for those affected by CRSV.[138]

Unfortunately, supportive staff with adequate resources and training, as well as their own professional support system do not always occur. An interviewee reported how intimate examinations, including for forensic purposes, were initially not being conducted in a dignified manner with adequate privacy.[139] Forensic clinicians are also not immune to the influence of stigmatizing socio-cultural norms.[140] A senior member of a forensic institute spoke of how, in spite of ethics attached to the medical profession, it is difficult to ensure that all physicians do not let their own stereotypes negatively affect a victim's experience, especially when non-forensic experts are asked to get involved in evidence capture.[141] Unfortunately, there are reports of sexual assault occurring when victims receive post-rape care.[142] This can prevent victims from coming forward to seek a forensic examination and therapeutic care. Several victims I interviewed were hesitant to have an FME due to concerns over how they would be treated, especially in low-resource settings where exams and sampling may be more limited.[143] Crucially, forensic clinicians need to be taught that there is no place for 'virginity testing' when assessing for sexual violence, and that this futile practice with no evidential basis exposes victims to further psychological, physical, and social harm.[144] Unfortunately, Olson and García-Moreno identified some forensic textbooks that have not been updated to exclude this gender discriminatory practice.[145]

Some victims of forced sterilization in Peru had investigations performed years later to ascertain what procedure resulting in forced sterilization had been carried out without their consent, due to the lack of documentation. Many described these investigations as lacking trauma-sensitive care despite appearing routine to

[136] Alison Livingstone, Presentation, Child Sexual Abuse, F2 Safeguarding Training, 2019.

[137] BASHH, n 60, p17.

[138] For an example of specialized sexual and reproductive healthcare for victims of sexual violence outside of conflict see, The My Body Back Project, https://mybodybackproject.com/, accessed 1 August 2025.

[139] Expert Roundtable, 2019.

[140] C12, Bogotá, Colombia, March 2019; C9, Bogotá, Colombia, September 2018; C15 FG1, Bogotá, Colombia, March 2019; U1, Kampala, Uganda, July 2018.

[141] C9, Bogotá, Colombia, September 2018.

[142] Julienne Corboz et al, Enhancing a Survivor-Centred Approach to Healthcare Provision in Afghanistan: Understanding and Addressing the Barriers Faced by Male Victims/Survivors of Sexual Violence, *Child Abuse and Neglect* 142(2) (2022) 105854.

[143] C13, Bogotá, Colombia, March 2019; C15, Bogotá, Colombia, March 2019.

[144] Rose McKeon Olson and Claudia García-Moreno, Virginity Testing: A Systematic Review, *Reproductive Health* 14(61) (2017), doi:10.1186/s12978-017-0319-0. While the hymen can be inspected for injuries with approved techniques and consent, most trauma heals quickly without obvious signs of injury. No form of virginity testing is acceptable including the two-finger per vaginal examination.

[145] ibid

clinicians.[146] Where the case proceeds to trial, further fear surrounds questioning that is not trauma-informed, causing further harm due to the perpetuation of rape myths,[147] as well as the lack of measures such as video or remote testimony.[148] Therefore when an FME is performed, it is important to consider other harms that may ensue down the line but also the potential for delayed transformative positive consequences associated with criminal proceedings.[149]

In some countries, it is mandatory for healthcare professionals to report sexual violence to the police (eg Colombia). This is irrespective of whether victims wish for police involvement, are undecided, or wish to preserve evidence for a potentially later date when they are ready. Victims may decide to undergo an FME as they desire the linked therapeutic care such as STI prophylaxis and emergency contraception, without having to explain themselves further. Victims can feel retraumatized by the lack of control when professionals make a mandatory report of their incident, or become traumatized by insensitive investigative proceedings, especially when special protections are not afforded to them.[150] Thus, certain harms can ensue from FMEs where this is not pre-emptively communicated with the victim. Where there are safeguarding concerns, such as that of children or vulnerable adults at risk, clinicians have an overriding obligation to involve other authorities such as the police and social services. In other countries, such as Northern Ireland, healthcare professionals only need to report to the police if certain information was given by the victim, such as the potential identity of the perpetrator or location of the crime.[151] Therefore, the limits of confidentiality need to be explained early to avoid further harm to the victims or others at ongoing risk. However, healthcare professionals can explain to victims that there is no duty to report to the police if such information is not disclosed by the victim, thus hopefully promoting engagement of victims to self-refer and receive therapeutic care to reduce downstream consequences (eg HIV) while respecting their decision to avoid police involvement at that time. This demonstrates strategies to mitigate the harm caused by sexual violence and maintain trust in the medical profession.

Both the harms and positive consequences arising specifically out of FMEs for those affected by CRSV in conflict-affected settings or in host countries need

[146] P2 FG1, Lima, Peru, May 2019.

[147] Rebecca Campbell et al, The Prosecution of Sexual Assault Cases with Forensic DNA Evidence: Survivors' Testimony Experiences, *Psychology, Public Policy, and Law* 31(2) (2025) 204-216, doi: 10.1037/law0000453.

[148] The Council of Europe Convention on Preventing and Combating Violence against Women and Domestic Violence 2014, Article 56(1)(a)–(i) and (2).

[149] Jelke Boesten, Transformative Gender Justice: Criminal Proceedings for Conflict-Related Sexual Violence in Guatemala and Peru, *Australian Journal of Human Rights* 27(3) (2021) 487–504.

[150] Sir John Gillen, Gillen Review, Report into the Law and Procedures in Serious Sexual Offences in Northern Ireland, 2019, paras 2.11–2.14 and Article 18(3) Council of Europe Convention on Preventing and Combating Violence against Women and Domestic Violence.

[151] For example in Northern Ireland, Section 5, Criminal Law Act (Northern Ireland) 1967, https://www.legislation.gov.uk/apni/1967/18/section/5, accessed 1 August 2025.

greater attention. Training to clinicians may need to be adapted to include expertise in areas such as torture, migration, and other pre-existing vulnerabilities,[152] as well as the potential for reparations or access to other care later. Where legal and technology infrastructure exists, there can still be frustration that forensics focus too heavily on physical injuries[153] and do not embody the longitudinal and complex trauma that can stem from sexual violence. The remaining part of this chapter aims to shed more light on the reality of consequences.

3.2.2 Infectious diseases

The transmission of sexually transmitted infections (STIs) is one of the most commonly reported physical complications, as high as 83 per cent in some studies of victims in conflict zones, despite the development of prophylaxis for some infections.[154] Armed conflict itself can also increase the spread of infectious diseases.[155] The likelihood of contracting an STI depends on the prevalence of the infection (how common it is in a population),[156] co-morbidities (eg immunocompromise), types of sexual activity, sexualized drug use, multiple sexual contacts, and whether risk-reducing strategies were used (eg the male condom).[157] STIs can be classified according to their causative organism (bacterial, viral, fungi, or parasitic) and whether they can be treated or cured. This section does not examine every possible STI but rather illuminates some of the most serious ones and draws upon empirical research to reflect on the multifaceted impact of STIs when the option for timely diagnosis and treatment is not offered to victims.

The first 72 hours after a rape or sexual assault is time-sensitive for medical interventions, such as Human Immunodeficiency Virus (HIV) prophylaxis,[158] and treatments that can be given within a short timeframe after the event, like

[152] Rubini et al, n 113.

[153] Janice Du Mont and Deborah White, The Uses and Impacts of Medico-Legal Evidence in Sexual Assault Cases: A Global Review, Sexual Violence Research Initiative, 2007, p41.

[154] C Watts et al, Sexual Violence and Conflict in Africa: Prevalence and Potential Impact on HIV Incidence, *Sexual Transmitted Infection* 86(3) (2010) 93–99.

[155] Marta Vasylyev et al, The Infectious Disease Burden Among War Related Internally Displaced People in the Lviv Region of Ukraine, *Germs (București)* 14(4) (2024) 322–343.

[156] Point prevalence is the proportion of the population who has the disease, condition, or characteristic at a specific point in time. Period prevalence refers to 'over a period of time' and includes new and existing cases.

[157] National Institute for Health and Care Excellence, Reducing Sexually Transmitted Infections, NG221, 15 June 2022; Harry Coleman et al, British Association for Sexual Health and HIV (BASHH) Summary Guidance on Testing for Sexually Transmitted Infections, 2023.

[158] Tetanus is recommended as part of wound care. It is not transmitted sexually but can enter via broken skin. The tetanus vaccine can be given but Immunoglobulin is generally not available in low resource settings. WHO, Clinical Management of Rape and Intimate Partner Violence Survivors Developing Protocols for Use in Humanitarian Settings, 2020, p23. For guidance related to specific STIs see, BASHH, Guidelines, https://www.bashh.org/resources/guidelines, accessed 1 August 2025.

vaccination courses for Hepatitis B and tetanus.[159] While data is limited in conflict situations, it appears that most victims will not be able to report within 72 hours.[160] Testing for STIs should be offered to victims of sexual violence depending on their incubation period and whether the diagnosis of an STI will have forensic significance. Tests for STIs are only reliable after a certain amount of time has passed (ie the incubation period),[161] which varies between organisms.[162] By way of example, testing for the STIs Chlamydia trachomatis (chlamydia), and Neisseria gonorrhoeae (gonorrhoea) at first presentation, in addition to two weeks after the sexual violence, may help to determine whether the bacterial infection pre-dates the incident or resulted from the sexual violence.[163] To demonstrate this further, if a person was not sexually active before the incident, such as a child, or the sexual violence involves penetration at a site for the first time,[164] or it has been many years since their last sexual contact, then positive identification of an STI could form evidence of the incident.[165] The forensic significance of STIs in some cases alongside the benefit of preventing bacterial infection needs to be balanced, particularly if they are unable to return for repeat testing and treatment at a later date.[166] Some guidelines outside conflict settings advise against routine antibiotic use for STIs following sexual violence except in specific cases, such as when the perpetrator is confirmed to have an infection and an emergency intrauterine device is required

[159] Most victims of sexual violence in conflict areas do not seek medical assistance within this critical time period, with the majority coming forward within a year and some also suffering repeated rapes over a year. Some research also indicates that other STIs are more prevalent than HIV (testing dependent on availability). For example, one study in South Kivu found that 66 per cent of victims tested positive for STIs compared to 1.5 per cent for HIV—Birthe Steiner et al, Sexual Violence in the Protracted Conflict of DRC Programming for Rape Survivors in South Kivu, *Conflict and Health* 3(3) (2009), 1–9, http://doi.org/10.1186/1752-1505-3-3.

[160] In conflict affected Ukraine, between February 2016 and June 2017, a sample of victims of CRSV took four days longer to report the incident compared to other gender-based violence. See Capasso et al, n 119.

[161] The incubation period refers to the time from first exposure to an infectious organism and the start of signs or symptoms, or onset of disease.

[162] Generally, test for HIV after at least 45 days (4th generation test); syphilis and Hepatitis B and C between three and six months.

[163] BASHH, n 60, p27.

[164] In females, it is important to note that due to the movement of vaginal secretions, a positive rectal infection may also be the result of vaginal penetration. Therefore, testing in both sites is important if there is a history of penile–vaginal penetration.

[165] Royal College of Pathologists. Guidance for Handling Medicolegal Samples and Preserving the Chain of Evidence, March 2017.

[166] The use of doxycycline for prophylaxis of bacterial STIs (syphilis, chlamydia) outside of sexual violence has been studied in certain population groups with research ongoing. It has been incorporated into some clinical guidelines; see, Laura H Bachman et al, CDC Clinical Guidelines on the Use of Doxycycline Postexposure Prophylaxis for Bacterial Sexually Transmitted Infection Prevention, United States, 2024: Morbidity and Mortality Weekly Report (MMWR) *Recommdations and Reports* 73(2) (2024) 1–8 (No RR-2), http://dx.doi.org/10.15585/mmwr.rr7302a1. See also, John Saunders et al, British Association for Sexual Health and HIV (BASHH) UK National Guideline for the Use of Doxycycline Post-Exposure Prophylaxis (DoxyPEP) for the Prevention of Syphilis, 2025. https://www.bashh.org/_userfiles/pages/files/saundersetal2025britishassociationforsexualhealthandhivbashhuknationalguidelinefortheuseof.pdf, accessed 22 November 2025.

for contraception.[167] However, the World Health Organization recommends presumptive treatment of bacterial STIs (chlamydia, gonorrhoea, and syphilis) on the first visit as well as any additional treatment based on positive results in humanitarian settings.[168] During conflict, the risk of harm from STIs needs to be considered so drugs are given in line with local protocols and with a single dose of antibiotics preferred given the possibility that victims may not be able to return.[169]

HIV is amongst the most serious infections which may arise from being a victim of sexual violence. It is a virus that targets the body's immune system, specifically attacking CD4 T cells—a type of white blood cell that plays a crucial role in fighting infections. HIV can progress to the most advanced stage without effective treatment—known as Acquired Immunodeficiency Syndrome (AIDS). It can be transmitted through unprotected sexual contact with an infected person where the virus is detectable in their blood.[170] If the person presents within 72 hours, then a risk assessment on HIV acquisition is performed and post-exposure prophylaxis (PEP) offered if the risk of transmission is considered significant (over 1 in 1000).[171] PEP, in the form of antiretroviral therapy, reduces replication and transmission of the virus.[172] Ideally, PEP for HIV is started within 24 hours but it can be given up to 72 hours, and preferably with counselling to improve adherence to the 28-day course of medications, given the potential side effects.[173] Although medical responses have become more efficacious over time, some are largely unchanged from the early 2000s, such as the early initiation of antiretroviral treatment (ART) upon a positive diagnosis of HIV.[174] Infected victims may be unable to access testing and early treatment aimed at suppressing the virus as well as monitoring for complications and reducing vaccine-preventable diseases. They are more susceptible to infection or experience more severe consequences from infection.[175]

[167] BASHH, n 60, p29; FSRH CEU statement on antibiotic cover for urgent insertion of intrauterine contraception in women at high risk of STIs, 22 May 2019.

[168] WHO, n 158, pp25–26.

[169] The Centers for Disease Control and Prevention (CDC) recommend routine prophylaxis against bacterial infections for the vast majority of adults and adolescents after sexual violence. See CDC, Sexually Transmitted Infections Treatment Guidelines, 2021. Carolyn J Sachs, Megan Ladd, and Brooke Thomas, *Sexual Assault Infectious Disease Prophylaxis, National Library of Medicine* (updated 2023), https://www.ncbi.nlm.nih.gov/books/NBK482239/, accessed 1 August 2025.

[170] HIV can also be transmitted via mother-to-child transmission, infected blood products, and sharing needles. Persons on treatment with an undetectable viral load in their blood do not transmit the virus. HIV/British Infection Association Adult HIV Testing Guidelines 2020, *HIV Medicine* 21(6) (2020) 1–26, p3.

[171] If the HIV status of the perpetrator is unknown, then the prevalence of detectable HIV viraemia in their presumed country of origin (https://aidsinfo.unaids.org) can be used to calculate the risk of transmission in combination with the type of exposure (eg penile–vaginal penetration): BASHH, n 60, p29; Adrian Palfreeman et al, British HIV Association/British Association for Sexual Health and HIV/British Infection Association Adult HIV Testing Guidelines 2020, *HIV Medicine* 21(6) (2020) 1–26, p5.

[172] BASHH & BHIVA, UK Guideline for the use of HIV Post-Exposure Prophylaxis, 2021.

[173] World Health Organization, Guidelines for HIV Post-Exposure Prophylaxis, 2024.

[174] WHO, Sexual Violence (Chapter 6), in Etienne G Krug, Linda L Dahlberg, James A Mercy, Anthony B Zwi, and Rafael Lozano, World Report on Violence and Health, World Health Organization (2002), p147–182. ART are drugs used to treat HIV infection.

[175] British HIV Association Guidelines on the use of Vaccines in HIV-Positive Adults, 2015.

For example, opportunistic infections take advantage of a lowered immune system which can lead to disability or be life-threatening.

The type of sexual violence impacts on the risk of HIV transmission.[176] For example, sexual violence involving penetration such as through rape or gang rape,[177] which is also seen in sexual slavery, can result in HIV transmission.[178] In particular, penetrative anal sex carries a higher risk of transmission. Inevitably, the increased number of sexual perpetrators involved in these acts can also exacerbate the risk of HIV acquisition.[179] Some perpetrators themselves may engage in high-risk sexual behaviour with multiple sexual partners and non-condom use, heightening the risk of HIV transmission.[180] Concurrent trauma such as mutilation, bodily injury, or genital trauma, including penetration of the vagina and anus with sharp instruments or weapons that may be contaminated with blood or certain bodily fluids (eg genital secretion and blood-stained saliva),[181] also influence the risk of HIV and other infections.

The public health impact of HIV can be worsened by limited access to PEP and screening for sexually transmitted infections in a conflict environment. Late diagnosis and therefore delayed testing is one of the major contributors to HIV-associated morbidity and mortality.[182] While there have been significant improvements in life expectancy and quality of life for persons living with HIV, this largely depends on prompt detection and the availability of combination antiretroviral treatment.[183] It is difficult to accurately estimate the age at which untreated HIV-positive victims of rape may die.[184] However, the median survival time is eight to ten years in adults from the time anti-HIV antibodies become detectable, which

[176] Jennifer Klot, Judith Auerbach, and Miranda Berry, Sexual Violence and HIV Transmission: Summary Proceedings of a Scientific Research Planning Meeting, *American Journal of Reproductive Immunology* 69 (2013) 5–19, p7.

[177] Gang rape refers to multiple perpetrator rape.

[178] Catherine Hankinsa et al, Transmission and Prevention of HIV and Sexually Transmitted Infections in War Settings: Implications for Current and Future Armed Conflicts, *AIDS* (16) (2002) 2245–2252.

[179] Ingrid Ba and Raja S Bhopal, Physical, Mental and Social Consequences in Civilians Who Have Experienced War-related Sexual Violence: A Systematic Review (1981–2014), *Public Health* 142 (2017) 121–135.

[180] Klot et al, n 176, p6.

[181] Note some bodily fluids are not a risk, eg urine, sweat, sputum, and non-blood stained saliva. WHO/EHT/CPR, Prevention of Transmission of HIV, 2004 (updated 2007). https://cdn.who.int/media/docs/default-source/integrated-health-services-(ihs)/csy/surgical-care/imeesc-toolkit/best-practice-safety-protocols/clinical-procedures-safety.pdf?sfvrsn=7898e9b1_5, accessed 1 August 2025.

[182] In the UK, late diagnosis is the most important factor in HIV-related morbidity and mortality. UK National Guidelines for HIV Testing 2008. September 2008. Prepared jointly by the British HIV Association, the British Association of Sexual Health and HIV, and the British Infection Society https://bhiva.org/wp-content/uploads/2025/01/GlinesHIVTest08.pdf, accessed 1 August 2025.

[183] Sirinya Teeraananchai et al, Life Expectancy of HIV-Positive People After Starting Combination Anti-Retroviral Therapy: A Meta-Analysis, *HIV Medicine* 18(4) (2017) 256–266. Note, a discrepancy in life expectancy exists between countries based on income, with 10 additional years on average in high income countries, ibid p257.

[184] Caroline Sabin, Do People with HIV Infection Have a Normal Life Expectancy in the Era of Combination Antiretroviral Therapy? *BMC Medicine* 11 (2013) 251.

occurs typically within a few weeks after contraction (although other variables will affect this, such as intravenous drug use and nutritional status).[185] For those with a significant interval from transmission to diagnosis and treatment, there could be particular HIV-related complications that may prove fatal, or that may impact the quality of life of those who survive contracting the disease until it is detected. Moreover, this harm can be compounded by the lack of social understanding and empathy towards those affected, with victims facing discrimination and social isolation.[186]

A number of public and private medical organizations I engaged with attempted to provide free ART to HIV-positive victims of sexual violence during and post-conflict, with varying success. Treatment was often interrupted (where not medically indicated) given supply difficulties,[187] and some victims had been lost to follow-up due to displacement.[188] It is unknown whether these victims have been able to access other ART, but this is deemed unlikely in many cases.[189] As such, sub-optimal treatment regimens pose a higher risk of transmitting HIV to others, and if the period of non-treatment is prolonged, compliance after reintroduction may be more difficult.[190] Several victims spoke of unreliable public health sources, including ART, as part of comprehensive health reparations. One Colombian victim told me, 'Women who have HIV, they need a special medication, and they are not getting it'.[191] Therefore the implications of non-adherence and disruption of supply can mean that there remain long-term risks for victims infected with HIV.

Future sexual activity of HIV-infected individuals risks further onward transmission and harm to partners. This can occur where victims are not informed of preventative strategies or the factors that increase transmission, such as whether their viral load is above negligible levels or the availability of sperm washing,

[185] ibid. See also K. Porter et al, The Practical Significance of Potential Biases in Estimates of the AIDS Incubation Period Distribution in the UK Register of HIV Seroconverters, *AIDS* 13 (1999) 1943–1951. The projected life expectancy in HIV-positive children under 3 years old can be as low as 2.8 years. See Andrea Ciaranello et al, Cost-effectiveness of First-Line Antiretroviral Therapy for HIV-infected African Children Less Than 3 Years of Age, *AIDS*, 29(10) (2015) 1247–1259.

[186] WHO, Sexual Health, Human Rights and the Law, 2015, p22.

[187] This was related to a number of factors including cost, funding, the type and availability of drugs, stolen consignments, and insecurity disrupting delivery. In well-controlled HIV-positive patients with an adequate immune system and monitoring, treatment interruption may be a therapeutic strategy to increase overall compliance and reduce drug associated toxicity. However, where this is not medically indicated, unintended interruption to ART may lead to complications from HIV as well as increasing risk of transmission to others. See Georgui Dubrocq and Natella Rakhmanina, Antiretroviral Interruptions: Impact on HIV Treatment and Transmission. *HIV AIDS*, 10 (2018) 91–101.

[188] C15 FG1, Bogotá, Colombia, March 2019; C2, Bogotá, Colombia, September 2018; U10 FG2, Lira, Uganda, July 2018.

[189] C2, Bogotá, Colombia, September 2018.

[190] A Jiamsakul, et al, TREAT Asia HIV Observational Database (TAHOD) Effects of Unplanned Treatment Interruptions on HIV Treatment Failure—Results From TAHOD, *Tropical Medicine and International Health* 21(5) (2016) 662–674.

[191] C15 FG1, Bogotá, Colombia, March 2019.

which can impact their decisions to personally conceive children. Such transmission of HIV may not be initially apparent to a victim. This point was raised during my fieldwork—one Ugandan doctor found that women appear at his clinic complaining of other ailments, but if undergoing surgery, they have to take a mandatory HIV test. This meant that many found out at this point that they were HIV positive, despite having been in the community for years, with some reported to have potentially had multiple partners and children, especially within the LRA.[192]

Other STIs that may affect victims of sexual violence include Treponema pallidum (syphilis), gonorrhoea, chlamydia, (ano)genital herpes simplex virus (HSV), Hepatitis B, and infections that can be more prevalent in tropical regions, such as lymphogranuloma venereum (LGV).[193] Contracting one STI also increases the risk of contracting others. Genital chlamydia trachomatis may be asymptomatic at presentation, but in cases of delayed or missed treatment, long-term consequences of pelvic inflammatory disease (PID),[194] infertility, pelvic pain, and life-threatening ruptured ectopic pregnancy may ensue.[195] As one victim who has PID said, this not only causes her severe pain but also strains the relationship with her partner:

> When this happens to you, you can't has normal relationships, and your man gets upset, he says you this, you that, who knows what you did. But I can't, my ovaries hurt a lot, when I have intercourse, the next day, my ovaries are swollen. I feel a lot of pain, low pain, pain in the lower abdomen.[196]

Another victim experienced similar suffering:

[192] U4, FG1, Gulu, Uganda, July 2018.

[193] LGV is caused by an invasive type of chlamydia infection (L1, L2, L3 serovars). This list of possible STIs is not conclusive. Human Papilloma Virus (HPV) can also be sexually transmitted. HPV can be spontaneously cleared from the body or can cause pre-cancerous cellular change or cancer of the cervix or anus after many years. HPV accounts for 90 per cent of cervical cancer, which is globally the fourth most common cancer in women as at 2018. Cervical cancer remains one of the main causes of cancer-related deaths in women in the African region. See Marc Arbyn et al, Estimates of Incidence and Mortality of Cervical Cancer in 2018: A Worldwide Analysis, *The Lancet Global Health*, 8 (2020) 191–203, pp191–192. See Human Papillomavirus and Related Cancers, Fact Sheet 2018, HPV Information Centre, June 2019, https://hpvcentre.net/statistics/reports/COD_FS.pdf, accessed 1 August 2025. Certain public health strategies are effective at reducing the HPV-related cervical cancers of this common STI (cervical screening and the HPV vaccination). Therefore, it may not be appropriate for the convicted person to be liable for such harm.

[194] PID refers to inflammation of pelvic structures (such as fallopian tubes, uterus, and ovaries) as a result of the spread of untreated infection from the neck of the uterus (cervix). This can lead to adhesions, blocking of the fallopian tubes, and infertility. Untreated genital chlamydial infection carries a 1–30 per cent risk of progressing to PID, see Nwokolo N C, Dragović B, Patel S, Tong C Y W, Barker G & Radcliffe K, 2015 UK national guideline for the management of infection with Chlamydia trachomatis, Int J STD AIDS, 27(4) (2016), p 251-267, p253.

[195] J Tscholl, M Letson, and H Williams, Sexually Transmitted Infections in Child Abuse, *Clinical Pediatric Emergency Medicine* 17(4) (2016) 264–273.

[196] Respondent 2, C15 FG1, Bogotá, Colombia, March 2019.

> the pain is terrible, and I went to the doctor because the pain is terrible, it goes from the hip all the way down, as if you were going to give birth. I went here to get medication, but there isn't any, the only thing I got is Naproxen, with another medication, but the pain is still there, very deep. The only way I can get rid of the pain is to have it all removed. But I know, this is a harm caused by the violation, and doctors don't want to accept it, and right now, to my gynaecologists, how could I say: what happened is that I was carnally accessed (raped) by many men, and since then I have this condition.[197]

According to interviews with civil society organizations and healthcare practitioners in Uganda and Colombia, STIs in male victims of sexual violence can have significant physical and psychological effects that persist more than a decade after the crime.[198] Specifically, for former child soldiers who suffered sexual violence, the continuing effects of STIs can make social and economic reintegration particularly difficult.[199] One Ugandan victim who had been abducted by the LRA and returned years later spoke about the difficulty of forming new sexual relationships, as they had contracted STIs in the bush that made them infertile.[200] Victims had also experienced neurological consequences (eg headaches and memory loss) from late-stage syphilis.[201] Some victims who had suffered sexual slavery were also exposed to multiple traumatic physical and psychological incidents that had a deep impact on their ability to socially reintegrate, concentrate in education initiatives, and hold down jobs.[202] While most of this discussion has focused on the direct victim, for women and girls, it can also have an indirect impact on their fetuses and children.

Victims who become pregnant from rape, or were pregnant at the time of rape, can be at risk of contracting an STI. This may pose significant risks to the pregnancy and to their fetus.[203] Disruptions to maternal and child healthcare in

197 Respondent 4, C15 FG1, Bogotá, Colombia, March 2019.

198 U10 FG2, Lira, Uganda July 2018.

199 Kennedy Amone-P'Olak et al, Sexual Violence and General Functioning Among Formerly Abducted Girls in Northern Uganda: The Mediating Roles of Stigma and Community Relations—the WAYS Study, *BMC Public Health* 16(64) (2016) p4.

200 UG FG1, Gulu, Uganda, July 2018.

201 U11, Gulu, Uganda, July 2018. Late syphilis occurs in one third of untreated persons, generally after 10-20 years. However, symptomatic late syphilis can also appear as soon as 1–7 years, depending on the body system or tissue affected. Therefore, the symptomatic manifestations are highly variable. Other examples include: destructive inflammatory lesions (called gummas) that commonly affect the skin but can occur in any organ; cardiovascular disease leading to heart failure; and neurosyphilis which can give rise to a range of symptoms that affect movement and sensation. See Margaret Kingston et al, UK National Guidelines on the Management of Syphilis 2015, *International Journal of STD & AIDS* (2015) 1-26, p3–5.

202 U4 FG1, Gulu, Uganda, July 2018; and see Amone-P'Olak et al, n 199.

203 For instance, a first infection of genital herpes (Herpes Simplex Virus), particularly in the third trimester, or within six weeks of birth, poses a significant risk of transmission to the newborn. Therefore treatment as well as antiviral suppressive therapy and delivery via caesarean section would be recommended. See, Emily Clarke et al, Joint British Association for Sexual Health and HIV and Royal College of Obstetricians and Gynaecologists National UK Guideline for the Management of Herpes Simplex

conflict,[204] or due to being sexually enslaved, can prevent infectious disease screening, treatment in pregnancy, and specific measures to reduce transmission to the baby during pregnancy and birth.[205] For instance, syphilis may be contracted through contact with an infectious lesion or transferred to the fetus transplacentally leading to congenital disease (a condition or disease present at birth) which can manifest early or late (after two years).[206] Untreated acquired infections may progress to secondary syphilis (25 per cent) and tertiary (late) disease with potentially gummatous (destructive skin lesions), neurological, and cardiovascular consequences.[207] Syphilis in pregnancy can also lead to miscarriage, preterm labour, and stillbirth.[208] However, adverse pregnancy outcomes can be decreased by early detection and treatment, which aims to eradicate parental disease, reduce vertical transmission to the fetus, or treat any fetal infection.[209] This section does not consider each infection that has significant risks in pregnancy but exemplifies longitudinal harms. A negative screening for an STI in the first trimester of pregnancy does not mean that the pregnant person cannot contract it later on in the pregnancy and so healthcare practitioners need to consider retesting, such as in cases of suspected rape.[210]

3.2.3 Pregnancy and reproductive violence

Of the many impacts arising from sexual violence, pregnancy has received the most attention, followed closely by sexually transmitted infections.[211] As a consequence

Virus (HSV) in Pregnancy and the Neonate (2024 update), *International Journal of STD and AIDS* 36(1) (2024) 1–20.

[204] Kameela Miriam Alibhai et al, Factors Impacting Antenatal Care Utilization: A Systematic Review of 37 Fragile and Conflict-Affected Situations, *Conflict and Health* 16 (2022) 33 https://doi.org/10.1186/s13031-022-00459-9.

[205] WHO recommends a minimum of eight contacts during pregnancy, and where quality antenatal care is not given this can result in preventable stillbirths and maternal deaths. WHO Recommendations on Antenatal Care for a Positive Pregnancy Experience: Summary Highlights and Key Messages from the World Health Organization's 2016 Global Recommendations for Routine Antenatal Care, January 2018, https://iris.who.int/bitstream/handle/10665/259947/WHO-RHR-18.02-eng.pdf , accessed 1 August 2025.

[206] Kingston et al, n 201.

[207] ibid. Gummatous lesions are destructive inflammatory lesions with central necrosis (cell death). They usually affect skin and bone, but can occur in any organ, and on average appear after 15 years. Neurosyphilis can cause a progressive dementing condition and affects blood vessels in the brain, potentially leading to stroke. Cardiovascular syphilis can affect the main artery of the body (the aorta) as well as vessels of the heart.

[208] ibid.

[209] ibid.

[210] ibid.

[211] Leah Woolner, Myriam Denov, and Sarilee Kahn, 'I Asked Myself If I Would Ever Love My Baby': Mothering Children Born of Genocidal Rape in Rwanda, *Violence Against Women* 25(6) (2019) 703–720.

of being impregnated through rape, a person is not only consigned to the physiological implications of pregnancy and potentially to obstetric and maternal medical problems, but may also be compelled to assume the social identity of a mother/parent and society's related discourse. To put the risks of unwanted pregnancy into perspective, if conducted in line with best practice, abortion is safer than childbirth.[212]

Emergency contraception (EC) represents another time-sensitive intervention. It should be offered to victims not wishing to conceive who are at risk of pregnancy, based on the type of sexual violence they experienced (eg penile–vaginal penetration) and whether they were using any existing contraception. Healthcare professionals advise on the suitability of different forms of EC, which include oral hormonal tablets and the copper intrauterine device (Cu-IUD), referring to updated protocols.[213] If medically appropriate, the Cu-IUD should be offered to all as it is the most effective method of EC.[214] It does require an intimate examination so healthcare professionals must exercise vigilance and reaffirm consent if there are signs of distress.[215] The victim may prioritize pregnancy risk reduction over forensic capture of specimens if there is no skilled professional available to collect and handle samples around the same time, but any injuries can still be noted.[216] Moreover, victims may not have access to EC or to a skilled professional able to fit a Cu-IUD due to factors relating to conflict.

The risks of unwanted pregnancy can be exacerbated when conflict has led to deteriorations in healthcare, increased maternal mortality,[217] and low birth weight in newborns.[218] The limited evidence available indicates that there may also be a positive relationship between conflict and miscarriage, premature births, and still births, but higher quality studies are needed.[219] Conducting research is

[212] There are various key medical elements of a safe abortion see, Best Practice in Comprehensive Abortion Care, Best Practice Paper No 2, Royal College of Obstetricians and Gynaecologists, June 2015, p1.

[213] Faculty of Sexual and Reproductive Healthcare (FSRH), Guideline, Emergency Contraception, Amended 2023; WHO, n 158, pp60–61.

[214] ibid.

[215] BASHH, n 60, p28

[216] ibid. Oral EC and Cu-IUD can be offered up to 120 hours post unprotected sexual intercourse (UPSI). However, the Cu-IUD can also be offered up to five days after the earliest likely date of ovulation. EC is not 100 per cent effective, so pregnancy can still ensue, and victims should be advised to test for pregnancy 21 days after the UPSI.

[217] Maternal mortality ratio (MMR) refers to the number of maternal deaths during a defined time period per 100,000 live births for that same time period. This indicator depicts the risk of death during pregnancy. To put this into perspective, the SDG target for the global MMR is less than 70 per 100,000 live births by 2030, and no greater than 140 per 100,000 in any country. The global MMR in 2017 was 211 per 100,000 live births. See the United Nation's Sustainable Development Goals Report 2020, pp28–29, https://unstats.un.org/sdgs/report/2020/The-Sustainable-Development-Goals-Report-2020.pdf, accessed 1 August 2025.

[218] Kien Le and My Nguyen, Armed Conflict and Birth Weight, *Economics and Human Biology* (2020), doi: 10.1016/j.ehb.2020.10092.

[219] James 39 Keasley, Jessica Blickwedel, and Siobhan Quenby, Adverse Effects of Exposure to Armed Conflict on Pregnancy: A Systematic Review, *BMJ Global Health* 2 (2017), doi:10.1136/bmjgh-2017-000377.

a potentially difficult undertaking with displaced persons and the lack of continuity of care. Women living in areas with high levels of sustained conflict can be susceptible to inadequate antenatal care—in the form of missed care during the first trimester, fewer than the minimum number of antenatal checks, insufficient screening for infectious diseases that could be passed to the newborn, and the absence of a skilled birth attendant at delivery.[220] In conflict, this reduced quality of care can be due to limited resources (eg medicines, equipment, and blood products), lack of specialized training, and an inability to travel to the hospital offering maternity care.[221] The security situation can influence birth choices, such as choosing the risks of abdominal surgery (caesarean section), which can be timed during the day, versus the fear of giving birth at night when the security situation can be precarious and doctors may struggle to access hospitals.[222] While these risks relate to both wanted and unwanted pregnancy, becoming pregnant as a result of rape—and losing the ability to choose whether to be subjected to these risks in a conflict situation—can be an aggravating factor.[223] A victim who was abducted by the LRA and suffered sexual slavery described the consequences arising from the lack of maternity care.

> If you're abducted as a young girl, been forced into having sex and also giving birth at an early age - there are many main challenges. In captivity we were giving birth but there wasn't any qualified medical person to do that. So, the girls were giving birth and there was no one to really give them the special attention. There was no hospital. That is why many of them developed complications like fistula.[224]

In the context of the LRA there was evidence from primary research that the armed group did attempt to mitigate some potential harms from combatant injuries and pregnancy complications.[225] However, medical assistance generally occurred when armed factions were settled in camps for a while and through the abduction of healthcare professionals. One victim held captive by the LRA explained:

[220] Bianca Zieglar et al, Antenatal Care Utilization in the Fragile and Conflict-Affected Context of the Democratic Republic of the Congo, *Social Science and Medicine* (2020) 262, DOI: 10.1016/j.socscimed.2020.113253; and Margaret Hogan et al, Maternal Mortality for 181 Countries, 1980–2008: A Systematic Analysis of Progress Towards Millennium Development Goal 5, *The Lancet* 375(9726) (2010) 1609–1623 DOI: 10.1016/S0140-6736(10)60518-1.

[221] Hyam Bashour, Mayada Kharouf, and Jocelyn DeJong, Childbirth Experiences and Delivery Care During Times of War: Testimonies of Syrian Women and Doctors, *Frontiers in Global Womens Health* 2 (2021), doi: 10.3389/fgwh.2021.605634.

[222] ibid.

[223] WHO, Congo, Country Profile, WHO Director-General Roundtable with Women Leaders on Millennium Development Goal 5.

[224] U13, Gulu, Uganda, July 2018.

[225] ibid.

> The other thing that was also helpful to the LRA is that for a time they also abducted medics. Those people who are like doctors were abducted in case they would also help, sometimes they were abducted even with some of the medications. They would always assess and see whether such a condition would require provision and they'd give advice.[226]

In essence, medical support was primarily for combatants and was not a reliable source of care for pregnant women who did not have recourse to a hospital in the event of an emergency. There were also further problems for the children who survived delivery, such as not receiving their required WHO vaccination schedule, and as result many became sick, increasing the burden on women who had to look after them and try to feed them while marching through the jungle.[227] Conflict situations raise questions about how armed groups mitigate certain harms from rape, such as through offered or forced contraception or abortion, as well as potential motivations to care for children (or forced wives) of their members. Their respect for the protection of healthcare and what care they are willing to commit to for sexual and reproductive health may shape the downstream consequences reparations contend with.[228]

Some authors highlight how difficult it is to articulate the pain arising from rape, and how victims, due to social shaming, silently cope even when opportunities to speak arise.[229] This in turn can hinder attempts to seek psychological support for pregnancy as a result of rape.[230] Where there was family acceptance of the raped victim and their child, sometimes the children born out of rape were raised as the mother's sibling in order to avert community humiliation.[231] Forced adoption can also occur where children are placed outside of the family network, sometimes in a place unknown to the woman.[232] Others opt for socially and politically palatable rape 'scripts' or resort to more subtle forms of communication to convey harms arising from pregnancy.[233] However, interviews with victims and transitional justice actors revealed that the adoption of language that is easier to digest might also reflect attempts to psychologically repair and mitigate short-term social

[226] ibid.

[227] Eunice Apio, Uganda's Forgotten Children of War, in R C Carpenter (ed), *Born of War: Protecting Children of Sexual Violence Survivors in Conflict Zones*, Kumarian (2007) 94–109, pp99–100.

[228] See Ezequiel Heffes, Armed Groups and the Protection of Health Care, *International Law Studies* 95 (2019) 226–243.

[229] Judith Lewis Herman, *Trauma and Recovery, From Domestic Abuse to Political Terror*, Pandora (1992) pp175–197; and Elizabeth Stanko, *Intimate Intrusions: Women's Experience of Male Violence*, Routledge (1985).

[230] U4 FG1, Gulu, Uganda, July 2018.

[231] U5, Gulu, Uganda, July 2018.

[232] C5, Bogotá, Colombia, September 2018.

[233] Jelke Boesten, *Sexual Violence During War and Peace. Gender, Power, and Post-Conflict Justice in Peru*, Palgrave Macmillan (2014) pp91–92.

consequences.[234] Yet this can also contribute to the silencing of future generations, inadequately redresssing the harm arising from pregnancy.

There are accounts of victims of sexual violence rejecting their children born out of rape and difficult intra-familial relationships.[235] One victim of a gang rape in Colombia spoke about how other victims she worked with considered harming or killing their children as 'they can't stand even their own children' or others wanted to abort the child rather than have to live with it.[236] Infanticide by the traumatized parent, or community or family members who may ostracize them, is considered a risk in some circumstances.[237] Maria in Peru, discussed at the start of this section, spoke about how she felt 'dirty' after the rape, that she could not live with herself and considered suicide, and having a child made her worry that this was 'an illness that you pass on to your children unconsciously, without even knowing'.[238] In Uganda, one victim who had been abducted, sexually enslaved, and forced to have the children of an LRA commander, said that she was accepted by her family's community, but her children were not, causing some of them to return to the bush.[239] Another victim of sexual violence during Peru's conflict spoke of how she became over-protective of her children for fear of losing a relationship that offered meaning to her life, as well as anxieties that her children would suffer sexual violence.[240]

A further issue is abortion after rape. In Peru, where abortion can only be performed to save the life of the expectant mother or pregnant person, or to prevent permanent and serious harm,[241] raising children from rape can be interpreted as an extended punishment. However, the raising of children also held the potential of societal reintegration as the mothers were viewed as being 'cleansed' through motherhood.[242] That said, pregnancy after rape can sometimes be a wanted pregnancy and even have a positive impact on a woman's recovery and sense of purpose, despite difficulties such as inheritance for her children. A study of mothers with children born of Rwanda's genocidal rape concluded that motherhood might exert a 'protective factor', despite the social rejection these mothers faced.[243] There

[234] U5 and U11, Uganda, July 2018; P2 FG1, Peru, May 2019; and C15 FG1, Colombia, March 2019.

[235] Gilmore, n 47, ICC-01/04-02/06-2623-Anx2-Red2, p30.

[236] C15 FG1, Bogotá, Colombia, March 2019.

[237] I Joachim, Sexualised Violence in War and its Consequences. Violence Against Women in War: Handbook for Professionals Working with Traumatized Women, Mabuse-Verlag GmbH (2005) 63–110.

[238] P6, Lima, Peru, May 2019.

[239] U4 FG1, Gulu, Uganda, July 2018.

[240] P5, Lima, Peru, May 2019.

[241] Cynthia Beavin, Deborah Billings, and Susana Chávez, Activist Framing of Abortion and Use For Policy Change in Peru, *Sexual and Reproductive Health Matters* 27(1) (2019) 160–167, p160. Peru's abortion laws can be found in the penal code—Código Penal (1991), Ley de 3 Abril 1991, Capitulo II, Artículos 114–120.

[242] Boesten, n 233, p84.

[243] Odeth Kantengwa, How Motherhood Triumphs over Trauma among Mothers with Children from Genocidal Rape in Rwanda, *Journal of Social and Political Psychology* 2(1) (2014) 417–434, p417. This touches upon post-traumatic growth (PTG), which refers to psychological growth and finding

is the potential of a therapeutic relationship between the caregiver and child when the child is differentiated from the trauma of how they were conceived, as well as the victim feeling a sense of belonging in the nurturing role. One Ugandan described how having a child out of rape helped them on their path to recovery,

> It's not very easy to restore a person after sexual violence, except maybe if children came out of it then it's easier to. If you assist that child who came out of sexual violence then that is one way of restoring, but for someone that does not come out with a child it's very hard to actually take away that feeling in their mind.[244]

Importantly, the management of unwanted pregnancy through abortion can be illegal at the time the rape occurs. Victims who are abducted and kept in sexual slavery or restricted confinement are denied the choice of terminating a pregnancy. This is further compounded by the grounds for legal abortion in a certain country, which may not include rape as permissible grounds.[245] The three case studies at the time of CRSV had restrictive abortion laws with varying degrees of punishment for those assisting with the abortion as well as the pregnant person. As discussed, Peru only allows abortion to preserve the life of the woman or avoid permanent harm to her.[246] In Uganda, abortion laws are unclear, but generally abortion is only permitted to preserve the life of the mother.[247] In Colombia, until 2022, abortion laws were restrictive and permitted only under three grounds: when the pregnant person's physical and mental health are at risk; when fatal fetal abnormality exists; and in rape, incest, artificial insemination, or embryo transfer.[248] Yet criminalization of abortion leads to a higher rate of unsafe abortion.[249] Moreover, when a mother dies from unsafe abortion, it is unlikely any children she has under the age of five will survive.[250] The potential cascade of harms flowing from rape can

meaning in traumatic experiences in the years after the event, including sexual violence. PTG can occur irrespective of whether negative psychological outcomes arise. Therefore, its presence should not be taken as an indicator that psychological support is not required. See Emilio Ulloa et al, A Literature Review, *Journal of Aggression, Maltreatment and Trauma* 25(3) (2016) 286–304.

[244] U4 FG1, Gulu, Uganda, July 2018.

[245] Marge Berer, Abortion Law and Policy Around the World, In Search of Decriminalization, *Health and Human Rights* 19(1) (2017) 13–27, p15.

[246] Article 119 of the Penal Code.

[247] The Constitution of the Republic of Uganda (1995), Article 22(2) states: 'No person has the right to terminate the life of an unborn child except as may be authorized by law.' Yet this law is not enacted and instead the Penal Code is relied upon. The Penal Code Act (Cap 120), as amended through the Penal Code (Amendment) Act 2007 (Act No 8 of 2007), Sections 141–143, 212, and 224. If a person acts in good faith and does not knowingly terminate a pregnancy then they will not be held responsible. There is also ambiguity on whether the threat to life is immediate or more medium to long term.

[248] See Constitutional Court of Colombia, Sentencia C-355/06 (May 2006).

[249] See Moses Mulumba et al, Access to Safe Abortion in Uganda: Leveraging Opportunities Through the Harm Reduction Model, *International Journal of Obstetrics & Gynaecology* 138(2) (2017) 231–236, p232.

[250] Presentation by Professor Kristina Gemzell Danielsson, Chair of FIGO Committee Human Rights, Refugees and Violence against Women 2018–2021, 7 February 2020, Winter Meeting, Ulster

be limited where there is greater liberalization of abortion law[251] and a repository of skills available to ensure implementation of safe abortion, as well as access to other complementary reproductive health services.[252] Before 2022, Colombia's narrow legal abortion framework allowed abortion in cases of rape, yet accessing legal abortion for this reason required reporting to the authorities, which could be viewed as an additional harm that deterred victims from seeking a safe abortion.[253] In February 2022, the Colombian Constitutional Court's decision, which legalized abortion without condition up to 24 weeks and, after 24 weeks under the rape exception, was a welcome change.[254] Given the general conservative nature of the medical profession, it is likely that there will be continued social resistance in changing the culture towards supporting abortion.

Unsafe abortion may result in death and is a major contributor to maternal mortality globally (8–15 per cent).[255] Furthermore, where death does not occur, between 435 and 5,298 per 100,000 women experience severe complications.[256] These may include haemorrhage, anaemia, pelvic infection, sepsis, subfertility or infertility, anaesthetic or surgical risks if a hysterectomy or another procedure is required (such as evacuation of retained products of conception in cases of an incomplete abortion), and psychological impacts.[257] Recent research data also

Obstetrical and Gynaecological Society: Diep Thi Ngoc Nguyen et al, Risk of Childhood Mortality Associated with Death of a Mother In Low-and-Middle-Income Countries: A Systematic Review and Meta-Analysis, *BMC Public Health* 19 (2019) 1281, http://doi.org/10.1186/s12889-019-7316.

[251] Manuel Gonçalves-Pinho et al, The Impact of a Liberalisation Law on Legally Induced Abortion Hospitalisations, *European Journal of Obstetrics, Gynecology, and Reproductive Biology* 203 (2016) 142–146.

[252] This includes family planning clinics and screening for STIs. See Best Practice in Comprehensive Abortion Care, Best Practice Paper No 2, Leading Safe Choices, Royal Obstetricians and Gynaecologists, March 2022, pp4 and 10.

[253] C14, Bogotá, Colombia, March 2019.

[254] Constitutional Court Ruling C-055/22, 21 February 2022.

[255] World Health Organization, Maternal mortality, WHO Fact Sheet, 7 April 2025. Available at: https://www.who.int/news-room/fact-sheets/detail/maternal-mortality accessed 23 November 2025; World Health Organization, Abortion, WHO Fact Sheet, 17 November 2025. Available at: https://www.who.int/news-room/fact-sheets/detail/abortion, accessed 23 November 2025; Therese McGinn and Sara Casey, Why Don't Humanitarian Organizations Provide Safe Abortion Care? *Conflict and Health* 10(8) (2016) 1–7, p2. WHO, Department of Reproductive Health and Research, Unsafe Abortion: Global and Regional Estimates of the Incidence of Unsafe Abortion and Associated Mortality in 2008, 6th Edition, Geneva, 2011, https://www.who.int/publications/i/item/global-and-regional-estimates-of-the-incidence-of-unsafe-abortion-and-associated-mortality, accessed 18 October 2020.

[256] McGinn and Casey, n 255.

[257] Facility-based Treatment for Medical Complications Resulting From Unsafe Pregnancy Termination in the Developing World, 2012: A Review of Evidence from 26 Countries, *BJOG: An International Journal of Obstetrics and Gynaecology* 123(9) (2016) 1489–1498. Haemorrhage refers to bleeding. Anaemia is when there is a deficiency in red blood cells and/or they do not function normally. Sepsis is a systemic and sometimes life-threatening bodily response to infections. Infertility is defined as 'the period of time people have been trying to conceive without success after which formal investigation is justified and possible treatment implemented', see Infertility Summary, National Institute of for Health and Care Excellence, August 2018. Hysterectomy refers to surgical removal of the uterus, which may be total (removal of the cervix or neck of the uterus) or subtotal, where the cervix is left in situ.

suggests that as many as half of the women who undergo an unsafe abortion seek care for complications. This highlights both the heightened risk of harm to women, girls and pregnant persons who choose this option, and that, due to prevailing circumstances and positions of local and international organizations, options for accessing safe pregnancy terminations may have been limited.[258] One such long-term consequence increasingly being understood from unsafe abortion is an abnormally invasive placenta in a subsequent pregnancy. This occurs as a result of the techniques used in unsafe abortion, i.e. sharp curettage causing lateral uterine scars and deep implantation of the placenta, which can cause life threatening bleeding.[259] Overall, there can be reduced support services for unintended or unwanted pregnancy during and in the aftermath of conflict that narrows options for pregnant persons and potentially impacts their mental, physical and social wellbeing.

The sexual and reproductive violence nexus

In terms of reproductive violence, harm is often overlooked or subsumed within analyses of physical consequences as a result of sexual violence. Altunjan defines reproductive violence as 'acts which affect the victim's reproductive system, organs, process, or capacity to reproduce that does not necessarily entail a sexualized component'.[260] Nevertheless, it is worth distinguishing reproductive violations from sexual ones to some extent given the differentiated long-term physical harm it causes to victims, as well as to their own dignity, future, family and even group/community. Reproductive violence has been seen within broader gender-based violence as limiting decision making and the choice of women to access and control certain resources, such as contraception and termination of pregnancy/abortion services, to even the 'arbitrarily different moral norms for men and women' around reproduction.[261] As the previous section discussed, pregnancy can be an intended outcome of rape (or through assisted reproductive technologies), and so its reproductive violence is distinct from sexual violence, but also remains linked to it.[262]

The conflation of reproductive violence with sexual violence arguably risks objectifying and sexualizing bodies further. Grey views reproductive violence as

[258] Anibal Faundes et al, Preventing Unsafe Abortion: Achievement and Challenges of a Global FIGO Initiative, *Best Practice and Research Clinical Obstetrics and Gynaecology* 62 (2020) 101–112.
[259] A Iacovelli et al, Risk Factors for Abnormally Invasive Placenta: A Systematic Review and Meta-Analysis, *Journal of Maternal and Fetal Neonatal Medicine* 33(3) (2020) 471–481.
[260] Tanja Altunjan, *Reproductive Violence and International Criminal Law*, Springer (2021) p9.
[261] J Barzelatto, Understanding Sexual and Reproductive Violence: An Overview, *International Journal of Gynecology & Obstetrics* 63(Suppl) (1998) s13–18, s14.
[262] Rosemary Grey, The ICC's 'Forced Pregnancy' Case in Historical Perspective, *Journal of International Criminal Justice* 15(5) (2017) 905–930, p930.

a subset of sexual violence and is worth distinguishing the more specific harm to an individual's reproductive autonomy as 'the ability to freely determine one's reproductive choices, including whether and in what circumstances to reproduce'.[263] One leading civil society organization in Colombia, Women's Link, has been proactive in seeking accountability for reproductive violence which they define as violent behaviour that prevents women and girls' reproductive rights, in particular, the

> right to enjoy the highest possible standard of health, including sexual and reproductive health services, the right to decide freely and autonomously the number and spacing of children, and the right to access information and means to make decisions regarding reproductive autonomy, amongst others. Forced pregnancy, abortion, sterilization and contraception in the context of the armed conflict all constitute reproductive violence.[264]

Accordingly, there is a range to the scope of reproductive violence that looks beyond the physical violence against individuals, to how their choice and agency is inhibited to reproduce, but also to be a parent. Despite this broad scope, Rubio-Marín is concerned that reproductive violence will be entangled by similar narratives that dominate sexual violence, such as a tactical weapon of war that affects women and girls.[265] Thus, gendering harm and reducing women and girls to their sexual worth rather than redressing the full breadth of reproductive harm risks neglecting a key aspect of sexual violence during conflict. This was apparent across the three case studies, by state agencies and armed groups. In Colombia, one civil society actor said that this was an important part of addressing harm as it touches upon 'different experiences in how sexual reproductive life was lived and was controlled and policed in the armed group'.[266]

Sexual and reproductive violence can be interrelated, which complicates the categorization of harms.[267] For instance, reproductive violence can have consequences on sexual wellbeing and integrity that require further discussion for reparations. By way of example, pregnancy can be considered a form of punishment for rape victims, particularly where a safe and free abortion as an option

[263] Rosemary Grey, Reproductive Crimes in International Criminal Law, in I Rosenthal, V Oosterveld, and S SáCouto (eds), *Gender and International Criminal Law*, OUP (2022).

[264] A Violence Without Name: Reproductive Violence in the Colombian Armed Conflict, Women's Link, June 2020.

[265] Presentation by Ruth Rubio-Marín, United Nations Workshop on Reparations and Conflict-Related Sexual Violence, United Nations Headquarters, New York, 1 November 2019.

[266] C1, Bogotá, Colombia, September 2018.

[267] See Suzanne Dedden et al, Hysterectomy and Sexual (Dys)Function: An Analysis of Sexual Dysfunction after Hysterectomy and a Search for Predictive Factors, *European Journal of Obstetrics & Gynecology and Reproductive Biology* 247 (2020) 80–84, p80.

is denied.[268] In Uganda, former LRA wives who were victims spoke of how they assumed that their perpetrators were sometimes motivated by punishment.[269] Similar concerns were expressed by civil society organizations, where family members had been forced to commit sexual acts against each other to humiliate them, which had the potential to complicate family dynamics, such as in the case of an incestuous pregnancy.[270]

The denial or non-consensual provision of sexual and reproductive health services for victims of sexual violence has increasingly been viewed as a form of violence and discrimination in its own right.[271] For instance, the procedure of forced sterilization can itself be interpreted as sexual violence.[272] Sterilization is a permanent surgical form of contraception in females and males.[273] When forced or coerced sterilization occurs, fully informed valid consent is not obtained.[274] As reproductive potential can be closely entwined with sexuality and societal worth, including in the Peruvian indigenous communities targeted, these women reported that they felt sexually unattractive and undesirable to potential male partners as they were not able to conceive further pregnancies.[275] The impact of reproductive surgery on femininity, sexual function, and mental health has been revealed outside of conflict settings where informed consent is obtained.[276] Forced sterilization during conflict or under authoritarian regimes directly impacts the living person

[268] Brooke Magee, Pregnancy as Punishment for Low Income Sexual Assault Victims: An Analysis of South Dakota's Denial of Medicaid-Funded Abortion for Rape Incest Victims and Why the Hyde Amendment Must be Repealed, *George Mason University Civil Rights Law Journal* 27(1) (2016) 77–118.

[269] U4 FG1, Gulu, Uganda, July 2018.

[270] U10 FG2, Lira, Uganda, July 2018.

[271] Report on Violence Against Women and Girls in Latin America, Inter-American Commission of Human Rights, OEA/SerL/V/II Doc 233/19, 14 November 2019.

[272] UN Secretary General reports include enforced sterilization, forced pregnancy, and forced abortion as part of conflict-related sexual violence. Conflict-Related Sexual Violence, 30 March 2021, S/2021/312 para 5.

[273] Clinical Effectiveness Unit – Faculty of Sexual and Reproductive Healthcare to the Royal College of Obstetricians and Gynaecologists, Clinical Guidance, Male and Female Sterilisation, 01/FSRH/Sterilisation/2014, https://www.cosrh.org/Common/Uploaded%20files/documents/cec-ceu-guidance-sterilisation-cpd-sep-2014.pdf accessed 23 November 2025.

[274] Sunneva Gilmore and Luke Moffett, Redressing Forced Sterilisation: The Role of the Medical Profession, *BJOG: An International Journal of Obstetrics and Gynaecology* 127 (2020) 923–926, p923; Open Society Foundations, Against Her Will. Forced and Coerced Sterilization Worldwide. Stop Torture in Healthcare, 2011; Lydia Guterman, The Global Problem of Forced Sterilization, Open Society Foundation Voices, 2011, http://www.opensocietyfoundations.org/voices/global-problem-forced-sterilization, accessed 3 December 2019. For more information on the current accepted principles of obtaining consent for female sterilization, see B Dickens, Female Contraceptive Sterilization: FIGO Committee for the Ethical Aspects of Human Reproduction and Women's Health, *International Journal of Gynaecology and Obstetrics* 115 (2011) 88–89.

[275] P2 FG1, Lima, Peru, May 2019.

[276] Christina Cackler, Valerie Shapiro, and Maureen Lahiff, Female Sterilization and Poor Mental Health: Rates and Relatedness among American Indian and Alaska Native Women, *Women's Health Issues* 26(2) (2016) 168–175, pp174–175; Phyllis Leppert, Richard Legro, and Kristen Kjerulff, Hysterectomy and Loss of Fertility: Implications for Women's Mental Health: Social Determinants of Women's Mental Health, *Journal of Psychosomatic Research* 63(3) (2007) 269–274, pp269 and 273; and Rachel Cooper et al, Hysterectomy and Subsequent Psychological Health: Findings from a British Birth Cohort Study, *Journal of Affective Disorders* 115 (1–2) (2009) 122–30, p129.

and their future progeny.[277] The forcible sterilization of Quechua-speaking poor rural indigenous people in Peru during the 1990s by the Fujimori regime, most of whom were females, exploited a number of intersecting vulnerabilities including ethnicity, gender, and class.[278] These crimes were excluded from the official state narrative of the conflict in the Peruvian Truth Commission's Report (CVR), where sexual violence took priority.[279]

Sexual and reproductive violence usually draws attention to the lack of family planning choice rather than enforced policies.[280] Forced abortion has been interpreted as a form of sexual violence.[281] Forced abortion also overlaps with obstetric violence because it uses medical and invasive procedures without a person's consent.[282] Interviews with women victims of CRSV in Colombia referred to the other acts of obstetric violence that occurred during and post-conflict, even if not conceptualized as strictly fulfilling the criteria for administrative reparations. For instance, one victim spoke of sexist notions regarding women's bodies as objects of sexual pleasure for men (including comments by medics during labour) and being viewed not as human beings with their own autonomy and dignity.[283] The Inter-American Court of Human Rights has found that sexist and stereotyped roles regarding women's bodies represents a form of violence and discrimination.[284] Gender norms also play out within armed groups and in other settings. In Colombia, a public health professor argued that victims within FARC were making false claims about the sexual violence they suffered to garner public sympathy.[285] In 2019, the Colombian Constitutional Court recognized that female victims in FARC did suffer sexual and reproductive violence, meaning that the government was obliged to recognize them as victims for the purposes of the reparations programme.[286]

[277] See Gilmore and Moffett, n 274.

[278] At least 275,000 females and 21,000 males from rural indigenous and mostly Quecha-speaking communities are estimated to be forcibly sterilized. See Matthew Brown and Karen Tucke, Unconsented Sterilisation, Participatory Story-Telling, and Digital Counter-Memory in Peru, *Antipode* 49(1) (2017) 186–203.

[279] Final Report of The Truth and Reconciliation Commission, Volume 6, 2003, http://www.cverdad.org.pe/ifinal/index.php, accessed 1 August 2025; and Rebecca K Root, *Transitional Justice in Peru*, Palgrave Macmillan (2012) p90.

[280] Joanne Neenan, *Closing the Protection Gap for Children Born of War: Addressing Stigmatisation and the Intergenerational Impact of Sexual Violence in Conflict*, LSE Centre for Women, Peace and Security (2017) p9.

[281] Civil Society Declaration on Sexual Violence, 2019, p19. See ABColombia, Colombia, Women, Conflict-Related Sexual violence and the Peace Process, November 2013.

[282] OEA/SerL/V/II Doc 233/19, n 271, para 183.

[283] C3, Bogotá, Colombia, September 2018.

[284] OEA/Ser.L/V/II. Doc.233/19, n 271, para 182.

[285] C12, Bogotá, Colombia, February 2019.

[286] Helena was a victim of forced recruitment and forced abortion—Corte Constitucional—Sentencia SU 599—2019 (víctimas de violencia sexual en conflicto armado), 11 Deciembre 2019 [Constitutional Court— Judgment SU 599—2019 (victims of sexual violence in armed conflict), 11 December 2019].

A final form of reproductive violence is forced contraception, which deprives an individual of 'reproductive autonomy', where the denial of access to such medicines or devices is not a violation per se, but becomes one through the denial of choice.[287] There is extensive evidence on the mechanism and effects of contraception that helps to situate these harms, and sophisticated eligibility criteria to guide decision making for clinicians and their patients.[288] The choice to use short and long-acting contraception is an individual one and will depend on any relative or absolute contraindications a person may have, as well as how the method and potential side-effect profile fits into a person's life. As previously discussed, sexual violence can also cause subfertility or infertility arising from complications (eg sexually transmitted infections, unsafe abortion) which can have a significant impact on victims, particularly in communities where reproductive potential is intimately linked to attractiveness, gender roles, and marriageability.[289] These can be related to gynaecological and other physical complications.

3.2.4 Gynaecological and other physical complications

The physical consequences for victims of sexual violence can include genital injuries (e.g., genital tears/lacerations, swelling, bruising) as well as complications such as fistulas.[290] Younger age is also associated with the increased number of genital injuries following rape,[291] which is important considering former child soldiers and civilians can be less than 15 years old.[292] One form of gynaecological consequence from sexual violence is a fistula, which is an abnormal connection between two body parts such as organs, blood vessels, or other body surfaces. Fistulae related to sexual violence involve the genito-urinary and/or intestinal system.[293]

[287] Commentary to The Hague Principles on Sexual Violence, 2019, p18.

[288] See WHO, Department of Reproductive Health, Medical Eligibility Criteria for Contraceptive Use, 5th Edition, WHO/RHR/15.07, 2015; UK Medical Eligibility Criteria for Contraceptive Use, Faculty of Sexual and Reproductive Healthcare, 2016 (amended September 2019).

[289] U6, Lira, Uganda, July 2019.

[290] AO Longombe, KM Claude, and J Ruminjoc, Fistula and Traumatic Genital Injury from Sexual Violence in a Conflict Setting in Eastern Congo: Case Studies, *Reproductive Health Matters* 16(31) (2008) 132–141. Studies from victims of sexual violence in conflict zones have revealed varying rates of rectal and vaginal fistulae ranging from 9 per cent–40.7 per cent. Genital trauma is also prevalent, with some studies reporting 28.7 per cent suffering severe genital tears.

[291] Rachel Baker and Marilyn Summers, Relationship of Genital Injuries and Age in Adolescent and Young Adult Rape Survivors, *Journal of Obstetric, Gynecological and Neonatal Nursing* 37(3) (2008) 282–289.

[292] There are various grades of tears (ie depth into muscles) that can weaken the pelvic floor to varying degrees, especially for those with young, still developing bodies. As the pelvic floor provides supports to the bowel and uterus, this can give rise to urine, faecal, or flatus incontinence (particularly if care or advice is absent) or even prolapse of pelvic organs over time. Pelvic organ prolapse can arise from other causes that place a strain on the pelvic floor (such as increased abdominal pressure from pregnancy, coughing, or tears during childbirth).

[293] For instance, passages created between the bladder and the vaginal wall.

This debilitating condition has a profound impact on quality of life and vital body functions, and is also subject to complications such as infection.[294] Sexual dysfunction is another consequence of this form of physical injury or from secondary psychological harm,[295] which can also affect male victims.[296] Fistulae can lead to reduced self-esteem, social and marital rejection, and community isolation.[297] The type and extent of acquired genito-urinary or recto-genital fistula will depend on the pathogenesis and way in which the injury was inflicted.[298] In conflict situations a fistula may develop from direct vaginal trauma, erosion from a foreign body, a pelvic abscess, an infected vaginal vault haematoma, or as a result of an obstetric injury from a pregnancy which may have been as a result of rape.

Death may also result from physical complications arising from sexual violence, potential sequelae or concurrent injuries. Penetrating pelvic trauma, which extends within the bony confines of the pelvis to involve urinary or intestinal organs or vasculature, can lead to life-threatening conditions.[299] It can, for example, cause haemorrhagic shock where emergency haemostasis is not possible, or septic shock, arising from fistula, pelvic abscess, urosepsis, miscarriage, or atypical infection from acquired immune deficiency associated with HIV. Women may have suffered a miscarriage, postpartum (after birth) mental illness,[300] ruptured ectopic pregnancy[301] (with higher rates in cases of pelvic inflammatory disease), and complications from labour dystocia. These factors increase maternal and neonatal mortality.[302] A number of women spoke about these complications, which also created difficulties with their partner, with some of them even remarrying to get over the problem.[303] In some ways this reflects women trying to navigate their society's moral norms, in that having a husband (even if it is the rapist) can normalize the

[294] N Dossa and others, Fistula and Other Adverse Reproductive Health Outcomes Among Women Victims of Conflict-Related Sexual Violence: A Population-Based Cross-Sectional Study, *BIRTH* 41(1) (2014) 5–13.

[295] Eugene Kinyanda et al, War Related Sexual Violence and It's Medical and Psychological Consequences as seen in Kitgum, Northern Uganda: A Cross-Sectional Study, *BMC International Health and Human Rights* 10(28) (2010) p7.

[296] Sarah Chynoweth, Julie Freccero, and Heleen Touquet, Sexual Violence Against Men and Boys in Conflict and Forced Displacement: Implications for the Health Sector, *Reproductive Health Matters* 25(51) (2017) 90–94, p92.

[297] Traumatic Gynecologic Fistula: A Consequence of Sexual Violence in Conflict Settings, The ACQUIRE Report, May 2006, p14; Sarah Wilson et al, Psychological Symptoms Among Obstetric Fistula Patients Compared to Gynecology Outpatients in Tanzania, *International Journal of Behavioural Medicine* 22(5) (2015) 605–613.

[298] M Stamatakos et al, Vesicovaginal Fistula: Diagnosis and Management, *Indian Journal of Surgery* 76(2) (2014) 131–136.

[299] Hornez et al, Penetrating Pelvic Trauma: Initial Assessment and Surgical Management in Emergency, *Journal of Visceral Surgery* 153(4) (2016) 79–90.

[300] Postpartum refers to the 12-month period after childbirth. See Eleanor Swift et al, Young Women Are the Most Vulnerable to Postpartum Mental Illness: A Retrospective Cohort Study in UK Primary Care, *Journal of Affective Disorders* 277 (2020) 218–224.

[301] Ectopic pregnancy refers to a pregnancy outside the uterus (specifically outside the uterine endometrium).

[302] Neonatal refers to the first four weeks of life.

[303] U4 FG1, Gulu, Uganda, July 2019.

past and allow them to move on by not being stigmatized as a 'fallen' woman, which would bring dishonour on their family.[304]

In subsequent pregnancies, female victims of sexual violence can suffer other consequences such as a higher risk of perineal tears due to genital mutilation, psychological impacts of re-experiencing pain in sexual or reproductive organs, and fears in the first stage of labour. There is also evidence to suggest that they may also sometimes avoid healthcare support in labour or for gynaecological problems, as intimate vaginal examinations may be perceived as invasive and painful, and victims may lack confidence in medical personnel.[305] However, even in the absence of severe physical injuries, sexual violence also increases the risk of developing gynaecological disorders in later life, namely heavy and abnormal menstrual bleeding.[306] Oral rape can also cause injuries, as well as expose a victim to infectious diseases.[307] There is decreased participation in preventative healthcare among victims of sexual violence, such as for pre-cancerous cervical screening,[308] as well as clinical breast examinations and mammograms for breast cancer.[309] Men are less likely to engage in screening for prostate cancer, which involves a blood sample to measure prostate-specific antigen (PSA).[310] If the PSA is elevated above the normal range, an intimate examination and prostate biopsy may be required.[311] The relationship between the experience of sexual violence and reproductive health outcomes throughout the lifecycle needs further research, including any potentially trauma-informed interventions and alternative approaches that could minimize retraumatization.[312]

Aside from the potentially pervasive impacts of untreated sexually transmitted infections, which has been discussed above, male victims of sexual violence can

[304] Boesten, n 33, p115.

[305] A. Gisladottir et al, Obstetric Outcomes of Mothers Previously Exposed to Sexual Violence, *PLoS ONE* 11(3) (2016) 1–12. Note the first stage of labour refers to painful contractions and progressive cervical dilatation to 10 cm. Whereas the second stage is the finding of full cervical dilatation (10 cm) with or without expulsive contractions or maternal effort. The third stage refers to the time from the birth of the baby to the expulsion of the placenta and membranes.

[306] Tayla Hassam et al, Sexual Assault as a Risk Factor for Gynaecological Morbidity: An Exploratory Systematic Review and Meta-Analysis, *European Journal of Obstetrics and Gynecology and Reproductive Biology* 255 (2020) 222–230.

[307] Emmeline Brew-Graves and Louise Morgan, Injuries and Allegations of Oral Rape: A Retrospective Review of Patients Presenting to a London Sexual Assault Referral Centre, *Journal of Forensic and Legal Medicine* 34 (2015) 155–158.

[308] Lillian Bengtson, and Shannon Lynch, Trauma, PTSD, and Self-Efficacy: Predictors of Cervical Cancer Screening in Sexual Violence Survivors, *Journal of Interpersonal Violence* 40(7–8) (2025) 1865–1887.

[309] Héctor Alcalá, Jessica Keim-Malpass, and Emma Mitchell, Sexual Assault and Cancer Screening Among Men and Women, *Journal of Interpersonal Violence* 36(11–12) (2021) NP6243–NP6259.

[310] ibid. This involves taking a blood sample and measuring prostate-specific antigen (PSA). If it is elevated, an intimate examination and biopsy of the prostate gland may be required.

[311] National Institute for Health and Care Excellence, How Should I Assess a Person with Suspected Prostate Cancer? Last revised September 2024, https://cks.nice.org.uk/topics/prostate-cancer/diagnosis/assessment/, accessed 1 August 2025.

[312] British Association for Sexual Health and HIV National Guidelines for the Management of Individuals Disclosing Sexual Violence in Sexual Health Services, 2022, p14.

also suffer anogenital and perineal injuries.[313] Males are more likely to have anorectal trauma than females.[314] This may vary from abrasions and fissures, to abscesses and perforations that can require surgical interventions, and may impact rectal continence and self-esteem in the long term.[315] Men have reported urinary and faecal incontinence,[316] as well as blood in the urine (haematuria) and haemorrhoids.[317] Some men (and women) may seek medical assistance for the immediate physical harms of rape such as genito-rectal bleeding or anal fissures, but not disclose how these injuries were sustained.[318] They may also be particularly susceptible to other violent physical injuries to their limbs (including bone fractures), head, and abdomen,[319] as well as reproductive consequences such as erectile dysfunction.[320] Weapons can be used to exert other violence and some may suffer from the effects of non-fatal strangulation, which is examined later. While the discussion so far has been on physical harm caused by sexual violence, it is in many ways artificial to define them as separate or distinct from the psychological harm that also results and can be intertwined with it.

3.2.5 Breast injuries

Sexual violence can encompass acts of a sexual nature affecting one or both breasts. This can range from unwanted kissing or touching of the breast(s) to injuries that

[313] Richard Tewksbury, Effects of Sexual Assault on Men: Physical, Mental and Social Consequences, *International Journal of Men's Health* 6(1) (2007) 22–35, p26; and John Thomas and Jonathan Kopel, Male Victims of Sexual Assault: A Review of the Literature, *Behavioural Sciences* 13(4) (2023) 304.

[314] Iain McLean, Val Balding, and Cath White, Forensic Medical Aspects of Male-on-Male Rape and Sexual Assault in Greater Manchester, *Medicine, Science and the Law* 44(2) (2004) 165–169.

[315] L Kiss et al, Male and LGBT Survivors of Sexual Violence in Conflict Situations: A Realist Review of Health Interventions in Low-and Middle-Income Countries, *Conflict and Health* 14(11) (2020), https://doi.org/10.1186/s13031-020-0254-5.

[316] Incontinence refers to loss of control. This may be of the urinary system resulting in loss of urine, or from the anal sphincter complex resulting in flatus (gas) or faecal loss. Ines Yagi et al, Characteristics and Impacts of Conflict-Related Sexual Violence against Men in the DRC: A Phenomenological Research Design, *Social Sciences* 11(2) (2022) 34; Elisa Rubini et al, Negative consequences of conflict-related sexual violence on survivors: a systematic review of qualitative evidence, International Journal for Equity in Health 22(1) (2023) 227, doi.org/10.1186/s12939-023-02038-7.

[317] Haemorrhoids (aka piles) are swellings containing enlarged blood vessels in and around the anus and rectum. They can be asymptomatic, but if their blood supply is affected, they can cause itching, pain (including with defecation), bleeding, and mucus discharge. Ines Yagi et al, Characteristics and Impacts of Conflict-Related Sexual Violence against Men in the DRC: A Phenomenological Research Design, *Social Sciences* 11(2) (2022) 34; Peninah Kansiime, Claire van der Westhuizen, and Ashraf Kagee, Barriers and Facilitators to Physical and Mental Health Help-Seeking Among Congolese Male Refugee Survivors of Conflict-Related Sexual Violence Living in Kampala, *Social Work & Social Sciences Review* 19(3) (2018) 152–173.

[318] Jayne Walker, John Archer, and Michelle Davies, Effects of Rape on Male Survivors: A Descriptive Analysis, *Archives of Sexual Behaviour* 34(1) (2005) 69–80, p73; and Michelle Lowe and Paul Rogers, The Scope of Male Rape: A Selective Review of Research, Policy and Practice, *Aggression and Violent Behavior* 35(1) (2017) 38–43, p40.

[319] Rubini et al, n 316.

[320] Tewksbury, n 313, p27.

damage superficial and deep structures of the breast or chest region. For conflict-related sexual violence, the intention behind injuries may include destruction or mutilation of breast tissue to impair the sexual attractiveness of a female's body or breast function.[321] In other instances, injury may occur due to restraining the victim,[322] or for the perpetrator's own gratification. Breasts are considered an intimate body region that can impact body image, relationships, and psychosexual functioning.[323] Thus, it is important to dedicate a section towards this largely overlooked harm when examining the impact of sexual violence.

There is a growing consensus that trauma to breasts is a form of gender-based violence as it predominantly affects women and girls.[324] While a harmful practice, breast flattening or ironing[325] has been misused as a protective mechanism against sexual violence especially where breast development is linked to a female's transition into womanhood.[326] It is not known whether this practice is more prevalent in conflict settings but it could represent a motivation to reduce other harms from certain forms of sexual violence as well as associated societal shame (eg rape and extramarital pregnancy).[327] Breast flattening generally falls under the radar for reasons that include being kept as a secret between mother and daughter.[328] More research is needed on the factors that influence its practice, but it presents its own set of health problems and can be challenging to detect.[329] A full examination of this practice is beyond the remit of this book.

There is a paucity of research on breast injuries in general,[330] with a particular void on that relating to breast injuries from sexual violence irrespective of whether it is conflict related. The studies that exist largely focus on injuries in athletes (including contact sports), trauma from surgery, or tumours in breast cancer, and less

[321] Lebeza Alemu Tenaw et al, Medical and Psychological Consequences of Rape Among Survivors During Armed Conflicts in Northeast Ethiopia, *PLoS ONE* 17(12) (2022) e0278859.

[322] Jack Crane, Interpretation of Non-Genital Injuries in Sexual Assault, *Best Practice & Research Clinical Obstetrics & Gynaecology* 27(1) (2013) 103–111.

[323] Tanja Zimmermann, Intimate Relationships Affected by Breast Cancer: Interventions for Couples, *Breast Care* 10 (2015) 102–108; Leslie Schover, The Impact of Breast Cancer on Sexuality, Body Image, and Intimate relationships, *CA: A Cancer Journal for Clinicians* 41(2) (1991) 112–120.

[324] G Tshimbidi, W Ngwisanyi, and C-A Benn, Bizarre Foreign Body of the Breast Secondary to Gender-Based Violence, *South African Journal of Surgery* 60(3) (2022) 216–217 https://doi.org/10.17159/2078-5151/SAJS3868.

[325] Breast flattening or ironing generally involves 'the repetitive pounding, pressing, ironing, rubbing, or massaging of a pubescent girl's breasts, often using hard or heated objects, in order to attempt to stop or delay them from growing or developing, make them flatter, or make them disappear'. See Fikrejesus Amahazion, Breast Ironing: A Brief Overview of an Underreported Harmful Practice, *Journal of Global Health* 11:03055 (2021).

[326] ibid.

[327] Francesca Robinson, Breast Ironing, *BMJ* (2019) 365:l1790, doi: 10.1136/bmj.l1790.

[328] Rebecca Tapscott, Understanding Breast 'Ironing': A Study of the Methods, Motivations, and Outcomes of Breast Flattening Practices in Cameroon, Feinstein International Center, May 2012.

[329] Alessandra Glover Williams and Fiona Finlay, Breast Ironing: An Under-Recognised Form of Gender-Based Violence, *BMJ, Archives of Diseases in Childhood* 105 (2020) 90–91.

[330] Deirdre E McGhee and Julie R Steele, Changes to Breast Structure and Function Across a Woman's Lifespan: Implications for Managing and Modeling Female Breast Injuries, *Clinical Biomechanics* 107 (2023) 106031.

frequently injuries from road traffic accidents (such as seatbelt trauma).[331] As with genital and other co-existing injuries in an acute setting, this may be due to blunt force trauma, penetrating injury, or thermal injury. The lack of research again reflects the general need for greater health research in women's health issues.[332]

The classifications of breast injury include McGhee and Steele's system, which is adapted from Song et al, and takes into account acute and delayed manifestations from a range of injury mechanisms.[333] Injuries can impact the skin, muscles, neurovascular system, lymphatics (which drains fluid), as well as adipose (fat), and glandular tissue.[334] Deeper injuries may involve structures such as the lungs, heart, and bony structures (eg the sternum). In the medium to long term, potential sequelae of breast injury include fat necrosis (death of body tissue), superficial thrombophlebitis (inflammation) of the vessels on the breast or chest wall (Mondor's disease), or deeper venous thrombosis (blood clots).[335]

Thorough assessments of potential breast trauma from sexual violence may not be possible where healthcare facilities are not operational or available, such as ultrasound and biopsy in addition to an external examination (inspection and palpation). Without expertise, breast injury may be under-recognized.[336] Nevertheless, there needs to be more research on long-term harms from a range of breast injuries in certain groups, such as on lactating or pregnant females or those with developing breasts.[337] Optimal management may not be possible, and even necessary surgical care may lead to iatrogenic or secondary injury.[338] Additionally, long-term care in the form of reconstructive surgery, under the rubric of rehabilitation in reparations, may be overlooked.

Breast injuries depend on the physiological changes throughout a person's lifespan— similar to genital injuries—as well as any pre-existing medical conditions (such as malignancy or dermatoses[339]). Sexual violence which involves the breast region can pose specific challenges and have implications for persons who are pregnant or lactating. This could result in breastfeeding (or chest feeding) difficulties

[331] Killian Bibby et al, A Systematic Review, *Sports Medicine* (54) (2024) 1921–1930 https://doi.org/10.1007/s40279-024-02027-y.

[332] Sanne A E Peters et al, Women's Health: A New Global Agenda, *BMJ Global Health* (2016) 1:e000080.

[333] McGhee and Steele, n 330. Their classification is divided into acute presentation (Class 1) and delayed presentation (Class 2), which is defined as from three weeks to four years, as well as subdivisions into minor injuries (Class 1A & 2A), major injuries (Class 1B & 2B). See also the Teo and Song Classification System, Christopher Tam Song, Isabel Teo, and Colin Song. Systematic Review of Seat-Belt Trauma to the Female Breast: A New Diagnosis and Management Classification, *Journal of Plastic, Reconstructive & Aesthetic Surgery* 68(3) (2015) 382–389.

[334] See McGhee and Steele, n 330 for a review of breast structure and function.

[335] ibid.

[336] Helena Bentley et al, Underreported and Underrecognized: A Comprehensive Imaging Review of Breast Injury, *Emergency Radiology* 30(6) (2023) 777–789, https://doi.org/10.1007/s10140-023-02167-0.

[337] McGhee and Steele, n 330.

[338] Bentley et al, n 336, p788.

[339] Dermatoses refers to a skin condition, defect, or lesion which may be localized or systemic.

which in turn impact neonatal health and potentially related longer-term health outcomes for the mother/lactating parent and child.[340] This can be acutely felt in situations of ongoing conflict where there may be impaired nutritional interventions, namely for infant formula or basic postnatal nutrition.[341] These cascading effects are not fully appreciated. Among females experiencing interpersonal violence (IPV), the relationship to breastfeeding is complicated, with some studies showing no association. On the other hand, a systematic review of IPV concluded that there appears to be impaired breastfeeding, owing to shame, in those with a history of any violence, especially in childhood.[342] The purported theories include depression, stress, and anxiety from sexual violence impairing the milk ejection reflex,[343] as well as pain in breast or nipple tissue. While not adequately explored in research, there may be body negativity, a feeling of lack of situational control with breastfeeding, and problems with delineating the maternal role from the sexual one,[344] especially if breast trauma is related to sexual violence.

Indirectly, there may be a lack of breastfeeding support within conflict environments, including trauma-informed support that is sensitive to previous sexual violence experiences. Victims who have become pregnant may have experienced a traumatic birth due to difficulties in accessing maternity services in conflict,[345] which may impact breastfeeding.[346] The physiology of lactation and breastfeeding is multifaceted and relies on hormonal regulation.[347] Stress and low mood can arise from the difficulties relating to conflict or birth trauma, reducing oxytocin release, which can lead to breastfeeding challenges, and potentially negative mental

[340] Chestfeeding refers to feeding a baby with milk from your chest. It is a more inclusive term for trans or non-binary persons. See Chestfeeding If You're Trans or Non-Binary, National Health Service, https://www.nhs.uk/pregnancy/having-a-baby-if-you-are-lgbt-plus/chestfeeding-if-youre-trans-or-non-binary/, accessed 1 August 2025.

[341] Shailja Shah et al, Delivering Nutrition Interventions to Women and Children in Conflict Settings: A Systematic Review, *BMJ Global Health* (2021) 6:e004897, doi:10.1136/bmjgh-2020-004897.

[342] Researchers have called for higher-quality studies and a meta-analysis on breastfeeding practices in the context of interpersonal and sexual violence, given the many confounds involved. See eg Anne Katrine Normann et al, Intimate Partner Violence and Breastfeeding: A Systematic Review, *BMJ Open* 10(10): e034153 (2020), doi:10.1136/bmjopen-2019-034153.

[343] ibid.

[344] ibid.

[345] Hyam Bashour, Mayada Kharouf, and Jocelyn DeJong, Childbirth Experiences and Delivery Care During Times of War: Testimonies of Syrian Women and Doctors, *Frontiers in Global Women's Health* 2 (2021), https://doi.org/10.3389/fgwh.2021.605634.

[346] For example, a good position and attachment of the infant at the breast is important for maintaining milk production. There may also be trauma to the nipple and breast if the infant latch is superficial. However, help with this may not be possible by trained professionals. Cheryl Tatano and Sue Watson, Impact of Birth Trauma on Breast-feeding A Tale of Two Pathways Beck, *Nursing Research* 57(4) (2008) 228–236; Hülya Türkmen, Hacer Yalniz Dilcen, and Bihter Akin, The Effect of Labor Comfort on Traumatic Childbirth Perception, Post-Traumatic Stress Disorder, and Breastfeeding, *Breastfeeding Medicine* 15(12) (2020) http://doi.org/10.1089/bfm.2020.0138.

[347] For an explanation on the anatomy and physiology of breastfeeding, see Karen Wambach and Catherine Watson Genna, Anatomy and Physiology of Lactation, in Karen Wambach and Becky Spencer, *Breastfeeding & Human Lactation*, 6th Edition, Jones & Bartlett Learning (2021) ch 3, pp49–84.

health outcomes.[348] It is also important to consider that physical and psychological trauma can result from difficult breastfeeding experiences itself, and it is unknown whether this could be potentially triggering for the victim or compound their trauma. That said, breastfeeding is also associated with improved mental health outcomes,[349] including in women with perinatal mental health conditions.[350] This phenomenon may be partly explained by the release of the hormone oxytocin when breastfeeding which also opposes the hormone cortisol, decreasing the stress response.[351] It can, as a result, strengthen the parent–child bond and exert some protective effect against postnatal depression.[352] Breastfeeding can represent a healing and empowering experience in those with a history of sexual trauma.[353] Ultimately, breastfeeding experiences are multifactorial and complicated after trauma; there remains uncertainty around whether sexual violence involving the breast adds further complexity.

3.2.6 Non-fatal strangulation

Strangulation is defined as the obstruction of air passages and/or blood vessels in the neck due to external pressure on the neck.[354] Strangulation can be fatal, but non-fatal strangulation (NFS) also causes serious harm to victims. A victim may not give a history of strangulation or exhibit visible external injury, but serious physical and psychological consequences can follow if it is not detected.[355] Non-fatal strangulation should be considered in victims of sexual violence.[356] In domestic settings, NFS is strongly linked to sexual assault.[357] It represents another

[348] Megan Yuen et al, The Effects of Breastfeeding on Maternal Mental Health: A Systematic Review, *Journal of Women's Health* 31(6) (2022) 787–807.

[349] ibid; and Abigail Wheeler et al, The Positive Cycle of Breastfeeding-Mental Health Outcomes of Breastfeeding Mothers Following Birth Trauma, *Healthcare (Basel)* 13(6) (2025) 672, doi:10.3390/healthcare13060672.

[350] Perinatal mental health conditions are defined as occurring during pregnancy and up to one year following birth. A range of perinatal mental health disorders can be positively affected by breastfeeding, such as PTSD, depression, and eating disorders. See Hayley Billings et al, Breastfeeding Experiences of Women with Perinatal Mental Health Problems: A Systematic Review and Thematic Synthesis, *BMC Pregnancy & Childbirth* 24(1) (2024) 582 https://doi.org/10.1186/s12884-024-06735-1.

[351] Anushree Modak, Vaishnavi Ronghe, and Kavita Gomase, The Psychological Benefits of Breastfeeding: Fostering Maternal Well-Being and Child Development, *Cureus* 15(10):e46730 (2023).

[352] ibid; Yuen, n 348.

[353] Lauren Sobel et al, Pregnancy and Childbirth After Sexual Trauma Patient Perspectives and Care Preferences, *Obstetrics & Gynecology* 132(6) (2018) 1461–1468.

[354] Catherine White et al, 'I Thought He Was Going to Kill Me': Analysis of 204 Case Files of Adults Reporting Non-Fatal Strangulation as Part of a Sexual Assault Over a 3 Year Period, *Journal of Forensic and Legal Medicine* 79 (2021) 102128.

[355] Institute For Addressing Strangulation, Guidelines for Clinical Management of Non-Fatal Strangulation in Acute and Emergency Care Services, February 2024, p4; and White et al, n 354.

[356] ibid.

[357] Studies from forensic centres caring for sexual assault victims who present for examination/therapeutic support report differing rates of NFS. White et al, n 354, reported NFS in 9.28 per cent of sexual assault cases over three years. NFS is likely under-reported and not always detected clinically.

form of coercion, control, and intimidation. However, reliable data does not exist in relation to CRSV. NFS is frequently reported to occur in victims of intimate partner violence and have an increased risk of lethality,[358] but also occurs where the perpetrator is not a partner or ex-partner.[359] Thus, it is important to consider that victims of sexual slavery can be repeatedly raped and may also endure the effects of NFS.

Research has revealed the gendered nature of the violence, with most victims being female or identifying as women.[360] One study which examined sexual assault characteristics in women victims of NFS who had a forensic examination found that weapon use was positively associated with NFS.[361] There is a gap in understanding regarding the relationship between conflict (including post-conflict), where weapons use including small arms occurs, and NFS in victims of sexual violence. Mortality is increased during and after conflict where there no disarmament,[362] but we do not know if fatal and non-fatal consequences from strangulation associated with sexual violence is more prevalent.

The immediate consequences of NFS are varied and can include: hypoxia, which is insufficient oxygen to the brain manifesting as loss of consciousness; cardiac dysthymia (abnormal heartbeat); damage to the spinal cord and nerves; as well as injury to blood vessels potentially resulting in a thrombus (blood clot) or tearing.[363] Delayed airway problems generally occur within six hours,[364] and could be life threatening. Recovery can be full but long-term difficulties can occur from injuries to anatomical structures in the area.[365] An acquired brain injury can result from NFS, which may lead to problems in speech and language, cognition, and emotional regulation; ideally this would be assessed at three months post-incident.[366] Vascular problems can occur up to 12 months afterwards, such as

Alongside under-reporting of sexual violence in general, true prevalence may be higher. Victims may also present to emergency services, which may not be captured in some statistics.

[358] Lindsay M Cannon et al, Examining Trends in Non-Fatal Strangulation Among Sexual Assault Survivors Seeking Sexual Assault Nurse Examiner Care From 2002 to 2017, *International Journal of Gynecology & Obstetrics* 149 (2020) 106–112.

[359] White et al, n 354.

[360] ibid; Vanita Parekh et al, Non-Fatal Strangulation versus General Assault in a Clinical Forensic Medicine Cohort: Characteristics of Patient, Perpetrator and Presentation, *Journal of Forensic and Legal Medicine* 102 (2024) 102651–102651.

[361] Grace McKee et al, New Perspectives on Risk Factors for Non-fatal Strangulation and Post-Assault Imaging, *Journal of Interpersonal Violence* 37(9–10) (2022) 8226–8236.

[362] David R Meddings, Weapons Injuries During and After Periods of Conflict: Retrospective Analysis, *BMJ* 315 (1997) 1417-1420.

[363] FFLM, Institute For Addressing Strangulation, Non-Fatal Strangulation: In Physical and Sexual Assault, July 2023, https://fflm.ac.uk/wp-content/uploads/2023/02/Non-fatal-strangulation-in-physical-and-sexual-assault-Prof-C-White-July-2023.pdf, accessed 1 August 2025.

[364] FFLM, Institute For Addressing Strangulation, Guidelines for Clinical Management of Non-Fatal Strangulation in Acute and Emergency Care Services, February 2024, p5

[365] Anatomical structures potentially affected include muscles in the neck, vocal cords, blood vessels, the thyroid gland, and the hyoid bone. See T Plattner, S Bolliger, and U Zollinger, Forensic Assessment of Survived Strangulation, *Forensic Science International* 153 (2005) 202–207.

[366] FFLM, Institute For Addressing Strangulation, n 364, p6.

carotid artery dissection, which is a tear in the layers of a main artery in the neck and can present as a stroke.[367] Psychological consequences (eg depression and anxiety) are frequently confounded with other types of violence (such as sexual violence) that can make delineation of outcomes from each act of violence unfeasible.[368] Victims have reported a fear of dying as a result of the act by perpetrators.[369] If there are symptoms and signs that suggest serious injury, imaging in the acute setting is recommended, as well as potential specialist input.[370] However, this may not be possible in conflict settings or where victims are enslaved.

3.3 Mental Health and Psychosocial Impacts

Sexual violence can also cause a range of mental health problems.[371] In female victims of rape, psychological morbidity is more common than physical injury, and if untreated can lead to lifelong problems.[372] The Inter-American Court has held that rape amounts to psychological torture because it aims 'not just to humiliate the victim but also her family or community'.[373] International criminal law has also held that rape is carried out to intentionally cause psychological harm through 'intimidation, degradation, humiliation, discrimination, punishment, control or destruction of a person'.[374] Some long-term psychological conditions are not unique to sexual violence and so can occur in other circumstances, such as post-traumatic stress syndrome (PTSD) and its complex variant CPTSD.[375] PTSD can occur following a single traumatic event, whereas the latter results from prolonged exposure to trauma with no foreseeable recourse to escape, such as in cases of sexual slavery.[376] A child born out of rape can also represent a repetitive trauma given the

[367] ibid.

[368] Helen Bichard et al, The Neuropsychological Outcomes of Non-Fatal Strangulation in Domestic and Sexual Violence: A Systematic Review, *Neuropsychological Rehabilitation* 32(6) (2022) 1164–1192.

[369] White et al, n 354.

[370] Imaging is usually in the form of a Computed Tomography (CT) scan of the vessels in the next +/- head +/- chest depending on the injury described and clinical presentation. This is advised to be performed if the victim presents within four weeks but can be done later than this in an outpatient setting. Guidance exists for clinicians on red flag symptoms and signs that indicate the need for further investigation and potential intervention, see FFLM, Institute For Addressing Strangulation, n 364.

[371] Mental health refers to psychological, psychiatric, and emotional consequences. See Santiago Martínez Torre et al, Key Mental Health Differences in Conflict-Related Sexual Violence and How Sex, Severity, and Early Intervention Impact on Improvement: A Retrospective Observational Study, *Conflict Health* 18(1) (2024) 61.

[372] Ruxana Jina et al, FIGO Guidelines, Report of the FIGO Working Group on Sexual Violence/HIV: Guidelines for the Management of Female Survivors of Sexual Assault, *International Journal of Gynecology & Obstetrics* 109(2) (2010) 85–92, p86.

[373] *Fernando Mejía v Peru*, No 5/96 CASE 10.970, 1 March 1996.

[374] *Jean-Paul Akayesu*, ICTR-96-4-T, 2 September 1998, para 687.

[375] For information on diagnostic criteria of PTSD/CPTSD, see WHO, International Classification of Diseases, 11th Edition (ICD-11), 2018.

[376] See YSG Hoffman et al, Complex PTSD and its Correlates Amongst Female Yazidi Victims of Sexual Slavery Living in Post-ISIS Camps, *World Psychiatry* 17(1) (2018) 112–113.

reminder of their experience.[377] PTSD is one of the most frequently reported psychological outcomes in men and women following CRSV.[378]

Other psychological consequences include anxiety, mood disorders (eg depression), and substance abuse.[379] These can negatively impact a person's quality of life, with victims suffering emotional distress even without a formal psychological diagnosis.[380] In contrast to non-sexual violence, victims of sexual violence are more likely to have negative relationships with themselves manifesting as low self-esteem, self-criticism, and less secure attachments.[381] There is a significant amount of research related to mental health and sexual violence, and in particular PTSD.[382] Psychological symptoms, including amnesia and disassociation, can also prevent victims from giving an account of their CRSV, which can lead to rejection in asylum applications[383] and may potentially have consequences for applying for reparations or urgent assistance. A person's environment may also limit improvement in symptomology, such as post-conflict hostilities or instability and socio-economic depravity.[384] Victims who have been displaced or migrated to other countries might have negative experiences in their new communities. It is worth highlighting certain long-term sequelae as well as delineating other mental health impacts that require consideration.

The trauma of rape and other forms of sexual violence, including the use of weapons and violence,[385] along with feelings of shame and social rejection can also cause suicidal ideation.[386] One victim explained why she felt life was not worth living for herself or her children,

> I was at a point of committing suicide, because a person that suffered sexual violence, feels like they are nothing, feels dirty, disgusted by yourself, and I cannot live.[387]

[377] Elisa van Ee and Jorin Blokland, Bad Blood or My Blood: A Qualitative Study into the Dimensions of Interventions for Mothers with Children Born of Sexual Violence, *International Journal of Environmental Research and Public Health* (16)23 (2019) 4810.

[378] Rubini et al, n 316.

[379] Evelyne Josse, 'They Came With Two Guns': The Consequences of Sexual Violence for the Mental Health of Women in Armed Conflicts, *International Review of the Red Cross*, 92(877) (2010) 177–195.

[380] *Jean-Pierre Bemba*, Public Redacted Version of Report on Mental Health Outcomes of Rape, Mass Rape, and Other Forms of Sexual Violence, Stanford University, School of Medicine, ICC-01/05-01/08-3417-Conf-Anx.A, p14.

[381] Jason Schnittker, What Makes Sexual Violence Different? Comparing the Effects of Sexual and Non-Sexual Violence on Psychological Distress, *SSM-Mental Health* 2 (2022) 100115

[382] Ba and Bhopal, n 179.

[383] Rubini et al, n 316.

[384] S Priebe and others, Course of Post-Traumatic Stress Disorder Following War in the Balkans: 1-Year Follow-Up Study, *Psychological Medicine* 43(9) (2013) 1837–1847.

[385] Elizabeth Dartnall and Rachel Jewkes, Sexual Violence Against Women: The Scope of the Problem, *Best Practice and Research Clinical Obstetrics and Gynaecology* 27(2013) 3–13.

[386] Josse n 379, p186; and 'I Lost My Dignity': Sexual and Gender-Based Violence in the Syrian Arab Republic, A/HRC/37/CRP.3, 8 March 2018, para 100.

[387] P5, Lima, Peru, May 2019.

Moreover, research conducted in the Democratic Republic of Congo indicates that the delay in addressing the assault emotionally aggravates the victim's isolation and psychological wellbeing.[388] Family members of rape victims are also at considerable risk of psychological damage, particularly when they have witnessed the sexual violence or been forced to participate in the rape.[389] Victims are sometimes raped in front of family members, which may in turn raise difficult emotions and feelings of shame, guilt, betrayal, and powerlessness.[390] The Inter-American Court has recognized that rape of a victim in front of a family member increases the 'humiliation of the victim and the trauma for both of them'.[391] Victims can experience persistent fear, shame, avoidance of being seen out in public, dodging situations that trigger memories of the crime, and difficulties in re-establishing intimate relationships.[392]

The relationship of victims to their bodies and their gender identity can also be negatively affected by sexual violence.[393] In particular, sexual slavery and captivity can give rise to a syndrome of chronic trauma which may in turn result in alterations in victims' personal identity and body image.[394] In severe cases, victims can feel dehumanized, unworthy of being loved, and/or experience an erosion of their personality.[395] Victims of sexual violence can experience psychosexual difficulties (arising from the act or a health complication, eg incontinence), making it difficult to participate in sexual relations and are also associated with negative sexual health outcomes (eg inhibited arousal, orgasm difficulties).[396]

Psychosexual dysfunction can be understood as a disturbance of sexual functioning that may originate in mental or emotional difficulties rather than physical disorders alone.[397] It garners less attention as a harm from sexual violence (and

[388] N Dossa et al, Mental Health Disorders Among Women Victims of Conflict-Related Sexual Violence in the Democratic Republic of Congo, *Journal of Interpersonal Violence* 30 (13) (2015) 2199–2220.

[389] Harvard Humanitarian Initiative and Oxfam International, 'Now, The World is Without Me': An Investigation of Sexual Violence in Eastern Democratic Republic of Congo, 2010, p1.

[390] Kimberly Theidon, Hidden in Plain Sight: Children Born of Wartime Sexual Violence, *Current Anthropology* 56(12) (2015) s191–200, s195.

[391] *Fernández Ortega et al v Mexico*. Judgment, Inter-American Court of. Human Rights, 15 April 2010, para 91.

[392] Susan Swiss and Janet E Giller, Rape as a Crime of War: A Medical Perspective, *Journal of the American Medical Association (JAMA)* 270(5) (1993) 612–615, p614.

[393] Inger Skjelsbæk, Victim and Survivor: Narrated Social Identities of Women Who Experienced Rape During the War in Bosnia-Herzegovina, *Feminism and Psychology*, 16(4) (2006) 373–403, p395.

[394] Judith Herman, *Trauma and Recovery: From Domestic Abuse to Political Terror*, Pandora (1997) pp93–94. See Chapter 4.

[395] Herman, n 394, p93.

[396] Sheraz Ahmad, Adult Psychosexual Dysfunction as a Sequela of Child Sexual Abuse, *Sexual and Relationship Therapy* 21(4) (2006) 405–418; Fiona Cowan and Leila Frodsham, Management of Common Disorders in Psychosexual Medicine, *Obstetrician and Gynaecologist* 17(1) (2015) 47–53; and Catalina Vechui, The Impact of Sexual Assault on Sexual Function: Strategies for Treatment and Prevention, in W O' Donohue and P Schewe (eds), *Handbook of Sexual Assault and Sexual Assault Prevention*, Springer (2019) p353.

[397] Cowan and Frodsham, n 396; Caroline Hunter, Interaction of Mind and Body in Psychosexual Medicine, in P Brough and M Denman, *Introduction to Psychosexual Medicine*, Third Edition, Palgrave (2019) p50.

trauma in general) than direct physical consequences, despite its mind-body connection,[398] potential somatizations such as pain, and sometimes interlinked physical conditions.

The psychosexual consequences of conflict-related sexual violence has not been adequately explored in research and may present with the added complexities that war brings to people's lives and intimate relationships. However, one study found that severe sexual problems were reported more frequently in victims of conflict-related sexual violence compared to non-sexual trauma from the Second World War.[399] There is also less literature available on the assessment of psychosexual dysfunction after sexual violence (as an adult or a child) compared to forensic aspects.[400] Further still, drug therapies for mood disorders as a result of the conflict or CRSV can themselves increase the risk of psychosexual dysfunction.[401] The victim may have a physical or psychological disability from sexual violence that could be impacting their sense of attractiveness, or symptoms that cause difficulty in sexual activity (eg fatigue or pain).[402] Society's assumptions and attitudes towards a disability or from the stigma of sexual violence might be affecting a person's ability to live a fulfilled sexual life. Maladaptive coping mechanisms such as alcohol dependence can also impact sexual functioning.[403] Health-related programmes that have been set up for health consequences are often not long term in nature or tailored to specialized needs,[404] and may increase tendency towards self-repair options that come with their own risks.

One Peruvian victim who suffered multiple rapes spoke of her difficulties with sexual pleasure and arousal as well as the impact it has had with her partner:

> In terms of sex, I am very cold, it is difficult, for me to have sex, I think that's why my second partner doubted me, because I was so cold, it would bring back memories of what happened to me so I would feel bad, feel cold, so I couldn't and I can't have sex.[405]

[398] Ruth Skrine, Blocks and Freedoms in Sexual Life, *A Handbook of Psychosexual Medicine*, CRC Press (2005) pp1–15.

[399] In a matched pairs study, sexual problems were reported in 80.9 per cent of CRSV victims versus 19 per cent in non-sexual conflict trauma. See Philipp Kuwert et al, Long-Term Effects of Conflict-Related Sexual Violence Compared with Non-Sexual War Trauma in Female World War II Survivors: A Matched Pairs Study, *The Archives of Sexual Behavior*, 43 (2014) 1059–1064, doi:10.1007/s10508-014-0272-8.

[400] Jenny Petrak and Barbara Hedge (eds), *The Trauma of Sexual Assault: Treatment, Prevention and Practice*, Wiley Series in Clinical Psychology (2009) p187.

[401] A R Shewale, A Shah, and J Painter, Risk of Psychosexual Dysfunction Between Users of Selective Serotonin Reuptake Inhibitors and Serotonin Norepinephrine Reuptake Inhibitors, *Value in health* 17(3) (2014), A210–A210; Tarun Narang and Shubh Singh, Psychosexual Disorders and Dermatologists, *Indian Dermatology Online Journal* 7(3) (2016) 149–158, p151.

[402] Nichola Chater, Sex and Disability, in Brough and Denman, n 397, 71–79.

[403] Narang and Singh, n 410, p151.

[404] Mahlet Woldetsadik, Grace Acan, and Okwir Isaac Odiya, The Enduring Consequences of Conflict-Related Sexual Violence: A Qualitative Study of Women Survivors in Northern Uganda, *Conflict and Health* (2022) 16(1) 16, https://doi.org/10.1186/s13031-022-00448-y.

[405] P5, Lima, Peru, May 2019.

This can, in turn, be an obstacle to conception when biological children are part of a person's life plan, which can negatively affect victims' intimate relationships, sexual identity, and perceived societal role. The same victim continued to describe how her goals for a loving intimate relationship and further children became re-negotiated because of the psychosexual impact that she did not receive care for.

> I had another relationship, and he asked me to get engaged, and I was like, 'I am not looking for a husband, I am looking for a father for my daughter.' I realised I didn't love him.[406]

Sexual dysfunction is a complex class of disorders that have an increased association with PTSD in those sexually victimized.[407] Yet psychological treatments for PTSD often misses opportunities to screen and address potential sexual dysfunction through a unified treatment approach; often leaving such consequences unaddressed.[408] Psychotherapies or physical treatments for psychosexual dysfunction may not be available from specialists especially during or immediately after conflict, leading to potentially further loss of positive sexual and reproductive outcomes.[409] Pharmacological treatments that do exist have largely been for males rather than females who disproportionately represent victims of sexual violence.[410] The impact on sexual dysfunction in male victims of sexual violence can also result in interpersonal difficulties that in turn challenges men's honour and social role. For instance, one transitional justice actor who works with male victims relayed the cascading impacts of sexual disorders:

> male victims say I sustained some injuries while in captivity and because I can't function sexually as a man, my wife complains, she wants to leave, she wants to go out'. And that is really a difficult feeling to deal with as a man because it's challenging who you are, it means you're not good enough as a man, that's why your woman wants to go and sleep with another man.[411]

For victims of sexual violence who suffer harm that results in permanent physical disability, it is important to appreciate the compounding harm disability can do to

406 ibid.

407 Vechui, n 396, pp353–365.

408 ibid p365.

409 For more information on psychosexual medicine applied to sexual disorders, see Institute of Psychosexual Medicine (IPM) Prospectus 2014. Margaret Denman, The Institute of Psychosexual Medicine Approach to Psychosexual Medicine as Practised by Health Professionals, pp1–2; Caroline Hunter, Psychological Background to Psychosexual Medicine, pp39–49; Nicola Carter, Physical Treatments for Sexual Problems, pp57–70, in Brough and Denman, n 397.

410 Sheraz Ahmad, Adult Psychosexual Dysfunction as a Sequela of Child Sexual Abuse, *Sexual and Relationship Therapy* 21(4) (2006) 405–418, p407. Phosphodiestease Type 5 inhibitors (eg Sildenafil) for erectile dysfunction. For more information on physical treatments such as drug therapies, see Nicola Carter, Physical Treatments for Sexual Problems, in Brough and Denman, n 39, pp57–70.

411 U1, Kampala, Uganda, July 2018.

their mental health. This is particularly true of those who face social rejection as well as chronic health issues. As the Convention on the Elimination of All Forms of Discrimination Against Women (CEDAW) has recognized, such individuals can 'suffer from a double discrimination linked to their special living conditions'.[412]

Victims of sexual violence may not associate the physical or psychological harm they continue to suffer since the rape, even if it includes vaginal discharge, recurrent urinary tract infections, or pelvic pain.[413] A coordinator in a Colombian feminist organization who provides psychosocial and legal assistance to victims of sexual violence spoke of how often they encountered this phenomenon. They stated, 'it is kind of shocking but there are a lot of times when women don't relate their issues and sexual troubles in reproductive health with the sexual violence they suffered'.[414] Victims whose ethnic, religious, or cultural background may inhibit them from speaking openly about their physical and psychological health may not feel able to articulate their suffering in psychological terms and instead may experience continued feelings of being 'infected', 'dirty', 'impure', or transmitting 'bad luck'.[415] A Peruvian victim who suffered rape in Ayacucho while fleeing a massacre expressed how feelings of being unclean affected her daily life.

> When I was working in a woman's house, I showered 2 or 3 times a day, and the woman used to say to me "do you want to be white? Why do you shower so much?" I used to wash my clothes with bleach, and I always liked white clothes, but I didn't know why, and if there was a stain I would wash it with bleach, I always preferred white clothes, I don't know, I think that that was a way of cleaning, cleaning what happened to me.[416]

Sexual violence may also have a pernicious effect on victims' economic situation, including disruption of their education or job, medical costs, being thrown out of the family home, and destitution, which can increase the vulnerability of victims and their dependents.[417] For instance, pregnancy resulting from rape can place further economic strain on their family as another person to feed in a precarious environment,[418] and victims in Uganda often spoke about giving up their education

[412] CEDAW General recommendation No 18: Disabled Women, 1991.
[413] Swiss and Giller, n 392, p614.
[414] C14, Bogotá, Colombia, March 2019.
[415] Psychology Beyond Borders, Psychosocial Adjustment and Social Reintegration of Children Associated with Armed Forces and Armed Groups: The State of the Field and Future Directions, 2008, p27; and Swiss and Giller, n 392, p614.
[416] P5, Lima, Peru, May 2019.
[417] Sahla Aroussi, Women, Peace, and Security and the DRC: Time to Rethink Wartime Sexual Violence as Gender-Based Violence? *Politics and Gender* 13(3) (2017) 488–515, p491; and Sahla Aroussi, Perceptions of Justice and Hierarchies of Rape: Rethinking Approaches to Sexual Violence in Eastern Congo from the Ground up, *International Journal of Transitional Justice* 12 (2018) 277–295, p284.
[418] Kirsten J Fisher, *Transitional Justice for Child Soldiers: Accountability and Social Reconstruction in Post-Conflict Contexts*, Palgrave MacMillan (2013) p175.

to support their child.[419] A focus group I conducted with nine Colombian women victims revealed that economic hardship and social isolation was linked to sexual violence in each of their lives. For instance, one victim in the group said:

> It is because most of us are single mums and head of the household - mothers who depend on getting a call for cleaning a house. We can´t tell our son: you see, son, I was raped, I was beaten, I had a son, a brother of yours, and he was taken away. You have that constant pain here. Apart from having no economy, no job, no stability. We have to live marginalized.[420]

In social terms, sexual violence can cause the 'disintegration of the moral and social fabric' of communities.[421] Attacks on civilians and the use of rape often results in the forcible displacement of the civilian population, which can, in turn, further weaken community protection against rape.[422] This can cause clear tensions within families, whereby victims are rejected by their partners and forced to leave their homes. A Peruvian victim of sexual violence expressed how familial rejection made it more difficult to support herself as she got older. She stated, 'we have been in need for more than twenty years, from diseases to abandonment on the part of our husbands and possibly by our families because at this age we are alone, we are sick, we do not count economically'.[423] These consequences are not limited to adults; children also face similar, and often aggravated, harms because of sexual violence.

3.3.1 Children and sexual violence

Children can suffer specific physical and psychological harms from sexual violence. This applies not only to them being young victims, but also those born as a result of rape. Many of the impacts on children are similar to those experienced by adults, such as chronic pelvic pain and sexually transmitted infections, but early forced sexual contact can amplify the severity of the complications.[424] Where trauma occurs to the anogenital area, some children may have no lasting physical

[419] O3, virtual interview, October 2018.

[420] C15 FG1, Bogotá, Colombia, March 2019; and U4 FG1, Gulu, Uganda, July 2018.

[421] Marion Pratt and Leah Werchick, Sexual Terrorism: Rape as a Weapon of War in Eastern Democratic Republic of Congo: An Assessment of Programmatic Responses to Sexual Violence in North Kivu, South Kivu, Maniema, and Orientale Provinces, USAID/DCHA Assessment Report (2004) p7.

[422] Gloria Gaggioli, Sexual Violence in Armed Conflicts: A Violation of International Humanitarian Law and Human Rights Law, *International Review of the Red Cross* 96(894) (2014) 503–538, p505.

[423] P2 FG1, Lima, Peru, May 2019.

[424] A C Kasherwa and J M Twikirize, Ritualistic Child Sexual Abuse in Post-Conflict Eastern DRC: Factors Associated with the Phenomenon and Implications for Social Work, *Child Abuse and Neglect* 81 (2018) 74–81.

injury due to healing, but there can be significant changes in neurological and social functioning.[425] Children can also be seen as a sub-group of victims given the harm they suffer and scale of sexual violence they can be subjected to. In Uganda, some 24,000 to 38,000 children were abducted by the Lord's Resistance Army, which had a particular impact on girls, who were often kept as 'wives' for commanders, making their escape more difficult and captivity longer (an average of four and a half years).[426] This also had a disruptive impact on their education and ability to socially reintegrate.[427] CRSV can lower girls' academic performance,[428] which can limit their future career opportunities. In Colombia, sexual and gender-based violence had a higher occurrence in displaced populations, where children are more likely to be exposed to sexual violence.[429]

Early adolescent pregnancy is associated with a higher rate of adverse pregnancy outcomes.[430] This may be attributed to the biological immaturity of female victims less than 15 years of age and poor antenatal care due to neglect and social rejection. In Uganda, one doctor noted that a number of his patients—children abducted by the LRA and kept as sex slaves—had long-term complications from childbirth due to their underdeveloped anatomy, meaning that when giving birth in the bush they were often cut to facilitate the delivery of the baby, and sometimes by non-skilled birth attendants.[431] These controlled incisions are referred to as episiotomies, where they were cut along the perineum but not as far as the rectum, yet some still suffered from recurrent infections or incontinence. Preterm birth, stillbirth, low birthweight, and intrauterine growth restriction (IUGR) are among the perinatal complications of impregnated females aged 13 to 15 that have been reported in the research. This contributes to a high-rate of adverse neonatal outcomes in terms of neonatal morbidity and mortality.[432] The resulting bereavement and loss can compound the trauma of sexual violence. There is also some research on whether victims of sexual violence, including children who are forced to witness sexual violence, experience developmental delays,[433] but the findings

[425] Randell A Alexander, Medical Advances in Child Sexual Abuse, *Journal of Child Sexual Abuse* 20 (2011) 481–485, pp484–485.

[426] Phuong Pham, Patrick Vinck, and Eric Stover, *Abducted: The Lord's Resistance Army and Forced Conscription in Northern Uganda*, Berkeley-Tulane Initiative on Vulnerable Populations (2007), p18 and 24.

[427] U1, Kampala, Uganda, July 2018.

[428] Derebe Madoro and Aneleay Cherinet, Sexual Violence, its Outcome and Associated Factors Among Female from Conflict Affected Setting, Ethiopia, *Health Science Journal* 17(6) (2023) 1028.

[429] Up to 2024, children made up 19.7 per cent of victims within the Colombian Victims' Unit.

[430] Less than 15 years old is considered early adolescent. M Kaplanoglu et al, Gynecologic age is an Important Risk Factor for Obstetric and Perinatal Outcomes in Adolescent Pregnancies, *Women and Birth* 28 (2015) 119–123.

[431] U6, Gulu, Uganda, July 2018.

[432] Kaplanoglu et al, n 430.

[433] Madoro and Cherinet, n 428.

are mixed, and further research is required.[434] For former female child victims, the greater the degree of physical injury caused by rape, the more likely labour is to be prolonged or obstructed in subsequent pregnancies.

Sexual violence can have lifetime complications for young victims. Similar to adults, these can include fistulas, urogenital injuries, and urinary and faecal incontinence, which can in turn cause victims to socially isolate themselves from their family and community.[435] One victim of sexual slavery in Uganda mentioned fistulas as a common occurrence amongst girls who were abducted and raped, which was only compounded by a lack of proper medical care when giving birth.[436] One civil society actor in Colombia who was raped spoke about how she was pregnant at the time of the violation and, as a result, was infected with an STI, causing her lifelong complications.[437] Another Ugandan obstetrician and gynaecologist spoke about the physical complications of children who are sexually enslaved, including secondary infertility due to blocked fallopian tubes.[438]

There is also a higher prevalence of long-term physical health symptomology in children who have suffered sexual violence, namely gastrointestinal, gynaecological, and pain disorders.[439] A number of explanations have been posited to explain these trends, such as the psychological stress and traumatogenic effects of sexual violence leading to biological dysfunction in later life. Victims of sexual slavery can be further demoralized and their dignity degraded by being reduced to commodities to be abused, traded, and disposed of.[440]

Child sexual abuse also has mental health consequences in the short and long term, which are more likely to be pervasive if episodes were recurrent or took place over a long period of time.[441] Other exacerbating factors include a close connection or relationship between the person and their perpetrator. Therefore, children who were sexually enslaved or suffered sexual or reproductive violence within armed groups or families may experience severe negative mental health effects.[442] While the psychological impact on children of being used as soldiers (PTSD, hostility, relationship problems, functional disabilities, and cognitive impairments) is well documented,[443] those who are raped and kept in sexual slavery

[434] E von Sneidern et al, Association between Adverse Childhood Experiences (ACEs) and Developmental Delay of Preschool Children in a Rural Area of Colombia, *Journal of Child and Adolescent Trauma* 10(3) (2017) 225–232.

[435] Longombe, Claude, and Ruminjo, n 290.

[436] U4 FG1, Gulu, Uganda, July 2018.

[437] C15 FG1, Bogotá, Colombia, March 2019.

[438] U6, Gulu, Uganda, July 2018.

[439] Ahona Guha et al, Long Term Healthcare Utilisation Following Child Sex Abuse: A Follow Up Study Utilising Five Years of Medical Data, *Child Abuse & Neglect* 106 (2020) 104538.

[440] Kirsten J Fisher, *Transitional Justice for Child Soldiers: Accountability and Social Reconstruction in Post-Conflict Contexts*, Palgrave MacMillan (2013) p173.

[441] Kasherwa and Twikirize, n 424, p8.

[442] ibid.

[443] Daya Somasundaram, Child Soldiers: Understanding the Context, *BMJ* 324(7348) (2002) 1268–1271.

can also suffer short-, medium-, and long-term harm. In the short term, upon their release, former abductees and child soldiers are often transitioned through reception centres and undergo a Disarmament, Demobilisation and Reintegration (DDR) programme.[444] Girls are often neglected in DDR programmes,[445] and those that do cater for them may overly focus on gender-based violence and leave unaddressed the psychological trauma of having committed atrocities.[446] Research on child soldiers suggests that in the medium to long term, girls can experience more psychological and adjustment problems than boys, being more vulnerable to depression and PTSD,[447] which may in part be explained by their experience of rape and stigma, although these factors are often not measured for both males and females.[448]

The layers of stigma and rejection faced by former child soldiers who have experienced sexual violence stem not only from their association with an armed group and its atrocities, but also reflect different gendered harms.[449] This can include girls and women returning from the bush with children or sexually transmitted infections, and compared to men, are seen as posing risks to the communities they return to, which can be a further source of stigma.[450] The consequences of harm arising from being a child soldier and suffering sexual slavery can depend on the nature, duration, and intensity of the violence experienced, witnessed, or perpetrated, which can be mediated by the child's age (cognitive maturity) and personal characteristics (degree of resilience, knowledge, skills, and abilities), and by the social context of those around them.[451] In communities where marriage is highly valued and can provide economic security and protection for

[444] See Katherine Muldoon et al, After Abduction: Exploring Access to Reintegration Programs and Mental Health Status Among Young Female Abductees in Northern Uganda, *Conflict and Health* 8 (2014) Article 5.

[445] S McKay, M Robinson, and M Gonsalves, Girls Formerly Associated with Fighting Forces and Their Children: Returned and Neglected, Coalition to Stop the Use of Child Soldiers, 2006.

[446] Theresa Stichick Betancourt et al, Sierra Leone's Former Child Soldiers: A Follow-Up Study of Psychosocial Adjustment and Community Reintegration, *Child Development* 81(4) (2010) 1077–1095.

[447] Brandon Kohrt et al, Comparison of Mental Health Between Former Child Soldiers and Children Never Conscripted by Armed Groups in Nepal, *Journal of the American Medical Association* 300(6) (2008) 691–702.

[448] See Theresa Betancourt et al, Sierra Leone's Child Soldiers: War Exposures and Mental Health Problems by Gender, *Journal of Adolescence Health* 49(1) (2011) 21–28. Some research suggests that worse mental health outcomes can be prevalent for male and female combatants who suffer sexual violence, see Kirsten Johnson et al, Association of Combatant Status and Sexual Violence with Health and Mental Health Outcomes in Postconflict Liberia, *Journal of the American Medical Association* 300(6) (2008) 676–690.

[449] Myriam Denov, Coping with the Trauma of War: Former Child Soldiers in Post-Conflict Sierra Leone, *International Social Work* 53(6) (2010) 791–806, p799.

[450] Dyan Mazurana and Susan McKay, *Where are the Girls? Girls in Fighting Forces in Northern Uganda, Sierra Leone, and Mozambique: Their Lives during and After War,* International Centre for Human Rights and Democratic Development (2004) 25–29.

[451] Kitwe Mulunda Guy, Child Soldiers as Zones of Violence in The Democratic Republic of Congo: Three Cases on Medico-Legal Evidence of Torture, *Torture* 19(2) (2009) 137–144, p139–140.

women, for example, this harm may include being rejected or ostracized because they are no longer virgins.[452]

The landmark study on Adverse Childhood Experience (ACEs), which can include physical, emotional, and sexual abuse, found a graded relationship between the level of exposure to trauma and negative health outcomes as adults.[453] This included depression, alcohol misuse, and early death such as through suicide.[454] There is ongoing research into how these early-life stressors impact development pathways as well as on how to prevent negative impacts and promote resilience: a concept that is discussed later.[455] Interestingly, the absence of a trauma-informed approach may actually inhibit recovery, exacerbate traumatic reactions, and act as a barrier to health-seeking behaviour in adult victims of sexual abuse.[456]

3.3.2 Intergenerational trauma and indirect victims

There is increasing psychological research indicating the intergenerational harms of gross violations and conflict on victims.[457] Research suggests that the noxious effects of trauma may be psychologically transmitted from one generation to the next, as evidenced by the increases in depressive and anxiety disorders found amongst the descendants of Holocaust survivors, for example.[458] This can impact on the structure and mental health of families across generations.[459] For example, in Northern Ireland, studies have found that the transgenerational effect of the conflict can manifest in the form of economic hardship, psychological impact, and carer responsibilities for parents and grandparents of direct victims.[460] The terms 'intergenerational' and 'transgenerational' are often used interchangeably, but for

[452] Denov, n 449, p799.

[453] Vincent J Felitti et al, Relationship of Childhood Abuse and Household Dysfunction to Many of the Leading Causes of Death in Adults The Adverse Childhood Experiences (ACE) Study, *American Journal of Preventative Medicine* 14(4) (1998) 245–258.

[454] ibid.

[455] Gordon Asmundson and Tracie Afifi (eds), Adverse Childhood Experiences: Using Evidence to Advance Research, Practice, Policy, and Prevention, Academic Press (2020) pp26–28.

[456] Kirsten Havig, The Health Care Experiences of Adult Survivors of Child Sexual Abuse: A Systematic Review of Evidence on Sensitive Practice, *Trauma, Violence & Abuse* 9(1) (2008) 19–33.

[457] See, for instance, B Bezo and S Maggi, Living in 'Survival Mode': Intergenerational Transmission of Trauma from the Holodomor Genocide of 1932-1933 in Ukraine, *Social Science and Medicine* 134 (2015) 87–94; and N Field, S Muong, and V Sochanvimean, Parental Styles in the Intergenerational Transmission of Trauma Stemming From the Khmer Rouge Regime in Cambodia, *American Journal of Orthopsychiatry* 83(4) (2013) 483–494.

[458] P Fossion et al, Transgenerational Transmission of Trauma in Families of Holocaust Survivors: The Consequences of Extreme Family Functioning on Resilience, Sense of Coherence, Anxiety and Depression, *Journal Of Affective Disorders* 171 (2015) 48–53; and H Wiseman and J Barber, Anger, Guilt, and Intergenerational Communication of Trauma in the Interpersonal Narratives of Second Generation Holocaust Survivors, *American Journal of Orthopsychiatry* 76(2) (2006) 176–184.

[459] ICC-01/04-01/06-1729-Anx1, pp3 and 25.

[460] *Transgenerational Trauma: Dealing with the Past in Northern Ireland*, WAVE Trauma Centre, March 2014.

the purpose of this book, intergenerational harm refers to direct exposure and consequences of trauma, such as children born of war, whereas transgenerational harm concerns the broader social, biological, and indirect environmental impact on epigenetic transmission.[461]

Intergenerational trauma can be considered direct and more proximate to the index individual such as when children are born as a result of rape. Intergenerational trauma refers to maternal exposure to traumatic environments and its impact on the children born, whereas transgenerational trauma refers to more indirect forms of transmission across generations and amongst family members. Children born of rape can often be overlooked in policies and reparations designed to address sexual violence.[462] While the direct impact of sexual violence against mothers on children born of rape is well documented, some researchers have suggested a strong prevalence of transgenerational trauma among all children of victims of sexual violence.[463]

In other contexts, this transgenerational trauma manifests itself in psychological problems in children who have watched their mothers being raped or suffering, with mothers themselves experiencing difficulties, including struggling to control impulses and tension, behaving aggressively towards their children, and being unable to bond with, and express emotions towards, their children.[464] One victim in Peru reflected on the repairs her children benefited from,

> my daughters needed therapy as well, because I was a violent mother, with my daughters, I did realise that it was because of the sexual violence, so it is necessary for people who have suffered rape, to see a psychologist, someone that understands them because they are not able to speak about it . . . a person who is damaged passes it on to their family, it is like an infectious illness.[465]

A Peruvian clinical psychologist who provided therapy to victims of sexual violence and their families also commented,

> the children felt that they were not loved, that their mother rejected them, and they didn't know why. Yet it was very difficult for the women to establish that relationship with their child, because sometimes when they looked at them, their

[461] This reflects that the correlation between traumatic environments on DNA remains contested, as research in this area is ongoing.

[462] Eithne Dowds, Children Born of Sexual and Gender-Based Violence in Conflict: Exploring the Boundaries of International Criminal Law, in W Aschauer et al (eds), *Children and War Past and Present*, Helion & Company, Vol III (2021).

[463] Medica Mondiale, 'We Are Still Alive. We Have Been Harmed But We Are Brave and Strong': 'Research on the Long-Term Consequences of War Rape and Coping Strategies of Survivors in Bosnia and Herzegovina, 2014, pp36–37.

[464] ibid pp89–92.

[465] P5, Lima, Peru, May 2019.

> children reminded them of their aggressor. Over years we help build a relationship, show both that they were not guilty and after all their difficulties the women realized they loved their children and they were part of them.[466]

These difficulties can lead to feelings of shame, guilt, self-blame,[467] identity crises,[468] and frustration at being continuingly labelled a victim of sexual violence nearly two decades after the events. Within families in Sierra Leone, children born as a result of rape are sometimes rejected as having 'bad blood' by the husbands of the women who have been raped.[469] In Uganda, this is a prevalent issue given the number of women and girls abducted and held in sexual slavery by groups such as the LRA, where thousands of children born of war returned home to their mothers' communities.[470] Whereas in Colombia and Peru there has been similar stigma for children born as a result of rape and their mothers, it is not on the same scale. These children also face stigma and social exclusion that can result in poverty and social deprivation as they are pushed to the margins of society. Combined with the psychological issues these children may face, such factors can lead to poor health outcomes including malnutrition, vulnerability to abuse, and susceptibility to disease.[471]

Some girls and women who suffer sexual violence may neglect, reject, harm, or kill the child born out of rape, viewing the baby as a reminder of the violation and a symbol of their suffering.[472] Therefore, children born out of rape can be rejected at multiple levels: first, by their own mothers; second, by the broader family, who may refuse to accept a descendent of the man who committed the rape; and third, by the broader community.[473] Children can also struggle to reconcile their affection, attachment, and loyalty to their fathers with the fathers' responsibility for committing atrocities, in particular the sexual violence inflicted on their mothers.[474] When children born out of rape are preparing for marriage as adults and a potential marriage partner enquires who their parents are, their inability to provide a clear

[466] P6, Lima, Peru, May 2019.

[467] Medica Mondiale, n 463.

[468] Ingvill Mochmann, Children Born of War—A Decade of International and Interdisciplinary Research, *Historical Social Research* 41(1) (2017) 320–346, p338.

[469] Megan MacKenzie, *Female Soldiers in Sierra Leone: Sex, Security and Post-Conflict Development*, New York University Press (2012) p126. Or 'bad seed', in that their fathers as perpetrators risk passing it down through the family line—Mark Drumbl, *Reimagining Child Soldiers in International Law and Policy*, OUP (2012) p8.

[470] A pilot project by the Justice, Law and Order Sector (JLOS) identified around 6,000 children born of rape returning to communities in order to assist their birth registration. See Carol Natukunda, Uganda: Gov't To Register Children born During LRA War, *New Vision*, 12 May 2019.

[471] Mochmann, n 468, p338.

[472] MacKenzie, n 469, pp127–128; and Theidon, n 390, s193.

[473] C15 FG1, Bogotá, Colombia, March 2019; U4 FG1, Uganda, July 2018.

[474] Myriam Denov and Anaïs Cadieux Van Vliet, Children Born of Wartime Rape on Fatherhood: Grappling with Violence, Accountability, and Forgiveness in Postwar Northern Uganda, *Peace and Conflict: Journal of Peace Psychology* 27(4) (2021) 597–605.

answer can be stigmatizing and may lead to problems in their relationships.[475] This can also cause problems in the workplace, when, for example, applying for jobs or completing registration forms.[476] Even when maternal acceptance occurs, however, children can express negative feelings and frustration towards their mother because of her inability to tell them who their father is, particularly in cases of multiple perpetrator rape.[477] This uncertainty and the children's associated resentment towards their mothers can lead to family and community tensions.

3.3.3 Stigma

Stigma refers to the way in which individuals or groups are marked as having less moral or social value than others. The Preventing Sexual Violence in Conflict Initiative (PSVI) report on stigma recognizes that when it comes to sexual violence, defining the concept is elusive, as it affects individuals in different ways and manifests differently across contexts, reflecting both external/imposed and internal (self-blame/shame) components.[478] In broader terms, Goffman outlines stigma as having a discrediting effect on an individual, underlining a 'special discrepancy between virtual and actual social identity', and going beyond a mere attribute to reflect a 'special kind of relationship between attribute and stereotype'.[479] He framed stigma as being a perspective that is 'generated in social contexts', in which individuals can manage its effects through identity management strategies, such as concealment. As such stigma can function as a means of 'social control'.[480] He also suggested that stigma was historically specific to its context, but this has been subsequently moved away from by Goffman and others.[481] Pescosolido and Martin refer to a stigma complex to better capture the nature and effects of the phenomenon as,

> the set of interrelated, heterogeneous system structures, from the individual to the society, and processes, from the molecular to the geographic and historical,

[475] U10 FG2, Uganda, July 2018.

[476] Sexual Violence Patterns, Causes, and Possible Solutions. An Interview with Julienne Lusenge, Solidarite Feminine pour la Paix Integrale (SOFEPADI), Democratic Republic of Congo, in Buss et al, *Sexual Violence in Conflict and Post-Conflict Societies: International Agendas and African Contexts*, Routledge (2014) 58–65.

[477] Gilmore, n 47, ICC-01/04-02/06-2623-Anx2-Red2, para 57.

[478] Preventing Sexual Violence in Conflict Initiative: Shaping Principles for Global Action to Prevent and Tackle Stigma, PSVI (2016) p4. The Hague Principles on Sexual Violence do not define stigma and it only appears once in the document despite intending to 'inform and expand upon understanding of the concept and consequences of sexual violence'.

[479] Erving Goffman, *Stigma: Notes on the Management of Spoiled Identity*, Prentice Hall (1986) pp4–5.

[480] ibid pp138–139.

[481] See Imogen Tyler and Tom Slater, Rethinking the Sociology of Stigma, *The Sociological Review Monographs* 66(4) (2018) 721–743, p729.

> that constructs, labels, and translates difference into marks. In turn, reactions from the internal to individual to those by even remote association, to a cultural bundle of prejudice (i.e., values, beliefs, attitudes, intentions) and discrimination (from other individuals, organizations, and institutions) are produced. This cultural bundle both shapes and is shaped by larger contexts that attempt to reduce them and subject them to larger, often unacknowledged, feedback loops, as well as intended and unintended consequences.[482]

Alternative approaches to responding to stigma through educating people about the effects and conditions have failed to substantively challenge its continued use.[483] Tyler and Slater suggest that this ignores the 'social and political function of stigma as a form of power'.[484] This moves beyond stigma as a social process to also consider how it is structurally rooted in societies. This structural stigma is the result of 'stigmatic assumptions becom[ing] embedded in social policies and practices'.[485] Other research has critiqued the individual or structural approach by suggesting that stigma is a culturally 'thick phenomenon' based in a range of communal practices, such as naming children.[486] Stigma has also been defined as a 'moral experience', which reflects the lived social experience of individuals and communities in the local world of their daily life, whether it is the workplace, home, or neighbourhood.[487] This means that stigma is a 'highly pragmatic, even tactical response to perceived threats, real dangers, and fear of the unknown'.[488] This resonates with the study of stigma in the sociology of punishment, where the labelling of offenders as outcasts served as a means to maintain social cohesion by 'spoiling' their reputation through degradation of their social status.[489] As MacDonald and Kerali summarizes, in conflict situations, 'Stigma and stigmatization are analysed as moral experience in those quotidian post-war spaces in which relationships and communities are being reconstructed, and in which war has ended but violence and social suffering endure'.[490] This has significant implications for responding to stigma around sexual violence, which is often predicated on communal values rather than confronting structures of power.

482 Bernice Pescosolido and Jack Martin, The Stigma Complex, *Annual Review of Sociology* 41(1) (2015) 87–116, p101.

483 Tyler and Slater, n 481, p729.

484 Ibid.

485 Chris Bruckery and Stacey Hannem, *Stigma Revisited: Implications of the Mark*, University of Ottawa Press (2012) p5.

486 Theidon, n 390, s194.

487 Lawrence Hsin Yang et al, Culture and Stigma: Adding Moral Experience to Stigma Theory, *Social Science and Medicine* 64(7) (2007) 1524–1535, p1528.

488 ibid.

489 Sarah Lageson and Shadd Maruna, Digital Degradation: Stigma Management in the Internet Age, *Punishment and Society* 20(1) (2018) 113–133, p116.

490 Anna MacDonald and Raphael Kerali, Being Normal: Stigmatization of Lord's Resistance Army Returnees as 'Moral Experience' in Post-War Northern Uganda, *Journal of Refugee Studies* 33(4) (2020) 766–790, p770.

Stigma related to sexual violence is a social process, culturally imbued and morally experienced, which is 'embedded in the pre-war and war-related gendered social inequalities.'[491] As one practitioner in Uganda found with girls and women returning from being abducted by the LRA, it is 'a question on your morality, on your sexuality and that is the questions your family's own honour and respecting the area of other people. So, the stigma is the family and community's own way of dealing with those contestations caused by the conflict.'[492]

Stigma has the effect of continuing the suffering of rape in a victim's everyday life that degrades their value and social position. For example, in Sierra Leone, former child soldiers who suffered sexual violence were reluctant to come forward to engage with the SCSL or the TRC due to fear that doing so would lead to punishment or upset their marriage or family arrangements.[493] In Ethiopia, community members considered women who had been raped as benefitting from sexual violence through preferential support from donors or non-governmental agencies,[494] and so they became further stigmatized. Prioritizing victims of sexual violence creates a hierarchy of victimhood, which can exacerbate tensions in communities where many people have suffered from an array of violence.

There are some harms that victims are very reluctant to speak of; even if victims can speak about being raped, the intimate details may not be disclosed, which can complicate efforts to provide appropriate treatment.[495] Victims may be seen as spoiled for marriage, ruining their prospects, 'status and access to key resources such as economic security, land, and protection.'[496] This can signify social disapproval of the 'socially deviant behaviour' from local social norms to exclude them from social institutions such as marriage.[497] This reflects on the family' perception of the moral worth of their daughters for marriage, which can limit their social prospects or status and bring shame on the family within the community.[498] Stigma can also be used to maintain community or cultural values around marriage by ensuring succession and purity within a group.[499] Stigma can be layered in reinforcing the victim's silence, whether through moral or social shame, or insensitive treatment by investigative bodies in understanding the victim's harm and thus perpetuating silence. As one Peruvian victim explained,

[491] Teddy Atim, Dyan Mazurana, and Anastasia Marshak, Women Survivors and Their Children Born of Wartime Sexual Violence in Northern Uganda, *Disasters* 42(Suppl) (2018) S61–S78, p64.

[492] U1, Kampala, Uganda, July 2018.

[493] Chris Coulter, *Bush Wives and Girl Soldiers: Women's Lives through War and Peace in Sierra Leone*, Cornell University Press (2009) pp172–173.

[494] Lebeza Alemu Tenaw et al, Medical and Psychological Consequences of Rape Among Survivors During Armed Conflicts in Northeast Ethiopia, *PLoS ONE* 17(12) (2022) e0278859.

[495] U4 FG1, Gulu, Uganda, July 2018; and Gilmore n 47, ICC-01/04-02/06-2623-Anx2-Red2ICC.

[496] Atim, Mazurana, and Marshak, n 491, p64.

[497] Coulter, n 493, p212.

[498] ibid.

[499] Gina Vale, Liberated, Not free: Yazidi Women After Islamic State Captivity, *Small Wars and Insurgencies* 31(3) (2020) 511–539, p529.

> I lived 23 years, with that pain, I wasn't able to tell anyone, not even family members, because I only knew what happened to me, how humiliating and disgusting it would be to tell someone what happened, so it was only me that knew it.[500]

Victims of sexual violence may face stigma from not only the violence, but also secondary consequences such as infection; they can face further stigma as 'injurious truths' for having, or being labelled as having, HIV.[501] One sexual violence expert also noted that stigma could manifest itself not just from the sexual violence, but its complications in leaving a woman unable to have further children, or medical complications.[502] Some physical and psychological harms caused by sexual violence can also reinforce silence, such as stigma surrounding mental health, urinary and faecal incontinence, or odorous physical wounds.[503] That said, all victims do not necessarily uniformly share social consequences of sexual violence. Negative reactions can range from some victims being told to get on with their lives, facing ostracism, domestic violence, or further sexual violence to silence them.[504] According to the coordinator of a Colombian victims group, women victims who summon the courage to speak about sexual violence are criticized for not doing so earlier, or are disparaged when they do, and depicted as unnecessarily complaining. She stated, 'community members and neighbours will say, "look, there she goes, the one who was raped." That is the usual comment. They call us miserable women.'[505]

The act of sexual violence as something that is done to the body can also generate stigma.[506] It also risks detracting from the impact on the victim's body to the actions of the perpetrator. Yet some health consequences of sexual violence can also lead to body stigma. By way of an example, urinary and faecal incontinence can result in perceived 'uncleanliness'. In addition, infertility can be attached with notions of reproductive inadequacy to fulfil social roles.[507] Bodily stigma can also occur in a background where body systems and their functions are considered taboo subjects. For instance, menstruation in female reproductive systems and defaecation in gastrointestinal systems. Across interviews with victims and civil society actors, there was a sense that these social taboos, as well as the shame and stigma of affected bodily functions, was an important vector in discouraging victims to seek medical assistance for ailments. These societal reactions to bodily

[500] P6, Lima, Peru, May 2019.
[501] Rebecca J Cook and Bernard M Dickens, Reducing Stigma in Reproductive Health, *International Journal of Gynecology and Obstetrics* 125 (2014) 89–92, p90.
[502] U1, Kampala, Uganda, July 2018.
[503] U4 FG1, Gulu, Uganda, July 2018.
[504] See Rebecca Campbell et al, Social Reactions to Rape Victims: Healing and Hurtful Effects on Psychological and Physical Health Outcomes, *Violence and Victims* 16(3) (2001) 287–302.
[505] C15 FG1, Bogotá, Colombia, March 2019.
[506] Tami Spry, In the Absence of Word and Body: Hegemonic Implications of 'Victim' and 'Survivor' in Women's Narratives of Sexual Violence, *Women and Language* 18(1) (1995) 27–32.
[507] U10 FG2, Lira, Uganda, July 2018.

manifestations and societal stigma seemed to permeate into the self-worth of victims, sometimes to the extent of rejection of their physical form. A gender expert working on victim issues for over thirty years shared their observations on why victims are reluctant to take care of their body,

> Sexual violence victims decide to leave their bodies, like 'this is not my body'. It is something that I can't explain. They don't care about their body. That means they don't want to go to the doctor. And if they have to pay for it, the less they want to go to the doctor.[508]

There is an interesting contradiction with victims in Colombia reporting healthcare reparations as inadequate, while also being unwilling to engage in positive health-seeking behaviours. This cannot only be attributed to the stigmatizing and harmful culture that can exist in a healthcare profession.[509] Rather, this speaks to victims' relationships with their bodies, and how depictions of an acceptable body are linked with societal norms of ableism, the governing of sexual relationships, and innocence in victims of sexual violence.[510] Rehabilitating harms can appear to be complicated and even in tension with victims' preferences, which calls for an examination of the processes that explain seemingly contradictory outcomes and the power struggles involved in attaining reparations that are concerned with restoring health in the fullest sense.[511]

Across the three case sites, victims spoke of how the symptoms they continue to bear are daily reminders of their victimization, not only for themselves, but also for their community, who observe their pain or notice their reclusively.[512] One victim spoke of how their body, by being biologically female, had betrayed them and she was struggling to reconcile her sexual and gender identity.[513] Several gender experts I interviewed made similar comments. One said,

> We noticed that these women don't want to talk or take care of their bodies. Sometimes they hate their bodies: 'because of my body I got in that situation. My body reminds me of the situation all the time.'[514]

In turn, victims may not wish to use their body if they do not feel empowered, not only for self-advocacy but also to pursue reparations or undergo the application process.[515]

[508] C4, Bogotá, Colombia, September 2018.
[509] C3 and C4, Bogotá, Colombia, September 2018.
[510] See Joseph Fischel and Hilary O'Connell, Disabling Consent, or Reconstructing Sexual Autonomy, *Columbia Journal of Gender and Law* 30(2) (2015) 428–528.
[511] See Chapters 6 and 7.
[512] C15 FG1, Bogotá, Colombia, March 2019.
[513] ibid.
[514] C4, Bogotá, Colombia, September 2018.
[515] C1, Bogotá, Colombia, September 2018.

Children born as a result of rape also face derogatory name calling, such as 'killer' or 'children of the rebel' in Uganda,[516] or *paraquito* in Colombia for those born as a result of paramilitary rapes.[517] Such children can face a 'double burden stigmatization' of their father being a rebel and them being born out of wedlock.[518] In Uganda, Apio notes that naming practices by the mother also reflect the difficult experiences and bad circumstances surrounding childbirth, so that 'the baby is turned into a living reminder of her suffering'.[519] These naming practices can be both formal through the mother and informal through the community, and can affect 'these children's identity, sense of self, and ability to reintegrate'.[520] While some social workers in reintegration centres in Uganda tried to rename these children and thereby distance them from the bad memories of the past towards something more positive, their mothers were reluctant to change their names.[521]

Respondents identified some of the broader sociological understandings of stigma as something 'negative' that society attaches to a person's past or identity, or that a victim self-attributes reflecting their own perceived guilt or self-blame.[522] In Colombia, one respondent found that there was a was 'a double stigma: first, the patriarchal bias that believes that if victims are women, "they probably did something wrong or something to deserve it" and second, the political context, "they must be implicated with one side of the conflict"'.[523] One Ugandan sexual violence expert saw stigma, not as a necessarily direct result of sexual violence in itself, but the social norms around victims that 'regulates [their] sexuality, marriage, identity, belonging—those are the underlying factors'.[524] In many ways she saw this as how society defines individuals based on gender and cultural notions of family honour, morality, and sexuality that degrades the social and familial values of those seen as tainted by sexual violence as a means to respond to conflict.[525] In Uganda, one community psychologist saw stigma as having profound individual psychological consequences for victims, where they suffer from self-neglect, isolation and social exclusion resulting in being labelled 'lazy'.[526] This marginalization is only compounded by community misunderstanding of the mental health impacts of sexual

516 U4 FG1, Gulu, Uganda, July 2018.

517 Tatiana Sanchez Parra, The Hollow Shell: Children Born of War and the Realities of the Armed Conflict in Colombia, *International Journal of Transitional Justice* 12(1) (2018) 45–63, p47.

518 Eithne Dowds, Children Born of Sexual and Gender-Based Violence in Conflict: The International Criminal Court, Ecological Environments and Human Development, *Children and Society* 33 (2019) 226–238, p233.

519 Eunice Apio, Uganda's Forgotten Children of War, in Carpenter, n 227, 94–109, p101.

520 ibid.

521 ibid.

522 C15 FG1 and C16, Bogotá, Colombia, March 2019.

523 C12, Botoga, Colombia, February 2019.

524 U1, Kampala, Uganda, July 2018.

525 ibid.

526 U5, Gulu, Uganda, July 2018.

violence, with some local people avoiding contact with victims, seeing them as 'mad', and being mentally ill as 'contagious'.[527]

Male victims of sexual violence whose perpetrators are also male can experience greater intolerance in some communities due to homophobia.[528] Victims may be unwilling to identify themselves as harmed from rape and may use alternative language, as evidenced in colloquial phrases such as 'faire du mal' (doing harm) to demarcate the experience of sexual violence.[529] Indeed, labelling a reparation pathway as a measure to address sexual violence may discourage or further stigmatize victims by making their suffering more visible and subjecting them to competition with other individuals in their community over resources.[530] Some victims of sexual violence turn to prostitution, face being trafficked, or engage in more informal transactional sex that can be less stigmatizing in some communities than the other options.[531] In turn, this can lead to further human rights abuses and harm, particularly when it is accompanied by requests not to use barrier protection (condoms), sometimes with the appeal of a higher payment fee to validate this activity.[532] This increases STI transmission and other sequelae, as documented above.[533] This phenomena has been documented in particular where peacekeepers have sought these services from sex workers, sometimes engaging in more violent sexual acts compared to local clients.[534]

Stigma can also affect victims' health-seeking behaviour. Stigma and shame can inhibit victims from coming forward to seek medical support, particularly where travelling and the expense of the journey may put them at risk of being discovered, rejected by family members, and thrown out of their home.[535] One interviewee, who works with a number of victims of sexual violence, found that pregnant women laboured without accessing health services out of fear of stigmatization if it was discovered that the child had been conceived as a result of rape.[536]

[527] ibid.

[528] Douglas Page and Samuel Whitt, Confronting Wartime Sexual Violence: Public Support for Survivors in Bosnia, *Journal of Conflict Resolution* 64(4) (2020) 674–702, p692.

[529] As highlighted by victims at the ICC in the *Bemba* case—Public redacted version of 'Decision on the tenth and seventeenth transmissions of applications by victims to participate in the proceedings', ICC-01/05-01/08-2247-Red, 19 July 2012, para 37 citing the Internal Report of the field interpreters, 29 November 2011, ICC-01/05-01/08-1960-Conf-Exp-Anx2. See also in Cambodia, Katrina Natale, 'I Could Feel My Soul Flying Away From My Body' *A Study on Gender-Based Violence During Democratic Kampuchea in Battambang and Svay Rieng Provinces*, Cambodian Defenders Project (2011).

[530] Kristin Kalla, Advancing Justice and Making Amends Through Reparations: Legal and Operational Considerations, in Fionnuala Ní Aoláin et al (eds), *The Oxford Handbook of Gender and Conflict*, OUP (2018) 253–264, p259.

[531] Aroussi, Perceptions of Justice and Hierarchies of Rape, n 417, p285.

[532] Jasmine-Kim Wastendorf, *Violating Peace: Sex, Aid and Peacekeeping*, Cornell University Press (2020) p86.

[533] ibid, p87.

[534] ibid, pp86–87.

[535] Report of the Panel on Remedies and Reparations for Victims of Sexual Violence in the Democratic Republic of Congo to the High Commissioner for Human Rights, OHCHR 2011, para 74.

[536] C15 FG1, Bogotá, Colombia, September 2018.

In Colombia, the prevalence of sexual violence and fear of stigma meant that some women used silence to cope, leading to under-reporting.[537]

In some contexts, due to the stigma associated with coming forward, medical personnel have supplied victims with traditional or local ingredients with which to self-treat their rape and 'cleanse' themselves, for example by trying to cause a termination of the pregnancy/abortion, often resulting in the death of the pregnant person.[538] Conversations with healthcare practitioners and community leaders in Colombia, Uganda, and Peru suggest that this form of treatment has been informally practised and often resulted in worse health outcomes for victims.[539] The Colombian protocol for healthcare practitioners in its 2019 iteration pays particular attention to the need for healthcare workers to be sensitive to the effects of stigma in victims being evasive or not forthcoming on sexual violence in initial consultations and history taking, as well as efforts needed to avoid stigma and to specifically tackle discrimination. However, the programme of healthcare rehabilitation to victims of sexual violence did not assess for ongoing stigma or satisfaction amongst victims.[540] One Colombian civil society actor commented that violence needs to be conflict-related in order for an individual to be eligible as a victim for services, which has led them to find that,

> how we understand the conflict is how we understand women. So this in turn this becomes its own stigma, because women cannot easily get away from it and easily highlight other harms that they might have suffered. So they have to understand themselves and their harms through that lens.[541]

Stigma can go beyond social exclusion and marginalization to also involve repeated violence. In Colombia, victims of sexual violence received death threats for publicly speaking out about their sexual violence and/or for advocating for their right to reparations. One Colombian victim discussed how her own activism had exposed her children and their families to similar intimidation,

> We have received threats. I used to have a bodyguard, but they took him away. They (the government) assigned him for a year. Because of the threats, my daughter sold everything from the little house she had, and she moved to Argentina with her three children and husband.[542]

[537] See Maitane Arnoso Martínez et al, Conflicto armado, impacto psicosocial y reparación en Colombia: la voz de las mujeres [Armed Conflict, Psychosocial Impact and Reparation in Colombia: Women's Voice], *Universitas Psychologica* 16(3) (2017) 1–12.

[538] Giulia Baldi and Megan MacKenzie, Silent Identities: Children Born of War in Sierra Leone, in Carpenter, n 227, 78–93, p84; and Theidon, n 390, s193.

[539] C3, Bogotá, Colombia, September 2018.

[540] C13, Bogotá, Colombia, March 2019.

[541] C3, Bogotá, Colombia, September 2018.

[542] C15 FG1, Bogotà Colombia, March 2019.

Lesbian and other LGBTIQ + individuals have also been subjected to higher levels of sexual violence and threats in Colombia; in some cases sexual violence was used to 'correct' such women.[543] As such, stigma can be multifaceted, affecting victims in different ways and over time, by excluding them socially as well as from support and care. Despite the increased risk of sexual violence, there remains gaps in understanding the harm to LGBTIQ+ populations.[544]

3.3.4 Post-traumatic growth

Post-traumatic growth (PTG) is considered a positive psychological outcome following stress and trauma, as well as a process through which development and transformation to the person's benefit occurs.[545] PTG is centred on psychological wellbeing through engagement with life challenges and is associated with positive changes in personality and assumptive worlds.[546] The three broad elements of PTG evolve around changes in life philosophy, perceptions of self, and relationships.[547] It is important to be cognizant that negative psychological outcomes can co-exist with PTG,[548] and that the relationship between the two has shown diverse results in different populations.[549] There are numerous self-reported validated measurement scales for PTG, of which the most renowned is the PTG Inventory (PTGI).[550] Yet, prescribed categories in these scales may not capture the spectrum

[543] Sebastián Giraldo-Aguirre, Victimización y sobrevivencia de mujeres y hombres considerados homosexuales en el marco del conflicto armado en Colombia [Victimization and Survival of Women and Men Considered Homosexual in the Context of Armed Conflict in Colombia], *Cadernos Pagu* 58 (2020) 1–37, p16.

[544] Inter Agency Standing Committee, Guidelines for Integrating Gender- Based Violence Interventions in Humanitarian Action: Reducing Risk, Promoting Resilience and Aiding Recovery, 2015.

[545] R Lev-Wiesel and M Amir, Post-Traumatic Growth Among Holocaust Child Survivors, *Journal of Loss and Trauma* 8(4) (2003) 229–237; R Tedeschi and L Calhoun, The Posttraumatic Growth Inventory: Measuring the Positive Legacy of Trauma, *Journal of Traumatic Stress* 9 (1996) 455–471; R Tedeschi and L Calhoun, Posttraumatic Growth: Conceptual Foundations and Empirical Evidence, *Psychological Inquiry* 15(1) (2014) 1–18.

[546] Stephen Joseph and P Alex Linley, Positive Psychological Perspectives on Posttraumatic Stress: An Integrative Psychosocial Framework, in Stephen Joseph and P Alex Linley (eds), *Trauma, Recovery, and Growth: Positive Psychological Perspectives on Posttraumatic Stress*, John Wiley & Sons (2008) ch 1, pp10–11.

[547] ibid.

[548] Lev-Wiesel and Amir, n 545.

[549] Other examples include Levine et al who found no relationship between PTSD and PTG, but Kirkner and Ullman found than reduced PTSD was associated with more PTG: Sarah E Ullman, Correlates of Posttraumatic Growth in Adult Sexual Assault Victims. *Traumatology*, 20(3) (2014) 219–224; Shira Z Levine et al, Examining the relationship between resilience and posttraumatic growth, *Journal of Traumatic Stress* 22(4) (2009), 282–286; Anne Kirkner and Sarah E Ullman, Sexual Assault Survivors' Post-Traumatic Growth: Individual and Community-Level Differences, *Violence Against Women* 26(15–16) (2020).

[550] Tedeschi and Calhoun, The Posttraumatic Growth Inventory, n 545. This is a 21-item scale with five dimensions: new possibilities; relating to others; personal strength; appreciation for life; and spiritual change.

of growth that may be unique to certain groups, such as victims of CRSV, and in-depth interviews may be more appropriate for difficult-to-reach populations with complex trauma.[551] In particular, victims of CRSV can have different alterations to growth (eg being more cautious),[552] compared to other types of trauma, which may not be included in scales with set criteria. There also remains uncertainty regarding the PTGI's ability to objectively measure actual growth rather than what is perceived to be positive change.[553] Measurement scales often do not appreciate cultural or community differences in what is understood as growth post-trauma.

Sexual violence is associated with significant rates of psychological distress including PTSD as discussed earlier.[554] However, PTG is possible where victims of CRSV have not availed of psychosocial therapies and have remained silent for years but have been retrospectively diagnosed with PTSD.[555] A study by Anderson and colleagues on victims of CRSV in Bosnia and Herzegovina found the most growth in victims' relationship to others (eg closeness to others) followed by new possibilities (eg life's purpose). It is important to consider the impact of CRSV to PTG's third dimension of sense of self and identity, which is explored in Chapter 4, and whether this is a major limiting factor to PTG. Interestingly, victims of childhood sexual violence who blame themselves can have greater difficulties adjusting.[556] The dynamic nature of PTG is important to understand how victims navigate the temporal nature of potential harms and options for repair. The psychological distress from CRSV may act as a vehicle for some degree of growth,[557] with the person aiming to self-repair or regulate by evening up the negative consequences.[558]

The interplay between resilience and PTG is somewhat contested, but generally they are considered as separate yet linked phenomena. PTG has been viewed

[551] Mike Slade et al, Post-Traumatic Growth in Mental Health Recovery: Qualitative Study of Narratives, *BMJ Open* 9(6) (2020).

[552] Patricia Frazier and Margrit Berman, Posttraumatic Growth Following Sexual Assault, in S Joseph and P Linley (eds), n 546, p167.

[553] P Frazier et al, Does Self Reported Posttraumatic Growth Reflect Genuine Positive Change? *Psychological Science* 20 (2009) 912–919, doi:10.1111/j.1467-9280.2009.02381; Kirkner and Ullman, n 549, 1987–2003.

[554] Frazier and Berman, n 552, p167.

[555] Anderson, Kimberley et al, Predictors of Posttraumatic Growth among Conflict-Related Sexual Violence Survivors from Bosnia and Herzegovina, *Conflict and Health* 13(1) (2019) 23–23.

[556] Rachel Lev-Wiesel, Beyond Survival: Growing out of Childhood Sexual Abuse, P157, in Joseph and Linley, n 546.

[557] ibid.

[558] Other studies on non-CRSV would support the theory that a certain degree of stress might be conducive to PTG, but when it is beyond a certain individual threshold for a person then growth is less likely to occur. Jónsdóttir and colleagues found PTG was associated with moderate severity of PTSD, whereas low or high symptoms of PTSD had less PTG. See Erla Katrín Jónsdóttir, Rannveig Sigurvinsdottir, and Bryndís Björk Ásgeirsdóttir, Associations Among Posttraumatic Growth, Demographic Characteristics, Posttraumatic Stress Symptoms, and Trauma Type, With a Focus on Sexual Violence, *Journal of Traumatic Stress* 36(5) (2023) 849–860.

as synonymous with resilience.[559] Others conceptualize resilience as a return to baseline pre-trauma making them further vulnerable to insult, whereas PTG goes beyond this, reflecting the ability to withstand further trauma without being damaged. In reality, many victims of sexual violence are unable to return to their baseline and are concerned with non-recurrence of the trauma. PTG can still occur with multiple and cumulative traumas;[560] however, analysing outcomes that indicate resilience between events is generally not feasible. When viewed holistically with a person's potentially full plethora of harms, PTG could be viewed as a form of resilience when it acts as a counter to mitigating the extent of harm (such as rejecting stigma) or managing the demands of their life in the aftermath of physical harm. The traumatic experience could also be accommodated negatively, leading to further psychological harm.

Post-traumatic growth can occur on a wider scale where communities are considered to grow after adversity, or where a group of individuals experience similar growth patterns after collective trauma.[561] Communities may experience a positive shift in beliefs and spirituality[562] after experiencing armed conflict, or its civilians CRSV. There may be a relationship between resilience factors such as community support and connectivity with others that can facilitate psychological confrontation of traumatic events and PTG.[563] Thus, growth can occur through trauma but also through some of the opportunities and measures implemented in its aftermath. By considering all the consequences flowing from CRSV we can better conceptualize how reparations may be a vector for individual and/or group post-traumatic growth.

3.4 Conclusion

Sexual violence causes a range of harm beyond the explicit and common ones often reported in the literature. Victims of CRSV can also experience none, some, or a range of these harms, in one, several, or multiple-perpetrator incidents. This can make the harm suffered by a victim unique and difficult to categorize for a reparation programme. As such, a one-size-fits-all approach to reparations, such as compensation, may inadequately remedy victims' harm. While there remains a need to consider disaggregated data (eg by gender identity) to discern health

[559] Janine Natalya Clark, Resilience, Conflict-Related Sexual Violence and Transitional Justice. A Socio-Ecological Framing, Routledge (2022) pp190–191.
[560] Jónsdóttir et al, n 558.
[561] Carolina Botero-García et al, Posttraumatic Growth and Resilience on Conflict-Related Sexual Violence: A Set of Systematic Reviews of Literature, *Social Sciences* 12 (291) (2023), doi.org/10.3390/socsci12050291.
[562] Richard Tedeschi et al, The Posttraumatic Growth Inventory: A Revision Integrating Existential and Spiritual Change, *Journal of Traumatic Studies* 30(1) (2017) 11–18.
[563] Botero-García et al, n 561.

consequences to certain population groups, this approach may not always appreciate intersectional harms as well as group-based harm such as to communities. Having a more robust understanding of harm can enable us to explore appropriate reparations for conflict-related sexual violence in Chapters 5 and 6. Engaging with forensic and mental health enables a broader understanding of harm suffered by victims of CRSV, as well as prompting those in the field to consider how reparations can be sought through other medico-legal opportunities. This chapter also highlighted a thicker understanding of stigma and how it functions as power that requires more than education to tackle it. Together the physical, psychological, and social harm of CRSV can have short-, medium,- and long-term consequences for victims, their families, and community. As discussed in Chapter 2, the effect of such sexual violations over time can have a pernicious effect on a victim's health, quality of life, and dignity. Together with the difficulty of reparations adequately responding to these harms, such measures take years or even decades to be implemented, and can make it too late for many victims to mitigate the chronic physical and psychological harms from which they suffer. Both these issues of stigma and time have implications for victims' vulnerability and resilience, as examined in Chapter 7. This deeper appreciation of the harm caused by CRSV can also shape the identities of those directly affected, which can compel or impede such individuals from seeking redress.

4

Sexual Violence and Identity

Victim, Survivor, and Patient

While attention to victims of conflict-related sexual violence (CRSV) in transitional justice has been growing, the impact of such violence on victims' identity and experiences of claiming redress has been largely neglected. This chapter explores how an individual's identity after CRSV, whether as victim, survivor, or patient, is constructed and deconstructed by the individual and society. As this chapter explores, identity can create barriers for individuals affected by CRSV and complicate their efforts to obtain reparations. The chapter begins by discussing the nature of identity in different disciplines, with a particular focus on identity as an intersection between understandings of the self (internal) and society (external). I then examine how transitional justice scholarship has approached the notion of identity. The subsequent sections explore the three primary identities associated with those who experience CRSV: victim, survivor, and patient. Victim and survivor are focused on, given their prevalence in transitional justice and reparations. The final section introduces the identity of 'patient', which is commonly used in medicine but not in reparations, and which is used here for contrast and to add to the debates around identity for CRSV.

The discussion on victim identity draws upon victimology literature, exploring the relevance of notions such as passivity and silence, harm and suffering, innocence and blame—all of which, I will argue, shape understandings of, and engagement with, victims in transitional justice. I then explore ideas associated with being identified as a 'survivor', drawing in particular from feminist scholarship that challenges the assumed passivity of victimhood and focuses instead on agency and empowerment. Drawing then upon the medical literature, I examine issues related to stigma, the role of dignity, healing, and the treatment of patients. Identity is an important way for individuals affected by CRSV to perform or mask their suffering. It is also a lens through which affected communities see such violence and construct reparation measures to respond to them. Appreciating how identity can inhibit or encourage individuals affected by CRSV to engage in reparations is vital to gaining a deeper understanding of reparations in victims' everyday lives.

Redressing Rape in War. Sunneva Gilmore, Oxford University Press.
DOI: 10.1093/9780198919735.003.0004

4.1 A Critical Understanding of Identity

Identity is difficult to define,[1] but it has been accepted that individuals can have multiple identities that can change over time.[2] Identity is understood in sociology as fluid, a social construct, and a way for individuals and groups to present themselves to others. For Goffman, identity is part of the performance of personhood that individuals present when interacting socially with others.[3] The internal 'self' consists of conscious and unconscious attributes,[4] while the external identity or 'mask' is what the individual truly aspires to.[5] In relation to gender identity specifically, Butler takes this further by arguing that gender is 'performative' in that it expresses what is 'purported to be' in society.[6] As depicted through the multifaceted lens of 'identity politics', identity has been a powerful tool in the formation of 'cultural scripts' in both 'ordinary' settled democracies and in the context of 'extraordinary' mass conflict, where transitional justice has traditionally operated.[7] From the perspective of political science, Fearon views identity as comprised of 'socially distinguishing features that a person takes a special pride in or views as unchangeable but socially consequential'.[8] These categories of identity appear to have 'rules of membership'[9] that similarly dictate the identity's discourse or narrative, which have important implications for victims, survivors, and patients.

In transitional societies, it is often the case that the identity politics that fuelled violence or authoritarian abuses also shape the debates over appropriate transitional responses.[10] Violence can be a product of identity, with the perpetration of atrocities being a key part of the 'doing' or 'performing' of identities.[11] This is

[1] Erikson developed the concept during the 1950s and 1960s, which has since been subjected to interdisciplinary critiques. On the concept's definitional dilemmas, see Erik Erikson, *Identity and the Life Cycle*, Norton (1959); and James Fearon, *What is Identity (As We Now Use the Word)?* Department of Political Science, Stanford University (1999).

[2] See Rogers Brubaker and Frederick Cooper, Beyond 'Identity', *Theory and Society* 29(1) (2000) 1–47.

[3] Erving Goffman, *The Presentation of Self in Everyday Life*, Doubleday (1959).

[4] Mardi Horoqitz, Self-Identity Theory and Research Methods, *Journal of Research Practice* 8(2) (2012) M14.

[5] Goffman distinguishes between frontstage and backstage in how people present themselves to others. The front stage is where individuals perform through 'impression management', whereas the backstage provides a space of 'work control' where they can 'buffer themselves from the deterministic demands that surround them'. Goffman, n 3, pp70–71.

[6] Judith Butler, *Gender Trouble: Feminism and the Subversion of Identity*, Routledge (1990) p25.

[7] Erving Goffman, *Relations in Public: Microstudies of the Public Order*, Allen Lane, The Penguin Press (1971); and Goffman, n 3.

[8] Fearon's full definition as 'an "identity" refer to either (a) a social category, defined by membership rules and (alleged) characteristic attributes or expected behaviors, or (b) socially distinguishing features that a person takes a special pride in or views as unchangeable but socially consequential (or (a) and (b) at once)'. Fearon, n 1, p36.

[9] Paige Arthur, *Identities in Transition: Challenges for Transitional Justice in Divided Societies*, CUP (2011) 1–14.

[10] ibid.

[11] Clare Bielby and Jeffrey Stevenson Murer, *Perpetrating Selves: Doing Violence, Performing Identity*, Springer (2018) p3.

exemplified where CRSV is intended to destroy the identity of the person and their 'sense of self in the aftermath'.[12] Sexual violence in this context can even be constitutive of identity, reducing victims to contested identities such as Tutsi women, or essentializing Muslim men as perpetrators.[13] In the aftermath of violence, societies transitioning from conflict may not only be addressing past violations, but deepening divisions over identity.[14] Some of those affected by CRSV may experience a painful fracturing of their identity that requires reparation to help restore a harmonious 'self-state' of their own personal identity.

Beyond the experiences of harm discussed in the last chapter, identity and lived experience can impact upon individual and group engagement with transitional justice mechanisms. Reparation programmes can be identity-centric with entitlement contingent on identity status, such as those in which only women are recognized as victims of rape, and sometimes go so far as redressing the 'wounded identities' of the state or society.[15] However, given that reparations can take decades to be implemented, there is a temporal aspect to identity. Some individuals may see their past identity as that of a fighter or an activist, but now, struggling with ongoing health problems, poverty, or marginalization as a consequence of conflict, position themselves as a victim.[16] The victim identity can be 'usable' by reducing 'real-world complexity to an easily consumable conflict narrative'.[17] Much of the discussion of identity in the transitional justice literature has concentrated on gender,[18] race,[19] or collective victimhood and new political identities after conflict.[20] There has also been an increasing turn towards intersectionality, which considers the relationship between multiple identity constructs.[21] Intersectionality

[12] Inger Skjelsbaek, Victim and Survivor: Narrated Social Identities of Women Who Experienced Rape During the War in Bosnia-Herzegovina, *Feminism and Psychology* 16(4) (2006) 373-403, p381; and Denise Sandole and Carl F Auerbach, Dissociation and Identity Transformation in Female Survivors of the Genocide Against the Tutsi in Rwanda: A Qualitative Research Study, *Journal of Trauma & Dissociation* 14(2) (2013) 127–137.

[13] Kirsten Campbell, The Gender of Transitional Justice: Law, Sexual Violence and the International Criminal Tribunal for the Former Yugoslavia, *International Journal of Transitional Justice* 1 (2007) 411–432, p429.

[14] Arthur, n 9, pp3–4.

[15] Lawrie Balfour, Reparations after Identity Politics, *Political Theory* 33(6) (2005) 786–811, p786.

[16] Natascha Mueller-Hirth, Temporalities of Victimhood: Time in the Study of Postconflict Societies, *Sociological Forum* 32(1) (2017) 186–206, p192.

[17] Micheál Hearty and Kevin Hearty, Naming and Framing Victims: Identity, 'Usable' Victimhood, and the Spectral Turn in Transitional Justice, *International Review of Victimology* 30(1) (2024) 70–88, p72.

[18] Fionnuala Ní Aoláin, Gendered Under-Enforcement in the Transitional Justice Context, in S Buckley-Zistel and R Stanley (eds), *Gender in Transitional Justice*, Springer (2012) 59–87, p71; and Louise Chappell, The Role of the ICC in Transitional Gender Justice: Capacity and Limitations in Susanne Buckley-Zistel and Ruth Stanley (eds), *Gender in Transitional Justice*, Palgrave (2012) 37–57, p44.

[19] Madeleine Fullard and Nicky Rousseau, Truth Telling, Identities, and Power in South Africa and Guatemala, in Arthur, n 9, 54–86, pp74–80.

[20] Nevin Aiken, *Identity, Reconciliation and Transitional Justice: Overcoming Intractability in Divided Societies*, Routledge (2013) pp18–19.

[21] Kimberlé Crenshaw, Demarginalizing the Intersection of Race and Sex: A Black Feminist Critique of Antidiscrimination Doctrine, Feminist Theory and Antiracist Politics, *University of Chicago Legal*

can help to safeguard those who have experienced CRSV from being judged in isolation where predisposing discriminations exist (eg on the basis of gender or ethnicity) or arise as a result of the harm.[22]

For the purposes of this chapter, identity is understood as playing an important role in understanding victims of sexual violence, their everyday experiences of living with its consequences, and their experiences of seeking appropriate reparations. Importantly, identity reflects both how individuals see themselves and how they present themselves to others or perform to social expectations. This chapter does not address the intersecting identities victims of CRSV may face,[23] many of which are highly contextual.[24] Rather, it focuses on three categories of identity: victim, survivor, and patient—and explores how they are 'performed' or 'usable' in the context of seeking reparations. An intersectional analysis will be weaved through the discussions on victims, patients, and survivors.

4.2 Victim Identity

The identity of 'victim' is commonly invoked to identify those who suffer harm. The United Nations defined victims as:

> persons who individually or collectively suffered harm, including physical or mental injury, emotional suffering, economic loss or substantial impairment of their fundamental rights, through acts or omissions that constitute gross violations of international human rights law, or serious violations of international humanitarian law. Where appropriate, and in accordance with domestic law, the term 'victim' also includes the immediate family or dependants of the direct victim and persons who have suffered harm in intervening to assist victims in distress or to prevent victimization.[25]

Forum 1 (1989) 139–167; Sumi Cho, Kimberlé Williams Crenshaw, and Leslie McCall, Toward a Field of Intersectionality Studies: Theory, Applications, and Praxis, *Signs* 4 (2013) 785–810.

[22] Ana Martin Beringola, Intersectionality: A Tool for the Gender Analysis of Sexual Violence at the ICC, *Amsterdam Law Forum* 9(2) (2017) 84–109, p96.

[23] The focus of this thesis is on females, but the role of masculinity is an important identity intersection that is receiving increasing attention. See Brandon Hamber, Masculinity and Transitional Justice: An Exploratory Essay, *International Journal of Transitional Justice* 1(3) (2007) 375–390; and Philipp Schulz, *Male Survivors of Wartime Sexual Violence: Perspectives from Northern Uganda*, University of California Press (2020) pp6–8.

[24] Salient ones would be ethnicity (eg Afro-Colombians) and age (such as child soldiers), but it is beyond the scope of this thesis to focus specifically on these at length.

[25] UN Basic Principles and Guidelines on the Right to a Remedy and Reparation for Victims of Gross Violations of International Human Rights Law and Serious Violations of International Humanitarian Law, A/RES/60/147, 16 December 2005, Principle 9.

While victim as a legal definition can be used to demarcate those worth recognizing, who is considered and presents themselves as a victim can be more broadly captured under the notion of 'victimhood'. As a social construct, victimhood is used to convey moral notions of innocence[26] and injustice; it speaks to the human tendency to explain atrocity through blame, even when the event is deemed 'uncontrollable'.[27] In line with Goffman's dramaturgy of identity, self-labelling or the naming of an individual or a group as a victim is 'a performative act that has the power to validate, and therefore "produce" a subject with this particular identity and the attributes that go with it (vulnerable, passive, helpless etc.)'.[28] Claiming victimhood as an identity is not only performative in Goffman's terms, it is also instrumental and 'usable' in claims-making for redress against those responsible.[29] It can be used to mobilize other similarly suffering victims and to generate moral support from society.[30] Using international definitions can leverage legal change for victims who do not fit within society's norms of innocence, such as female combatants who were subjected to forced abortions within FARC.[31] Thus, identifying as a victim is a means of 'claims-making' against another to invoke a reaction from the state, those responsible, or wider society.[32]

In his domestic analysis of crime, Christie suggests that there is a hyper-focus on 'ideal victims' who are imbued with the moral virtues of innocence and vulnerability, which justifies and legitimizes the intervention of the state and its role in controlling crime.[33] In transitional justice, the innocent victim has a more politically contested position, in that it sits atop the 'apex of a hierarchy of victimhood and becomes a symbol around which contested notions of past violence and suffering are constructed and reproduced'.[34] This idealism and politicization is in stark contrast to the experience of suffering or victimization that can be neglected or marginalized in transitional justice interventions.[35] According to Fletcher and van der Merwe:

[26] Richard Quinney, Who is the Victim? *Criminology* 10 (1972) 314–323, p321.

[27] Trudy Govier, *Victims and Victimhood*, Broadview Press (2015) p19.

[28] Valerie M Meredith, Victim Identity and Respect for Human Dignity: A Terminological Analysis, *International Review of the Red Cross* 91(874) (2009) 259–277, p262.

[29] Hearty and Hearty, n 17.

[30] Kieran McEvoy and Kirsten McConnachie, Victims and Transitional Justice: Voice, Agency and Blame, *Social and Legal Studies* 22(4) (2013) 489–513, p504.

[31] See Cherilyn Elston, Nunca Invisibles: Insurgent Memory and Self-representation by Female Ex-Combatants in Colombia, *Wasafiri* 35(4) (2020) 70–78.

[32] Kieran McEvoy and Kirsten McConnachie, Victimology in Transitional Justice: Victimhood, Innocence and Hierarchy, *European Journal of Criminology* 9(5) (2012) 527–538, p531.

[33] Nils Christie, The Ideal Victim, in E A Fattah (ed), *From Crime to Victim Policy*, Macmillan (1986) 17–30.

[34] McEvoy and McConnachie, n 30, p532.

[35] McEvoy and McConnachie ibid, p534; and Luke Moffett, *Justice for Victims before the International Criminal Court*, Routledge (2014) p24.

> Victims are never a simple, unidimensional category, either in terms of their own complex needs or in terms of the fluidity of identities that characterize an ongoing conflict ... The constructed nature of victims in transitional justice works against addressing the complex nature of victims' experiences and identities. They may hold multiple and conflicting views, certainly collectively but also individually, that transitional justice is ill equipped to address.[36]

Such debates over the identity of 'victim' and victimhood were not originally a concern of victimology, which focused instead on the character and circumstances of those who were affected by crime in an effort to distil the factors that made certain groups more susceptible to violence.[37] However, since the 1990s more critical accounts have emerged that have focused on the lived experience of victims, victimhood, and victims who are 'hidden' due to prevailing social norms and state practices.[38] In particular, critical victimology examines the 'role of the law and the state in the victimisation process as well as the potential for human actors both to sustain and to change the conditions under which they act'.[39] In the 2000s, cultural victimology began to gain traction as a means through which to better understand how victims are perceived symbolically in society. In particular, cultural victimologists considered how victims are positioned within public discourses, as well as the 'nature of victimization *itself* in addition to the social standing of the person or group being victimised'.[40]

Cultural victimology enriches the discussion on all forms of reparation for CRSV, by explaining which victims are considered deserving of full redress and the impact of reparations on victims of such violence. Ferrell et al claims that cultural victimology is 'attuned to human agency, symbolic display, and shared emotion'.[41] At the heart of its approach is an ethical cautioning about how certain forms of suffering are made public and others are obscured. The culture of victimhood consists of many individual and collective actors who decide how to portray their suffering. The reaction of the wider society then frames reparations not just in terms of who is an eligible victim, but also in terms of the context in which the harm occurred, that is, the nature of the harms and the responsible actors. Thus, the term 'victim' is externally ascribed when society determines that an individual meets the criteria for victimhood. The individual is then placed in what Carrabine

[36] Laurel Fletcher and Hugo van der Merwe, Editorial Note, *International Journal of Transitional Justice* 8(1) (2014) 2–3.

[37] Hans Von Hentig, *The Criminal and his Victim: Studies in the Socio-Biology of Crime*, Archon (1976); and Martin F Wolfgang, 'Victim Precipitated criminal Homicide, *Journal of Criminal Law and Criminology* 48(91) (1957) 1–11.

[38] McEvoy and McConnachie, n 32, p530.

[39] Rob Mawby and Sarah Walklate, *Critical Victimology*, Sage (1994) p177.

[40] Matthew Hall, Victims of Crime: Culture, Politics and Criminal Process in the 21st Century, *Northern Ireland Legal Quarterly* 68(4) (2017) 469–490, p470.

[41] Jeff Ferrell, Keith Hayward, and Jock Young, *Cultural Criminology An Invitation*, Sage (2008) p190.

et al term the 'hierarchy of victimisation'.[42] One's position on this hierarchy is influenced by public favour; an individual is likely to rank lower when they themselves have also perpetrated the same or another crime, or are considered to have exposed themselves to unnecessary risk, such as sex work.[43] This framework will be used in Chapter 7, when discussing stigma and vulnerability.

In public health, where systematic reviews of quantitative and qualitative studies on harm have been conducted, they can have a narrow focus on what constitutes CRSV, and the population of interest is often limited to civilian victims.[44] This fails to capture specific consequences of CRSV within armed groups or to former combatants and can perpetuate notions of a deserving or ideal victim within medical spheres, which I argue does not take a holistic medico-legal approach. Furthermore, intimate partner and domestic violence can also be excluded due to perceptions on what is inextricably linked or caused by the conflict.

Public reactions can also be moulded by the individual persons or groups that 'shout the loudest', instrumentalizing and amplifying the importance of one particular type of suffering over others.[45] Referring to the media's hyper-attention to CRSV in the Democratic Republic of Congo, for example, Heaton blames the sensationalism surrounding this one type of victim and the restrictive narrative of rape as a weapon of war for creating an 'incomplete comprehension of the conflict overall'.[46] With the promise of resources and pervasive incentives for those presenting with a certain type of victimhood, victims have adopted the preferred public discourse even where rape did not occur in the conflict context.[47] In the Democratic Republic of Congo, this strategy was adopted to help normalize the discussion of sexual violence and dispel the stigma generally attached to it. As such, individuals consider the overall culture of victimhood when presenting themselves. They have to consider the general identity of 'victim' to be true or they may choose to silence the specifics of their victim identity (eg intimate partner violence rather than CRSV), which can mean that individuals become 'party to a range of interactions' with the social identity of victim.[48] This resonates strongly with the

[42] Eamonn Carrabine et al, *Criminology: A Sociological Introduction*, 2nd Edition, Routledge (2009) pp159–161.

[43] ibid, p16.

[44] Elisa Rubini et al, Negative consequences of conflict-related sexual violence on survivors: a systematic review of qualitative evidence, International Journal for Equity in Health 22(1) (2023) 227, doi.org/10.1186/s12939-023-02038-7; Ingrid Ba and Raja S. Bhopal, Physical, mental and social consequences in civilians who have experienced war-related sexual violence: A systematic review (1981–2014), *Public Health* 142 (2017) 121–135.

[45] Kieran McEvoy and Ruth Jamieson, Conflict, Suffering and the Promise of Human Rights in D Downes, C Chinkin, and C Gearty (eds), *Crime, Social Control and Human Rights Essays in Honour of Stan Cohen*, Willan (2007) 422–441, p425.

[46] Laura Heaton, The Risks of Instrumentalizing the Narrative on Sexual Violence in the DRC: Neglected Needs and Unintended Consequences, *International Review of the Red Cross* 96 (894) (2014) 625–639, pp625–626.

[47] ibid.

[48] Gabe Mythern, Cultural Victimology: Are We All Victims Now? in S Walklate (ed) *The Handbook of Victims and Victimology*, Routledge (2007) 464–483, p466.

broader literature on identity and its performativity. That said, building on the previous chapter, it is worth considering the aspects of victim identity in relation to harm and suffering, innocence and blame, and passivity and silence in more depth, given that they can inform victim identity and individuals' engagement with reparation processes. These themes reflect some of the prevailing cultural conceptions in victimology that hierarchize the innocence of a victim as most deserving of society's attention for redress, and denies that identity to other individuals, despite the harm and suffering they have experienced.

4.2.1 Harm and suffering

Victim identity is contingent on the infliction of harm and the experience of suffering, alluding to the damage or adverse effects a person endures.[49] Suffering, when understood as a consciousness of pain, may heighten a person's sense of 'self' or purpose, and give meaning to their identity for the rest of their life. The course a person's life takes after the infliction of harm is immensely variable. Not all perceived harms evoke suffering, nor manifest in the short term. According to Conaghan, 'our concept of harm is thoroughly social',[50] and the internalization of society's harmful gender norms will also impact whether a person externally identifies as a victim and seeks redress. Feminist critiques of harm have helped to unearth hidden gendered harms.[51] In the context of CRSV, this pertains to how individuals' sexual harm seeps into the community, both in the smaller unit of family and friends and the wider society. Ní Aoláin calls these ripples 'communities of harm'.[52] Some social spheres are uneasy about disrupting the outward appearance of 'cheerful social life' in a new democracy by engaging with victimhood.[53] Furthermore, society may disallow victims from owning their suffering.

Given the shame and stigma that they can experience, victims of sexual violence often remain silent or are not forthcoming about their suffering. Even when individuals who suffer CRSV say they are victims, others may deny or disparage their claims because they exhibit none of the physical consequences that others assume would be self-evident in such circumstances, such as pregnancy, vaginal bleeding, or STIs. This is even evident in some reparation claims before the Iraqi Yazidi [Female] Survivor Law, where claimants who do not have sufficient documentary

[49] Govier, n 27, p26.

[50] Joanne Conaghan, Law, Harm and Redress: A Feminist Perspective, *Legal Studies* 22(3) (2002) 319–339, p322.

[51] Fionnuala Ní Aoláin, Exploring a Feminist Theory of Harm in the Context of Conflicted and Post-Conflict Societies, *Queen's Law Journal* 35(1) (2009) 219–244, p223; and Catherine MacKinnon, Sexual Harassment: Its First Decade in Court, in C MacKinnon (ed), *Feminism Unmodified*, Harvard University Press (1987) 103–116.

[52] ibid.

[53] Govier, n 27; and U4 FG1, Gulu, Uganda, July 2018.

evidence have to provide witnesses to confirm they were captured and held as sex slaves by ISIS to be eligible, which can be difficult when many witnesses were killed, displaced, or fearful of speaking out and being labelled collaborators.[54] As Bowyer has observed, for victims 'the reality of [their] suffering is self-evident, but it is far from self-evident to others'.[55] Silence around these issues is commonplace even outside the context of conflict.[56] During fieldwork for this study, for example, victims considered it rude to correct outsiders' interpretations of their suffering, including non-governmental organizations (NGOs) carrying out transitional justice work.[57] Many of those interviewed kept their true sense of identity (eg as a survivor) hidden in case revealing it would impact their ability to receive reparations, from medical treatment to housing support.[58] Departures from the traditional view that 'one should keep one's pain and suffering to oneself'[59] may encourage freedom of self-expression and reduce fragmentation of identity, but it may be onerous for victims in conservative cultures. Sincere depictions or performances of suffering may be undermined by others misconstruing their suffering as a claim to 'innocence' in the conflict, or to gain financial/material reparations. Displays of suffering reinforce that a person has been harmed; as such, they can distract from the circumstances in which that harm took place. In essence, while it is difficult to deny a person their own experience of suffering, perceived harm may be politicized in transitional justice processes for reparation. For victims, this can lead them to lean into the notions of passivity and helplessness or silence, after suffering CRSV.

4.2.2 Passivity and silence

In Western societies, the term 'victim' is imbued with a cultural connotation of passivity and helplessness, which reflects the suffering of individuals who were too weak to defend themselves and therefore garner sympathy from society.[60] The term 'victimhood' can often evoke an image of passivity. The subtle and innovative strategic methods a person may utilize to create or replicate the sensation of control do not typically feature in victim discourses. Drawing upon the impact of identity on 'self', some victims have set aside the requisite of passivity: some detail

[54] Luke Moffett and Christoph Sperfeldt, Assessing the Implementation of the YSL, IOM (2024)—on file with the author.

[55] Timothy James Bowyer, *Beyond Suffering and Reparation: The Aftermath of Political Violence in the Peruvian Andes*, Springer (2019) p2.

[56] Judith Butler, *Frames of War: When Is Life Grievable*? Verso (2009).

[57] O2, virtual interview, November 2018.

[58] U4 FG1, Gulu, Uganda, July 2018.

[59] Govier, n 27, p4.

[60] Van Dijk argues that this is rooted in the Christian theology of the sacrifice of Christ but may also reflect media, policy, and social constructs. See Jan Van Dijk, Free the Victim: A Critique of the Western Conception of Victimhood, *International Review of Victimology* 16(1) (2009) 1–33.

dissociative mind techniques, others reward their resilient 'self' with the freedom of their imagination, and a number may even abuse their peers, by stealing rations in refugee camps, for example, or placing others in harm's way to protect themselves. While the conception of 'victim' as a key identity may not reflect local contextual understandings, it does enable victims to tap into legal rights that they can use to pressurize the state to act. Some victims can resist notions of passivity and speak out, demanding that their rights be fulfilled. One interviewee, who now runs a women's support network for those who have suffered sexual violence, put this in her own terms:

> When I was forcedly displaced, because I was going to be murdered by the perpetrators after the sexual assault, I turned to sexual exploitation. And while doing that, I tried to kill many men. Because I thought: if I was raped by three men, why do I have to sell my body to men? Why can't I be violent against men as well?[61]

While other victims interviewed belonged to armed groups and rejected notions of passivity in some ways, they did share the belief that the victim identity was a tool for claims-making and struggling for change. As one victim in Colombia said: 'We use [the word "victim"] to make demands, and I don't think that another word is necessary, because with that word we have achieved everything we have managed to get.'[62]

A presumption of passivity and vulnerability can also be observed in some organizations' preference to overprotect individuals on the basis of their presumed trauma and vulnerability, ultimately depriving them of the autonomy that should be returned to them.[63] Identity politics should also reconsider identity-driven gatekeepers that reproduce damning identity-narratives, in which 'one is the victim and the other is the saviour',[64] thereby recreating a divide between 'the incapable and passive victim' and 'the expert and superior NGO'. Whilst ethically it is vital to limit retraumatization, safeguards do not have to centralize around a strict policy where individuals are presumed to be unable to make their own choices.

Cohen suggests that passivity and silence can be considered 'implicatory denial', in that violations are known but victims also suffer from inaction by society in not doing the 'right' thing about it.[65] Silence sits in contrast to identity as performance,

[61] I have withheld the interview reference here to protect this individual's identity.

[62] C15 FG1, Colombia, March 2019.

[63] See Janine Natalya Clark, De-Centring Trauma: Conflict-Related Sexual Violence and the Importance of Resilience Discourse, *International Journal of Human Rights* 22(6) (2018) 801–821. There is a similar trope in fieldwork where the overprotection of victims is based on their trauma. July 2018 in Uganda and September 2018 in Colombia.

[64] Tshepo Madlingozi, On transitional Justice Entrepreneurs and the Production of Victim, *International Journal of Transitional Justice* 2(2) (2010) 208–228, p210.

[65] Stanley Cohen, *States of Denial*, Polity (2000) p9.

as it is the 'absence of speech'.[66] Silence can also reflect the involuntary non-participation of victims due to their economic, social, or linguistic exclusion from transitional justice. Victims may be silent as a result of 'silencing', which itself may be due to marginalization, discrimination, blaming, or may be self-imposed.[67] In other words, while silence may appear to be a 'choice', it can be imposed by the environments or structures in which victims live.[68] Victims may also be unable to articulate or find the appropriate vocabulary to articulate their suffering, which, according to Obradović-Wochnik, adds another layer of silence.[69] In Uganda, women were compelled to silence their preferred identity when in the company of revered professionals who might be able to help them, namely NGOs and medics, due to stigma or the risk of secondary harm.[70] In other contexts, silence can be imposed on victims because their experience of suffering goes against 'dominant narratives of conflict, victimization and organizational collective memory',[71] such as with females within armed groups.

The value of silence is debatable in societies transitioning from mass atrocities, with some seeing silence as morally reprehensible and a 'cruel pact of denial'.[72] Others point to non-Eurocentric cultures, where silence as a means of forgetting is valued for avoiding antagonism.[73] In such a way, silence can be a 'medium of expression, communication, and transmission of knowledge . . . that is not dependent on speech'.[74] Silence can seem at odds with the expressive goals of transitional justice in confronting society with its past and setting the record straight.[75] Ross argues that silence is assumed to be 'intrinsically damaging, and speech healing', and this view can have a 'high cost' for victims of sexual violence, for whom it can be humiliating to speak about 'intimate matters' in public.[76] Nevertheless there are increasing demands for states and transitional justice mechanisms to 'break the silence' around sexual violence and thereby the impunity of perpetrators in order

[66] Carol Kidron, Toward an Ethnography of Silence: The Lived Presence of the Past in the Everyday Life of Holocaust Trauma Survivors and Their Descendants in Israel, *Current Anthropology* 50(1) (2009) 5–27, p6.

[67] Jelena Obradović-Wochnik, The 'Silent Dilemma' of Transitional Justice: Silencing and Coming to Terms with the Past in Serbia, *International Journal of Transitional Justice* 7 (2013) 328–347, p335.

[68] ibid pp335–336.

[69] ibid p343.

[70] U4 FG1, Uganda, July 2018. This is analysed in Chapter 6.

[71] Cheryl Lawther, Transitional Justice and Constructing Victims and Victimhood, in Cheryl Lawther and L Moffett (eds), *Research Handbook on Transitional Justice*, Edward Elgar (2023) 174-190, p187.

[72] Martha Minow, *Between Vengeance and Forgiveness*, Beacon Press (1998) p16.

[73] Alexander Laban Hinton, *The Justice Façade: Trials of Transition in Cambodia*, OUP (2018) p234; and Kidron, n 66, p6.

[74] Kidron, n 66, p7.

[75] Janine Natalya Clark, Finding a Voice: Silence and its Significance for Transitional Justice, *Social and Legal Studies* 29(3) (2020) 355–378, p358.

[76] Fiona Ross, An Acknowledged Failure Women, Voice, Violence, and the South African Truth and Reconciliation Commission, in R Shaw, L Waldorf, and P Hazan (eds), *Localizing Transitional Justice: Interventions and Priorities after Mass Violence*, Stanford University Press (2010) 69–91, p83.

to prevent its repetition. Beyond the issue of stigma, highlighted in the previous chapter, victims of sexual violence remain silent because they do not want to be defined for the rest of their lives as only a 'rape victim',[77] suggesting that some identities stick more in the public mind than others. As a method of identity management of the self, remaining silent can be 'a means to protect the self and others, holding experience at bay or within so that its harm cannot ramify outward'.[78]

Silence can also be a survival strategy. For those who suffer, not identifying as a victim and remaining silent about their harm can be a means for them to maintain their self, and resist being defined by their identity as a victim. Ross notes that when bearing witness to the South African Truth and Reconciliation Commission, women avoided speaking about sexual violence in order to speak more about the broader impact of violence on their family and everyday struggles they faced under Apartheid.[79] Silence used in this way does not involve acquiescing, consenting, or 'passively accepting the status quo', but 'positively adapting to them and silently negotiating for the best possible outcome'.[80] Silence can reflect a period of time before victims mobilize and organize to challenge such silencing. One victim of sexual slavery in Uganda, for example, who faced stigma upon returning home found that silence was imposed on her:

> I had to be in silence, all of the suffering, hushed, because you don't want to tell this to anyone, because nobody in my family knew, not my children, no one, I was repressed, I fell in depression and anxiety, I still live like this, I still do.[81]

The woman is now part of a group of women who suffered similar experiences and meet to talk about their harm, not only to support each other, but to 'break the silence' and position themselves as engaging the community to prevent its recurrence. As another victim in the group said, 'Sexual violence was not an invention of the war, it was used as a weapon of terror, but sexual violence happens in the places that should be a shelter: home, school, university, inside society itself'.[82] As such, by breaking the silence, these victims were not only going beyond their own identity but challenging the discourse and social norms around the occurrence of sexual violence. Silence can be a way for victims to exercise agency, a way to remember the loss of a loved one in their own day-to-day activities, or a form of silent memorialization.[83] It can also represent a 'mode of resistance', which continues to

[77] Rosalind Shaw and Lars Waldorf, Localizing Transitional Justice, in Shaw et al. ibid., 3-26, p12.
[78] Ross, n 76, p89.
[79] ibid.
[80] Clark, n.63, pp366–367.
[81] U4 FG1, Gulu, Uganda, July 2018.
[82] U4 FG1, Gulu, Uganda, July 2018.
[83] Lauren Dempster, *Transitional Justice and the 'Disappeared' of Northern Ireland*, Routledge (2019) pp34–36.

be largely unrecognized.[84] Thus, the silence of victims needs to be kept in mind when designing and delivering reparations, in particular for those who have suffered sexual violence, and sensitively creating a space for them to come forward.

4.2.3 Innocence and blame

Victims are often considered blameless, in that someone else is responsible for their harm or misfortune. This conception can also reflect moral perceptions that a victim is innocent in the wrongdoing that has befallen them. To be considered blameless and worthy of the 'victim' identity, a person must keep themselves out of harm's way, otherwise they are blamed for their own misfortune.[85] Yet irrespective of the circumstances (eg even walking to gather firewood in daylight), victims of CRSV are often blamed, usually because of a facet of their identity, such as their sexual orientation, gender, or ethnicity. As such, victims may perpetually feel undeserving and hierarchize themselves by default. The struggle with identity becomes ever more acute as they try to summon the strength to epitomize society's unachievable stereotype of the 'true' victim as completely innocent, while simultaneously asking for their 'weaknesses' of pain and suffering to be redressed.[86] However, as acknowledged by Christie, gender norms are variable and weakness does not universally evoke sympathy.[87] In some societies, for example, a socially constructed 'ideal' victim does not exist, as persons suffering the crime are not considered victims: they are perceived as having fewer rights than others (eg because they are female) or as objects that things are done to; they are held responsible for the harm done to them in some way, to the extent that their weakness is a temptation for their offender and their behaviour is treated as suspect, including their refusal to accept the construct that they had a 'role' in their own victimization. Equally, victim profiles have become essentially feminized, racialized, and infantilized in international arenas, which, as Schwöbel-Patel argues, dangerously reduces their suffering to gender and neglects victims who identify as men.[88] Nonetheless, Christie's themes of victimhood are cross-cutting, and metaphorical typologies prompt international law to consider the ideal and non-ideal CRSV victim in each context.

[84] Régine Michelle Jean-Charles, Toward a Victim-Survivor Narrative: Rape and Form in Yvonne Vera's *Under the Tongue* and Calixthe Beyala's *Tu t'appelleras Tanga, Research in African Literatures* 45(1) 2014) 39–62, p45. In reference to Myriam Chancy in Framing Silence: Revolutionary Novels by Haitian Women; and Clark, n 75.

[85] Christie, n 33.

[86] Christine Schwöbel-Patel, The 'Ideal' Victim of International Criminal Law, *European Journal of International Law* 29(3) (2018) 703–724, p709.

[87] Christie, n 33, p21.

[88] Schwöbel-Patel, n 86, p711; and C S Mibenge, *Sex and International Tribunals: The Erasure of Gender from the War Narrative*, University of Pennsylvania Press (2013).

The identity of 'victim' is increasingly being interrogated to reflect that not all individuals fit into neat categories of innocent victim or evil perpetrator; rather, some can also be 'complex victims'.[89] This term reflects the experience of individuals who suffer violations but are also responsible for causing harm to others.[90] In the context of CRSV, a prime example of complex victims are female combatants who are subjected to reproductive violence, such as forced contraception and abortion. For example, in Colombia, it has been estimated that the FARC-EP carried out over 1,000 forced abortions per year.[91] The decision of the Constitutional Court of Colombia in the case of Helena aligns with this view. Helena (a pseudonym) was forcibly recruited to the FARC when she was 14 years old. During her time in the armed group, her commander exerted control over her sexual and reproductive autonomy by enforcing a 'no pregnancy' policy including the use of mandatory contraception which involved a self-injection monthly.[92] This form of long-acting, reversible contraception decreases bone mineral density and is therefore considered appropriate for those under 18 only after other methods have been considered.[93] However, Helena did fall pregnant and was subjected to a forced abortion, resulting in physical and psychological harm.[94] Helena was initially denied victim status according to Law 1448 of 2011 (Victims Law) and therefore deemed ineligible for reparations from the Victims Unit. This was overturned by the Constitutional Court which considered the case of forced abortion and contraception of an armed group member as amounting to sexual violence related to the conflict.[95] Recognizing such fighters as victims highlights that individuals do not fit into neat categories. As Lawther argues, it is important to acknowledge 'the complexities and contradictions of the victim identity [as it] is part of recognizing the complex and messy reality of conflict and the personal, social and political contexts in which victimization and involvement in conflict occurs'.[96]

Aside from unsafe medical procedures, methods such as abdominal trauma have been used to deliberately induce miscarriages and women have been killed to prevent births; such acts have been recognized by international criminal justice bodies, although recognition of the commission within an armed group is an

[89] See Erica Bouris, *Complex Political Victims*, Kumarian Press (2007).

[90] See Luke Moffett, Reparations for 'Guilty Victims': Navigating Complex Identities of Victim–Perpetrators in Reparation Mechanisms, *International Journal of Transitional Justice* 10(1) (2016) 146–167.

[91] Women's Link Worldwide, Una violencia sin nombre: violencia reproductiva en el conflicto armado colombiano [A Nameless Violence: Reproductive Violence in the Colombian Armed Conflict] (2020), para 25.

[92] Case SU599/19, Constitutional Court of Colombia, 11 December 2019, pp4–8.

[93] This also includes an evaluation of risks and benefits every two years for those wishing to continue progestogen-only injectable forms of contraception. See Progestogen-only Injectable Contraception, Faculty of Sexual and Reproductive Health: Clinical Effectiveness Unit, October 2020, pp4–5.

[94] Case SU599/19, Constitutional Court of Colombia, 11 December 2019, pp4–8.

[95] Case SU599/19, Constitutional Court of Colombia, 11 December 2019.

[96] Lawther, n 71, p179.

emerging area.[97] For instance, in the *Ntaganda* case at the ICC, former child soldiers subjected to sexual slavery and rape were recognized as victims, and even the children born of the defendant were eligible to be recognized as direct victims.[98] Similarly, in the subsequent case of *Ongwen*, girls and women who were abducted, raped, and kept in sexual slavery were recognized as victims. These included Ongwen's 'wives', who were forcibly detained, raped, and forced into pregnancy.[99] In such circumstances during times of conflict, victim identity is not clear cut; the more complex experience of some individuals, especially those involved with armed groups, complicates notions of blamelessness, passivity, and innocence and creates controversy around reparations for such individuals. In light of this discussion, it is worth reflecting more broadly on victim identity and CRSV informed by the victimology literature and data collected from my fieldwork.

4.2.4 Reflections on 'victim' identity

The facets of the 'victim' identity discussed above are all inextricably linked and work in unison to reinforce ideas of ideal victimhood that have begun to create unease for actors involved in CRSV. The overuse of the term 'victim' or its harm narrative risks inducing 'compassion-fatigue' and de-sensitization.[100] Positioning individuals as other, more relatable entities (such as patient, parent, or child) may have greater appeal to the rest of society.[101] One Ugandan health practitioner considered that using identity labels such as 'victim' or 'survivor' is stigmatizing, as it triggers 'extra secondary psychological thought' that reminds individuals of the dreadful situation they underwent, and instead preferred using 'client'.[102] This was shared by another Ugandan doctor who considered 'client' as 'softer' and more 'neutral' than 'victim' or 'survivor'.[103] In contrast, one victim of rape in Peru felt that the words 'survivor' or 'victim' carried no stigma.[104] One Colombian doctor also suggested that the use of 'victim' was not stigmatizing, but instead helped to

[97] The *Akayesu* judgment of the ICTR acknowledged that Hutu militia beat and tortured pregnant women—whose pregnancy resulted from sexual relations with Tutsi men—with the aim of inducing miscarriages. In other instances, the pregnant women were killed. See Transcript, *Akayesu* (ICTR-96-4-T), Trial Chamber I, 17 January 1997, 428, 437; Civil Society Declaration on Sexual Violence, 2019, p19: Rosemary Grey, The ICC's First 'Forced Pregnancy' Case in Historical Perspective, *Journal of International Criminal Justice* 15(5) (2017) 905–930.

[98] *Ntaganda*, Judgment, ICC-01/04-02/06-2359, 8 July 2019, para 979; Reparations Order, ICC-01/04-02/06-2659, 8 March 2021, para 123.

[99] *Ongwen*, Judgment, ICC-02/04-01/15-1762-Red, 4 February 2021, paras 3056–3062.

[100] See Elaine Zook Barge, Breaking Cycles of Violence: Building Healthy Individuals and Communities. The Center for Justice and Peacebuilding, Village STAR Manual 2011, Eastern Mennonite University (2007).

[101] Govier, n 27, p5.

[102] U6, Lira, Uganda, July 2018.

[103] U7, Lira, Uganda, July 2018.

[104] P14, Lima, Peru, May 2019.

distinguish individuals from ordinary patients, and allowed them access to a programme that offered them 'special and continuing attention' for their harm.[105] One public health expert in Colombia expressed the view that those individuals who preferred being called 'victims' did so not to reflect the 'essence' of their experience, but rather as a 'strategy'.[106] This reflected the stage they were at in seeking justice, receiving reparations, and more generally in their recovery. It also depended on whether they enjoyed a stronger political position than those for whom the public feels only a generalized sympathy for their suffering.[107]

Exclusively focusing on constructions of victimhood risks bypassing or silencing those who do not wish to be embroiled in the politics of victimhood and publicize their suffering. Some individuals remain silent and avoid publicly identifying as a victim despite living with the harmful consequences of sexual violence and try to manage their suffering by themselves, which is discussed in further detail in Chapter 7. Van Dijk suggests finding alternative terms or identities for victims of crime; some languages spoken in China and Japan, for example, use more neutral terms, such as 'harmed party'.[108] Therefore, moving to more neutral identities is not without precedent. As highlighted by cultural victimology, the discourse behind identities will be shaped by society's vision of justice. Perhaps a more neutral term, such as 'survivor' or 'patient', can help broach some of these issues when dealing with those affected by CRSV.

4.3 Survivor Identity

Rock observes that victims may have reservations over their victim status, exacerbated by the rise of competing survivor identities at a time when strength and resilience in the aftermath of trauma are highly rated by society.[109] The powerless and passive discourse is so strongly imprinted that some victims feel 'locked in' and that reconstructions of identity are extremely arduous.[110] In interviews with war victims in Afghanistan, Saeed observed that educated professionals self-identified as survivors, whereas less affluent individuals opted for the term 'victim'.[111] These differences were attributed to the sense of empowerment felt through education and financial comfort, which conflicted with depictions of passivity. Indeed in Iraq, in contrast to the depravations carried out by ISIS, those who were sexual enslaved by them wanted to be identified as 'survivors', which is symbolically reflected in

[105] C8, Bogotá, Colombia, September 2018.
[106] C12, Bogotá, Colombia, February 2019.
[107] C12, Bogotá, Colombia, February 2019.
[108] Van Dijk, n 60, pp1–2.
[109] Paul Rock, *Constructing Victims' Rights: The Home Office, New Labour, and Victims*, OUP (2004).
[110] Van Dijk, n 60, pp2–3.
[111] Huma Saeed, Victims and Victimhood. *International Journal of Transitional Justice* 10(1) (2016) 168–178, p176.

the law (Yazidi [Female] Survivor Law). Though some who benefited from the law have noted that the term 'survivor' has become common parlance in reminding people that a person was sexually violated, which like the victim identity, can be all consuming of a person's external identity in society.[112]

'Survivor' and its verb form, 'survive', frequent the discourse on a wide range of lethal and non-life-threatening events, including surviving an illness, attempted suicide, and marital divorce.[113] A number of international NGOs have framed their work around survivors, such as 'All Survivors', which works on male sexual violence, and the Global Survivors Fund, which advocates for reparations for those who suffer sexual violence during conflict. This reflects broader trends in domestic practice in addressing sexual and domestic violence that transform the victim identity, with its associations of passivity and weakness, to the more empowering identity of 'survivor' to reflect individuals' resilience.[114] However, survivor-centred approaches to reparations can weigh heavily on the individual, giving less attention to the wider ecosystem and the interplay of factors that led to CRSV and need transforming.[115] This section investigates the apparent origins of the term 'survivor' in disciplines that care for individuals who have suffered sexual violence, as well as the implications in theory and practice of the survivor identity for CRSV. While victim and survivor are often used interchangeably at times by different actors, there is a strong discourse underlying both that is worth critically examining.

The identities of victim and survivor in relation to conflict- and non-conflict-related sexual violence are extensively used in praxis. Feminist scholars have argued that these terms should be applied to advance the best interests of vulnerable groups or highlight hidden violence against women and children. However, their usage also has generated a myriad of unintended consequences that continue to prevail in the context of sexual violence. For instance, the stigmatizing origins of the term 'victim' arguably can be traced back to efforts in the 1970s to highlight domestic and sexual violence; women 'traded off' the passive, innocent 'victim' role so that the violence they had experienced would be taken seriously.[116] This follows from feminist scholarship that proposed the survivor identity to challenge the depiction of female victims of domestic violence as inferior, both in strength

112 Moffett and Sperfeldt, n 54.

113 Michael Papendick and Gerd Bohner, 'Passive Victim—Strong Survivor'? Perceived Meaning of Labels Applied to Women Who Were Raped, *PLoS ONE* 12(5) (2017) 1–21; and Laura Anderson and Karen Gold, 'I Know What It Means But It's Not How I Feel', *Women & Therapy* 15(2) (1994) 5–17.

114 See Jennifer Dunn, 'Victims' and 'Survivors': Emerging Vocabularies of Motive for 'Battered Women Who Stay', *Sociological Inquiry* 75(1) (2005) 1–30; and Kaitlin Boyle and Kimberly Rogers, Beyond the Rape 'Victim'—'Survivor' Binary: How Race, Gender, and Identity Processes Interact to Shape Distress, *Sociological Forum* 35(2) (2020) 323–345.

115 Janine Natalya Clark, *Conflict-Related Sexual Violence and Transitional Justice. A Social-Ecological Framing*, Routledge (2023) p278.

116 Amy Leisenring, Confronting 'Victim' Discourses: The Identity Work of Battered Women, *Symbolic Interaction* 29(3) (2006) 307–330.

and substance, to the extent of being eternally 'in need' of saving from outsiders. In response, the survivor rubric emerged to confer perseverance and the ability to cope.[117]

While 'victimism' encouraged public empathy that brought about some change, such as making intra-marital rape illegal,[118] it also positions those affected as lacking agency. The principal tactic adopted by the original survivors' movement was awareness-raising by encouraging survivors to disclose their experience of trauma in meetings with each other and then to the wider public.[119] Metaphorical language from the inception of the survivor movement, such as on 'breaking the silence', to encouraging 'speak out', are being reinvigorated for the conflict arena,[120] which may not reflect the wishes of those affected by such violations.[121] Drawing upon Spry, using survivor language for sexual and gender-based violence (SGBV) may narrow the scope of our analysis.[122] Both 'victim' and 'survivor' act as a hegemonic barrier to the expression of women's experiences.[123] As a replacement for 'victim', and its negative connotations, 'survivor' was not universally embraced by feminists.[124] Conventional terminology compressed the nature of violence into physical terms, reducing the body to 'that [which] things are done to'.[125] Individuals may be entrapped by the choice of language, which can recycle the harm into vernacular forms. Spry goes so far as describing both *victim* and *survivor* as 'the assailant's language',[126] distracting from the 'otherness' of the experience of harm, loss, and intersectionality.

Govier claims 'survivor' is inappropriate when a certain amount of hardship has not been endured or significant obstacles not encountered. Determining this threshold of hardship is extremely subjective and relies on the concept of due deference commonly found in victimhood: only the person harmed knows the depths of their suffering.[127] These perceptions of hardship and 'innocence' are rooted in the meaning of 'survivor' in both the superficial and deep sense, although even the former can present significant daily challenges to those 'merely' trying to stay alive

[117] Anderson and Gold, n 113.

[118] Kathleen Barry, *Female sexual slavery*, New York University Press (1979) p44.

[119] See Ellen Bass and Louise Thornton, *I Never Told Anyone: Writings by Women Survivors of Child Sexual Abuse*, Harper Collins (1983).

[120] Ruth Seifert, The Second Front: The Logic of Sexual Violence in Wars, *Women's Studies International Forum* 19(1/2) (1996) 35-43, p37.

[121] Jelke Boesten and Marsha Henry, Between Fatigue and Silence: The Challenges of Conducting Research on Sexual Violence in Conflict, *Social Politics* 25(4) (2018) 568–588, p577.

[122] Tami Spry, In the Absence of Word and Body: Hegemonic Implications of 'Victim' and 'Survivor' in Women's Narratives of Sexual Violence, *Women and Language* 18(2) (1995) 27–32, p27.

[123] ibid.

[124] Julie Osmond speech in relation to a documentary commissioned by INTERVICT states that American feminists' proposal to replace victim with survivor was met with near universal approval, in Van Dijk, n 60, p3.

[125] Goffmann, n 7, p27

[126] Spry, n 122.

[127] Govier, n 27, pp67–69.

physiologically. Interestingly, studies have revealed that 'survivor', as opposed to 'victim' in non-conflict sexual violence is perceived as more life-threatening and grievous. This finding highlights that constructions of both identities are muddied and vary with time period and context.

As Papendick and Bohner have noted, 'survivor' is frequently used in reference to coping with the long-term effects of sexual violence, describing a harmed person who is no longer suffering, or at least not to the same degree. Therefore, advocates of 'survivor' framings may downplay the existential impact of CRSV,[128] the moral wrongfulness of the act, or its consequences for identity in later life. Reparations, which usually come years after CRSV, if at all, have come to be associated with the concept of the long-term survivor. Therefore, it may be pertinent to use terminology which encourages reparation in the immediate or short term; in this sense, 'victim' or 'patient' may be more appropriate. In the case of the Yazidi [Female] Survivor Law, if a person dies before they can make a claim, their family are not eligible, providing a stark limitation to remedying such sexual violence to only those who live. The passage of time implied in the transition from 'victim' to 'survivor' may give the impression that the consequences of sexual violence are no longer as great because the person has coped thus far, that is, that the temporal distance from the harmful act is inversely proportional to the severity of need. Similarly, survivor-resilience strategies can be perceived as mitigating the harm when the person is continuing to struggle with unmet needs. Interviewees who had suffered CRSV in Colombia, for example, disliked the term 'survivor' as it implied that 'the danger has passed',[129] and they considered their life after CRSV as 'not truly surviving'.[130] Surviving may also connote the experience of overcoming difficult circumstances, rather than the wrongful acts or crimes of others that cannot be so easily overcome. As one interviewee put it:

> [T]he word 'survivor' is related to . . . [the idea that] for example I survive a disease, I survive a natural disaster, or I survive an accident. But I am not a survivor of sexual violence. I don't survive sexual violence. The women who were victims of sexual violence, who were tortured, assassinated, they don't survive sexual violence.[131]

Many of these debates about the use of 'survivor' are being replicated in the context of transitional justice. The remainder of this section examines how the identity of survivor is engaged with in societies moving away from conflict under transitional justice, before discussing the intersections with medicine.

[128] Govier, n 27, p55.
[129] C3, Bogotá, Colombia, September 2018.
[130] C15 FG1, Bogotá, Colombia, March 2019.
[131] C3, Bogotá, Colombia, September 2018.

4.3.1 Survivor identity in transitional justice

Resilience has come to be associated with survivor identities; the term is believed to have originated as a reactionary resistance to the broken narrative of 'victim', which over-emphasizes passivity and powerlessness.[132] It can also reflect that being resilient and surviving does not change the status quo and may be the only way a person can exist due to a lack of alternatives.[133] Clark argues that the 'trauma model', which has been widely adopted by NGOs, risks overshadowing alternative and resilient discourses, noting that female survivors of sexual violence 'are often portrayed as "finished" products—as women who will always be deeply traumatised because they were raped'.[134] Paradoxically, positive psychology's concept of post-traumatic growth acknowledges that victims can grow beyond just surviving after trauma,[135] which does not fit with NGOs' imagining of the term survivor. In this context, the use of 'survivor' may help to recount successes as well as struggles,[136] in that *survivor* is a transitional identity that connotes the closure of one part of a person's life and the beginning of a more optimistic future.[137] Clark argues that rather than being something normative that survivors of CRSV 'ought to be' resilient, instead efforts should be made to create and facilitate 'environments that enable and foster resilience.[138] This is discussed in more depth in Chapter 7, but it is important to keep in mind in subsequent chapters when discussing reparation programming.

The survivor identity has come to be associated with certain blameless discourses in transitional justice, as typified by the young female civilian survivor of genocide or sexual violence. One can be a 'survivor' of deliberate human atrocity or natural disasters, regardless of one's innocence or otherwise. In relation to CRSV, predisposing patriarchal currents and gender stereotypes may extend to all individuals' profound guilt and remorse regardless of actual levels of responsibility for the harm. This may be reinforced by post-conflict societal stigma. Feelings such as guilt or remorse are not inevitable, but these 'survivor' attributes may traverse all individuals. An individual's self-condemnation may impact on their ability or willingness to move forward, arising as it does from the belief that no action they take will be beneficial given the chain of events leading to the previous traumatic situation. Equally, the valourization of the 'against all the odds' survivor may

[132] Boyle and Rogers, n 114, p328.
[133] Clark, n 115, p3.
[134] Clark, n 63, p805.
[135] Rachel Lev-Wiesel, Beyond Survival: Growing out of Childhood Sexual Abuse, in Stephen Joseph and P Alex Linley (eds), Trauma, Recovery, and Growth: Positive Psychological Perspectives on Posttraumatic Stress, Wiley (2008) p154.
[136] Govier, n 27, p53.
[137] Rachel Klimmek and Jennifer Wenzel, Adaptation of the Illness Trajectory Theory to Describe the Work of Transitional Cancer Survivorship, *Oncology Nursing Forum* 39(6) (2012) E499–510.
[138] Clark, n 155, p4.

pressurize other individuals into adopting a similar outlook or engaging in actions with which they are uncomfortable. Likewise, the 'survivor to thriver' trope is commonly associated with CRSV victims who have not just overcome their trauma but also transitioned to a more productive and positive position in life.[139] As the experience of sexual violence victims demonstrates, being a survivor in the deep sense means adapting to one's environment or situation, igniting the active, competent 'self'.[140]

While 'survivor' is often associated with notions of innocence, the identity of victim-perpetrators and complex perpetrators (that is, persons who perpetrate to survive) are often tangled up with the perception that sexual violence is sometimes committed as 'an act of survival'. In some circumstances, the ramifications of a person choosing not to commit sexual violence can range from ostracization and reduced 'protection' from warring parties to threats of sexual violence, such as genital mutilation and forced stripping, or execution. Cohen has problematized our assumptions about dominant rape narratives, suggesting alternatives to the weapon-of-war discourse.[141] Cohen states that internal cohesion incentives promote the commission of rape, either willingly to enhance solidarity, or under duress.[142] These motives may be interpreted as survival strategies. Survivor justifications can be used to absolve a person of their responsibility, casting them as less complicit because they succumbed to the 'external' pressures of group identity to survive, and precipitating 'internal' struggles of self. As such, 'survivor' may be a closely held identity for some perpetrators of CRSV. This uncomfortable narrative of 'perpetrating to survive' in transitional justice may be ancillary to the claim of 'survivorship' and reparation.

In sum, the survivor identity needs to be contextualized. Survivor as an identity can be used by a range of actors including perpetrators, bystanders, and those who suffer, which risks morally equating the experiences of victims with perpetrators and undermining its value as a distinctive identity. That said, it can also serve to mediate the experience of victims, enabling them to move forward from past abuses. This underscores the need to take greater care when using the term and not to assume that the pioneering replacement of 'victim' with 'survivor' meets the needs of all persons or is without consequence. In the early stages of post-trauma, survivor identity may be conducive to healing, but it can lose its beneficial effect if it is not renegotiated into an 'evolving sense of self'.[143] In this sense, the survivor identity is applicable not only to transitional justice but also to medicine.

[139] Christine Dinsmore, *From Thriving to Surviving. Incest, Feminism and Recovery*, State University of New York Press (1991) p190.
[140] Govier, n 27, pp29–30.
[141] Dara Kay Cohen, *Rape During Civil War*, Cornell University Press (2016) pp17–55.
[142] ibid pp26–31.
[143] Alexis Phillips and Judith Daniluk, Beyond 'Survivor': How Childhood Sexual Abuse Informs the Identity of Adult Women at the End of the Therapeutic Process, *Journal of Counseling and Development* 82(2) (2004) 177–184, p178.

4.3.2 Survivor as a medical concept

There are some healthcare guidelines in relation to sexual violence or abuse that use the term 'survivor'. Schachter et al consciously choose *survivor* over *victim* in many situations to 'acknowledge the strength and resourcefulness of individuals' and thereby to confer a different type of recognition of victims, which is less concerned with their experience of trauma. The authors are aware that the words 'survivor, patient, client, or individual' have different connotations, and yet are interchangeably used and without scrutiny to refer to those seeking care.[144] It may be instructive to draw upon findings in medicine with regards to the use of 'survivor' terminology to ensure the term is not diminished by overuse, nor represented as a subject of fascination for researchers. Compared to any other medical specialty, oncology has overwhelmingly featured survivor narratives.[145] Survivor terminology preceded the identity phenomenon in oncological research and guidelines: 'cancer survivor rates' are often depicted as percentages and accorded to every stage of a carcinoma.

Holistic cancer care has hypothesized the benefits of the 'survivor' discourse in terms not only of the physical but also 'the social, psychological, spiritual, and existential impact of cancer on one's life for the remainder of one's life'.[146] The assumed psychological benefits of the term 'survivor'[147] may explain why its use has concentrated on chronic medical conditions, or those requiring intense treatment and surveillance. Park et al found that in persons who have lived through cancer, survivor narratives yielded better psychological outcomes and contributed to positive interactions with healthcare providers.[148] There are no such empirical studies on the use of 'survivor' in the context of CRSV. Nevertheless, survivor inferences in any setting may help to redirect focus to the remainder of a person's life, liberating that person of their trauma despite physical co-morbidities and their psychosocial effects. The cancer literature reflects a similarly indiscriminate belief in the positive impact of the survivor identity on a person's life, irrespective of their lifespan: 'the term survivorship represents living after a diagnosis of cancer, regardless of how long a person lives'.[149] That said, the term 'survivor' is clearly inappropriate for some patients, such as those with terminal cancer, for

[144] Candice Schachter et al, *Handbook on Sensitive Practice for Healthcare Practitioners: Lessons from Adult Survivors of Childhood Sexual Abuse*, Ottawa: Public Health Agency of Canada (2011) pp3–4.

[145] Survivor as an identity has also been developed further by corporate marketing and fundraising bodies for research. For cause-related health marketing, see Clare Patton, Breast Cancer Cause-Marketing: Reworking the Social Contract, *Commercial Law Practitioner* 24(3) (2017) 43.

[146] Crystal Park, Ianita Zlateva, and Thomas Blank, Self-identity After Cancer: 'Survivor', 'Victim', 'Patient', and 'Person with Cancer', *Journal of General Internal Medicine* 24(Suppl 2) (2009) 430–435, p430.

[147] See Michael A Andrykowski, Emily Lykins, and Andrea Floyd, Psychological Health in Cancer Survivors, *Seminars in Oncology Nursing* 24(3) (2008) 193–201; and Park et al, n 146.

[148] Park, Zlateva, and Blank, n 146.

[149] ibid, p430.

whom survival is not possible, and can place an onus on the person to exhibit resilience. Others may live for some years and yet feel they are only partly surviving, instead existing as a shadow of their former self.[150] As a result, cancer patients often reject the term.[151]

Similarly, in post-conflict settings, the threat of SGBV can remain high, health complications prevail, and children suffer intergenerational harms, which can create difficulties for individuals who view themselves as survivors.[152] The gender-health interface was apparent in the victims interviewed for this book. Some women disfavoured the term 'survivor' because they felt it was not possible to truly 'survive' when living with a life-limiting health condition or when enduring, either directly or indirectly, the consequences of the harm for their children. Others saw their survival as dependent on continuing to receive the support they currently had, as one victim of forced sterilization explained: 'I have continuously received support from my psychologist, and it's like you have to live with the psychologist by your side to survive.'[153]

Drawing upon oncology perspectives,[154] the term 'survivor' applies to everyone who suffers sexual violence. However, Mullan, a medical physician who had cancer, suggests that survivorship is linked with expected behaviours, whereas *survival* as a concept might be more appropriate:

> Survival, in fact, begins at the point of diagnosis, because that is the time when patients are forced to confront their own mortality and begin to make adjustments that will be part of their immediate and to some extent, long-term future.[155]

Applying this perspective to CRSV, it may make the survivor identity more inclusive by incorporating the notion of survival. As currently conceived, the term 'survivor' can be criticized for excluding those who died during CRSV or from their concurrent injuries.[156] The focus on those who stay alive creates a hierarchy of survivors, with the most resilient at the apex. It is arguable that *survival* in the context of victimhood may more accurately represent a person's effort and resilience against poor odds.

[150] See Zilka Spahić Šiljak, Victim or Survivor? Choosing Identity After Wartime Sexual Violence, in Julianne Funk, Nancy Good, and Marie E Berry (eds), *Healing and Peacebuilding After War*, Routledge (2020) 121–132.

[151] Park, Zlateva, and Blank, n 146, p430.

[152] U13, Lira, Uganda, July 2018.

[153] P2 FG1, Lima, Peru, May 2019.

[154] Oncology is a medical specialty concerned with the understanding and treatment of cancer.

[155] Fitzhugh Mullan, Seasons of Survival: Reflections of a Physician With Cancer, *New England Journal of Medicine* 313(4) (1985) 270–273, p271.

[156] Govier, n 27, p30.

Survivor as a medical identity in forensics

The term survivor is also seeping into forensic work, with some framing forensic efforts around survivor-centred documentation.[157] This may become problematic as the legal terms of victim (and complainant) are important to understanding who has been subjected to the sexual offence. They also represent the neutrality and understanding of forensic physicians when conducting their work. Thus, 'survivor-centred forensic investigation' could risk undermining the legitimacy of this important work and the role of clinicians as neutral in these investigations. Using legal terms such as victim, which can be prefixed by 'alleged' for documentation purposes, focuses on the wrongfulness of the crime. It is not possible to be an alleged survivor. Forensic medicine evolved from the need to investigate and ascertain cause of death.[158] A dignified approach should still be centred on the victims and may overlap with what is considered 'survivor-centred', but has the advantage of bringing the sexual offences to the fore, while still upholding the integrity of these investigations. Furthermore, forensic pathology also crucially encompasses those who did not survive the violence, making it important to be respectful of those deceased victims and their families, as well as persons who feel they are not surviving according to the trope. Where options exist and informed consent is obtained, it is important to be mindful of additional sensitivities in language surrounding the products of conception resulting from an abortion or miscarriage.

In summary, the concepts of survival, survivor, and survivorship are interlinked. As with the term 'victim', however, being labelled or identifying as a survivor brings its own imbued notions. More neutral language that can overcome some of the baggage of 'victim' and 'survivor' may be found in the use of the patient identity.

4.4 Patient Identity

> I absolutely think there should be much more flexibility in terminology. I also think that these things that are changing should be approached as something that can change. I tend to refer to groups of people I know or in the general abstract sense as survivors but I fully recognise that is an individual choice. Somehow we need to bring back the humane element, the fact that we are talking about people rather than numbers or just the category of a crime. It becomes very challenging in judicial contexts like Kosovo. I also think that this discussion around patient or people, it comes back to this issue, does it have to be specifically limited to the crime and then how do you prove that.[159]

[157] Physicians for Human Rights, Strategic Plan 2025–2028, pp12 and 14

[158] Jonathan Wyatt et al, *Oxford Handbook of Forensic Medicine*, OUP (2011) pp4–5.

[159] I2, the Hague, October 2018.

Although individuals may self-ascribe their identity as a victim or survivor, or be labelled as such by others, a medical threshold must be crossed for an individual to be labelled as, or to claim the identity of, a patient. Whilst 'survivor' emerged as a response to the negative connotations of 'victims' suffering SGBV, the use of 'patient' as another alternative to 'victim' has not been promoted, as it is firmly associated with medicine. In some Western translations, 'patient' embodies the 'sick role', cultivating an impression of 'passivity and powerlessness' comparable to that of 'victim'.[160] In practice, however, there are many definitions of patient, even within the medical sphere. 'Patient' may be defined simply as a person who suffers. *Black's Medical Dictionary* defines the term as: 'A person with an injury, physical or mental disorder or disease, or abnormality who comes into the care of a health professional or of an institution responsible for providing care to such persons'.[161] However, 'patient' may also encompass well persons engaging with healthcare, such as primary prevention or screening. Similar to 'victim', 'patient' embodies a rights entitlement to the 'highest attainable standard of physical and mental health'.[162] In this section, the usefulness of a patient identity in achieving adequate reparation for CRSV is examined, including whether presumed medical neutrality can help allay the stigma of sexual violence in terms of blame and taboo.

Burns urges all disciplines to learn general ethics from 'the patient'.[163] Medicine and transitional justice have different priorities and values, and despite interacting with those who suffer, practitioners often work in 'parallel silos'.[164] Some principles in relation to care have infiltrated transitional justice. 'Victim-centred' is comparable to 'patient-centred' care, in that both terms place foreground suffering. The rights discourse has drawn greater attention to individuals' experience and enjoyment of rights, whether as reparations or healthcare, as key components of their dignity.[165] It is also intuitive to view these individuals as patients in order to 'repair' the harm, or, where this is not possible, to provide them with 'care'; this is most evident where public health resources are limited. Input from medical specialism may also contribute to broadening understanding of such crimes of a 'sexual nature', as well as cultural nuances in medical cross-territorial practice.

[160] Park, Zlateva, and Blank, n 146; and Talcott Parsons, Illness and the Role of the Physician: A Sociological Perspective, *American Journal of Orthopsychiatry* 21(3) (1951) 452–460.

[161] *Blacks Medical Dictionary*, 41st Edition A & C Black Publishers Limited (2005), http://medicine.kaums.ac.ir/UploadedFiles/Files/Blacks_Medical_Dictionary.pdf, accessed 1 August 2025. See also Reva Rubin, Theory of Clinical Nursing, *Nursing Research* 15(3) (1968) 210–212, p210, where she defines it as 'Persons undergoing subjectively involved experiences of varying degrees of tension or stress in a health situation'.

[162] Article 12(1), 1966 International Covenant on Economic, Social and Cultural Rights.

[163] Lawrence Burns, What Does the Patient Say? Levinas and Medical Ethics, *Journal of Medicine and Philosophy* 42 (2017) 214–235, p226.

[164] Sylvia Servaes and Natascha Zupan, In Larger Justice: Linking Health Care, Transitional Justice and Peacebuilding, *Journal of Peacebuilding and Development* 8(3) (2013) 64–68, p64.

[165] Burns, n 163, p215.

Having highlighted the relevance of the patient identity for transitional justice discussions on addressing CRSV, it is worth exploring the merit of medico-legal identities for CRSV. The following section is divided into three subsections exploring the themes of stigma and transformation of negative norms; the use of 'patient' as a dignified approach to redressing the harm of CRSV; and its role as empowerment; and ethical reparation.

4.4.1 Stigma and transforming negative norms

The two dominating identities in CRSV, victim and survivor, each encompass their own specific stigma that circulate around blame, passivity, and resilience. Thus, persons are expected to conform to the stereotype of a victim, a survivor, or both by making a 'healthy' transition from one to the other. In theory, medicine's neutral stance disregards any such expectations or predilections on a person who has suffered CRSV, thereby shifting focus to the resultant health consequences of the harm and prevention of complications. Stigma is lost in the objective to provide impartial care based solely on the person's status as a patient, discriminating on the basis of medical need alone.[166] For victims of CRSV, access to services is influenced not only by medical urgency but also by their financial resources, as economic barriers frequently impede consistent and timely care. However, the commonality of the patient identity when seeking healthcare for a sexual or intimate complaint following CRSV provides the basis for a dignified response to the harm inflicted, which maintains confidentiality and reduces fear of being exposed to the community. In Uganda, patient identities were appreciated for such discretion. Where medical professionals can give assurances of privacy, it may encourage those 'silently suffering' to seek help for sensitive health problems that may interfere with many aspects of their daily life. The utility of stigma mitigation is captured in the following statement from a female victim, as translated by an interpreter:

> She feels she would be more comfortable to say she's a patient like any other. People from the community, to identify ourselves as a victim because sometimes as she's talking to the medical person, probably there are people around her and then she feels like it's a sort of victimising her, victimisation.[167]

In practice, across all sites where empirical research was conducted, stigma was perceived to seep into the ethical practice of medics, albeit to varying degrees. In these cases, the value of the patient identity was diminished and trust in the

[166] General Medical Council (GMC), Good Medical Practice, 2013; WHO, A Human Rights-Based Approach to Health, 2010, p2.
[167] U13, Gulu, Uganda, July 2018.

altruistic efforts of healthcare providers was compromised. In Uganda, CRSV victims spoke of how a large segment of the population viewed themselves as victims irreconciled with the past, including those with elite or respectable positions in the community. Perceptions of bias in healthcare were evident in interviews with those affected by CRSV:

> If you identify yourself as a victim of the LRA war you find maybe the medic that you're talking to probably was also in one way or another affected by the conflict and then may not give you the necessary treatment, and then at some point may give you a wrong injection.[168]

A patient identity is not enough to ensure confidentiality and a dignified healthcare response. As with most identities, it depends on the adjuncts to the label. These can be condensed into four domains: where one is identified as a patient (context); by whom; for what purpose (appropriateness, intention); and in what manner (body language, vocality, visual aids, explanation for use). The latter was exemplified by one victim's view of 'the colour code' in Colombia, where women who have suffered sexual violence are given a purple armband, known as 'the purple code', to ensure doctors and nurses do not repeatedly ask the same sensitive questions unnecessarily. Yet this explicit mark attached to the physical 'self' becomes a visual target for further stigma. In Colombia, this quickly became common knowledge among other patients, visitors, and personnel not bound by equivalent medical ethics. As one female affected by CRSV found

> Yes, this armband is a label. And if we go backwards, from the first moment when the doorman meets the woman, he starts pointing at her: 'That woman over there has been raped.' So this is why we often decide not to go to the hospital and prefer to remain in silence.[169]

Coding is a standard safeguarding measure to ensure discretion and maintain confidentiality, usually featuring in patient records, handover sheets, or summary boards.[170] In abstract terms, the label 'patient' should function as a signal of possible suffering and a prompt to proceed with care and sensitivity.[171] However, the clinical focus can take for granted how identities/labels are (mis)construed. In my own medical practice with victims of sexual violence, we are often encouraged to frame the person as a patient, or given our evidential role in supporting a possible

[168] U4, FG1, Gulu, Uganda, July 2018.
[169] C4, Bogotá, Colombia, September 2018.
[170] See GMC, Confidentiality: Good Practice in Handling Patient Information, 2017, paras 81–85.
[171] Mireille Lavoie, Thomas de Koninck, and Danielle Blondeau, The Nature of Care in Light of Emmanuel Levinas, *Nursing Philosophy* 7(4) (2006) 225–234, p227.

future prosecution, as the 'complainant'. Often in building rapport with the patient, we use their name and avoid language like 'complainant', which can give an overly legalistic and objective stance to their suffering, and suggest that they are complaining or alleging harm without proof. This can undermine their trust and willingness to engage in the intimate forensic examination/collection process. While sometimes we have an obligation to notify the police, the choice often remains with the victim on whether they want to press charges. Forensic medical officers are there to treat the patient in a dignified way while documenting and collecting evidence alongside providing therapeutic treatment, which can range from counselling, STI screening, emergency contraception, and referral for surgery.

Whilst medicine's focus on the dignity of patients has inspired other disciplines,[172] such as palliative care and nursing, 'dignity fatigue' also permeates medical practice.[173] Care here is defined as 'a human trait, an affect or feeling, an interpersonal interaction, a moral imperative, and a series of therapeutic practices'.[174] A general overstretching of resources worsened by conflict, as well as increased demands on outcomes, can detract from 'bedside' standards.[175] Some forensic experts have acknowledged the need to 'regroup' and analyse the manner in which customary medical terms such as 'patient' are used.

> Yes, the terms used in the healthcare system should be, because sometimes aren't, more respectful and neutral so that a social revictimization does not occur to those who have been already assaulted. A lot of work is needed in changing many medical terms so that terms are much more respectful of human dignity.[176]

Meredith urges practitioners to use the term 'victim' with 'care', taking a dignity-orientated approach so as not to devalue the person.[177] Such an approach recognizes all the baggage that the identity of victim incurs, and to see those who suffer as human beings, to respect their dignity in terms of understanding their experience and circumstances, and to treat them with compassion. Yet a 'patient'-only approach may submerge the context in which harm occurs by focusing on the individual harm and not the broader circumstances in which such suffering occurred.

[172] Valerie Meredith, Victim Identity and Respect for Human Dignity: A Terminological Analysis, *International Review of the Red Cross* 91(874) (2009) 259–278.

[173] See Lillemor Lindwall and Vibeke Lohne, Human Dignity Research in Clinical Practice—A Systematic Literature Review, *Scandinavian Journal of Caring Sciences* 35(4) (2021) 1038–1049.

[174] Janice M Morse et al, *Advances in Nursing Science* 13(1) (1990) 1–14.

[175] ibid.

[176] C13, Bogotá, Colombia, March 2019.

[177] Meredith, n 172, p265.

4.4.2 Patient identity as empowerment

Victims may be dissuaded from presenting to healthcare facilities where they will be accorded another identity that traditionally implies a lack of control.[178] Others relinquish this role, using their harm and suffering to lament their status as victims. Yet the 'powerless' *victim* can acquire new skills and realization through reconstructions of 'active' *patient*-hoods. Modern medicine is acutely aware of some patients' tendency to abdicate responsibility for their own health. Hence, attempts to inject an ethos of partnership and joint decision-making in non-life-threatening situations is commonplace. A person may be passive in that a harm occurred largely outside their control, but they may be able to assert agency with regard to decisions during the initial assault or the aftermath. Accepting the patient or victim role should not unreasonably extend the perception of powerlessness to other contexts, even if related to the harm. Transition between identities over time may evoke responsible action.[179] In some settings, the desire to rebalance relationships has encouraged the cultivation of contemporary medical identities of *client* and *beneficiary*. Such identities dissuade the use of isolating medical lingo, demonstrating that healthcare professionals are not immune from the governance of other professions who have clients (from lawyers to hairdressers) or from the divides therein. In legal spheres, the professional–client relationship actually strengthens ethical obligations under the fiduciary principle. Nonetheless, as with other replacements for the term 'victim', caution must be exercised when applying the 'client' label, which is not always 'best suited' to those in most need of care.

4.4.3 Patient identity and ethical reparation

The use of patient terminology need not be restricted to the medical context. Although its aim is to rise above the usual 'identity politics', adopting a patient identity contributes to tensions by opening a portal through which everyone partied to the conflict can access reparations. This could be addressed through more active use of the 'patient' terminology in reparation processes by encouraging transitional justice practitioners to engage with the totality of harm when developing reparative strategies, to consider the patient as an 'access point' through which health impairments can be identified against the backdrop of CRSV, and to appreciate the interplay between health consequences and identity in the aftermath of sexual violence. Even when the harm is irreparable, palliation is predicated on the idea that the pain a patient experiences is never justifiable or useful.[180] Hence,

[178] See Park, Zlateva, and Blank, n 146.
[179] Viktor E Frankl, *Man's Search For Meaning*, Rider (2008) p140.
[180] Lavoie, de Konick, and Blondeau, n 171, p220.

if reparations are unable to deliver their mandate of repair, an ethic of care—commonly symbolized by the 'patient'—may be therapeutic and may serve to re-instate some civic trust.

As Burns observed, the 'practical and symbolic importance assigned to the patient physician relationship is largely the result of two factors: first, the physician's demonstrated (or hoped for) power to heal; and second, its inescapability'.[181] The first of these is the good intention to 'heal' or 'repair'; the second, 'inescapability', depends on the physician demonstrating a commitment to heal. Beyond the practical component of transitional justice relationships is the symbolic element, what De Greiff often refers to as civic trust.[182] However, it is within the smaller, daily relationships between state or transitional justice representatives—such as health-care practitioners who deliver rehabilitation programmes—that the two powerful effects of the patient–physician relationship described by can be emulated. As obligations to provide reparations are not legally enforceable, the latter can only be encouraged, although the overlap between the rehabilitation of health and human rights places a minimum duty of care on all physicians.

4.5 Conclusion

Identity is both a uniquely personal sense of self and a public construct. This chapter has unpacked some of the different identities that individuals who suffer sexual violence can 'perform' or 'mask' themselves with in order to seek redress. The tensions within the concept of identity are apparent in CRSV, where cultural barriers of stigma and discrimination continue to shape the way in which individuals affected by such violence can be recognized and access reparations. There is no escaping the positive and negative repercussions of any identity discourse;[183] however, this should not foster complacency towards label-induced harms. Orwell urges us to 'let the meaning choose the word', an approach which encourages the use of alternatives when the meaning of a word evolves, or its negative by-products become distracting.[184] Cameron rates language as inept at expressing women's primary concerns. The absence or silencing of alternative terminology in relation to sexual violence may perpetuate misunderstandings, which is particularly concerning where sexual health and the intimate body experiences remain taboo.[185] Furthermore, referring to women as victims or survivors classifies them

[181] Burns, nv163, p214.
[182] Pablo de Greiff, Justice and Reparations, in Pablo de Greiff (ed), *Handbook of Reparations* OUP (2006) 451–477, p463.
[183] Steven Angelides, Feminism, Child Sexual Abuse, and the Erasure of Child Sexuality, *GLQ: A Journal of Lesbian and Gay Studies* 10(2) (2004) 141–177, p162.
[184] George Orwell, *Why I Write*, Penguin (2014) p118.
[185] Deborah Cameron, Introduction, *The Feminist Critique of Language: A Reader*, Routledge (1990) p13.

as a 'reified status' of gender,[186] where their suffering is shaped by gender and its performativity, such as social expectations and taboos. Gender conceptualizations have progressed, but terminology on sexual violence has not.[187]

To ensure language imperfections do not become a barrier to engagement, transitional justice has the opportunity to open up the space for individuals to articulate their struggles and use alternative terminology. Doing so may enhance transitional justice in three ways: by liberating fixed victim/survivor discourses; by increasing gender and sexual sensitivity; and by unveiling taboo harms that can be redressed. Yet as Cohen cautions, finding new terminology can give a false sense of improvement when 'much the same groups of experts are doing much the same business as usual'.[188] Replacing terms with new ones is a 'poor way of preserving and learning from the past'.[189] It also undermines the struggle of victims to secure legal entitlements in domestic or human rights law that has created a discourse around their rights as victims. The established identities communicated by the terms 'victim' and 'perpetrator' are not easily discarded, given their institutional practicality. While it may be tempting to discount the value of identity, these terms may subconsciously permeate our 'self' and have proven to both fuel and impede post-conflict transitions. Given the complexity of human nature and the inherently sensitive nature of CRSV, a single identity is unlikely to satisfy all. However, it may be possible to develop language that offers a reasonable 'best fit', assisted by external adjuncts that aim to reveal the entire personhood, in all its endless configurations and components. In Northern Ireland, services and the Commission for Victims and Survivors use both terms, allowing individuals to self-identify. Having a best fit may also require reflexivity from transitional justice practitioners—including lawyers, advocates, service providers, and medical practitioners—to be responsive to each person, to treat them with dignity, and avoid simply reducing them to a single identity.

Transitional justice practitioners should conceptualize the three most important identities of those who have suffered CRSV more broadly, and make greater use of these identities to delineate its consequences. Identity can be another site in which post-conflict woes are perpetuated, but it can also be a sanctuary, unrestricted by the rigidities of material boundaries, and helping to illuminate those that may benefit from reparation. In response to the contentious issue of identity in relation to CRSV, a number of strategies are evident, including replacement, hybridity, and change. Yet identity transition need not involve changing categories; it can instead involve reconstructing an identity to address perceived negatives and cultivate its positives. As will be explored in further detail in Chapters 6 and 7, a merger of the

[186] Judith Butler, Performative Acts and Gender Constitution: An Essay in Phenomenology and Feminist Theory, *Theatre Journal* 40(4) (1988) 519–531, p520.
[187] Spry, n 113, p31.
[188] Stanley Cohen, *Visions of Social Control Crime, Punishment and Classification*, Polity (2005) p152.
[189] Tony Ward and Shadd Maruna, *Rehabilitation*, Routledge (2007) p7.

rights of the victim, the resilience of the survivor, and the ethical care to which patients are entitled could provide a more holistic approach to redressing CRSV, but each of these identities carries its own baggage that cannot be discarded simply by replacing one word with another. For these reasons, in the remainder of this book I will use the term 'victim' for its alignment with rights discourse and reparations in law, and 'victim' or 'patient' when speaking about harm; 'survivor' will generally not be used, as it is considered too inclusive. In the next chapter, I will consider reparations and their development as a mechanism for providing redress to those affected by CRSV.

5

The Evolution of Reparations for Conflict-Related Sexual and Reproductive Violence

5.1 Introduction

Reparations are considered a key legal and political tool to 'make good' harm caused by a responsible party,[1] and have been used for hundreds and even thousands of years to settle conflicts.[2] The starting point for reparations is in the theory of corrective justice, in that they are measures intended to rectify the wrong caused to the injured party.[3] As such, reparations are intended to return the victim to their original position before the violation through restoring to them all they have lost.[4] Reparations in international law are developed from domestic private law principles of civil claims of remedy against individuals and the state.[5] This is reflected in the seminal dictum in the *Chorzow Factory* case that 'reparation must, as far as possible, wipe-out all the consequences of the illegal act and re-establish the situation which would, in all probability, have existed if that act had not been committed'.[6] Reparations in international law serve to restore a breach by one state's wrongdoing as far as feasible to the injured state affected, such as removing troops from invading a neighbouring country. Yet reparations have rarely been ordered after conflicts between or within states, despite the increasing recognition of such acts as amounting to international crimes.

The emergence of human rights law shifted the remedial process from a horizontal, reciprocal relationship between states under international law to a vertical relationship entitling individuals and groups to claim for redress against the state.[7] Under human rights law reparations are measures intended to acknowledge

[1] See Luke Moffett, Reparations in Transitional Justice: Justice or Political Compromise? *Human Rights and International Legal Discourse* 11(1) (2017) 59–70.

[2] See Luke Moffett, *Reparations and War: Seeking Balance after Conflict*, OUP (2023).

[3] Dinah Shelton, *Remedies in International Human Rights Law*, OUP (2005) p19.

[4] *Restitutio in integrum status quo ante*—ibid p9.

[5] Luke Moffett, Transitional Justice and Reparations: Remedying the Past? in C Lawther, L Moffett, and D Jacobs (eds), *Research Handbook on Transitional Justice*, Elgar (2017) 377–400, p378.

[6] *Germany v Poland, The Factory at Chorzow* (Claim for Indemnity) (The Merits), Permanent Court of International Justice, File E. c XIII. Docket XIV: I Judgment No 13, 13 September 1928.

[7] Antonio Augusto Cançado-Trindade, *The Access of Individuals to International Justice*, OUP (2011) p200.

Redressing Rape in War. Sunneva Gilmore, Oxford University Press. © Sunneva Gilmore 2026.
DOI: 10.1093/9780198919735.003.0005

and remedy as far as possible suffering caused to individuals and groups as a result of gross human rights violations.[8] In this context, reparations feature as part of the right to remedy in that they have a procedural and substantive dimension, that is, to allow victims whose rights are violated to claim for relief.[9] In addition, international human rights law has increasingly recognized due diligence obligations of states, or at least subsidiary duties, to provide reparations to victims, even where this involves non-state or private perpetrators.[10] Over the past four decades, human rights law has developed the main corpus of practice and normative parameters of reparations,[11] which has increasingly turned to address sexual and gender-based violence.[12]

More recently, international criminal law bodies, such as the International Criminal Court (ICC), the Extraordinary Chambers in the Courts of Cambodia (ECCC), and the Extraordinary African Chambers (EAC) have recognized victims' rights to reparation, and ordered measures (or at least approved them) against a perpetrator following a conviction for sexual violence.[13] Although human rights law tends to focus primarily on state obligations to ensure effective and adequate remedies,[14] international criminal law has jurisdiction over individual criminal responsibility. This focus on individual responsibility can face the challenge of a convicted person's obligation to make reparations to their victims.[15] Over the past fifteen years there has been increasing attention to individuals' rights to reparations and conflict-related sexual violence (CRSV) at an international level. However, while there is growing academic and policy interest, there has been limited jurisprudence and state practice to put proposed approaches into effect.

Against this backdrop, this chapter considers the reparation principles that have gained traction for their relevance to sexual and other gender-based violence.

[8] See Moffett, n 5.

[9] Shelton, n 3, p91.

[10] CEDAW, General recommendation No 19: Violence against women, 11° session, 1992, UN Doc HRI\GEN\1\Rev1 at 84 (1994), paras 9 and 24(i); *Case of Velásquez Rodríguez v Honduras* (Merits) IACtHR Series C No 4 (29 July 1988) para 174; Principle 16, UN Basic Principles on Reparations.

[11] See Thomas Antkowiak, Remedial Approaches to Human Rights Violations: The Inter-American Court of Human Rights and Beyond, *Columbia Journal of Transnational Law* 46 (2008) 351–419.

[12] See Ruth Rubio-Marín and Clara Sandoval, Engendering the Reparations Jurisprudence of the Inter-American Court of Human Rights: The Promise of the *Cotton Field* Judgment, *Human Rights Quarterly* 33 (2011) 1062–1191.

[13] Previous ad hoc tribunals excluded such direct claims of reparations, see Anne-Marie de Brouwer, Reparation to Victims of Sexual Violence: Possibilities at the International Criminal Court and at the Trust Fund for Victims and Their Families, *Leiden Journal of International Law* 20 (2007) 207–237. See also Andrea Durbach and Louise Chappell, Leaving Behind the Age of Impunity: Victims of Gender Violence and the Promise of Reparations, *International Feminist Journal of Politics* 16(4) (2014) 543–562; Christoph Sperfeldt, The Trial Against Hissène Habré: Networked Justice and Reparations at the Extraordinary African Chambers, *International Journal of Human Rights* 21(9) (2017) 1243–1260; and Rachel Killean and Luke Moffett, What's in a Name? 'Reparations' at the Extraordinary Chambers in the Courts of Cambodia, *Melbourne Journal of International Law* 21(1) (2020) 115–143. The Kosovo Specialist Chambers can also award reparations under Rule 168.

[14] Shelton, n 3, p8.

[15] Article 75(2), Rome Statute of the International Criminal Court.

It then sets out the conceptual and historical development of reparations for mass atrocities in international criminal law, truth commissions, human rights jurisprudence, and civil society bottom-up efforts. It explores the nascent practice of reparations for CRSV, drawing from a medico-legal approach which incorporates medical evidence, fieldwork, legal rules, and jurisprudence. Throughout, the chapter highlights the framework and practices that currently exist for victims of CRSV. It then turns to consider the development of 'transformative reparation' theories and explores their implications for responding to CRSV. This discussion will complement the following chapter which will explore how the specific measures of reparations for CRSV have been constructed to remedy the harm in practice.

5.2 Identifying Principles of Reparations

While there are a range of principles and guidelines on reparations, many of the international treaties that provide for victims' right to remedy do not explicitly address sexual violence.[16] For example, the 2005 UN Basic Principles on Reparations establish victims' right to reparations for gross violations of human rights and serious breaches of international humanitarian law, outlining appropriate forms of reparations. The 2005 Principles include general principles on non-discrimination and access to relevant information concerning violations and reparation mechanisms, but no specific guidance on how these can be realized or adapted to suit issues such as sexual and gender-based violence.[17] This constructive ambiguity can allow a range of state practices to develop in line with such principles, but it provides little practical guidance on how such reparations should look or be designed and implemented in practice. One of the authors of the 2005 UN Basic Principles suggests that they do not create new legal obligations on states, but 'identify mechanisms, modalities, procedures and methods for the implementation of existing legal obligations under international human rights law and international humanitarian law'.[18] As such, the principles are 'meant to serve as a tool, a guiding instrument for states in devising and implementing victim-oriented policies and programmes'.[19] That said, the principles have been adopted in national reparation programmes, as well as the jurisprudence of the Inter-American Court of Human Rights (IACtHR) and the ICC.[20]

[16] See Article 8, Universal Declaration of Human Rights 1948; Article 13, ECHR; Article 2(3) ICCPR; Article 25(2), ACHR; and Article 7(1), ACHPR.

[17] Principles 24 and 25. The principle of non-discrimination did include gender and sexual orientation in its drafting, but it was dropped in the final version—Mahmoud Cherif Bassiouni, International Recognition of Victims' Rights, *Human Rights Law Review* 6(2) (2006) 203–279, p259.

[18] Theo van Boven, Victims' Rights to a Remedy and Reparation: The United Nations Principles and Guidelines, in C Ferstman and M Goetz (eds), *Reparations for Victims of Genocide, War Crimes and Crimes Against Humanity: Systems in Place and Systems in the Making*, Brill (2020) 15–37, p29.

[19] ibid p29.

[20] Bassiouni, n 17, pp278–279.

The lack of specific rights or obligations in international law regarding reparations for sexual violence is also mirrored in many human rights conventions, even those on the rights of women, such as the Convention on the Elimination of Discrimination against Women. While sexual violence is not explicitly addressed in this Convention,[21] its Committee (CEDAW) sought to remedy this deficit in General recommendation No 30 of 2013 by stressing the importance of prompt reparations for CRSV through court or administrative programmes.[22] In its own Committee decisions on violations of the Convention, Rubio-Marín and Tanck found that CEDAW has made a positive contribution in setting international standards and guidelines, in the face of weak engagement by other human rights bodies, even if this does not necessarily result in state compliance.[23] Importantly, in the past decade CEDAW has advanced a more coherent vision of gender-sensitive, integral, and transformative reparations in light of human rights obligations in states developing transitional policies and programmes for implementation.[24] Elsewhere, the 2014 UN Secretary General's Guidance Note on Reparations for CRSV holds that ensuring reparations for CRSV are effective and adequate requires a better understanding of the 'gendered-nature and consequences of the harm suffered for both males and females', taking into account gender inequalities including actual or perceived gender or other identity biases.[25]

In transitional justice, perhaps the most useful 'guiding principles' on the operation of reparation programmes come from de Greiff, the first appointed UN Special Rapporteur on Truth, Justice, Reparations and Guarantees of Non-Recurrence. De Greiff outlines a taxonomy of reparations to assess their effectiveness: completeness; comprehensiveness and complexity; integrity or coherence; finality; and munificence.[26] Completeness involves the coverage of the 'whole universe of potential beneficiaries'.[27] Comprehensiveness covers the distinct types of violations or harm, with complexity concerning the variety of measures, such as going beyond just compensation.[28] Integrity involves internal and external coherence, which refers to the relationship between different types of reparations and other transitional justice mechanisms respectively.[29] Finality pertains to whether a

[21] See Article 15, Convention on the Elimination of All Forms of Discrimination Against Women 1979.

[22] CEDAW, General recommendation No 30 on women in conflict prevention, conflict and post-conflict situations, October 2013, CEDAW/C/GC/30, paras 76 and 79.

[23] Ruth Rubio-Marín and Dorothy Estrada-Tanck, Transitional Justice Standards on Reparations for Women Subjected to Violence in the CEDAW Committee's Evolving Legal Practice, *International Journal of Transitional Justice* 14(3) (2020) 566–584, pp568–569.

[24] ibid p583.

[25] Clara Sandoval, *Guidance Note: Reparations for Conflict-Related Sexual Violence*, UN Secretary General (2014) p5.

[26] Pablo de Greiff, Repairing the Past: Compensation for Victims of Human Rights Violations, in Pablo de Greiff (ed), *Handbook of Reparations*, OUP (2006) pp6–13.

[27] ibid p6.

[28] ibid pp6–10.

[29] ibid pp10–11.

reparation programme closes off other avenues for victims to seek redress.[30] Lastly, munificence relates to the scope of a reparation programme's benefits.[31] It is apparent that there are a range of principles for reparations, but few have been developed in international law as a soft-law basis for informing how to address CRSV. Medicine does not have 'reparation principles' given that it is often seen as an adjunct to the legal nature of reparations. Yet as we will see, medical concepts and best practice are increasingly filling the space on effectively implementing reparations, especially around mitigating secondary victimization. It is worth turning to examine how sexual violence during times of conflict has been addressed in other international legal fields and practice.

5.3 Delivering Reparations for Conflict-Related Sexual Violence

Despite the absence of any specific treaty, convention provisions, or international guidelines on reparations for CRSV, over the past fifteen years there has been a growing body of jurisprudence and state practice on this issue. The following subsections explore responses to CRSV in the key areas of these developments, namely international criminal justice, truth commissions, human rights jurisprudence, and civil society-led initiatives. These areas provide background on the origins of reparations for CRSV, helping to understand, in the next chapter, the forms which are seen as appropriate for remedying such violations, including those that arise from court orders and domestic reparation programmes.

5.3.1 Responses to CRSV in international criminal justice

International criminal justice has historically overlooked CRSV. Following the Second World War, mechanisms introduced to deliver accountability or justice neglected to address CRSV; for example, the Comfort Women, the Rape of Nanking, and Soviet sexual violence in Eastern Europe.[32] This may have been due to reluctance on the part of victims to come forward immediately after the conflict, the male dominated investigation and prosecution teams, or the prioritization

[30] ibid p12.

[31] ibid pp12–13. Dixon similarly develops five principles to distinguish reparations from assistance in their delivery. The principles are responsibility, recognition, process, form, and impact. See Peter Dixon, Reparations, Assistance and the Experience of Justice: Lessons from Colombia and the Democratic Republic of the Congo, *International Journal of Transitional Justice* 10(1) (2016) 88–107, 95–102; and Killean and Moffett, n 13 in application of these principles in the context of the ECCC.

[32] See Anne-Marie de Brouwer, *Supranational Criminal Prosecution of Sexual Violence: The ICC and the Practice of the ICTY and the ICTR*, Intersentia (2005).

of abuses against prisoners of war and crimes against peace.[33] This trend of neglecting CRSV continued to some extent at the ad hoc tribunals established to address violations in the former Yugoslavia and Rwanda, even though they developed important jurisprudence on sexual violence as amounting to torture and genocide,[34] and included the professional participation of women.[35] Feminist critiques of international criminal law have highlighted that sexual violence is often deprioritized by prosecutors and it can be more difficult to ensure victim cooperation in criminal proceedings, as their protection is weighed against defendants' rights to confront their accuser.[36]

The prosecution of sexual violence remains problematic at the International Criminal Court, where the first two cases (*Lubanga* and *Katanga*) did not include sexual violence, despite its prevalence.[37] As discussed in Chapter 2, the emblematic case of *Bemba* on mass rape resulted in an acquittal,[38] and other cases involving sexual violence collapsed.[39] This reflects the selectivity of charges and convicted persons before international criminal justice bodies as well as the high evidential threshold for a conviction.[40] However, since 2019 there have been two high profile cases at the ICC—*Ntaganda* and *Ongwen*—which include convictions for sexual violence. In the *Ntaganda* case, a former commander of a militia in eastern Democratic Republic of Congo was convicted in July 2019 of, amongst other counts, sexual slavery and rape against civilians and child soldiers.[41] In March 2021, the Court, for the first time, also awarded reparations for sexual violence, including compensation and rehabilitation for victims of rape and sexual slavery,[42] discussed further in the next chapter. In the *Ongwen* case the Office of the Prosecutor made efforts to include SGBV charges, including sexual slavery and for the first time at the ICC, forced pregnancy and forced marriage. Indeed, the Prosecutor herself noted that the charging of a range of counts for sexual and

[33] See Christine Chinkin, Shelley Wright, and Hilary Charlesworth, *Feminist Approaches to International Law: Reflections from Another Century*, in D Buss and A Manji (eds), *International Law: Modern Feminist Approaches*, Hart (2005) 17–47.

[34] *Akayesu*, ICTR-96-4-T, 2 September 1998, paras 597–598 and 731–734; *Furundžija*, IT-95-17/1-T, 10 December 1998, paras 183–186; and *Kunarac, Kovac and Vukovic*, IT-96-23-T, 22 February 2001, paras 438–440. See Binaifer Nowrojee, 'Your Justice is Too Slow': Will the International Criminal Tribunal for Rwanda Fail Rwanda's Rape Victims? in D Pankhurst (ed), *Gendered Peace: Women's Struggles for Post-War Justice and Reconciliation*, Routledge (2007) 107–136.

[35] Fiona de Londras, Prosecuting Sexual Violence in the Ad Hoc International Criminal Tribunals for Rwanda and the Former Yugoslavia, in M Fineman (eds), *Transcending the Boundaries of Law: Generations of Feminism and Legal Theory*, Routledge (2010) 290–304, p298.

[36] ibid pp299–302.

[37] Anne-Marie de Brouwer, What the International Criminal Court has Achieved and can Achieve for Victims/Survivors of Sexual Violence, *International Review of Victimology* 16 (2009) 183–209, p194.

[38] Final decision on the reparations proceedings, ICC-01/05-01/08-3653, 3 August 2018, para 7.

[39] *The Impact of Litigation on Combating Sexual Violence and its Consequences in Africa*, FIDH (2019) pp102–103.

[40] Luke Moffett, *Justice for Victims Before the International Criminal Court*, Routledge (2014) p194.

[41] Judgment, ICC-01/04-02/06-2359, 8 July 2019.

[42] *Ntaganda*, Reparations Order, ICC-01/04-02/06-2659, 8 March 2021.

gender-based violence was intended to reflect the 'multidimensional harm' suffered by victims—demonstrating an internalization of previous critiques that CRSV had been neglected.[43] In March 2021, Dominic Ongwen was convicted of forced marriage and forced pregnancy, along with rape and sexual slavery—the reparations award in this case is the most extensive ordered by the ICC with total liability in excess of €52 million EURO. These two cases reflect the Court's efforts to compensate for failing to make visible sexual and gender-based violence in its prosecutorial selection of charges and perpetrators in its initial cases. There was also similar criticism and activism at the ECCC where civil society reproached the tribunal for the absence of SGBV in prosecutions. Their mobilization encouraged a 'shift in attitude' that led to its inclusion in subsequent cases.[44] As discussed in more depth in Chapter 6, the conviction of leaders of the Khmer Rouge for forced marriage resulted in the tribunal ordering such reparations through the funding of a dance project (Pka Sla Krom Angkar) to memorialize victims' suffering.[45]

The challenge of securing convictions for sexual violence at international courts has led to the suggestion that a higher evidential standard was used for sexual violence charges, especially during wartime.[46] There may have been a similar practice at the ad hoc tribunals; as SáCouto and Clearly argue, in times of war sexual violence is 'often tacitly encouraged or tolerated, even if not officially sanctioned, and the absence of explicit orders in these cases often makes it more difficult for the prosecution to link the perpetrator with the crime'.[47] This can be seen in the Extraordinary African Chambers against former Chadian president Hissene Habré, who, despite being convicted of personally committing rape against a victim who testified at the Court, was acquitted of this charge, but not others, on appeal, meaning that this victim was excluded from the final reparation order of compensation to over 7,000 victims of torture.[48] Criminal tribunals can be a

[43] Fatou Bensouda, "Prosecuting Sexual and Gender-Based Crimes at the International Criminal Court, SAIFAC Conference: International Law and Justice for Victims of the Gross Human Rights Violation of Sexual and Gender-Based Violence, 27 November 2019, p7.

[44] Rachel Killean, Constructing Victimhood at the Khmer Rouge Tribunal: Visibility, Selectivity and Participation, *International Review of Victimology* 24(3) (2018) 273–296; and Emma Palmer and Sarah Williams, A "Shift in Attitude"? Institutional Change and Sexual and Gender-Based Crimes at the Extraordinary Chambers in the Courts of Cambodia, *International Feminist Journal of Politics* 19(1) (2017) 22–38.

[45] Rosemary Grey, Yim Sotheary, and Kum Somaly, The Khmer Rouge Tribunal's First Reparation for Gender-Based Crimes, *Australian Journal of Human Rights* 25(3) (2019) 488–497.

[46] Brigid Inder, Prosecuting Sexual Violence in Conflict—Challenges and Lessons Learned A critique of the Katanga Judgment, Women's Initiatives for Gender Justice Global Summit to End Sexual Violence in Conflict, 11 June 2014.

[47] Susana SáCouto and Katherine Clearly, Importance of Effective Investigation of Sexual Violence and Gender-Based Crimes at the International Criminal Court, *Journal of Gender, Social Policy & the Law* 17(2) (2009) 337–359, p354.

[48] Given the lack of financial resources, this award has not been implemented. See Nader Diab, Challenges in the Implementation of the Reparation Award against Hissein Habré: Can the Spell of Unenforceable Awards across the Globe be Broken? *Journal of International Criminal Justice* 16(1) (2018) 141–163.

difficult space for victims of sexual violence to come forward and reflect on their direct harms in a sensitive manner. It remains to be seen whether the increasing recognition, prosecution, and awarding of reparations to victims of CRSV can effectively remedy victims' harm. This is particularly acute in the *Ntaganda* case, where his victims continue to face insecurity and ongoing conflict. This contrasts with truth commissions, which are often established at the end of hostilities or when a regime has ended.

5.3.2 CRSV in Truth Commissions

A similar pattern of historically overlooking CRSV is discernible with regard to domestic transitional justice in the 1970s and 1980s that emerged in Latin America through truth commissions, which focused on extrajudicial executions and disappearances through truth recovery bodies.[49] Truth commissions can provide a more official account of past violations and contribute to transforming some of the narratives and societal debate on the past, but also continue the silence around other violations, in particular sexual and gender-based violence.[50] Attention to other violations in Chile and Argentina slowly developed, namely torture and exile, but only recently have sexual and reproductive violations become apparent.[51] This could in part be explained by the focus on the explicit and widespread violations of thousands of individuals' civil and political rights, rather than attention on more hidden and structural atrocities.[52] This can be acutely seen in the South African Truth and Reconciliation Commission where sexual violence was not included in the political offences that were focused on, though 446 victims gave statements on sexual violence and three special hearings were held for women to speak of their experiences.[53] As Kusafuka suggests, this may have indicated that the commission struggled to discern sexual violence as a political offence or one that was personally motivated,[54] which has implications for whether such violations were considered

[49] See Priscilla Hayner, *Unspeakable Truths: Transitional Justice and the Challenge of Truth Commissions*, Routledge (2011).

[50] See Onur Bakiner, One Truth Among Others? Truth Commissions' Struggle for Truth and Memory, *Memory Studies* 8(3) (2015) 345–360.

[51] These reflected gendered notions of motherhood and the place of women alongside restrictive reproductive rights. See Catherine O'Rourke, Transitioning to What? Transitional Justice and Gendered Citizenship in Chile and Colombia, in S Buckley-Zistel and R Stanley (eds), *Gender in Transitional Justice*, Palgrave (2012) 136–160.

[52] Rosemary Nagy, Transitional Justice as Global Project: critical reflections, Third World Quarterly 29 (2) (2008) 275–289, p287.

[53] Ayumi Kusafuka, Truth Commissions and Gender: A South African Case Study, *African Journal on Conflict Resolution* 9(2) (2009) 45–67, pp47–48.

[54] ibid p52. This reflected that victims appeared before the human rights violations committee and perpetrators before the amnesty committee, which often did not consider sexual violence to be politically motivated, see Jeremy Sarkin and Sarah Ackermann, Understanding the Extent to which Truth Commissions are Gender Sensitive and Promote Women's Issues: Comparing and Contrasting these

ordinary or extraordinary, and thereby subject to amnesty, alongside the neglect of socio-economic violations and the gendered-nature of truth gathering.[55] As a result, the commission 'neglecting the link between what was considered "extraordinary" and "ordinary" violence, and produced a missed opportunity to examine the structural, ideological and systemic background of gender relations, especially the apartheid's structural abuses against women.'[56] The promise of the enfranchisement of women and transformation of their lives with the transition away from apartheid has failed to be realized, inhibited by the 'hierarchies of harm' that the TRC prioritized over sexual violence.[57]

In recent years, other truth commissions have been more cognizant of CRSV, reflecting the broader ambit of truth commissions to encourage wider engagement of all genders and to document the patterns and structures of violence. In the case of Liberia, its truth commission documented and highlighted the widespread and systematic use of rape against women and girls as a weapon of war, which was assisted by advocacy and mobilization of civil society and a gender committee to encourage victims to come forward.[58] Similarly, the involvement of victim and human rights organizations in the Peruvian Truth and Reconciliation Commission (CVR) helped to contribute to the recognition and documentation of forced prostitution, forced marriage, sexual slavery, forced abortion, forced pregnancy, and rape. Yet, the state's use of forced sterilization of mostly poor rural indigenous women under the Fujimori dictatorship was entirely excluded.[59] In addition, the violence against sexual minorities, and the MRTA killings of cross-dressers, were given only passing attention.[60] In Sierra Leone, the promise of psychological 'healing' in testifying before the truth commission, and expectations built up around accessing rehabilitation and other forms of reparation, were unmet despite victim and women groups' activism shaping the commission, ultimately resulting in a paltry outcome of some compensation and skills training for a fraction of victims of sexual violence.[61] In

Truth Commission Roles in South Africa, Guatemala, Peru, Sierra Leone and Liberia, *Georgetown Journal of International Law* 50 (2019) 463–516, p481.

[55] See Andrea Durbach, Towards Reparative Transformation: Revisiting the Impact of Violence against Women in a Post-TRC South Africa, *International Journal of Transitional Justice* 10(3) (2016) 366–387, p374; and Tristan Anne Borer, Gendered War and Gendered Peace: Truth Commissions and Postconflict Gender Violence: Lessons from South Africa, *Violence Against Women* 15(10) (2009) 1169–1193.

[56] Kusafuka, n 53, p51.

[57] Durbach, n 55, p384–385.

[58] Sarkin and Ackermann, n 54, p506.

[59] See Jocelyn Getgen, Untold Truths: The Exclusion of Enforced Sterilizations From the Peruvian Truth Commission's Final Report, *Boston College Third World Law Journal* 29(1) (2009) 1–34.

[60] This amounted to two pages in the twelve-volume report. See Katherine Fobear, Queering Truth Commissions *Journal of Human Rights Practice* 6(1) (2014) 51–68, pp57–58.

[61] Anne Menzel, The Perils of Recognising Local Agency: A Situational Concept of Agency and the Case of Victims of Sexual Violence and the Sierra Leone Truth and Reconciliation Commission (TRC), *Journal of International Relations and Development* 23 (2020) 584–606, pp600–602.

more contemporary truth commissions, the Gambian and Colombian commissions have embedded a gender-sensitive approach in their work and created special hearings for victims of sexual and gender-based violence,[62] and in Colombia, this has included violence against members of the LGBTI community.[63]

Other truth commissions have acknowledged further gender-based harms, such as inheritance laws that disallows female heirs, or unequal employment opportunities. The gender-sensitive approaches of truth commissions, such as those in Timor-Leste, Morocco, and Sierra Leone, illuminated the dual condition of victims, who suffered not only grave human rights abuses, but also historical economic and social injustices that predisposed them to marginalization.[64] Whilst gender was not uniformly integrated into Morocco's Equity and Reconciliation Commission (IER), the report rejected the Moroccan law of succession, recommending that both women and men have equal entitlement to land inheritance.[65] Nevertheless, truth processes have also reflected traditional or conservative narratives, which can silence or erase the testimony of women who do not fit into 'expected stereotypes (for example, selfless mother or innocent victim)'.[66] Indeed, Ni Aoláin finds that sexual violence and women have continued to be marginalized in the enforcement of transitional justice, minimizing its transformative potential and not fulfilling the positive presumptions that they would benefit from such transitions.[67] Despite the role of truth commissions in broadening the visibility of sexual violence, they have struggled to have their recommendations for reparations implemented.[68] This can reflect that truth commissions are there to uncover the truth and make recommendations for reparations to be implemented by the state, leading to 'expectation management', with victims who come before them expecting compensation and other forms of redress, but which can make such bodies seem patronizing or cause a 'deflation of hope'.[69] The contribution of truth commissions indicates the difficulty of addressing such violations in the aftermath

[62] Sunneva Gilmore, Julie Guillerot, and Clara Sandoval, *Beyond Silence and Stigma—Crafting a Gender-Sensitive Approach for Victims of Sexual Violence in Domestic Reparation Programmes*, RRV (2020) p11.

[63] Nicole Maier, Queering Colombia's Peace Process: A Case Study of LGBTI Inclusion, *International Journal of Human Rights* 24(4) (2020) 377–392.

[64] Julie Guillerot, Foundation for the Future, Morocco: Gender and the Transitional Justice Process, International Center of Transitional Justice, September 2011; and *The Rabat Report: The Concept and Challenges of Collective Reparations*, International Center of Transitional Justice (ICTJ) (2009).

[65] Morocco: Gender and The Transitional Justice Process, ICTJ (2011) p28.

[66] Fionnuala Ní Aoláin and Catherine Turner, Gender, Truth and Transition, *UCLA Women's Law Journal* 16 (2007) 229–279, pp259–260.

[67] Fionnuala Ní Aoláin, Gendered Under-Enforcement in the Transitional Justice Context, in S Buckley-Zistel and R Stanley (eds), *Gender in Transitional Justice*, Springer (2012) 59–87.

[68] See Luke Moffett, In the Aftermath of Truth: Implementing Truth Commissions' Recommendations on Reparations-Following Through for Victims, in J Sarkin (ed), *The Global Legacy of Truth Commissions*, Intersentia (2018) 143–168.

[69] Menzel, n 61, p318.

of conflict, but there remain increasing efforts to do so, in particular with sexual minorities.

5.3.3 Responding to CRSV in human rights jurisprudence

There has been some emerging jurisprudence from human rights bodies which recognizes CRSV, in particular from the IACtHR, which has a well-established body of case law on reparations.[70] In 2006, for the first time, the IACtHR was confronted with violations that were specifically directed towards female inmates based on their gender at the Miguel Castro Castro prison in Lima, Peru, between 6 and 9 May 1992.[71] These institutional abuses occurred during a period of conflict when non-state armed groups were presented by the state as the main perpetrators of human rights abuses. The court found that women endured further harms based on their gender and awarded additional sums of money for sexual violence linked to the specific type of harm endured,[72] setting an important precedent about the moral intangible damages related to gendered harms. The court also expressed some 'transformative' aims in the judgment by recommending human rights training. However, this element of the judgment was not gender-specific. It did not, for example, address issues such as medical rehabilitation for sexual violence or training of correctional officers on gender discrimination. Subsequent cases expanded on the need to ensure guarantees of non-repetition and to more elaborately construct notions of reparation that are proportional to material damages.[73]

A pivotal moment for addressing gender-based violence came in 2009 when the IACtHR was faced with the *Cotton Field v Mexico* case.[74] Gender discrimination was considered a factor that led to the disappearances and sexual violence committed against the three deceased female victims, as well as the lack of due diligence in the state's investigation of the case and treatment of their next of kin.[75] For instance, the police informed a mother whose daughter was missing that if 'anything happened to her, it was because she was looking for it, because a good girl, a good woman, stays at home'.[76] Whilst the case did not occur in the background of armed conflict, it was the first case where the perpetrators were non-state actors, and the decision shaped how evidentiary thresholds in sexual violence could be adapted

[70] This jurisprudence and that of the European Court and other human rights bodies are discussed further in Chapter 6.
[71] *Castro Castro Prison v Peru* (Merits, Reparations, and Costs) IACtHR Series No 160 (25 November 2006).
[72] Rubio-Marín and Sandoval, n 12, p1077.
[73] See Chapter 6 for forms of reparations.
[74] Transformative reparations or at least their potential is discussed in the next section of this chapter.
[75] Rubio-Marín and Sandoval, n 12, p1063.
[76] *González et al ('Cotton Field') v Mexico* (Preliminary Objection, Merits, Reparations, and Costs) IACtHR Series C No 205 (16 November 2009) para 198.

where evidence could not be presented because of the ineptness or unwillingness of the state to appropriately conduct an investigation. The Court was careful to encompass the expansive potential of gender-based harms by interpreting injured parties who were entitled to reparation as next of kin and extended family, amounting to a violation of their personal integrity through secondary victimization.[77] However, the case failed to consider the gravity of the loss of the mothers of the deceased victims, both in a moral and material manner. In addition, female members of the family had led the efforts to seek justice but the temporal, economic, and emotional investment was not fully incorporated into the reparation decision. Instead, only a presumed salary of the deceased's alleged occupation and presumed funeral costs were awarded, irrespective of the mothers' employment losses and other costs. Unlike in the *Castro Castro* case, the Court highlighted that Mexico could not provide information that ensured that its violence against women policies were effective and it did not order further policy measures, since they could not prove harms resulted from a lack of implementation.

As demonstrated by the case of *Castro Castro* and *Cotton Fields*, the IACtHR has strengthened conceptualizations of reparation for sexual violence.[78] It could be argued that these are not conflict-related cases given they occurred in a prison and in the city of Juarez. However, the political contexts of Peru and Mexico at the time reflect large-scale organized violence, whether against the Shining Path in the former or drug cartels in the latter, reflecting a situation of insecurity from various armed actors as well as state violations. As such, in times of emergency, the IACtHR defended victims' rights, even in the case of former members of Shining Path, recognizing their suffering and their entitlement to reparations. In the *Cotton Fields* case, the general insecurity did not justify the state abdicating its obligations to guarantee rights for all, but also to positively protect women from further violence. Despite these achievements, progress has arguably plateaued, perhaps owing to tensions surrounding what is appropriate given reparations' conceptual underpinnings in corrective justice, and whether it is able to exercise its capacity to catalyze structural change.[79] Relevant cases from other regional and UN human rights bodies are discussed in the next chapter.

5.3.4 'Bottom-up' responses to CRSV

In the face of state inaction, more informal civil society-led efforts have occasionally sought to acknowledge victims' harm and advance reparation claims.[80] One

[77] ibid para.424.
[78] See Rubio-Marín and Sandoval, n 12.
[79] ibid.
[80] Christine M Chinkin, Women's International Tribunal on Japanese Military Sexual Slavery, *American Journal of International Law* 95(2) (2001) 335–341.

notable example is the Women's International War Crimes Tribunal for the Trial of Japanese Military Sexual Slavery. The Tribunal was set up by civil society in 2000 to address the issue of 'Comfort Women'—hundreds of thousands of girls and women sexually enslaved by the Imperial Japanese Army during the Second World War and neglected in post-war settlements in the peace agreements.[81] The Tribunal sought to investigate, prosecute, and recommend reparations for sexual slavery committed against Korean women in Tokyo to highlight the criminal responsibility of the Japanese government who continued to deny responsibility.[82] The Tribunal set out twelve remedial measures for the Japanese government to carry out, including: acknowledgement of responsibility for the violations and the failure to investigate and prosecute such crimes; a full and frank apology with guarantees of non-repetition; compensation to redress the harm and deter its future occurrence; creation of an investigative mechanism to prosecute those responsible; establishment of a truth and reconciliation commission to create a historical record; creation of memorials, a museum, and a library dedicated to the victims' memory; sponsorship of both formal and informal educational initiatives, including in school textbooks; training for the military in gender and equality law; repatriation of survivors; disclosure and declassification of all relevant military and government documents; and location and return the remains of those deceased.[83]

While the judgment and recommendations for reparations had no legal effect, they served to highlight the victims' suffering and mobilize public attention to encourage Japan to redress the Comfort Women, and constituted the first and most comprehensive attempt to provide reparative measures to victims of conflict-related sexual violence. The reparations recommended by the Tribunal took into account the victims' harm, in particular under the headings of physical suffering; reproductive harm; psychological harm; harm to intimate relations and social/community life; silence; and poverty and social and economic hardship.[84] The judges' rigorous legal analysis of international law helped to cement the credibility of their recommendations and accounted for evidence that documented that harms were continuous and long term for victims of sexual violence.[85] This Tribunal and other women's hearings have been a proactive response to states'

[81] See Ethan Hee-Seok Shin, The Comfort Women Reparation Movement: Between Universal Women's Human Right and Particular Anti-Colonial Nationalism, *Florida Journal of International Law* 28(1) (2016) 87–158.

[82] See Tina Dolgopol, The Judgment of the Tokyo Women's Tribunal, *Alternative Law Journal* 28(5) (2005) 242–249.

[83] Transcript of Oral Judgment delivered on 4 December 2001 by the Judges of the Women's International War Crimes Tribunal on Japan's Military Sexual Slavery, delivered in The Hague, The Netherlands, 4 December 2001, by Women's Caucus for Gender Justice, www.iccwomen.org/wigjdraft1/Archives/oldWCGJ/tokyo/summary.html, accessed 1 August 2025.

[84] Dolgopol, n 82, p244.

[85] See ibid.

inaction to address sexual violence and break the silence surrounding it with victims as active citizens.[86]

As noted above, the 2005 UN Basic Principles on Reparations are silent on gender and sexual violence, as are the 2005 UN Impunity Principles. The Nairobi Declaration aimed to fill this gap by promoting a gender-sensitive approach.[87] Like the Women's Tribunal, the Nairobi Declaration was a 'bottom-up' effort by civil society organizations, reflecting the role of grassroots organizations coming together on the international stage to mobilize change. The Declaration makes an important contribution in three ways. First, by focusing states and reparation programmes to pay attention to contextual or gender-specific harm. Second, by calling for women and girls' participation in reparation processes to improve their ownership and inform appropriate forms of reparations. Third, by drawing upon pre-existing structural inequalities that may contribute to certain types of harm.[88] While only declaratory, the Nairobi Declaration is increasingly being embedded in the jurisprudence and practice of reparations for CRSV.[89] The Nairobi Declaration and the literature on reparations for sexual violence strongly recommend the importance of incorporating a gender-inclusive approach to the process, design, and implementation of reparations.[90] Therefore, it is worth distinguishing what gender-inclusive and gender-sensitive approaches entail, which is the focus of the next section. Suffice it to say, it can be seen from the analysis in this section that CRSV has taken a long time to receive attention through various bodies, even to the extent that victims themselves, with civil society allies, have had to establish processes for recognition. It is notable that such a gender or transformative perspective does not fully engage with a medico-legal approach in understanding the intersections of law, health, and the body, and the impact and consequences of CRSV, which have implications for envisioning the effective implementation of

[86] Andrea Durbach and Lucy Geddes, 'To Shape Our Own Lives and Our Own World': Exploring Women's Hearings as Reparative Mechanisms for Victims of Sexual Violence Post-Conflict, *International Journal of Human Rights* 21(9) (2017) 1261–1280. The 2011 Women's Hearing for sexual violence that occurred during the Khmer Rouge in Cambodia also served to raise awareness on reparations as an educational function and acknowledgement of victims' suffering, even if it did not result in the Cambodian government implementing a reparations programme—see Beini Ye, Transitional Justice Through the Cambodian Women's Hearings, *Cambodia Law and Policy Journal* 2 (2014) 23–37.

[87] Sheri Labenski, *The Right to Reparations for Sexual and Gender-Based Violence*, Centre for Women, Peace and Security (2020) p14.

[88] Valérie Couillard, The Nairobi Declaration: Redefining Reparations for Women Victims of Sexual Violence, *International Journal of Transitional Justice* 1(3) (2007) 444–453; and Nairobi Declaration on Women's and Girls' Right to Remedy and Reparation, March 2007, https://www.fidh.org/IMG/pdf/NAIROBI_DECLARATIONeng.pdf, accessed 1 August 2025.

[89] *Lubanga*, Order for Reparations, ICC-01/04-01/06-3129-AnxA, 3 March 2015, para 17. See Rashida Manjoo, Introduction: Reflections on the Concept and Implementation of Transformative Reparations, *International Journal of Human Rights* 21(9) (2017) 1193–1203, p1195.

[90] See Nairobi Declaration on Women's and Girls' Right to a Remedy and Reparation 2007; UN Guidance Note; *Lubanga*, ICC-01/04-01/06-3129, 3 March 2015, para 18; and Ellen Anna Philo Gorris, Invisible Victims? Where Are Male Victims of Conflict-Related Sexual Violence in International Law and Policy?, *European Journal of Women's Studies* 22(4) (2015) 412–427.

reparations for such violations (discussed in more depth in Chapter 7). Chapter 6 explores in more detail what reparations have emerged from these different bodies, but it is worth examining in more detail two key concepts which have emerged from the practice and theorizing around redressing CRSV: gender-sensitivity and transformative reparations.

5.4 A Gender-Sensitive Approach to Reparations

A gender-inclusive approach refers to the incorporation of all gender identities in reparation processes. Gender-sensitivity expands this understanding by seeking to comprehend how cultural and societal factors shape gender-exclusion and discrimination.[91] On this basis, gender-sensitivity in reparations can appreciate the differentiated impact, meanings, and motivations behind sexual violence on account of gender.[92] This should in turn inform the processes and contribute to forms of reparation. That said, to be truly gender-sensitive is to reflexively adopt an intersectional lens, so as to discern the ways in which gender interacts with other identities or forms of discrimination resulting in unique harms, and ultimately requires a multifaceted response.[93]

A gender-sensitive approach requires an understanding that women, men, and other gender identities must not be excluded or discouraged from coming forward to claim reparations. For instance, women's victimization is situated within pre-existing social inequalities, which disproportionately compounds their suffering. These include social and employment discrimination, cultural conventions regarding women's honour and chastity, lack of access to land and property rights, and exposure to intimate or sexual violence.[94] One victim of rape interviewed in Peru believed that such an approach was important in confronting both structural violations and encouraging people to treat victims with empathy, as she said those engaging with victims need to treat them,

> with mutual respect for people, no discrimination . . . if someone suffered a trauma or something, for them to be listened to, and a gynaecologist to be

[91] Renata Šribar, Glossary of Common Terms in Gender Equality and Feminist Theory, in Mirjana Ule, Renata Šribar, and Andreja Umek Venturini (eds), *Gendering Science: Slovenian Surveys and Studies in the EU Paradigms*, Echoraum (2015) p173.

[92] Jelke Boesten, *Sexual Violence During War and Peace. Gender, Power and Post-Conflict Justice in Peru*, Palgrave MacMillan (2014) p11.

[93] Kimberlé Crenshaw, Mapping the Margins: Intersectionality, Identity Politics, and Violence against Women of Color, *Stanford Law Review* 43(6) (1991) 1241–1299.

[94] Fionnuala Ní Aoláin, Catherine O'Rourke & Aisling Swaine, Transforming Reparations for Conflict-Related Sexual Violence: Principles and Practice. Harvard Human Rights Journal, 28 (1) (2015) 95–144, p102.

> working with a psychologist, hand by hand, to support people who have suffered sexual violence.[95]

One transitional justice practitioner in Colombia, in her work in rural areas with indigenous victims of sexual violence, found that concepts of gender and reparations were difficult to convey:

> we are not arriving to the communities and saying, 'this is the truth and you women have to behave in order to be empowered' or whatever. No, we have to listen to women. We need to listen to the authorities even though most of the time they are men and sometimes they really don't want to listen to women talking about rights. It is like a concept that is developing women, family and subsequent generations that is the gender concept that somehow translates into what indigenous women are more comfortable with.[96]

Women may face particular forms of blame and shame. A gender-sensitive approach can assist in getting victims to open up and speak about their experience and needs. One psychologist who worked closely with victims of CRSV suggested the need to empathize with them:

> it is undeniable that there are cases of sexual violence, and we are not ready to give people who have suffered this the treatment they need. Even when they do interviews, or when they gather testimonies, they don't consider that the person that is going to do this work needs to be very sensitive and be able to create enough empathy for the people to be able to share their experiences. [Victims of sexual violence], they think that they are guilty, mainly women, but there were also men who suffered sexual violence, and it is even more difficult for them to talk about it, so training is needed for the people who do this work with the affected people... The context has harmed them, and this [understanding] is very important for the recovery of women, because guilt is something that damages them a lot, restricts them, and impedes theirs process of recovery.[97]

In interviews with some healthcare practitioners, taking a gender-sensitive approach was more about educating the public, as in making people aware that they provided services for sexual violence to encourage victims to come forward. Such an approach did not necessarily encompass training their staff on sensitivity towards victims.[98] This may reflect that 'gender-sensitivity' is a top-down concept

95 P6, Lima, Peru, May 2019.
96 C10, Bogotá, Colombia, October 2018.
97 P5, Lima, Peru, May 2019.
98 U10, Lira, Uganda, July 2018.

that may not be well received by grassroots community victim support groups. Indeed, reference to 'gender sensitivity' was more prevalent amongst interviewees who worked for international organizations, sometimes by victims and rarely by healthcare practitioners, perhaps reflecting the vernacular of the field of civil society organizations working on CRSV. It can also reflect the complexity of articulating how to effectively remedy CRSV through only a gender lens, when controversial issues of contraception, termination of pregnancy, and children born as a result of rape can contravene local taboos or even domestic laws.

Interviews with victims of CRSV also revealed that during protracted conflicts sexual violence can occur throughout a person's life by multiple different actors from partners to members of armed groups.[99] While a gender lens can underscore the range of violations that occur to persons that identify as women and girls, it can result in international organizations focusing on explicit violent rape, as this is more likely to resonate with donors, rather than everyday sexual or domestic violence. Often such violence is not isolated or unconnected, but reflects a range of coercive, grooming, or exploitative situations that can be exacerbated by conflict, such as women having to engage in sex with fighters for food (eg in Sudan),[100] which can lead them to being raped by other armed groups or trafficked. However, there is a lack of consistent data to support such indications, as research often uses inconsistent terminology and methods that make it difficult to have a generalized picture of sexual violence in war and the everyday existence of women and girls.[101]

Yet, victim-blaming—whereby victims are made to feel complicit in their own victimization—traverses both private and public domains; in private, by partaking in matrimony with their perpetrator; and in public, by falsely casting the person as promiscuous or deceitful, and so seducing their perpetrator.[102] This can have implications for accessing reparations, where only 'conflict-related' violence is accepted for eligibility and access to services. In practice it may be medically difficult to separate incidents when victims of sexual violence have a complex history that has compounded their harm. For instance, several victims spoke of how they experienced sexual violence by a partner or family member before and/or after their conflict-related sexual violence.[103] They spoke of how they did not have recourse to support in non-conflict situations and were vulnerable to further violence if

[99] C3 and C4, Bogotá, Colombia, September 2018; and C15 FG1, Bogotá, Colombia, March 2019.

[100] Women forced to have sex with soldiers for food in Sudanese city, *The Guardian*, 22 July 2024.

[101] See Alys McAlpine, Mazeda Hossain, and Cathy Zimmerman, Sex Trafficking and Sexual Exploitation in Settings Affected by Armed Conflicts in Africa, Asia and the Middle East: Systematic Review, *BMC International Health and Human Rights* 16(34) (2016), https://doi.org/10.1186/s12914-016-0107-x.

[102] Views around complicity are similar to the report: Haley Clark and Antonia Quadara, Insights into Sexual Assault Perpetration Giving Voice to Victim/Survivors' Knowledge. Australian Government, Australian Institute of Family Studies. Research Report No 18 (2010) pp30–32.

[103] C3 Bogotá, Colombia, September 2018, C15 FG1, Bogotá, Colombia, March 2019 and U4 FG1, Pece, Gulu, July 2018.

they attempted to seek it.[104] The conflict magnified pre-existing inequalities and harmful gender norms which created an enabling environment for conflict-related sexual violence, but also limited opportunities to receive care after each episode and understand the impact in a chronological manner.

Practitioners or researchers treating or engaging with victims need to be cognizant of the continuum of harm victims can face and how insensitivity can silence them, continue to marginalize them, or prevent them from accessing the care or redress they need. Such insensitivity can also be reflected in perceptions and policies, such as in Colombia where some civil society actors highlighted that rehabilitation for victims of sexual violence mainly focused on psychological group supports, as 'women [face] barriers to access physical rehabilitation because the healthcare system is not sensitive enough regarding the specific and special attention a victim of sexual violence needs'.[105] As one Peruvian psychologist said, victims of CRSV can be treated in a disconnected way:

> gynaecologists, when they treat people they not only limit themselves to the physical aspects, to the organic elements, but to consider the emotional factor, because they don't consider that at all, it is like you treat people separately, the physical here and the psychological over there, not like a unit.[106]

Victims of sexual violence often face stigma from their family, community, and society that disincentives them from speaking out or punishes those who do.[107] One transitional justice practitioner also found that labelling victims can be gender insensitive and continue stigma, such as with those abducted into sexual slavery:

> while we should always avoid labelling someone as being, for example, a former wife, when they have been abducted. They are not a product of what happened to them, so we should always be careful of our language in that respect.[108]

Gender sensitivity requires seeing the whole victim and the barriers or burdens they may face in coming forward. The socio-economic background of the victim may inhibit them from spending days away participating in healthcare treatment or reparation processes when they are struggling to put food on the table, earn a living, and/or look after family members.[109] Administrative reparation programmes or court orders for such victims may also need to be informed by the

[104] ibid.
[105] C5, Bogotá, Colombia, September 2018.
[106] P6, Lima, Peru, May 2019.
[107] Principles for global action. Preventing and Addressing Stigma Associated With Conflict-Related Sexual Violence, PSVI 2017.
[108] O2, The Hague, January 2019.
[109] Jo-Anne Wemmers, The Healing Role of Reparations, in J Wemmers (ed), *Reparations for Victims of Crimes against Humanity: The Healing Role of Reparations*, Routledge (2014) 221–232, pp226–231.

reality of the socio-economic context and a gendered understanding of harms suffered.[110] In particular, facilitating access and exercising discretion aims to minimize or avoid stigma. This is not always achieved. In Sierra-Leone, the process of registration for reparations was sex-segregated; however, when women came together in large groups, they were asked to publicly identify the harm they had experienced. As a result, many women registered as 'widow' as opposed to 'rape victim' in the belief that by doing so they would receive support for their family and children as well as themselves.[111] Indeed, victims may be unwilling to identify themselves as harmed from rape and may use alternative language, as evidenced in some applications before the International Criminal Court, where victims used phrases such as 'faire du mal' (doing harm) to identify sexual violence.[112] Practical and procedural adaptations are therefore required to ensure that victims can not only avail of opportunities to feed into reparation design, but also apply and receive reparations in a manner that is appropriate for them.[113]

Men and boys, on the other hand, may suffer harm differently as a result of hypermasculinity, where sexual violence committed against them disrupts their gender and sexual identity, preventing them from being considered as vulnerable and speaking about their suffering.[114] At the same time, the physical impact of sexual violence against males can make them unable to live up to the 'hegemonic masculinity expectations' of their families and communities when performing manual labour to provide for their families. In this context, the provision of livestock and agricultural tools would help these victims improve their quality of life.[115] There may also be taboos and even criminal penalties for homosexual behaviour in certain contexts. As Schulz points out with his research on male victims of CRSV in northern Uganda, reparations can echo gendered understandings of payment as a dowry, making them feel inferior.[116] The invocation of these feelings in men speaks

110 Clara Sandoval, Reflections on the Transformative Potential of Transitional Justice and the Nature of Social Change in Times of Transition, in R Duthie and P Seils (eds), *Mosaics of Justice* (2017) 166–201, p170.

111 Ruth Rubio-Marín, Reparations for Conflict-Related Sexual and Reproductive Violence: A Decalogue, *William and Mary Journal of Women and the Law* 19(1) (2012–2013) 69–104, p87

112 As highlighted by victims at the ICC in the *Bemba* case—Public redacted version of 'Decision on the tenth and seventeenth transmissions of applications by victims to participate in the proceedings', ICC-01/05-01/08-2247-Red, 19 July 2012, para 37 citing the Internal Report of the field interpreters, 29 November 2011, ICC-01/05-01/08-1960-Conf-Exp-Anx2. See also in Cambodia—Katrina Natale, 'I Could Feel My Soul Flying Away From My Body' A Study on Gender-Based Violence During Democratic Kampuchea in Battambang and Svay Rieng Provinces, Cambodian Defenders Project (2011).

113 The ICC adopted the principle of gender-inclusive and sensitive to its design and implementation in the *Ntaganda* case—ICC-01/04-02/06-2659, paras 60–62.

114 Philipp Schulz, The 'Ethical Loneliness' of Male Sexual Violence Survivors in Northern Uganda: Gendered Reflections on Silencing, *International Feminist Journal of Politics* 20(4) (2018) 583–601, p595.

115 Philipp Schulz, Examining Male Wartime Rape Survivors' Perspectives on Justice in Northern Uganda, *Social and Legal Studies* 29(1) (2020) 19–40, pp33–34.

116 Philipp Schulz, 'Luk pe Coo,' or Compensation as Dowry? Gendered Reflections on Reparations for Conflict-Related Sexual Violence Against Men, *International Journal of Transitional Justice*, 12(3) (2018) 537–548, p547.

to the underlying patriarchal undertones throughout society that give rise to harm based on social constructs and cultural norms. Accordingly, gender can be an important facet in shaping appropriate reparations, but not the only lens to examine reparations for CRSV, given the social and cultural implications of sexual violence and stigma. Kalla suggests that being conscious of these issues, a gender-sensitive approach should 'adequately respond to women's and men's strengths and challenges' in claiming redress, such as reparations.[117]

Despite the expansive work by gender theorists,[118] a narrow gender lens can fixate on sexual violence against women, neglecting men, trans and non-binary gender identities as well as non-sexual gender-based violence.[119] In relation to the latter, the impacts on the health and wellbeing of women victims who experience non-sexual harm remain unappreciated in many transitional justice contexts. Women may disproportionately assume caregiver roles (dependents include children, elderly, extended family members), yet income calculations fail to encompass the full implications for women, given that many daily activities are traditionally unpaid. Loss of opportunity typically does not feature the inability to procreate as a result of sexual violence[120] or reduced marriage prospects with its associated financial security. A gender-sensitive approach might better recognize these realities.

A gender-sensitive approach might also consider that pre-conditions and consequences of sexual violence extend into many spheres, such as mental and physical health; disabilities; and adjustments in occupation, identity, community, or societal bonds. For instance, victims of sexual violence can experience psychosexual difficulties (arising from the act or a health complication, eg incontinence) making it difficult to participate in sexual relations.[121] The impact on sexual and gender identity has been narrowly understood in transitional justice (including reparations) and does not seek to adequately intersect norms around sexuality, reproduction, and society. Individual units of society are comprised of cultural norms on private and family life that need to be understood through sexual health and reproduction. In light of the need for a gender-sensitive approach, Rubio-Marín argues that reparations should be considered in light of their transformative potential.[122]

[117] Kristin Kalla, Advancing Justice and Making Amends Through Reparations: Legal and Operational Considerations, in F Ní Aoláin et al (eds), *The Oxford Handbook of Gender and Conflict*, OUP (2018) 253–264, p257.

[118] Allyson Jule, Gender Theory, in Alex C Michalos (ed), *Encyclopedia of Quality of Life and Well-Being Research*, Springer (2014) p107.

[119] Nagy, n 52, p287.

[120] Morocco: Gender and The Transitional Justice Process, ICTJ (2011) p27.

[121] Sheraz Ahmad, Adult Psychosexual Dysfunction as a Sequela of Child Sexual Abuse, *Sexual and Relationship Therapy* 21(4) (2006) 405–418; and Fiona Cowan and Leila Frodsham, Management of Common Disorders in Psychosexual Medicine, *Obstetrician and Gynaecologist* 17(1) (2015) 47–53. See Chapter 2.

[122] Ruth Rubio-Marín, Introduction: A Gender and Reparations Taxonomy, in Ruth Rubio-Marín (ed), *Unsettling Sexual Hierarchies While Redressing Human Rights Violations*, CUP (2009) 1–17, pp16–17.

The transformative approach towards reparations for CRSV is explored further in the following section and is worth discussing in more depth given the recent attention to it in the literature and perspectives from those interviewed.

5.5 Transformative Reparations and Conflict-Related Sexual Violence

5.5.1 Defining transformative reparations

Transformative justice arose as part of a critique of transitional justice in not adequately addressing structural violence. It has had particular support amongst those working on CRSV so as to 'address the underlying structures and systems in place that give rise to violence against women'.[123] Rubio-Marín suggests that a transformative approach to a reparations programme has the 'capacity to subvert, instead of reinforce, pre-existing structural inequalities', which is not limited to gender hierarchies.[124] For Uprimny, transformative reparations are not only corrective justice, but engage with distributive concerns of how resources are allocated in society and prioritize support for victims who need it.[125] Others have suggested that the transformative potential of reparations can occur on three interconnected levels: individual; institutional; and structural.[126] The individual level is concerned with ensuring access to remedies including the right to reparation given the personal nature of harm. Institutional transformation calls for legal and institutional reforms as part of the guarantee of non-recurrence, in addition to continuous professional training to ensure sexual and gender-based crimes are dealt with in a sensitive manner.[127] In some ways this can reflect gender-sensitivity, but goes beyond empathy and understanding, to structurally tackling systemic discrimination that exists during or outside of conflict.[128] However, what is perceived as transformation at these three levels is often viewed in a rather legalistic fashion with an emphasis on legal institutions and courts rather than broader social, health, or economic outcomes.[129]

[123] Manjoo, n 89, p1195.
[124] Rubio-Marín, n 122, p17.
[125] Rodrigo Uprimny Yepes, Transformative Reparations of Massive Gross Human Rights Violations: Between Corrective and Distributive Justice, *Netherlands Quarterly of Human Rights* 27 (2009) 625–647.
[126] Manjoo, n 89, p1196. Farmer takes a broad approach to structural violence, referring to socio-economic inequalities, such as racism to gender inequality and extreme poverty. See Paul Farmer, *Pathologies of Power: Health, Human Rights, and the New War On the Poor*, University of California Press (2005) pp8–9.
[127] Manjoo, n 89, pp1197–1199.
[128] ibid.
[129] ibid.

Durbach and Chappel view the transformative potential of reparations for sexual violence as comprising of recognition, representation, and redistribution.[130] The transformative potential is thus a means to ensuring political participation and equality of rights through women and girls' experiences being recognized and validated to affirm their standing in society. In addition, reparations are encouraged to assist in equitable access to economic resources as opposed to returning women and girls back to discriminatory socio-economic circumstances.[131] This transformative potential speaks more to the rights and empowerment discourse, civic participation, and the broader issues of trust that de Greiff discusses,[132] but perhaps neglects the everyday suffering and consequences of sexual violence, such as disability, stigma, and prevailing silence outside and after reparation processes.

Different conceptions of transformative reparations were discussed by interviewees. One UN official in Colombia saw it as countering silence and a culture of permissibility where,

> sexual violence is possible in a culture that tolerates sexual violence against women. Sexual violence is based on a culture that accepts that women's bodies are male property or the patriarchal culture property. Repairing the victim should imply dismounting that culture that promotes the existence of sexual violence. So, repairing the victim should not only be giving assistance and providing services but coming to a commitment to transform the society that allowed that victim to became one in the first place.[133]

Transforming a person's social and family life was often discussed by interviewees, though transformation on a wider scale was frequently not envisaged through reparations.[134] As one Colombian victim said, her suffering caused her 'personal life to change completely, it transformed me, and my main purpose is to help other women to transform as well'.[135] From discussions with victims, transitional justice practitioners, and health professionals, this transformation included a range of agendas from education[136] to plastic surgery for scars,[137] or improving the situation of certain marginalized groups, such as Afro-Colombians.[138] However, most interviewees were unfamiliar with the term, or did not see what it added to seeking

[130] Durbach and Chappell, n 13, pp551–552.
[131] ibid, pp548–549; and Sarah Williams and Emma Palmer, Transformative Reparations for Women and Girls at the Extraordinary Chambers in the Courts of Cambodia, *International Journal of Transitional Justice* 10(2) (2016) 311–331, p312.
[132] Pablo de Greiff, Justice and Reparations, in Pablo de Greiff (ed), *Handbook of Reparations*, OUP (2006) 451–477, pp463–464.
[133] C5, Bogotá, Colombia, September 2018.
[134] U5, Lira, Uganda, July 2018.
[135] C3, Bogotá, Colombia, September 2018.
[136] C14; and U10, Lira, Uganda, July 2018.
[137] O3, virtual interview, October 2018.
[138] C1, Bogotá, Colombia, September 2018.

individual reparations. For interviewees, transformation related to a need for change and hope that reparations would deliver it. As one Colombian victim said, 'a great thing it would be for us to have our own productive processes and transform ourselves into a role model for other women'.[139]

5.5.2 Transformative processes

The expectation and feasibility to deliver on structural or institutional transformation will vary according to who is deemed the responsible actor(s), the reparation mechanism (administrative or judicial), and the legal framework (permitting transformative aims). Reparation orders from international criminal courts declaring individual criminal liability are arguably not best placed to instigate reform for structural factors that contributed to conflict-related crimes, yet can have a symbolic transformative value.[140] Furthermore the convicted person may be indigent, leaving victims reliant on a trust fund or donor support rather than a State dedicated budget plan, which are often unsustainable and look more like development projects.[141] They are further constrained by only focusing on a subset of victims from selected crime sites when there is a large victim population,[142] compounded by criminal proceedings being often lengthy and without the anticipated verdict. Similarly, for domestic administrative reparation programmes, institutional reform and societal change may be beyond their capacity or effects. However, the process of designing and delivering reparations, particularly for administrative programmes, has been hailed in itself as reparative and even transformative.[143] Process-driven transformation was an emerging theme in fieldwork in Peru among political elites, yet contrasted with victims' interviews, in which they deemed education and health reparations as yielding more concrete transformation. Similar to apologies that partially denounce violations or accountability, an over-emphasis on process as reparation may be perceived by victims as states attempting to disregard their suffering or the seriousness of the violation.

139 C15, Bogotá, Colombia.

140 *Lubanga Dyilo*, Judgment on the Appeals against the 'Decision Establishing the Principles and Procedures to Be Applied to Reparations' of 7 August 2012, ICC-01/04-01/06-3129, 3 March 2015, para 34.

141 See Report by the Special Rapporteur on the promotion of truth, justice, reparation, and guarantees of non-recurrence, Pablo de Greiff, A/69/518, 8 October 2014, para 56; and Christoph Sperfeldt and Rachel Hughes, The Projectification of Reparation, *Journal of Human Rights Practice* 12(3) (2020) 545–565.

142 Williams and Palmer, n 131, p318.

143 See Brandon Hamber, The Dilemma's of Reparations: In Search of a Process-Driven Approach, in K De Feyter et al (eds), *Out of the Ashes: Reparation for Victims of Gross and Systematic Human Rights Violations*, Intersentia (2009) 135–149.

5.5.3 Transformative outcomes

Whilst transformation at the structural and institutional level is an ambitious, but important, aim of gender-sensitive reparations, a multi-dimensional approach considers the potential standalone impact of each form of reparation as well as in unison with other measures. Manjoo considers the change in practice where compensation is no longer seen as the dominant form of reparation as key to the theoretical progress of transformative reparations. Nonetheless, the individual transformative value of compensation cannot be ignored for many victims even where they have been informed of an array of reparative possibilities.[144] My fieldwork in Peru highlighted that some victims and representatives of victim groups prioritized economic compensation decades after the violation occurred and when it could no longer be used for immediate relief, perhaps due to its ideological link to moral harms and economic autonomy.[145] Furthermore, a number of the Peruvian victims spoke of how compensation represented a direct investment in the person as a citizen of the state.[146] Compensation can speak to the plurality and complexity of victims' needs as it offers them the choice to invest it in what is appropriate to them. As one NGO representative stated: 'Usually women use it to improve the conditions of their lives – from paying for their child's education to renovating their house.'[147] A Peruvian victim of sexual violence used their compensation to create a cemetery and memorial site where the belongings of their loved ones who were killed or disappeared could be buried, reflecting differing priorities and needs that are shaped by the multiple violations victims endured during conflict.[148]

From a medical perspective, doctors tend to consider individual transformation possible, referring to success stories such as surgical repair of genital fistulae, or division of adhesions from STIs that led to pelvic inflammatory disease and blocking the fallopian tubes and preventing pregnancy. Although health indicators such as mortality and morbidity can indicate transformation, typically these arise from development efforts affecting the entire population. One Ugandan healthcare practitioner described healthcare in supporting victims in broader development, as

> transforming the lives of the war victims is empowering them to stand against stigmatisation, against segregation and against all the harms that are directed

[144] Manjoo, n 89, p1196.

[145] P2 FG1, P3 FG2, and P6, Lima, Peru, May 2019. See similar expectations in Cambodia, Rachel Killean, Procedural Justice in International Criminal Courts: Assessing Civil Parties' Perceptions of Justice at the Extraordinary Chambers in the Courts of Cambodia, *International Criminal Law Review* 16(1) (2016) 1–38, p28.

[146] P2 FG1, P3 FG2, Lima, Peru, May 2019.

[147] C5, Bogotá, Colombia, September 2018.

[148] P6, Lima, Peru, May 2019.

> against their lives. So I will say transforming their lives would lead to transformation of the community where they are based.[149]

Rehabilitative indicators may more appropriately gauge transformation, particularly in victims of sexual violence, which is explored in the next chapter. In comparison to doctors, members of the community outreach team often expressed ambivalence regarding transformative potential of reparative interventions.[150] The reasons for this were not clear, but since they followed victims through their journey from the identification of needs to post receipt of treatment and other forms of reparation, they were likely to observe the complexities of managing multifaceted harm in daily life.

5.5.4 Critiques of transformative reparations

Some commentators suggest that expecting reparations to be a locus for societal transformation may overburden such legal measures.[151] According to Mani, the distinction between victims and perpetrators is futile when reparations strive to engage in larger social justice aims of reconciliation.[152] McGonigle and Fraser suggest transformative reparations are not a 'game changer', but more of an amalgamation as a 'synthesise or repackage' of existing human rights obligations on states to address victims' rights more holistically.[153] Indeed, they find the vernacular of 'transformative' is more rhetorically used as an advocacy tool for broader societal change.[154] Walker finds it is a 'false dilemma' for reparations, as state practice and human rights jurisprudence in the last few decades has moved beyond corrective justice and forms of compensation and restitution.[155] As such, seeing the transformative potential aims at a more modest understanding of what reparations by themselves can achieve in the face of systemic, socially ignored, or culturally accepted CRSV. Indeed, the victims interviewed who received reparations did not experience transformation beyond improving or alleviating some of their basic needs. Many of them they still faced stigma, marginalization, and discrimination. This may suggest reparations failing to meet their transformative potential in the face of political, social, and economic realities.

149 U6, Lira, Uganda, July 2018.

150 ibid.

151 Luke Moffett, Reparations for victims at the International Criminal Court: A New Way Forward?, *International Journal of Human Rights* 21(9) (2017) 1204–1222, p1212.

152 Rama Mani, *Beyond Retribution: Seeking Justice in the Shadows of War*, CUP (2002) p107.

153 Brianne McGonigle Leyh and Julie Fraser, Transformative Reparations: Changing the Game or More of the Same, *Cambridge International Law Journal* 8(1) (2019) 39–59.

154 ibid p58.

155 Margaret Urban Walker, Transformative Reparations? A Critical Look at a Current Trend in Thinking about Gender-Just Reparations, *International Journal of Transitional Justice* 10(1) (2016) 108–125, pp117–118.

Medical practitioners who worked with victims of sexual violence saw reparations as unable to be transformative because they often did not engage with 'sexual wellbeing'.[156] Others were more sceptical, seeing reparations as unable to deal with those who deny the occurrence of sexual violence or consider it acceptable, but acknowledging that providing healthcare can have a transformative impact on the life of a victim.[157] This was shared by other healthcare providers in Uganda who considered providing healthcare to victims of sexual violence as important for supporting their normal social functioning—helping them look after their families, go to school or work, and be more able to contribute to the community.[158] One victim of multiple instances of sexual violence said that such violations 'transform' her personal life 'completely', but she also now uses the experience to encourage other women to 'transform their lives' and be empowered by having 'a voice of our own'.[159] However, for most practitioners and victims, 'repair' was the key word in the conception of reparations and in the expectation of its implementation. 'Transformational' may be more aspirational and not reflect the expectations or experiences of those involved in CRSV.

5.6 Conclusion

Reparations for CRSV have taken decades to come to the fore in transitional justice debates and practice. They are now well established and part of the normative landscape that also challenges assumptions of doing justice to the past, looking beyond simply individual redress to tackling and transforming the structures that gave rise to such violations. These principles and practice are helpful in considering appropriate forms of reparations that have been made for CRSV by states and courts. However, there remain increasing efforts to broaden the understanding of victims' experiences so that those they engage with are gender-sensitive and do not cause secondary victimization. At the same time, efforts to seek reparations to transform the structures that contribute to CRSV have yet to meet their potential or be overburdened by the ability of reparation measures to transform society. It is apparent from some of the literature and fieldwork that transformative reparations risk overstating the benefits for victims' experiences, which are often more modest and detached from their harms.

Understanding the historical and legal context of reparations for victims of sexual violence sets the foundation for analysing the practice of implementing such measures. Chapter 6 examines the forms of reparations, which have been shaped

156 C8, Colombia, September 2018.
157 U11, Lira, Uganda, July 2018.
158 U7, Lira, Uganda, July 2018.
159 C4, Bogotá, Colombia, September 2018.

by the historical context, mainly developing from human rights jurisprudence and often focusing on remedying individual rights, as discussed in this chapter. The human rights basis of reparations has often meant that they have not addressed collective rights, broader goals of transformation, or sought to be gender-sensitive. Chapter 7 builds on the understanding of the forms of reparations, but explores the notion of vulnerability, drawing on the analysis of harm and identity, to better appreciate the consequences and lived experience of victims in engaging with and seeking reparation. Together with this chapter and the fieldwork referred to therein, they reflect a more complex picture of the nature of reparations and what it can and cannot do for victims of CRSV.

6

Remedying Conflict-Related Sexual and Reproductive Violence

The UN Basic Principles on Reparations (2005), drawing from the jurisprudence of regional human rights courts and state practice, outline five main measures of reparation: restitution; compensation; rehabilitation; measures of satisfaction; and guarantees of non-repetition. These measures are intended to be used together to respond to the different facets of harm suffered by victims of gross violations of human rights and serious breaches of international humanitarian law.[1] The forms of reparations have been distinguished between individual and collective measures, that is, those which personally benefit victims and those that have reparative effects for a group or community. In reality, the individual/collective distinction is often blurred as reparations are delivered to individual victims and particular groups or sectors in a society.

In the three case studies examined for this book, different forms of reparations were implemented. In Uganda, there has been no reparation programme, but instead a number of general assistance and reconstruction programmes.[2] The proposed National Transitional Justice Policy outlines that reparations will be 'comprehensive to facilitate victims' reintegration into society', with particular attention to the 'gender-challenges' the conflict created which include 'children born of war'. In reality, little of substance has been delivered to any victims from any sector,[3] though the recent conviction of former LRA commander Dominic Ongwen at the ICC will see some victims, in particular those subjected to forced pregnancy and sexual slavery, be eligible for reparations.[4] However, implementation remains severely constrained by Ongwen's indigence and ongoing funding deficiencies.

In Colombia, the 2011 Victims and Land Restitution Law governs most reparations, which intends to ensure comprehensive or integral reparations to satisfy victims' rights as well as to achieve 'reconciliation and lasting and sustainable

[1] Lisa Magarrell, Reparations for Massive or Widespread Human Rights Violations: Sorting Out Claims for Reparations and Social Justice, *Windsor Yearbook of Access to Justice* 22(1) (2003) 85–98, p89; and *Atala Riffo et al v Chile* (Merits, Reparations, and Costs) IACtHR Series C No 239 (24 February 2012) para 241.

[2] See Stephen Oola and Luke Moffett, *'Cul Pi Bal' Reparations for the Northern Uganda Conflict*, Reparations, Responsibility and Victimhood in Transitional Societies, RRV (2020).

[3] JLOS, National Transitional Justice Policy, Ministry of Internal Affairs, 2019, pp20–21.

[4] See Reparations Order, ICC-02/04-01/15-2074, 28 February 2024.

Redressing Rape in War. Sunneva Gilmore, Oxford University Press.
DOI: 10.1093/9780198919735.003.0006

peace'.[5] Reparations are deemed to include 'measures of restitution, compensation, rehabilitation, satisfaction and guarantees of non-repetition, in their individual, collective, material, moral and symbolic dimensions'.[6] These reparation measures are intended to be delivered alongside assistance measures to victims.[7] For victims of sexual violence, they have special protection and less onerous evidential requirements in order to benefit under the scheme.[8] Peru has a similar comprehensive reparations programme to Colombia.

In Peru, reparations were implemented in light of the truth commission's recommendations, to 'repair and compensate for the violation of human rights as well as the social, moral and material losses or damages suffered by the victims as a result of the internal armed conflict'.[9] The reparation plan PIR (Integral Reparations Plan) outlines six reparation programmes—a 'citizens' rights restitution programme; a reparations programme in education; health reparations; collective reparations; symbolic reparations; and a programme to promote and facilitate access to a solution of housing'.[10] Victims of rape were included within the reparation programme from the outset.[11] However, it excludes other forms of sexual violence, such as forced pregnancy, mutilation, and forced abortion documented in the CVR's report.[12]

This chapter explores the five forms of reparations focusing on the extent to which they address the needs of victims of CRSV. It concentrates on compensation and rehabilitation as these are the most common reparative measures practiced by states with regard to CRSV. The chapter also draws from my fieldwork—reflecting upon the experiences of victims, transitional justice practitioners, and healthcare professionals.

6.1 Restitution

Restitution is sometimes referred to as the 'purest' form of reparations since its focus is upon trying to fulfil the return or restoration of all that has been lost,

5 Article 8, Law 1448/2011.

6 Articles 25 and 69, which also states: 'Each of these measures will be implemented in favor of the victim depending on the violation of their rights and the characteristics of the victimizing act.'

7 Article 21, Law 1448/2011.

8 Articles 38, 41, 42, 137(2), and 181(3), Law 1448/2011.

9 CVR, Final Report, vol IX p154; Article 1, Law No 28592, 29 July 2005; and Julie Guillerot, *Reparations in Peru: 15 Years of Delivering Redress*, RRV (2019) p12.

10 Guillerot, n 9, p16.

11 Article 6, Law 28592.

12 Julie Guillerot, Linking Gender and Reparations in Peru: A Failed Opportunity, in Ruth Rubio-Marín (ed), *What Happened to the Women? Gender and Reparations for Human Rights Violations*, Social Science Research Council (2006) 136–193, p151. Forced sterilization is also excluded and was not documented in the CVR's report, see Sunneva Gilmore and Luke Moffett, Redressing Forced Sterilisation: The Role of the Medical Profession, *BJOG* 127(8) (2020) 923–926.

that is, re-establish the situation which existed before the wrongful act was committed.[13] In international law and human rights, restitution can include the restoration of rights or property.[14] However, restitution for sexual violence and other gross violations is much more challenging. For instance, in the *Loayza Tamayo* case, a professor in Peru was detained incommunicado, tortured, and claimed she was raped.[15] She received compensation and other forms of reparation, her employment rights were restored, including loss of salary, social security, and employment benefits, with lost career prospects and promotions considered under non-pecuniary compensation awarded by the Court. However, the Court paid no attention to the allegation of rape as it was seen as part of the coercive circumstances of her detention.[16] The threat or act of sexual violence can cause suffering that cannot simply be undone. Even the best medical treatments may not completely heal the physical and psychological damage done by such harm.[17] Legal discourses tend to gloss over the lived experiences of victims and survivors of such harms, and the language of restitution can sound naive at best.[18]

The notion of restitution for victims of sexual violence is closely linked with the other forms of reparation when framed as the re-establishment of a person's dignity, citizenship, and reputation.[19] For instance, in Uganda in 2019, a proposed restitution programme aimed to provide birth certificates to children born during captivity by the LRA, but by 2025 this had not materialized.[20] This is particularly important for women and girls, who despite being allowed to return to their communities, faced practical and legal barriers such as being unable to register the citizenship and birth of their children due to questions around their nationality and paternal lineage.[21] This can prevent these children from attending university, obtaining a loan, or buying a house, as they do not have citizenship, having been born in the bush.[22] One Ugandan woman, who was sexually enslaved by the LRA

[13] Article 35, Articles on Responsibility of States for Internationally Wrongful Acts; and Luke Moffett, *Justice for Victims Before the International Criminal Court*, Routledge (2014) p168.

[14] Mohamed Cherif Bassiouni, International Recognition of Victims' Rights, *Human Rights Law Review* 6(2) (2006) 203–279, p268.

[15] The Commission could not substantiate this claim, but agreed her treatment was inhumane and degrading. *Loayza Tamayo v Peru* (Judgment) IACtHR Series C No 33 (17 September 1997) para 58.

[16] *Loayza-Tamayo v Peru* (Reparations and Costs) IACtHR Series C No 42 (27 November 1998) paras 116–117.

[17] See Chapter 2.

[18] One victim specifically used the word 'restitution' when speaking about reparations, others spoke more about specific interventions such as psychological support, compensation, and medical treatment. Restitution and restoration more generally were used by six transitional justice practitioners and one Ugandan healthcare professional, reflecting its more professional vernacular than conceptualized or understood by victims and healthcare practitioners.

[19] Colleen Duggan and Ruth Jacobson, Reparation of Sexual and Reproductive Violence: Moving from Codification to Implementation, in Ruth Rubio-Marín, *The Gender of Reparations*, CUP (2009) 121–161, p154.

[20] Carol Natukunda, Gov't To Register Children Born During LRA War, *New Vision*, 12 May 2019.

[21] Virginie Ladisch, *From Rejection to Redress: Overcoming Legacies of Conflict-Related Sexual Violence in Northern Uganda*, ICTJ (2015) p23.

[22] Patrick Ocen, Victims: Front and Centre, Redress and Impunity Watch, October 2019.

and has advocated for her children born in the bush to benefit from this certification scheme, said that such restitutions are about 'restoring the life of the person after conflict . . . to restore what has been denied'.[23]

Other practical forms of restitution, such as those linked to property, have limited utility in remedying sexual violence. Duggan and Jacobson identify restitution that fundamentally restores the 'good name' of women victims of sexual violence may do little to subvert gendered values attached to women, namely marriage suitability, reduced autonomy, and reproductive capacity.[24] This may include returning women and children born of war to their paternal community to access inheritance and other rights.[25] The sensitivity and taboo status of subjects of a sexual nature may problematize restitution, as there may be a tendency to reference pre-existing gendered values rather than an alternative, more progressive view on women's citizenship and reproductive rights. However, recognition of individual's rights can improve their autonomy as rightholders and treat them with respect and dignity, which in turn challenge these pre-existing values. This also speaks to the importance of restoring rights to victims, but often needs to be accompanied by compensation and other measures to alleviate their suffering.

6.2 Compensation

Compensation is the provision of monetary awards that seek to quantify or provide a comparable value to the damage that has been caused or lost. The UN Basic Principles outline that compensation can include:

(a) Physical or mental harm;
(b) Lost opportunities, including employment, education and social benefits;
(c) Material damages and loss of earnings, including loss of earning potential;
(d) Moral damage;
(e) Costs required for legal or expert assistance, medicine and medical services, and psychological and social services.[26]

An individual payment can represent a tangible and symbolic recognition of victims' suffering. It can also give victims the choice and agency to use resources as they see fit.[27] Under international human rights law, compensation is largely

[23] U4, Gulu, Uganda, July 2018.
[24] Duggan and Jacobson, n 19, p155.
[25] See Amnesty International, 'Do Not Remain Silent': Survivors of Sexual Violence in South Sudan Call for Justice and Reparations, 24 July 2017.
[26] Principle 20.
[27] Ernesto Verdeja, A Normative Theory of Reparations in Transitional Democracies, *Metaphilosophy* 37(3–4) (2006) 449–469, p460; and Truth and Reconciliation Commission of South Africa Report (1998) vol 5, p179.

viewed as the 'next best' remedy where restitution of victims to their original position before the violation is not possible.[28] Symbolically, under international human rights law, compensation is also designed to 'affirm public respect for the victim and give public recognition of the wrongdoer's fault in failing to respect basic rights'.[29] Compensatory awards that do not acknowledge responsibility have been ruled as insufficient to be an adequate remedy commensurate with the harm caused by sexual violence and the state's human rights obligation to ensure an effective remedy.[30]

However, compensation can be a 'double-edged sword'—particularly for victims who have suffered serious harms.[31] While on the one hand compensation can help alleviate needs and meet costs to allow some form of quality of life for victims, on the other it can be a constant reminder of their violation.[32] Moon has argued that state reparations are sometimes used politically as an alternative to victims' desire for retributive justice.[33] Drawing on Argentina's Madres de Plaza de Mayo (mothers of the disappeared) and the military Junta's Dirty War of 1976–1983, the state attempted to limit prosecutions of those responsible via amnesties and pardons. As such, some of the madres considered financial and symbolic reparations (via memorials) as a means to buy their silence and halt truth recovery and prosecutions.[34] In a similar vein, in Colombia and Peru, victims also told me they were concerned that domestic reparations could be used as a 'trade-off' for prosecuting those most responsible for sexual violence.[35] Similarly, in Uganda, victims expressed concern that reparations funded by the state would be insufficient to meet their needs, and that they too desired prosecutions.

Compensation may also produce 'ambivalence' amongst some victims, generating feelings of guilt and shame for accepting a monetary amount for their suffering.[36] This can often be seen when such awards are not associated with an acknowledgement of responsibility making victims feel that it is 'blood money' to

[28] Dinah Shelton, *Remedies in International Human Rights Law*, 2nd ed., Oxford University Press (2006), p21.

[29] ibid pp291–292.

[30] *Sharma v Nepal*, CCPR/C/122/D/2364/2014, Human Rights Committee, 25 May 2018, para 9.12.

[31] Brandon Hamber, Repairing the Irreparable, Dealing with the Double-Binds of Making Reparations for Crimes of the Past, *Ethnicity and Health* 5(3–4) (2000) 215–226, p219.

[32] See, for the experience in Croatia—Janine Natalya Clark, In from the Margins: Survivors of Wartime Sexual Violence in Croatia and an Early Analysis of the New Law, *Journal of Human Rights Practice*, 8(1) (2016) 128–147.

[33] Claire Moon, 'Who'll Pay Reparations on My Soul? Compensation, Social Control and Social Suffering, *Social and Legal Studies* 21(2) (2012) 187–199.

[34] ibid p193.

[35] In Peru, victims of forced sterilization felt that senior ministers and ex-President Fujimori, who were responsible for creating the forced sterilization policy, should face trial rather than only targeting 'a few rogue doctors'. P2 FG1 and P3 FG2, Lima, Peru, May 2019, Lima Peru; and C3, Bogotá Colombia, September 2018.

[36] Thomas M Antkowiak, Remedial Approaches to Human Rights Violations: The Inter-American Court of Human Rights and Beyond, *Columbia Journal of International Law* 46 (2007–2008) 351–419, p388.

silence them.[37] In a similar vein, the Japanese government originally offered the so-called 'Comfort Women' a fund for reparations, but without acknowledging the Japanese Empire's responsibility for their sexual enslavement.[38] Similarly, in Bosnia and Herzegovina, victims of conflict-related sexual violence receive monthly pensions comparable to citizens with disabilities, rather than reparations.[39] In effect, this frames the harms wrought by sexual violence as social welfare rather than acknowledging the responsibility of 'their side' for such atrocities.[40] This sentiment was shared by a Ugandan civil society actor who said:

> I know mothers who told me 'I can never even receive any money even if they brought money as reparations, it would be like selling the blood of my child for that money, I can never take anything in place of the life of my child'[41]

The process of awarding compensation requires attempting to quantify the unquantifiable in the context of serious human rights violence such as sexual violence.[42] As discussed in chapter 3 on harm, the economic quantification of compensation in terms of adequacy is exacerbated by mass victimization at a time when society may also be undergoing economic recovery. Therefore, amounts of compensation are often shaped by what is economically feasible for the local state. In determining appropriate levels of compensation, those involved may be required to make judgements on material amounts based on the severity of the harm caused as well as what are sometimes referred to as 'moral' damages for harmed caused by violations.[43] Such moral damages can include awards for the damage to a victim's dignity and reputation due to stigmatization or the effect on a woman's ability to marry or access social benefits.[44] The European Court of Human Rights has held that compensation for moral harm is justified as gross violations cause 'evident trauma, whether physical or psychological, pain and suffering, distress, anxiety, frustration, feelings of injustice or humiliation, prolonged uncertainty,

[37] Hamber, n 31, p222; and Verdeja, n 27, p460.
[38] Carlton Waterhouse, The Good, the Bad and the Ugly: Moral Agency and the Role of Victims in Reparations Programs, *University of Pennsylvania Journal of International Law* 31(1) (2009) 257–294, pp276–277.
[39] Lejla Hadzimesic, Consequences of Conflict-Related Sexual Violence on Post-Conflict Society: Case Study of Reparations in Bosnia and Herzegovina, in F Ní Aoláin et al (eds), *The Oxford Handbook of Gender and Conflict*, OUP (2017) 508–520, p510.
[40] ibid.
[41] U1, Kampala, Uganda, July 2018.
[42] Brandon Hamber, The Dilemmas of Reparations: In Search of a Process-Driven Approach, in K de Feyter et al (eds), *Out of the Ashes: Reparation for Victims of Gross and Systematic Human Rights Violations*, Intersentia (2005) 135–149, p137.
[43] *B.J. v Denmark*, Views of 10 May 2000, CERD/C/56/D/17/1999, para 7; and *Velásquez Rodríguez v. Honduras*, Inter-American Court of Human Rights, Judgment of 29 July 1988, Series C No. 4, para. 48.
[44] Gabriella Citroni, *Between Stigma and Oblivion, A Guide on Defending the Rights of Women Victims of Rape or other Forms of Sexual Violence in Bosnia and Herzegovina*, Trial (2012) p56.

disruption to life, or real loss of opportunity'.[45] Such non-pecuniary compensation is intended to recognize the 'moral damage' and severity of the harm, but is not intended to act as a 'financial comfort or sympathetic enrichment at the expense' of the state.[46] Again, this is a difficult balance to strike between not impoverishing or enriching victims, yet being unable to adequately quantify the harm suffered, meaning that such amounts are based on equity.[47]

This contrasts with pecuniary or material awards of compensation that provide a quantifiable amount of money for measurable damages to assets, loss of opportunities, and loss of income or property. However, international—or indeed national—court-based assessments for adjudicating individual instances of human rights violations may be far higher than domestic reparation programmes, creating an asymmetrical system in the value assigned to similar victimization.[48] In calculating pecuniary or economic damage, it is important to be aware of the ways in which local gender roles may shape compensation claims. For instance, in many communities, for women who work at home looking after family, or working on family land (where they do not receive any income), calculations of appropriate compensation levels cannot be made on the basis of income, loss of earnings, or the equivalent.[49] As a result of forced disappearances or killings of male family members, women (and children) may also have had to fulfil multiple roles that were previously undertaken by men, sometimes whilst enduring their own health problems as a result of sexual violence.

Quantifying such non-pecuniary harm to compensate for sexual violence represents judicial discretion based on fairness or equity. As the Inter-American Court of Human Rights (IACtHR) has explained for non-pecuniary compensation, it is intended to cover the 'suffering and distress' or detriment to their 'significant values', and can be justified

> through acts or works that are public in terms of their scope or repercussion, such as transmitting a message of official condemnation of the human rights violations involved and of commitment with efforts to ensure that they never happen again, that have the effect of honoring the memory of the victims, recognizing their dignity and providing consolation to their next of kin.[50]

[45] *Varnava and Others v Turkey*, App nos 16064/90, 16065/90, 16066/90, 16068/90, 16069/90, 16070/90, 16071/90, 16072/90, and 16073/90, ECtHR, 18 September 2009, para 224.

[46] ibid.

[47] Luke Moffett, Transitional Justice and Reparations: Remedying the Past?, in Cheryl Lawther, Luke Moffett & Dov Jacobs (eds), *Research Handbook on Transitional Justice*, Edward Elgar (2017) 377–400, p394

[48] See Clara Sandoval, Two Steps Forward, One Step Back: Reflections on the Jurisprudential Turn of the Inter-American Court of Human Rights on Domestic Reparation Programmes, *International Journal of Human Rights* 22(9) (2018) 1192–1208.

[49] The World Bank, World Development Report: Gender Equality and Development, 2012, ch 5.

[50] *Case of Molina Theissen v Guatemala* (Reparations and Costs) IACtHR Series C No 108 (3 July 2004) para 66.

In other cases involving multiple violations including sexual violence, the Court did not distinguish a specific amount for each violation.[51] It has been argued that economic damage should be also interpreted as including loss of educational opportunities, employment, or social benefits, as well as the material implications of the birth of children as a result of rape, fertility issues for women and men, and lifelong sexual and reproductive health problems.[52] For instance, in *Plan de Sánchez v Guatemala*, while rape did not feature in the merits judgment, it did in the reparations decision; nevertheless the Court provided a base rate to all survivors of $20,000 USD for non-pecuniary damage, with no specific consideration or award for victims of sexual violence.[53] Rubio-Marín and Sandoval have noted that in this case the Court neglected the specific harm that female victims experienced during the massacre.[54] In a sense, being the wife, daughter, or sister to survive a genocidal act as an indirect victim, eclipsed these women's own personal direct sexual victimization. In the later case of the *Village of Chichupac and neighbouring communities v Guatemala*, rape was recognized in other measures of the Court's reparation order, but it was again not reflected in the compensation award.[55]

A gender-sensitive approach to compensation would consider all the consequences flowing from sexual violence, both pecuniary and moral harms. For instance, in the *Cantu v Mexico* case, Rosendo Cantu, a 17-year-old indigenous woman, was beaten and raped by eight soldiers,[56] which had a profound effect on her life.[57] In calculating the non-pecuniary compensation the judge considered that Rosendo was a child at the time of the rape, the nature and seriousness of the violations, the suffering caused to her and her daughter, how she was treated by the authorities, the time that had elapsed since the rape, the denial of justice, and the change in their living conditions and other consequences they suffered.[58] As a result the court awarded her $60,000 USD and $10,000 USD for her daughter for having to live in exile and inciting disruption to her family.[59] This was awarded

[51] *Loayza-Tamayo v Peru* (Judgment, Reparations, and Costs) IACtHR Series C No 42 (27 November 1998) para 139; and *Molina Theissen v Guatemala* (Reparations and Costs) IACtHR Series C No 108 (3 July 2004) para 70.

[52] See Fionnuala Ní Aoláin, Catherine O'Rourke, and Aisling Swaine, Transforming Reparations for Conflict-Related Sexual Violence: Principles and Practice. *Harvard Human Rights Journal*, 28(1) (2015) 95–144.

[53] *Plan de Sánchez Massacre v Guatemala* (Reparations) IACtHR Series C No 116 (19 November 2024) paras 87–89.

[54] Rubio-Marín and Sandoval (2011) pp1072–1073.

[55] *Members of the Village of Chichupac and neighboring communities of the Municipality of Rabinal v Guatemala* (Preliminary Objections, Merits, Reparations and Costs) IACtHR Series C No 328 (30 November 2016) paras 324–328.

[56] *Rosendo Cantú et al v Mexico* (Preliminary Objection, Merits, Reparations, and Costs) IACtHR Series C No 216 (31 August 2010) paras 72–75.

[57] ibid para 277.

[58] ibid para 279.

[59] ibid.

alongside other forms of reparations, including scholarships to higher education for Rosendo and her daughter.[60]

In other cases, the Inter-American Court has recognized a range of sexual violence as compensable, including forced nudity,[61] groping and sexual assault,[62] penetration of the vagina with a finger,[63] and sexual torture, including threats of rape, pinching, and hitting intimate parts of the body (genitals, breasts, and mouth).[64] The European Court of Human Rights (ECtHR) has also awarded compensation for forced gynaecological assessment,[65] forced nudity,[66] and rape,[67] but often does not order other forms of reparations finding that the judgment and relevant compensation as just satisfaction.[68] The ECtHR regularly orders an overall sum without explicitly determining the amount of compensation per violation or any non-pecuniary and pecuniary distinction.[69] While the UN Human Rights Committee does not rule on specific amounts of compensation, in its first decision on conflict-related sexual violence in *Sharma v Nepal*, involving the claimant being disappeared and tortured including being threatened with rape. The Committee ruled that interim relief payments of 246,000 rupees ($2,500 USD) by the state were insufficient to be an adequate remedy commensurate with sexual violence.[70]

Medical expertise can also be unevenly adopted in an attempt to reduce credibility in cases of sexual violence in evidencing claims for compensation. For example, in *E.B v Romania*, the ECtHR recognized that domestic authorities did not seek input from a mental health specialist or psychologist regarding the context of the claimant's responses, or take into account the intellectual disability (oligophrenia) and depressive state of the claimant that may have heightened her vulnerability.[71] Instead, domestic authorities selectively emphasized the lack of genital injuries (despite apparent physical trauma not always manifesting from

[60] ibid para 257.

[61] The victims were awarded $10,000 USD for this—*Miguel Castro Castro Prison v Peru* (Merits, Reparations, and Costs) IACtHR Series C No 160 (25 November 2006) paras 305–307 and 432(h).

[62] *Case of Women Victims of Sexual Torture in Atenco v Mexico* (Preliminary Objection, Merits, Reparations, and Costs) IACtHR Series C No 371 (28 November 2018) para 187.

[63] The victim was awarded $30,000 USD non-pecuniary compensation for this rape—*Castro Castro*, n 61, paras 309 and 432(g).

[64] *Atenco*, n 62, paras 188 and 196.

[65] *Y.F. v Turkey*, App no 24209/94, ECtHR, Judgment on Merits and Just Satisfaction, 22 July 2003, para 48.

[66] *Valašinas v Lithuania*, App no 44558/98, ECtHR, Judgment, 24 July 2001, para 141.

[67] *Aydin v Turkey*, App no 23178/94, ECtHR, Judgment on Merits and Just Satisfaction, 25 September 1997, para 131.

[68] Helen Keller and Cedric Marti, Reconceptualizing Implementation: The Judicialization of the Execution of the European Court of Human Rights' Judgments, *The European Journal of International Law* 26(4) (2016) 829–850, p844.

[69] Article 41, ECHR. See James Gallen, The European Court of Human Rights, Transitional Justice and Historical Abuse in Consolidated Democracies, *Human Rights Law Review*, (2020) 1–30, p14.

[70] *Sharma v Nepal*, CCPR/C/122/D/2364/2014, Human Rights Committee, 25 May 2018, para 9.12.

[71] *E.B. v Romania*, App no 49089/10, ECtHR, Judgment, 19 March 2019, paras 59–60. Note, oligophrenia refers to a group of mental disorders characterized by reduced intellectual activity, which can be congenital or acquired in infancy.

rape), and discounted bruises on the victim's arms, as this trauma could not be reliably connected to rape. The failure to apply an adequate medico-legal approach at the investigation stage impeded subsequent or timely domestic-ordered reparations. The non-pecuniary damage awarded was higher than other similar cases (€12,000 USD) on the basis that psychological distress was endured through the state's failure to adequately respond to allegations, including seeking appropriate expertise.[72]

The Inter-American Court has recognized that violations of an individual's reproductive rights can also be compensable. For instance, in the *Castro Castro* case—where three women who were between 5 and 8 months pregnant were denied antenatal medical care during the military raid on the prison, forced to lie on their abdomens for long periods, and only received medical care during labour—they were awarded $5,000 USD.[73] In the *I.V. v Bolivia* case, while not a conflict case, the decision did not distinguish between the pecuniary and non-pecuniary compensation, awarding $50,000 USD for forced sterilization.[74] In the friendly settlement involving victims of forced sterilization cases in Peru, the state agreed to $10,000 USD compensation for each of the eight claimants.[75] In order to avoid creating a hierarchy of sexual harms (in which one is more compensable than another), in the *Atenco* case covering a range of sexual torture and rape, the Court awarded $70,000 USD to each of the victims and $15,000 USD to their next of kin.[76] The Court stated that these amounts were explicitly intended to reflect the gravity of these violations.

In terms of the practice in domestic reparation programmes, pecuniary and non-pecuniary compensation is not differentiated. Given the high number of victims that are often affected, claimants are stratified based on their violation and circumstances, rather than an individual assessment of their harm. For instance, in Croatia, victims of CRSV are entitled to 100,000 kuna (about €12,200 USD), or if there are aggravating circumstances this can be increased to 150,000 kuna (about €18,400 USD).[77] Victims are also entitled to a monthly allowance that is determined in the budget each year.[78] In comparison, in neighbouring Bosnia and Herzegovina, victims of CRSV only receive a monthly allowance,[79] and in Serbia, victims of sexual violence are excluded as they need to show physical and

[72] ibid para 72.

[73] *Castro Castro*, n 61, paras 197(57) and 432(f).

[74] *Case of I.V. v Bolivia* (Preliminary Objections, Merits, Reparations and Costs) IACtHR Series C No 329 (30 November 2016) para 358.

[75] *Friendly Settlement María Mamérita Mestanza Chávez and Peru*, Report No 71/03, Petition 12.191, 22 October 2003.

[76] *Atenco*, n 62, para 376.

[77] Such as forced pregnancy, forced abortion, forced birth, or sexual violence committed against a minor victim. HLC, The Legal and Institutional Framework in Serbia Regarding the Rights and Needs of Civilian Victims of War, 2017, p 45.

[78] In 2016, this amounted to 328 EUR: ibid.

[79] In 2016, this was 540 KM (260 EUR): ibid p50.

permanent harm, which is difficult in many sexual violence violations.[80] In Chile, annual pensions of between approximately $2,300 USD and $2,600 USD were awarded to survivors of sexual abuse.[81] In Peru, a fixed rate of $3,700 USD was awarded to eligible victims who suffered harm that resulted in disability or from sexual violence connected to the conflict, with the same amount to be apportioned amongst the next of kin of those killed or disappeared.[82] It is apparent that for similar forms of sexual violence, that is, rape, there is no agreed flat rate of compensation for non-pecuniary harm and perhaps there should not be one so as to reflect the circumstances of the victim. However, inequalities can still exist between domestic awards through administrative reparation programmes and court ordered ones, as in cases involving Peru at the IACtHR, where victims of sexual violence were awarded $30,000 USD,[83] which is in stark contrast to the $3,700 USD they would have received under the PIR.[84]

The inclusion of victims of CRSV within domestic compensation programmes is intended to deal with the past and is arguably an illustration of such crimes being given increased priority. By way of example, in the Philippines, the severity and therefore prioritization for reparations places victims of rape or sexual abuse at the same level as torture (6–9 out of 10), with disappearance or death being seen as the most serious at the top of the scale at 10.[85] In Sierra Leone, victims of CRSV were prioritized as a vulnerable group by the Truth and Reconciliation Commission, which included women and girls subjected to sexual slavery, rape, mutilation, and forced marriage, as well as men and boys who experienced sexual violence.[86] The Sierra Leone Truth and Reconciliation Commission justified the inclusion of CRSV victims in the priority group not based on an assessment of their income for compensation, but because of the particular stigma they faced and their inability to sustain themselves.[87]

However, as discussed above, not all reparation programmes adequately provide compensation for CRSV. Peru only included victims of rape. In Nepal the interim relief programme provided compensation to those who had been killed, displaced, or injured, but excluded victims of CRSV.[88] In Guatemala reparations were only available to female victims of sexual violence, not male victims.[89]

80 ibid pp10 and p30.

81 See Elizabeth Lira, The Reparations Policy for Human Rights Violations in Chile, in Pablo de Greiff (ed), *The Handbook of Reparations*, OUP (2006) 55–101.

82 Supreme Decree No 051-2011-PCM, 16 June 2011.

83 *Castro Castro*, n 61, para 433(c)(ix).

84 These victims were not eligible under the PIR, as they were convicted members of the Shining Path, which has created further tension among victims.

85 Section 19(2), Human Rights Victims Reparation and Recognition Act of 2013, Republic Act No 10368.

86 Sierra Leone Truth & Reconciliation Commission, Witness to Truth: Final Report of the Truth and Reconciliation Commission TRC, vol 2, ch. 4, Graphic Packaging Ltd (2004) para 95.

87 ibid ch 4, para 96.

88 Ruben Carranza, *Relief, Reparations, and the Root Causes of Conflict in Nepal*, ICTJ (2012) p10.

89 Duggan and Jacobson, n 19, 121–161, p138.

In Guatemala, for some of those female victims that did come forward to claim, it appears that some families or communities would pressurise them to speak out publicly with their stories of victimization and register with the reparation programme (PNR) to obtain compensation.[90] However, when they did come forward to claim compensation they were sometimes accused by elements of the local community of 'willingly giving sex to the enemy for money.'[91] In a similar fashion to the 'Comfort Women', these claims around compensation and aspects of victim competition, even community resentment, left some victims feeling further victimized, stigmatized, and silenced by virtue of having claimed compensation.[92] This can be particularly acute in cases of CRSV, given variable local understandings of the meaning of 'consent' and victims in some circumstances being labelled as prostitutes for making such compensation claims.[93]

Compensation itself can be a gendered notion. As noted in chapter 5, Schulz found that in Northern Uganda where hegemonic masculinities prevail, a small minority of male victims of sexual violence considered compensation as a similar form of dowry or customary payment related to a sexual relationship.[94] Compensation is regarded by some male victims as having somehow been 'feminised'[95] because such payments are regarded as 'for women'. In Peru the institution responsible for delivering reparations to victims, the Single Victim Registry (RUV), sought to ensure that payments went directly to victims, in particular women, as the husband or partner 'would expect to receive the money himself [as the one] responsible for administering money in the family'.[96]

There are also risks to victims of sexual violence receiving compensation, as one transitional justice practitioner in Colombia, where victims are eligible to receive an award to the equivalent of a 30-month minimum wage ($7,800 USD), noted,

> many women have problems with compensation because their family members or intimate circle don't know that they have been victims of sexual violence. If a woman gets home suddenly with a 25 million pesos cheque, this could be very problematic.[97]

Thus, a gender-sensitive approach needs to consider how compensation has a socio-cultural connotation for victims receiving money for their harm and how

[90] ibid.
[91] ibid p142.
[92] Waterhouse, n 38, p276.
[93] Chunghee Sarah Soh, The Korean 'Comfort Women': Movement for Redress, *Asian Survey* 36(12) (1996) 1226–1240, p1239.
[94] Philipp Schulz, 'Luk pe Coo,' or Compensation as Dowry? Gendered Reflections on Reparations for Conflict-Related Sexual Violence Against Men, *International Journal of Transitional Justice*, 12(3) (2018) 537–548, p547.
[95] ibid.
[96] P12, Lima, Peru, May 2019.
[97] C5, Bogotá, Colombia, September 2018.

this can be mitigated or sensitized so as to reduce further stigma, such as distinguishing it from a dowry in the Ugandan context.

The severity of the specific physical violation of sexual violence can also be compounded by inequality, destitution, and social dislocation, as well as family separation and isolation. As noted above, sexual violence has long-term ramifications for the economic future of the survivors. For example, in the Democratic Republic of Congo, and among Ethiopian refugees in Sudan, research found that agricultural output has reduced because women who were sexually violated were afraid to return to their 'normal' lives.[98] Similarly, a study of male survivors of sexual violence in the Democratic Republic of Congo found that all of them had abandoned their previous occupations as a result of fear and stigma, with the result that their families lacked 'funds to meet basic household needs such as food, medication, shelter and education for children'.[99] For women, the stigma attached to sexual violence and the consequences flowing from such stigma can be linked to the high value placed on ideals such as chastity, honour, and purity. The stigma attached to sexual violence can result in the breakdown of the family unit with severe economic consequences. In contexts where marriage represents women's best—and sometimes only—route to security, abandonment by their partner or the loss of their marriage prospects can be detrimental to their future and result in a lifetime of poverty.[100] Sexual violence can also have implications for indirect victims, in particular children born of rape. Thus, in Peru, children born of rape are recognized as a separate beneficiary of reparations, enabling them to claim compensation up until the age of 18 and preferential access to education.[101]

The moral and material damage caused by sexual violence may therefore require a combination of individual and collective reparations.[102] Compensation to each victim would be most appropriate, given the personal harm caused, but complemented with wider collective measures of rehabilitation, measures of satisfaction, and guarantees of non-recurrence. Compensation may take the form of a lump-sum payment, which can support a victim's agency to spend the money how they choose. Moreover, a lump sum can provide victims who have been stigmatized with the financial independence to start over, that is, to live elsewhere or find

[98] See J Kelly et al, Hope for the Future Again: Tracing the Effects of Sexual Violence and Conflict on Families and Communities in Eastern Democratic Republic of the Congo, Harvard Humanitarian Initiative (2011).

[99] M Christian et al, Sexual and Gender Based Violence Against Men in the Democratic Republic of Congo: Effects on Survivors, Their families and the Community, *Medicine, Conflict and Survival* 27(4) (2011) 227–246.

[100] See Harvard Humanitarian Initiative and Oxfam International; and Fionnuala Ní Aoláin, Gendered Under-Enforcement in the Transitional Justice Context, in S Buckley-Zistel and R Stanley (eds), *Gender in Transitional Justice*, Springer (2012) 59–87, p69.

[101] Ley 28592, Ley que crea el Plan Integral de Reparaciones (PIR), artículo 6(c) [Law 28592, Law establishing the Comprehensive Reparations Plan (PIR), Article 6(c)].

[102] REDRESS, A Report on Reparations and Remedies for Victims of Sexual and Gender Based Violence, 2016, p9.

alternative employment.[103] As one Peruvian transitional justice practitioner found with victims of sexual violence,

> they used the compensation to buy a small house, to improve the house they already own, to study, to get medical treatments, to start a business or strengthen the one they have.[104]

At the same time, some victims may be vulnerable, in debt, or psychologically traumatized, meaning that their money is misspent or misused, particularly where they are unable to hold their own bank account. Compensation payments made public may also incentivize further victimization. Perpetrating groups that are dissatisfied with the objectives of transitional justice or judicial decisions have threatened victims to give them the money.[105] Moreover, some schemes may be vulnerable to abuse. During an interview with Peru's Unique Victims Registry (RUV), the coordinators told me how the lower thresholds of evidence required in claiming compensation for CRSV may have contributed to unexpectedly high registrations for this violation, to the extent that an external auditor concluded that there were excessive false claims for CRSV, closing the register in the municipality of San Martin.[106] The abuse of compensation claims by other citizens was perhaps motivated by ongoing conditions of poverty and inequality, or prevalent sexual violence which was not explicitly linked to the conflict. Similar corruption has also been noted in Sierra Leone by community leaders claiming family members suffered CRSV.[107]

Some authors commentating on the role of compensation for other forms of violations have also raised the question of whether such awards should make victims self-sufficient for their own future.[108] This may be problematic especially where compensation is awarded for the use of approved 'productive projects' in which victims are then expected to sustain themselves.[109] However, for victims of CRSV, compensation can at least provide some financial security in a climate of stigma that limits or inhibits earning opportunities, may dissuade them from illegal and unregulated sex work, and offers support where they have been rejected by their home, community, or family. Instead of one-off payments, a regular pension every

[103] UN Guidance Note, p17.

[104] P12, Lima, Peru, May 2019.

[105] Luke Moffett, Struggling for Reparations in Northern Ireland, in C Ferstman and M Goetz (eds), *Reparations for Victims of Genocide, War Crimes and Crimes Against Humanity: Systems in Place and Systems in the Making*, Brill (2020) 678-709.

[106] P3, Lima, Peru, May 2019.

[107] Eva Ottendoerfer, Translating Victims' 'Right to Reparations' Into Practice: A Framework for Assessing the Implementation of Reparations Programs from a Bottom-Up Perspective, *Human Rights Quarterly* 40(4) (2018) 905–931, p927.

[108] Max Counter, Producing Victimhood: Landmines, Reparations, and Law in Colombia, *Antipode* 50(1) (2018) 122–141.

[109] ibid.

week, month, or year can assist victims to have some financial security in the long term. Yet in situations of mass victimization, the delivery of compensation can be slow. In the case of Colombia, only 10 per cent of compensation has been delivered and there was fatigue and frustration amongst victims of sexual violence waiting for redress. As one victim told me:

> compensation for female victims of sexual violence, is only for me. No member of the family is considered for compensation. Nevertheless, this compensation is not being delivered. The government say they are prioritizing elderly women, women with disabilities, women with terminal diseases. But that is it . . . only words. We get invitations to 2 or 3 workshops, we fill in forms and put our names in lists, and that's it, that is supposed to be reparation, and facilitators say 'we are smiling now'. We smile, we laugh off course, but what about the guarantee of reparations the state owes us. There is nothing there. That is a very serious problem, a problem that we ask urgently for help, from the international level, because to get it from our own country has been impossible.[110]

Compensation can assist in providing financial support in managing the consequences of their suffering, but it will often never be enough. In this regard, monetary compensation is insufficient by itself and, as noted above, it should be complemented with other rehabilitative and reparative measures.[111] As one Peruvian victim of sexual violence said, 'we received compensation for sexual violence reparation of 10,000 soles [$3,000 USD], but there was no psychological reparation, which is the most important reparation that they could give us, so that we can live a better life.'[112]

6.3 Rehabilitation

The notion of rehabilitation has different meanings across a range of disciplines. For example, within criminology, the term is associated with efforts to change deviant or criminal behaviour on the part of former prisoners or offenders.[113] As a result of sustained critique of the idea that rehabilitation was something done *to* ex-prisoners, or indeed as the rationale for practices which corrode the rights of such individuals, the term has also been broadened to include a range of familial,

[110] C15 FG1, Bogotá, Colombia, March 2019.
[111] *RPB v the Philippines*, CEDAW, 12 March 2014, Communication No 34/2011.
[112] P4, Peru, May 2019.
[113] Sonja Meijer, Rehabilitation as a Positive Obligation, *European Journal of Crime, Criminal Law and Criminal Justice* 25(2) (2017) 145–162, p146. F Allen, *The Decline of the Rehabilitative Ideal*, Yale University Press (1981); Francis T Cullen and Karen E Gilbert, *Reaffirming Rehabilitation*, Anderson (1982); and E Rotman, Do Offenders Have a Constitutional Rights to Rehabilitation?, *Journal of Criminal Law & Criminology* 77 (1986) 1023–1068, p1024.

environmental, or indeed personal variables which may assist offenders in desisting from crime.[114] Similarly, rehabilitation in medicine is referred to as the process that helps patients recover. This encompasses both medical treatment and a 'reiterative, active, educational, problem solving process focused on a patient's behaviour' and outcomes aimed at maximizing the patient's participation in their own recovery to minimize their pain and distress, as well as that of their family and carers.[115] Rehabilitation is not only about treating the disease, but also about recognizing the person 'behind the disease' and the effect of illness on their life and the lives of those close to them, to ensure that their recovery is designed to 'maximize a person's participation in society.'[116] Rehabilitation within the reparations literature is a catch-all phrase intended to encompass a range of care and services for victims, designed to achieve a similarly broad range of objectives.

Despite the breadth of rehabilitation as reparation, the 2005 UN Basic Principles on Reparations only dedicate one line to rehabilitation, providing little guidance on the scope of this obligation, covering merely 'medical and psychological care as well as legal and social services.'[117] The UN Committee Against Torture has emphasized that rehabilitation should be 'holistic' and aimed at the

> restoration of function or the acquisition of new skills required by the changed circumstances of a victim in the aftermath of torture or ill-treatment. It seeks to enable the maximum possible self-sufficiency and function for the individual concerned, and may involve adjustments to the person's physical and social environment. Rehabilitation for victims should aim to restore, as far as possible, their independence, physical, mental, social and vocational ability; and full inclusion and participation in society.[118]

Such rehabilitation may need to look beyond initial assistance for serious violations such as torture and sexual violence that requires long-term medical care.[119] The African Court of Human and People's Rights' General Comment on Torture goes further by requiring states to take measures to ensure 'adequate documentation . . . [and provide] unimpeded and regular access to comprehensive health care, including sexual and reproductive health-care services, physical rehabilitation,

[114] M Kay Harris, In search of Common Ground: The Importance of Theoretical Orientations in Criminology and Criminal Justice, *Criminology and Public Policy* 4(2) (2005) 311–328, p318.

[115] Derick Wade and Bareld de Jong, Recent Advances in Rehabilitation, *BMJ* 320 (2000) 1385–1388, p1386.

[116] M Cardol, B De Jong, and C Ward, On Autonomy and Participation in Rehabilitation, *Disability and Rehabilitation* 24(18) (2002) 970–974.

[117] UN Basic Principles, Principle 21.

[118] General Comment No 3 of the Committee against Torture, 19 November 2012, CAT/C/GC/3, para 11.

[119] ibid paras 13–14.

psychological and psychosocial support, and socio-economic support'.[120] The human rights jurisprudence on rehabilitation as a form of reparation is increasingly being seen as incorporating this curative function, as well as expanding more broadly to community development.[121] In a similar vein, the South African Truth and Reconciliation Commission recommended that rehabilitation should comprise community-based services and activities 'aimed at promoting the healing and recovery of individuals and communities that have been affected by human rights violations' aswell as promoting reconciliation and transforming the way services are provided in South Africa, including health, social, educational, and housing services.[122]

From a medical perspective, rehabilitative reparations for CRSV have included diagnostic testing, prophylactic therapy (especially when implemented in situations of ongoing post-conflict violence or insecurity, eg Colombia) as well as curative treatments (such as pelvic floor reconstruction or genital fistulae repair).[123] The WHO defines rehabilitation as 'the combined and coordinated use of medical, social, educational and vocational measures for training or retraining the individual to the highest possible level of functional ability'.[124] The WHO Rehabilitation 2030 Call for Action Strategy does not frame rehabilitation in terms of reparations, even when discussing violations and conflict, but sees it as part as the third most important health indicator (after mortality and morbidity) for those vulnerable and as part of its work around Sustainable Development Goal 3.[125] The range of rehabilitation indicators is vast; a barometer for both individual rehabilitation (eg quality of life and attainment of individual goals)[126] and that of a healthcare system (eg ratio of rehabilitation personnel or multidisciplinary teams per 10,000 people).[127] A combination of core indicators is required to ensure that adequate coverage or medical rehabilitative reach is matched with performance

[120] General Comment No 4 on the African Charter on Human and Peoples' Rights: The Right to Redress for Victims of Torture and Other Cruel, Inhuman or Degrading Punishment or Treatment (Article 5), 4 March 2017, para 61.

[121] For instance, *Plan de Sánchez*, n 53, paras 105 and 110. See Luke Moffett, *Justice for Victims Before the International Criminal Court*, Routledge (2014) p172.

[122] South African TRC Report vol 5, pp176 and 190.

[123] A Pinel and L Kemunto Bosire, Traumatic Fistula: The Case for Reparations, *Forced Migration Review* 27 (2007) 18–19; and L Lombard et al, Rehabilitation Experiences After Obstetric Fistula Repair: Systematic Review of Qualitative Studies, *Tropical Medicine and International Health* 20(5) (2015) 554–568.

[124] Disability Prevention and Rehabilitation, 28 April 1976, A29/INF.DOC/1, p13.

[125] WHO, Rehabilitation 2030, A Call for Action, August 2017: WHO, Rehabilitation 2030, First Meeting Report, 6–7 February 2017; WHO, Rehabilitation 2030, Second Meeting Report, 8–9 July 2019.

[126] NHS England Commissioning Board, D02/S/a NHS Standard contract for specialised rehabilitation for patients with highly complex needs (all ages), 2013, p4.

[127] WHO, Rehabilitation Indicator Menu: A Tool Accompanying the Framework for Rehabilitation Monitoring and Evaluation (FRAME), 2019, p18. There are six core indicators and 34 expanded ones for healthcare systems. Rehabilitation is aimed at good population functioning over time, which can be measured through surveys such as the WHO Model Disability Survey (MDS).

quality.[128] Aside from the conceptual and practical differences on rehabilitation, there is a gap in what amounts to effective rehabilitation as a form of reparation. As such, there is a schism between the two disciplines of law and medicine on rehabilitation that needs to be bridged more effectively to repair victims' harm.

Again in terms of medical rehabilitation, the IACtHR has ordered states responsible for gross violations of human rights to provide victims with appropriate medical treatment and medications free of charge.[129] The Court has also ordered states to ensure priority access and to provide financial support to cover transport and other directly related costs, with such treatment based on the needs of the victim following an individual assessment.[130] Preferential treatment for victims of CRSV may cause tensions from members of the population who cannot claim victimhood yet have experienced reduced standards of care given the conflict's impact on health infrastructure.[131] However, where the state is unable to provide such services in a timely manner for victims, the Court has required it to use specialized private or civil society institutions.[132] The Court has ordered rehabilitation measures where the state already had a multi-disciplinary team in place to provide medical treatment, assistance, and reintegration of victims of sexual violence into the community, including training programmes in indigenous communities on women's rights and the prevention of sexual violence.[133] In some cases, the Court has ordered the state to establish a health centre in the victims' community,[134] but in other cases where a centre already exists, it has required only that the state ensure the provision of specialist treatments for victims of sexual violence through the existing local centre.[135]

Victims' relationships to their bodies and their gender identity can be negatively affected by sexual violence.[136] As examined in Chapter 3, sexual violence can have serious, complex, and life-long physical and psychological consequences on victims. Rehabilitation can centre on quality of life that contributes towards a dignified life, such as regaining control (even if not complete cure) over urinary or faecal continence, which may perpetuate ideologies of rape victims being viewed as 'unclean' and 'impure', as well as aiding in the ability to undertake desired tasks

[128] Camila Gianella and Alicia Yamin, Struggle and Resistance: Using International Bodies to Advance Sexual and Reproductive Rights in Peru, *Berkeley Journal of Gender, Law and Justice* 33(1) (2018) 41–74, pp45–46.

[129] *Castro Castro*, n 61, para 449.

[130] *Atenco*, n 62, para 341.

[131] O3, virtual interview, October 2018. Sunneva Gilmore, Expert Report on Reparations for Victims of Rape, Sexual Slavery and Attacks on Healthcare, *The Prosecutor v Bosco Ntaganda*, International Criminal Court, 28 October 2020, Public Redacted Version, ICC-01/04-02/06-2623-Anx2-Red2, p79.

[132] *Cantú*, n 56, para 253.

[133] ibid paras 234-238.

[134] *Plan de Sánchez*, n 53, para 110.

[135] *Cantú*, n 56, para 260.

[136] Inger Skjelsbæk, Victim and Survivor: Narrated Social Identities of Women Who Experienced Rape During the War in Bosnia-Herzegovina, *Feminism and Psychology* 16(4) (2006) 373–403, p395.

or social activities.[137] Lira sees working with victims to assist them in recovering their sense of self and belonging, so as to 'give meaning to their own lives' as rehabilitation, emphasizing their agency, rather than simply their function.[138] However a victim's relationship to their body is also situated in the notion of identity, discussed in Chapter 4, and how they socially engage with others. For one victim, suffering sexual violence meant that their body became part of the war, reflecting broader narratives of rape as a weapon of war: 'My body was used in a war to spread terror. And I had nothing to do with war.'[139] One healthcare professional spoke about how some victims disassociated from their bodies and said

> I think it is because sexual violence victims . . . sort of decide to leave their bodies, like 'this is not my body'. They don't care about their body. That means they don't want to go to the doctor. And if they have to pay for it, the less they want to go to the doctor.[140]

Such dissociation can result in self-neglect, worsening the health of the victim and creating a barrier to seeking help and benefiting from reparation measures such as rehabilitation.

One victim of CRSV offered an anecdote to explain how important it was to rehabilitate her physical pain and also her body image. This led her to seek out new rehabilitative pathways distinct from the administrative reparations programme in Colombia. She explained that she was still subdued, in pain, and spent ten years without looking at herself in the mirror. She went on to say that she used to wear make-up and would apply it without using a mirror. However, one day she had to go for a laboratory test and she was wondering why people were staring at her. She decided to visit her friend afterwards:

> When I finally got to a friend's house, she said: what did you do to yourself? And I just answered, well regular make up, brown eyebrows. She said: No, go to the mirror, look at yourself. But I didn't want to. I refused. She finally said my eyebrows were blue. only now, with the (victims and professionals) network, I found the courage to look at myself in the mirror again. we have a mark . . . I think that mark is with you for the rest of your life, because they damaged you morally, psychologically, physically, everything, the mark is there, stamped for the rest of your life. . . . Well, in spite the 10 years that have gone by, one is still subdued to that pain, that sadness, our smile was damaged.[141]

[137] U4 FG1, U5 and U6, Gulu, Uganda, July 2018.
[138] Elizabeth Lira, Reflections on Rehabilitation as a Form of Reparation in Chile after Pinochet's Dictatorship, *International Human Rights Law Review* 5(2) (2016) 194–216, p216.
[139] C3, Bogotá, Colombia, September 2018.
[140] C4, Bogotá, Colombia, September 2018.
[141] C15 FG1, Bogotá, Colombia, March 2019.

One Colombian civil society actor summed up the impact of the conflict on women's bodies in this way:

> For example, if we only consider the universe of women victims, the armed conflict has left deep wounds in their bodies and lives, to recover from that has long-term implications but of course the repair done today helps to alleviate the damage and is a way of giving the minimum tools for women to begin the recovering of their life projects that were truncated.[142]

One Colombian transitional justice practitioner who works with CRSV victims tries to incorporate rehabilitation of the body and victims' body image in their work through a women's network,

> One of the things that we are doing with the network was how to recover the body for peace, that's how we called it in a project. We decided to do some workout. Because we realized that when they had to go and file the complaint before the legal authorities, they were nervous, upset, and that was because they had to recall their situation and they had to talk about their bodies, where did it happened, how she attacked. So, before a certain activity, we decided to do some sort of exercise and that started to work. We noticed that these women don't want to talk or take care of their bodies. Sometimes they hate their bodies: 'because of my body I got in that situation. My body reminds me of the situation all the time'.[143]

While the role of the body within reparations remains underexplored, this book does not align with Clark's view, which refers to the 'leakiness' of female bodies on the basis that normal female physiology 'leaks' through lactation, menstruation, and even childbirth. Despite Clark's intention to show the positive dimensions of women's bodies through a broad understating of what it means to leak (eg emotion, love, and sorrow),[144] framing bodily functions from a 'leakiness' perspective can be problematic. First, it does little to break taboos surrounding women and girls' reproductive health as being 'unclean', as well as other physical consequences (such as genital fistula and pelvic floor weakness) that can also cause leakiness to a greater degree. Second, leakiness implies a fault in the human body—somehow the body's apparatus comes loose and leaks, and affects only females. Whereas the male physique is self-contained, robust, and unrealistically invulnerable (see Chapter 7)- making leakiness a gendered term.[145] Instead, rehabilitation can

[142] C14, Bogotá, Colombia, February 2019.

[143] C4, Bogotá, Colombia, September 2018.

[144] Janine Natalya Clark, 'Leaky' Bodies, Connectivity and Embodied Transitional Justice, *International Journal of Transitional Justice* 13 (2019) 268–289, p278.

[145] Thomas Thurnell-Read, Off the Leash and Out of Control: Masculinities and Embodiment in Eastern European Stag Tourism, *Sociology* 45(6) (2011) 977–991, p979.

capture the potential of the human body to repair, while respecting the body in all its diverse forms. Also, where these female bodily flows are impaired, as in menstrual disorders, there can be considerable distress and impinge upon sexual and reproductive identity. Thus, leakiness can be desired, but referring to these physiological processes as such does little to dismantle the taboo surrounding these body systems and may add to the justification for objectifying women's bodies for their reproductive or sexual worth.

Injuries that are not only physical in nature are attached to the body of the victim. Despite this, violations of personal integrity can be narrowly limited to physical injuries resulting in disability,[146] thereby excluding categories of harm that may not cause permanent physical disability, such as mental health conditions and physical impacts like incontinence and complications relating to genito-urinary fistulae, which may not be included. Thus, the criteria used to determine severe harm and suffering, including any relevant disability model will be important in understanding the impacts of the violations. That said, an attempt to be thorough can be overly complex. Instead, the potential bodily manifestations of sexual violence could be considered more comprehensively, and the integration of medicine assists in ensuring that severe suffering is redressed.

Despite medical, social, and legal interventions, there is no guarantee of full rehabilitation for victims, or 'healing'. Instead, victims may experience ambivalence where they have to live with the 'impossibility of closure' or living with physical and emotional pain.[147] Hamber suggests that a 'good enough' approach to the modest possibilities of transitional justice and reparative processes in healing victims is more realistic in informing their expectations and pushing back against political demands for closing the door on the past.[148] Chapter 7 explores the notions of vulnerability and resilience, in particular self-repair, that resonates with these issues. There is some practice of integrating reparations or at least widening their effects by complementing them with other support structures. For instance, in Cambodia, the ECCC, together with specialist civil society organizations, used a range of targeted and gender-sensitive processes to encourage victims of sexual and gender-based violence to come forward, including providing psychological services and training on gender-sensitivity and SGBV, alongside 'women's hearings, self-help groups, one-to-one therapy sessions and forum theatre'.[149] This points to the comprehensive nature of reparations, that rehabilitation alone cannot

[146] Cristián Correa, Operationalising the Right of Victims to Reparation, in A Peters and C Marxsen (eds), *Reparations for Victims of Armed Conflict*, CUP (2021) 92–178, p144.

[147] Brandon Hamber, *Transforming Societies after Political Violence: Truth, Reconciliation, and Mental Health*, Springer (2009) p193.

[148] ibid.

[149] Rachel Killean, *Victims, Atrocity and International Criminal Justice: Lessons from Cambodia*, Routledge (2018) p142.

resolve, but which needs measures of satisfaction to repair the moral and social harm, in particular around stigma.

6.4 Measures of Satisfaction

Measures of satisfaction are a collection of actions and processes intended to publicly acknowledge the suffering of victims and embed in society's consciousness the wrongful nature of such violations.[150] Akin to non-pecuniary compensation, measures of satisfaction aim to redress the moral harm suffered by a victim and vindicate their good name and dignity.[151] In international law, satisfaction is used as a remedy to repair the damage to another state's reputation or honour.[152] In transitional justice, measures of satisfaction are sometimes referred to as 'symbolic reparations' as they provide a performative function in signifying the recognition of responsibility and victimhood.[153] The UN Basic Principles on Reparations refer to a range of measures intended to repair the moral harm suffered by victims,[154] such as investigations, apologies, recovery of remains, memorialization structures, or naming of public spaces, national commemoration days, rituals or ceremonies, and artistic or literary forms.[155] The South African Truth and Reconciliation Commission recommended that such measures are intended to

> 'facilitate the communal process of remembering and commemorating the pain and victories of the past ... [and] should entail identifying a national day of remembrance and reconciliation, erection of memorials and monuments, and the development of museums.[156]

As part of the armed conflict in Guatemala in the 1980s, the Guatemalan military disappeared civilian men who were claiming land titles, and then moved in and sexually enslaved the women of the community. In 2012, eleven women brought the Sepur Zarco case against two senior Guatemalan military officers responsible for the disappearances and sexual slavery. In 2016, the two officers were convicted and sentenced to 120 and 240 years. The domestic court also ordered that

[150] Shelton, n 28, p78; and *Myrna Mack-Chang v. Guatemala*, Judgment of 25 November 2003, Inter-American Court of Human Rights, Series C No 101, para 86.
[151] Frédéric Mégret, The International Criminal Court Statute and the Failure to Mention Symbolic Reparations, *International Review of Victimology* 6 (2009) 127–147, p129.
[152] Shelton, n 28, p54.
[153] Ruti Teitel, *Transitional Justice*, OUP (2000) p147.
[154] Moffett, n 121, p173.
[155] Brandon Hamber and Ingrid Palmary, Gender, Memorialization and Symbolic Reparations, in Ruth Rubio-Marín (ed), *The Gender of Reparations*, CUP (2009) 324–381, p325. See also Kieran McEvoy, Anna Bryson, and Carine Placzek, *Apologies in Transitional Justice*, United Nations Special Rapporteur on the Promotion of Truth, Justice, Reparations and Guarantees of Non-recurrence (2019).
[156] South African TRC Report vol 5, p175.

alongside compensation for each victim of sexual violence, the state was responsible for installing a health centre, improving educational provision in the community in particular to guarantee the right to education of girls and women, along with scholarships, taking steps for the provision of basic services in communities and homes of victims through development committees. It also required that the case of the women of Sepur Zarco should be included in the national curricula and textbooks, that a documentary should be produced on the case, translated the judgment into the 24 Mayan languages and designated 26 February as the Day of the Victims of Sexual Violence, Sexual Slavery and Domestic Violence. Finally, it also ordered the local municipality of El Estor to build a monument representing the search for justice by the Women of Sepur Zarco. In addition, the Ministry of National Defence was required to include courses on women's human rights and legislation on preventing violence against women in military training courses.[157] Notably, although this was a criminal case against individual perpetrators, as they were acting as officials of the state, the Court held that the state was responsible for implementing reparations.

More recently in the domestic criminal proceedings against military officers involved in the disappearance of Marco Antonio Theissen and the detention, torture, and rape of Emma Theissen, the Court, amongst other measures, ordered the erection of a monument in the name of Emma Guadalupe Molina Theissen in the facilities of the former military base where she and others were tortured and raped.[158] While the victims had claimed for a grant of the Emma Molina Theissen award for the best undergraduate dissertation on sexual violence against women, the court rejected this, instead ordering the Guatemalan government to create the Molina Theissen medal for humanitarian work or respect to human rights compliance.[159] This may reflect a more general effort to encourage members of the military to comply with such norms.

The scope of symbolic reparations can mean that any act of reparation, including the process around which the reparation occurs, may be interpreted as symbolic.[160] Material reparations that are considered appropriate and comprehensive can represent a sincere commitment to repair harm and acknowledge those injured or disabled as valued citizens, especially given their inability to fully repair or compensate the harm caused. For instance, a healthcare strategy could provide accessible psychological care by culturally sensitive and trained professionals for as long as necessary during the victim's life. However, traditionally, symbolic reparations are conceived as moral reparations that are distinct from more tangible forms. As Roht-Arriaza asserts, reparation is 'secondarily about compensation; its

[157] Sentencia C-01076-2012-00021 of 2º, 2 March 2016, pp509–511. The court awarded 500,000 quetzales (£50,000) to each of the victims, twice that ordered to next of kin of those disappeared.
[158] C-01077-1998-00002 of 1ro. Tribunal Primero de Sentencia Penal, 23 May 2018, p1074.
[159] ibid p1073.
[160] Hamber, n 31, p220.

symbolic aspects are paramount'.[161] As Chapter 7 explores, while this may be true for some victims and for society, sexual violence causes harms and vulnerabilities that require improvements to a person's wellbeing, quality of life, and dignity, that is, less about the political relationships with the state and more about a person's lived experience.

One measure of satisfaction that is often overlooked and is relevant for CRSV is dignification.[162] Dignification may be more important to victims in terms of raising public awareness and officially acknowledging their experiences, as well as countering the cultural, moral, and social practices and justifications that led to their occurrence. In Guatemala, dignification is intended to 'recognize and promote broader societal awareness of the suffering of women survivors during the armed conflict and de-stigmatize survivors by acknowledging that this violence was not their fault'.[163] Such dignification measures are intended to vindicate victims' dignity and contribute to the 'regenerating of the social fabric and strengthening social relations of coexistence'.[164] They include remembrance activities at the community, regional, and national levels; historical memory events; and documentation of victims' and survivors' experiences; commemoration of the national day of the dignity of victims each year; construction of headstones and mausoleums; psychological accompaniment; building of public parks in memory of victims; and renaming public spaces with victims' names.[165] In many ways these are comparable to measures of satisfaction, but they are centred on victims' dignity, increasing awareness of their experiences, reaffirming moral and social values, and as such contributing to non-repetition. However, dignification measures can seem hollow when victims face ongoing discrimination and inequalities, in particular in communities where basic social services and infrastructure are lacking.[166]

Art may also be useful in facilitating some dignification measures. In Cambodia one of the reparation projects approved in Case 002/02 was a dance production (*Pka Sla Krom Angkar*). Designed to reflect the forced marriage experience of women, it drew on the oral stories of victims during the Khmer Rouge as well as those who testified and participated before the ECCC.[167] While a dance production

[161] See Naomi Roht-Arriaza, Reparations Decisions and Dilemmas, *Hastings International and Comparative Law Review* 27(2) (2004) 157–219, p189.

[162] UN Basic Principles, Principle 22(d).

[163] Alison Crosby, M Brinton Lykes, and Brisna Caxaj, Carrying a Heavy Load: Mayan Women's Understandings of Reparation in the Aftermath of Genocide, *Journal of Genocide Research* 18(2–3) (2016) 265–283, p274.

[164] Artículo 39, Resolución de la Comisión Nacional de Resarcmiento, Número CNR-001-2015 [Article 39, Resolution of the National Reparations Commission, Number CNR-001-2015].

[165] ibid Artículo 40 [Article 40].

[166] Sanne Weber, Trapped between Promise and Reality in Colombia's Victims' Law: Reflections on Reparations, Development and Social Justice, *Bulletin of Latin American Research* 39(1) (2020) 5–21, p16.

[167] Rosemary Grey, Yim Sotheary, and Kum Somaly, The Khmer Rouge Tribunal's First Reparation for Gender-Based Crimes, *Australian Journal of Human Rights* 25(3) (2019) 488–497.

is problematic for ensuring effective redress if it is the only form of reparations for victims,[168] and the experiences of men are missing,[169] traditional culture can be an apposite means of using traditional cultural dance to publicly promote the dignity of victims and widen understanding of their experiences. In Kosovo 5,000 dresses donated by victims and supporters were displayed on a clothesline in a football stadium in the capital to symbolize the transition from being kept in a private closet to being exhibited in a public display ('symbolically "airing out the laundry" of the unspeakable and unspoken crime of wartime rape in Kosovo').[170] This demonstrated the role of art in memorializing rape, which contributed to making the 'victims visible', while preserving their anonymity, and increased the inclusion of sexual violence in the history and public discourse of the conflict. However, it is important to note that this initiative was carried out after mobilization of victims with different civil society and government actors, alongside other community sensitization and education efforts.[171]

In terms of conflict-related sexual violence being perceived as gender-based violence, there has been a limited repertoire of satisfaction measures. Victims do not always accept those measures that have been implemented, such as partial apologies and empathetic statements made by parties not directly responsible. For example, in total there have been eight out of the forty official apologies from the Japanese state from 2002 to 2005 that have been focused on the comfort women. These statements, in letters or public announcements, acknowledged only that the comfort women suffered harm, but not the responsibility of Japan.[172] Other satisfaction measures have been halted by inaccessibility to official documents including police and military records. This obstruction was noted by the Women's Tribunal, impeding any truth-telling mechanism, accountability, and an accurate depiction of the harms endured from the comfort system.[173] In terms of apologies and acknowledgments of responsibility, the ICtHR has required that in sexual violence cases, such measures involving state institutions should include senior government officials, conducted in public,[174] in the indigenous language of the victims where appropriate,[175] with the consultation of victims on how and when it should be carried out, and with a copy of the apology provided to victims[176] or disseminated through the media.[177] This has often been accompanied by the publication

[168] See Rachel Killean and Luke Moffett, What's in a Name? 'Reparations' at the Extraordinary Chambers in the Courts of Cambodia, *Melbourne Journal of International Law* 21 (2020) 115–143.

[169] Grey, Sotheary, and Somaly, n 167, p494.

[170] Anna Di Lellio, Feride Rushiti, and Kadire Tahiraj, 'Thinking of You' in Kosovo: Art Activism Against the Stigma of Sexual Violence, *Violence Against Women* 25(13) (2019) 1543–1557, p1547.

[171] ibid p1545.

[172] Hamber and Palmary, n 155, p369.

[173] Tina Dolgopol, The Judgment of the Tokyo Women's Tribunal, *Alternative Law Journal* 28(5) (2005) 242–249.

[174] *Castro Castro*, n 61, para 445; *Cantú*, n 56, paras 225–226; *Atenco*, n 62, para 347.

[175] *Cantú*, n 56, para 226.

[176] *Atenco*, n 62, para 347.

[177] *Castro Castro*, n 61, para 445.

and dissemination of the judgment's findings on violations in national daily newspapers and government websites.[178]

If the state does not play a role in the creation or support of measures of satisfaction, even if only in a limited capacity, then reparations are unlikely to be truly effective given the failure to acknowledge responsibility.[179] In such cases, victims may be left with no choice but to seek moral recognition and validation elsewhere. Civil society and transnational actors have been instrumental in carving out symbolic reparations for CRSV victims, notably the construction of the Statue of Peace, which faces the Japanese Embassy in Seoul, South Korea.[180] The statue, whether initially intentional or not, has been interpreted as a means to confront Japan into acknowledging their responsibility. Rooney suggests the statue has effectively shifted the shame from victims of sexual violence to the perpetrator, which has only been exacerbated in local communities by the lack of state remorse.[181] Each feature of the statue's design serves as a reminder of the ongoing struggle for accountability, such as the empty chair awaiting the perpetrator's public atonement.[182] In summary, despite Japan's compensation to the comfort women, the lack of internal cohesion between reparation measures means that all forms are diminished in significance to victims. However, there is potential for symbolic measures created by actors not implicated in the crimes to advocate for truth and acknowledgement of responsibility. Such measures by civil society may not amount to official reparations, as they are not made by a responsible party, but they can provide more visibility in society to victims' harm and the implicit guilt of those responsible. However, these gestures may be viewed by some as a charitable compromise rather than an effective remedy for victims' suffering.

There is increasing recognition that reparations should be culturally appropriate, and ideally be constructed by the victims or at least with significant consultation or co-creatorship.[183] The ambiguity of implementation of international norms on reparations, such as in the 2005 UN Basic Principles, may provide such flexibility for states to create bespoke reparations that are contextually relevant. Lengel posits that symbolic measures may also be survival mechanisms by victims of conflict-related sexual violence particularly through performative resistant remembering,[184] thus highlighting their therapeutic potential of enabling victims to

[178] *González* et al *('Cotton Field') v Mexico* (Preliminary Objection, Merits, Reparations, and Costs) IACtHR Series C No 205 (16 November 2009), para 468; and *Atenco*, n 62, para 344.

[179] Hamber and Palmary, n 155, p367; and Hilary Josephs, The Remedy of Apology in Comparative and International Law: Self-Healing and Reconciliation, *Emory International Law Review* 18(1) (2004) 53–84.

[180] Sierra Rooney, The Politics of Shame: The Glendale Comfort Women: Memorial and the Complications of Transnational Commemorations, *de arte* 53(2–3) (2018) 86–102, p97.

[181] Erika Doss, *Memorial Mania*, University of Chicago Press (2010) p264; and Rooney, n 180, p96.

[182] Rooney, n 180, p99.

[183] Hamber and Palmary, n 155, p366.

[184] Lara Lengel, Mediated Memory Work and Resistant Remembering of Wartime Sexual Violence, 1992-1995, *Feminist Media Studies* 18(2) (2018) 325–328.

process the past through a variety of mediums, whilst ensuring a legacy for future generations. Adopting a feminist critique, resistant remembering endeavours to reject the patriarchal depictions of women in memorials or similar representations that actually do not amount to satisfaction. Memorials that commemorate the achievements and suffering of women have often been constructed on stereotypes. As remembering is important to identity, it can be significant for victims of sexual violence to recount their narratives freely and also set a precedent for future generations.[185]

For instance, women from the Association Kuyanakuy in Peru created a quilt that displayed pre- and post-conflict community life. While the choice of a textile activity may be interpreted as reinforcing gendered roles, the quilt was a celebration of their skills and artistic expressionism. The quilt became an important symbol of truth through its circulation to other transitional justice mechanisms: first used as a form of testimony to the Peruvian Truth Commission in 2002, then during a vigil demanding truth and accountability, as well as featuring in festivals around the world.[186] The measure has been effective in reducing pressure on victims to reiterate their stories verbally, especially when they are of a sensitive nature and may still be distressing and disrupt a victim's return to community life. As well as the content or key messages, the uses and transitory nature of the quilt (or other form) require the approval of the victims to avoid any sense of the conflict being stolen from them.

Artistic interpretations of sexual violence may be presented in an abstract fashion that may not be immediately apparent to the observer or reflect victims' experiences. As such, prompts or presentations may be required to assist interpretation of the main narrative, such as with the *Pka Sla Krom Angkar* dance in Cambodia discussed above. That said, there are few examples of permanent statues or memorials for CRSV victims.[187] In essence, statues are for men and knitting for women (or similar temporary crafts). Although there are exceptions, the majority of statues that do commemorate women in conflict (as victims or as heroines) have been designed by men, and overwhelmingly depict women as nurturers or caregivers, self-sacrificing, passive, and agentless.[188] At the other extreme, where women are included in statues and memorials portraying gender-based or sexual crimes, there can be a sensationalizing of traditional gender roles or notions of passivity and suffering.[189] There is a monument in the centre of the village of

[185] Heather Fraser and Dee Mitchell, Feminist Memory Work in Action: Methods and Practicalities, *Qualitative Social Work* 14(3) (2015) 321–337.

[186] Hamber and Palmary, n 155, p366.

[187] Despite numerous Holocaust memorials being created since the 1970s, the experiences of women and sexual violence is often missing—see Sonja M Hedgepeth and Rochelle G Saidel, *Sexual Violence Against Jewish Women During the Holocaust*, Brandeis University Press (2010) p2.

[188] Hamber and Palmary, n 155; and Amy Rothschild, Victims Versus Veterans: Agency, Resistance and Legacies of Timor-Leste's Truth Commission, *International Journal of Transitional Justice* 11(3) (2017) 443–462, p460.

[189] Rothschild, n 188, p456.

Shabunda in South Kivu that depicts the despair of a woman, intended to symbolize the suffering of women during the conflict, including victims of sexual violence, widows, and those who died leaving orphans.[190] In other contexts, statues and memorials have been erected to commemorate sexual violence to ensure that it remains in the public consciousness and to encourage its non-repetition.[191] Monuments and statues can also be used as a form of resistance and to counter the silence of those responsible,[192] as in the case of the Comfort Women statue depicting a young girl and an empty chair.[193]

Colombian women victims of conflict-related sexual violence have resisted typical symbolic forms of reparations that are both gender-constrictive and prevent them from 'owning' their suffering. The Colombian sculptor Doris Salcedo designed and created an 'anti-monument' entitled 'Fragmentos' in conjunction with 15,000 victims of conflict-related sexual violence during the more than five-decade civil war. Through a process of melting and pounding, they transformed thirty-seven tonnes of weapons from the FARC into a contemporary floor that conveys a metaphysical space, representing the ongoing path in the complex peace process required after signing the 2016 Havana agreement.[194] However, for some commentators the valorization of violence through destroying the weapons deflected from any monumentalizing of suffering.[195] For others, the process of modifying the metal with other victims provided a way to express their pain and symbolically, at least, stand above the destroyed guns and display their resilience.[196] In addition, acknowledgement of responsibility occurred through the FARC's surrender of weapons and their approval of the design, even if they preferred a vision in which weapons symbolically liberated the country. It should also be noted that there were no weapons or materials from military or police forces in Colombia's anti-monument, suggesting a continued resistance by the state to recognize sexual violence committed by its forces.

[190] Office of the United Nations High Commissioner for Refugees (OHCHR), Report on Reparations for Victims of Gross Human Rights Violations, 2011, para 43.

[191] In 2023, Budapest will have a statue commemorating the use of rape during the Second World War—Fanni Kaszás, Budapest to Erect Statue Commemorating Wartime Sexual Violence Victims, Hungary Today, 30 January 2020. https://hungarytoday.hu/budapest-to-erect-statue-commemorating-wartime-sexual-violence-victims/, accessed 1 August 2025.

[192] In 2019, a sculpture memorializing the Lai Dan Han (children of mixed heritage resulting from sexual violence committed by Korean troops during the Vietnam War) was unveiled. The work depicts a mother and her child trapped in entwined vines to commemorate victims of sexual violence and children born of rape. See Jack Straw, We Must Strengthen Justice and Increase Accountability to End Sexual Violence in Conflict for Good, *The Telegraph*, 5 August 2019.

[193] Rooney, n 180, pp96–99.

[194] This is featured in an arts centre in Bogotá, which opened on 10 December 2017. Interviews with victims and professionals revealed that there has been less traction and interest in the anti-monument since the new government.

[195] Lengel, n 184, 325–328.

[196] C3, Bogotá, Colombia, September 2018.

Measures of satisfaction can take a collective dimension, such as educational programmes for the wider community or programmes for victimized indigenous communities. Collective measures are also necessary to address the root cause of stigmatization, even if it is difficult to ensure the level of positive impact. In *TPF v Peru*, CEDAW called for 'education and training programmes to encourage health providers to change their attitudes and behaviour in relation to adolescent women seeking reproductive health services and respond to specific health needs related to sexual violence'.[197] Similarly in *Gonzalez v US*, the IACtHR recommended that the United States

> continue adopting public policies and institutional programs aimed at restructuring the stereotypes of domestic violence victims, and to promote the eradication of discriminatory socio-cultural patterns that impede women and children's full protection from domestic violence acts, including programs to train public officials in all branches of the administration of justice and police, and comprehensive prevention programs.[198]

Training and education can jointly amount to satisfaction and guarantees of non-repetition, as the former often requires assurances that efforts have been made to prevent recurrence.

6.5 Guarantees of Non-Repetition

Guarantees of non-repetition refer to the efforts by a responsible party to take measures to prevent the violation from re-occurring. For states, this often involves institutional reforms and legislative amendments to improve governance, such as independence of the judiciary and civilian oversight of the military.[199] In international law, guarantees of non-repetition (GNR) are meant to end the breach and restore the legal situation affected by the violation, in that they 'serve a preventive function and may be described as a positive reinforcement of future performance'.[200] As de Greiff points out, in comparison to truth, justice, and reparations, guarantees of non-recurrence involve a function that can be satisfied by a broad range of measures.[201] The UN Impunity Principles justify the need for GNR 'to ensure respect for the rule of law, foster and sustain a culture of respect for human

[197] *TPF v Peru*, 4 November 2011, CEDAW Communication No 22/2009.

[198] Inter-American Commission on Human Rights, *Jessica Lenahan (Gonzalez) v US*, Report No 80/11 Case 12.626.

[199] Moffett, n 121, p175. UN Basic Principles, Principle 23.

[200] *Yearbook of the International Law Commission 2001*, vol 2(2), p88.

[201] Report of the Special Rapporteur on the promotion of truth, justice, reparation, and guarantees of non-recurrence, Pablo de Greiff, A/HRC/30/42, 7 September 2015, para 23.

rights, and restore or establish public trust in government institutions'.[202] Mayer-Reickh argues that guarantees of non-repetition are better understood as a 'distinct obligation rather than a subset of reparations'.[203] However, this overlooks victims' needs for the violation not to recur against them or their family in the future as part of their redress.

Some commentators view guarantees of non-repetition as central in transforming the gender discriminatory causes of CRSV.[204] De Greiff argues that 'institutional engineering' through GNRs is insufficient to transform society. This broadly taps into deeper concerns of top-down approaches in state-led technocratic transitional justice. He instead suggests that societal transformation to prevent the recurrence of violations requires cultural and personal interventions.[205] This has been a consistent issue raised by respondents in the fieldwork in Colombia and Uganda. At a minimum, ensuring GNR through adequately trained and monitored healthcare professionals can reduce the risk of secondary victimization. At most, creating cultures of empathy through better understanding of the experience of victims of CRSV, their stigmatization and potential for secondary victimization would ensure that healthcare professionals are attuned to these issues in their provision of care. Yet, as Mayer-Rieckh notes, cultural and individual change is more difficult and takes longer to achieve, due to institutional or organizational resistance, but once it is obtained it can be more resilient.[206] In Colombia, respondents brought up several times that, despite an extensive reparation programme being in place, healthcare professionals remained a barrier for victims coming forward. For example, as one interviewee argued:

> sexual violence is possible in a culture that tolerates sexual violence against women. Sexual violence is based on a culture that accepts that women's bodies are male property or the patriarchal culture property.[207]

In the *Atenco* case involving sexual torture of 11 women in police custody, the Court noted that the refusal of forensic doctors to identify signs of sexual violence, their lack of independence, and absence of a complaint mechanism against them contributed to impunity, requiring the Mexican government to guarantee the

[202] Principle 35.

[203] Alexander Mayer-Rieckh, Guarantees of Non-Recurrence: An Approximation, *Human Rights Quarterly* 39(2) (2017) 416–448, p424.

[204] Kristin Kalla, Advancing Justice and Making Amends Through Reparations: Legal and Operational Considerations, in Fionnuala Ní Aoláin et al (eds), *The Oxford Handbook of Gender and Conflict*, OUP (2018) 253–264, p260.

[205] A/HRC/30/42, 7 September 2015, para 32.

[206] Mayer-Rieckh, n 203, p438.

[207] C6, Bogotá, Colombia, September 2018.

independence of medical personnel.[208] The UN Basic Principles on Reparations envisages the obligation on states to protect medical and healthcare professionals and promote the 'observance of codes of conduct and ethical norms', that include medical, psychological, and social service professionals.[209] Such a reform of codes of conduct and ethical norms may be a route to building a culture of empathy within healthcare professionals, as explored more in the following chapters.

Reinstating civic trust in healthcare institutions may require reminders of 'dignified' codes of practice, which could amount to a form of symbolic and material reparation that starts with frontline healthcare personnel. Reduced ethical controls during conflict and post-conflict may mean it is easier to commit professional misconduct. Identifying as a patient should aim to reduce, not incite, further harm nor should it cause revictimization. In contrast to Colombia's interpretation of coding, patient adjuncts can be used to positively transform notions of CRSV stigma. Physicians for Human Rights in Kenya have proposed giving free healthcare cards to families of up to four members, to reduce stigma towards that one victim of sexual violence. Besides encouraging familial integration, indirect eligibility for medical care may enhance the health of the population.[210]

There remains a systemic cultural problem in how victims of CRSV are treated that permeates society in terms of stigma and silence. Indeed, the Nairobi Declaration was attuned to this in setting out that reparations 'must drive post-conflict transformation of socio-cultural injustices, and political and structural inequalities that shape the lives of women and girls' and that 'reintegration and restitution by themselves are not sufficient goals of reparation, since the origins of the violations of women's and girls' human rights predate the conflict situation'.[211] The profound harm experienced by direct victims and their families can be compounded by the underlying structural and socio-cultural context in which they live. The IACtHR has endorsed this position when considering the issue of reparations for women victims of sexual violence, stating that 'bearing in mind the context of structural discrimination in which the facts of this case occurred, [. . .] the reparations must be designed to change this situation, so that their effect is not only of restitution, but also rectification. In this regard, re-establishment of the same structural context of violence and discrimination is not acceptable'.[212] This issue permeates the following chapter on vulnerability and resilience with reparations for conflict-related sexual violence.

208 *Atenco*, n 62, para 364.
209 UN Basic Principles, Principle 23(d) and (f).
210 Meeting in Boston with PHR, November 2019.
211 Nairobi Declaration on Women's and Girls' Right to Remedy and Reparation (2007) para 3.
212 *Cotton Field*, n 178, para 450.

6.6 Conclusion

Despite being neglected in international and domestic responses to dealing with the past, there is increasing recognition of the need for comprehensive forms of reparations. As was argued in Chapter 2, stigma, social recrimination, and intransigence of state institutions have meant that reparations for CRSV is often neglected or hidden. This chapter sought to map out the nascent jurisprudence and state practice around reparations for CRSV, as well as the evolving concepts and principles of reparations. Compensation is often used to respond to sexual violence, reflecting a more fungible means to respond to sexual violence that may be unaddressed for years, but can carry connotations of blood money or insinuate the exchange of sexual services for money as prostitution. Restitution, while often concerned with restoration of property rights, also has a place for victims of CRSV, such as with the establishment of the official identification documents of children born as a result of rape within armed groups. Rehabilitation offers a real opportunity for improving victims' health and quality of life, but it is often inhibited by the years or decades it takes for victims to benefit from such measures, as discussed in Chapter 2 and 3. Other more public-facing reparative efforts, such as measures of satisfaction and guarantees of non-repetition, can play an important part in publicly acknowledging victims' harms and reforming the structures and institutions that caused such violations. All these different forms of reparations have been developed to more comprehensively respond to CRSV. The next chapter takes this further by considering the lived experience of victims and how vulnerability and resilience can shape their access to, and engagement with, reparations.

7

Vulnerable Bodies

Resilience, Sexual Violence, and the Utility of Reparations

7.1 Introduction

Vulnerability—whether to do with everyday hardships, disability, or social and institutional exclusion[1]—is a concern across a number of disciplines including medicine, bio-ethics, law, philosophy, sociology, victimology, development studies, and feminist scholarship.[2] However, it has yet to be addressed systematically in the field of transitional justice.[3] While it is well established that victims have a right to reparation, these norms often provide little guidance in meeting victims' particular vulnerabilities.[4] While a rights-based approach spells out a legal entitlement for victims, it does not assist in determining how states in their domestic reparation programmes prioritize or manage resources in the face of a victim population. Instead, terms like proportionality, margin of appreciation, and equity are used, which allow states some discretion in balancing resources with rights, but little regarding alleviating structural and other vulnerabilities victims may face. This has implications for the reach of reparations, which inevitably involve some sort of prioritization due to finite resources in transitional societies.

In practice, vulnerability has gradually emerged as a useful notion to guide prioritization of reparations for certain groups deemed 'especially vulnerable' and has been cited in the explanations given for specific reparation measures ordered. This has included explicit references in court decisions, and explicit and implicit references in administrative reparation schemes to rationalize scaling measures such as compensation amounts or rehabilitation programmes.[5] The increasing pull of

[1] Luke Moffett, Vulnerability, Resilience and the Responsive State in Transitional Societies: Seriously Injured Victims of the Troubles in Northern Ireland, in Tanya Ni Mhuirthile and James Gallen (eds), *Law, Responsibility and Vulnerability State Accountability and Responsiveness*, Routledge (2021).

[2] Human Development Report 2014 Sustaining Human Progress: Reducing Vulnerabilities and Building Resilience, UNDP (2014) p55.

[3] Emily E Harwell and Philippe Le Billon, Natural Connections: Linking Transitional Justice and Development Through a focus on Natural Resources, in Pablo de Greiff and Duthie (eds), *Transitional Justice and Development: Making Connections*, ICTJ (2009) 282–331, p285.

[4] Emily Camins, Needs or Rights? Exploring the Limitations of Individual Reparations for Violations of International Humanitarian Law, *International Journal of Transitional Justice* 10(1) (2016) 126–145.

[5] The Inter-American Commission of Human Rights outlines special protocols that take into account specific vulnerabilities of girls and adolescents when investigating and delivering justice related to sexual crimes. See Report on Violence Against Women and Girls in Latin America, OEA/SerL/V/II Doc 233/19, Inter-American Commission of Human Rights, 14 November 2019, paras 245 and 262.

Redressing Rape in War. Sunneva Gilmore, Oxford University Press.
DOI: 10.1093/9780198919735.003.0007

reparations to be attuned to structural vulnerabilities can echo back to the need to engage with transformative justice.[6] Nevertheless, the added value of incorporating vulnerability normatively and practically into thinking about reparations remains under-developed.

At the same time, focusing on vulnerability can fall into the trap of portraying victims as dependents, without agency and unable to manage the consequences of their harm. There is a growing attention to resilience, which taps into the survivor discourse discussed in Chapter 4 and appreciates those who suffer sexual violence can find empowerment, organize others similarly affected , or experience personal growth after such violations. This chapter engages with both the notions of vulnerability and resilience around reparations in particular, and how such measures may complement both perspectives and allow for a more nuanced approach to redressing the harm of a heterogenous victim population. In light of this analysis, the chapter also discusses the practice of self- and informal repair when carried out by victims as they await reparations that can take years or decades to be implemented.

This chapter draws on interdisciplinary literature and my own empirical findings from across the three case-studies of Colombia, Peru, and Uganda to explore the utility of vulnerability in relation to reparations for conflict-related sexual violence (CRSV). The chapter begins by outlining the broader literature on vulnerability. It then considers the pros and cons of vulnerability as an organizational framework in addressing the complexity of reparations for CRSV. It specifically examines how vulnerability can inform a more complex understanding of rehabilitation as a form of reparation. This is followed by an exploration of the vulnerability and resilience of victims of CRSV, drawing on the experience of interviewees and the notions of self- and informal repair. The final section of the chapter takes stock of how vulnerability may be utilized in an effective manner given the spectrum of harms and needs arising from CRSV.

7.2 Vulnerability: A Theoretical Basis

There is no universal understanding of vulnerability, but it is frequently linked to the notion of susceptibility or threat of harm.[7] Some scholars suggest that vulnerability implies an obligation to respond to suffering and thus may be

[6] See Luke Moffett, Reparations for Victims at the International Criminal Court: A New Way Forward? *International Journal of Human Rights* 21(9) (2017) 1204–1222, p1212.

[7] Robert E Goodin, *Protecting the Vulnerable: A Reanalysis of Our Social Responsibilities*, University of Chicago Press, (1985) p110; Kate Brown, 'Vulnerability': Handle with Care, *Ethics and Social Welfare* 5(3) (2011) 313–321, pp315 and 318. Vulnerability is derived from the Latin word *vulnus* (wound).

viewed as the basis for human rights claims more generally.[8] For example, Clark Miller views the vulnerability of others as the key source of human rights obligations.[9] Given the potentially large catalogue of vulnerabilities for any given population, the notion inevitably invites some consideration of prioritization or hierarchy regarding which groups and vulnerabilities should be addressed.[10] From a public health perspective, Grabovschi and colleagues organize vulnerability according to degrees of severity.[11] They define high vulnerability as multiple vulnerabilities, which in turn increase health needs and are thus associated with reduced quality and/or access to healthcare.[12] Given the complex and compounding nature of vulnerabilities with regard to CRSV, and the challenge of assessing which of these needs should be prioritized, it is useful to consider how vulnerability in such contexts is constructed and classified for the purposes of reparations.

Mackenzie, Rogers, and Dodds outline a taxonomy of vulnerability, which attempts to avoid crude biological interpretations by marrying the intrinsic vulnerability of the human condition with the identification of context-specific forms of vulnerabilities.[13] Essentially, there are two *linked* but different sources of vulnerability (inherent and situational) that can exist in the dispositional (potential) or occurrent (actual) state.[14] As such, vulnerability can be intrinsic to being a human being (inherent) or caused by the circumstances in which a person finds themselves (situational), which can be in the future (dispositional) or presently experienced (occurrent). Conflict-related sexual violence involves both inherent and situational sources of vulnerability as well as the potential for victims to have continuing and subsequent harms. The section therefore outlines the benefit of understanding the temporality of vulnerability. It concludes with a cautionary note on the potential for focusing on vulnerability to become disempowering.

[8] Bryan S Turner, *Vulnerability and Human Rights, Essays on Human* Rights, Pennsylvania State University Press, (2006) pp1–25.

[9] Sarah Clark Millar, *The Ethics of Need: Agency, Dignity and Obligation*, Routledge (2012) p12. Some needs are considered essential for species-specific survival, namely food, water, shelter, and medical care. See Norman Daniels, *Just Health: Meeting Health Needs Fairly*, CUP (2008) pp34 and 87. See also Judith Butler, *Precarious Life: The Powers of Mourning and Violence*, Verso (2004) p2. Butler considers vulnerabilities as stemming from the actions of others, such as violence or neglect. By the same rationale, so too must be the alleviation and reduction of any underlying factors that could heighten vulnerability since they were created by the actions of others.

[10] Alexander HMorawa, Vulnerability as a Concept of International Human Rights Law, *Journal of International Relations and Development* 6(2) (2003) 139–155, p142.

[11] Cristina Grabovschi, Christine Loignon, and Martin Fortin, Mapping the Concept of Vulnerability Related to Health Care Disparities: A Scoping Review, *BMC Health Services Research* 13(1) (2013), doi:10.1186/1472-6963-13-94.

[12] ibid.

[13] Catriona Mackenzie, Wendy Rogers, and Susan Dodds, Introduction: What Is Vulnerability, and Why Does It Matter for Moral Theory? in Catriona Mackenzie, Wendy Rogers, and Susan Dodds (eds), *Vulnerability: New Essays in Ethics and Feminist Philosophy*, OUP (2014) p7.

[14] ibid pp7–9.

7.2.1 Inherent vulnerability

'Inherent vulnerability' reflects the human condition as a universal and continuous exposure to injury affecting both bodily and social wellbeing.[15] As human beings we are inherently vulnerable to disease, illness, and accidents that can impair our quality of life, wellbeing, or result in death. Vulnerability is constantly in flux and varies across a person's life requiring varying levels of support at different times. For example, early and advanced age groups are amongst the most inherently vulnerable in most societies irrespective of the presence of conflict.[16] In analogous research, Charmaz's extensive work into the psychological and social consequences of chronic illness finds that for the person affected, long-term illness is not only about coming to terms with the medical condition/disease,[17] but primarily about the continuous struggle to define and maintain identity while managing the illness's intrusion in daily life.[18] Thus, when people have been affected by serious illness or incapacity, there may be periods of increased inherent vulnerability where a person struggles to adapt to their bodily limits and unite their body with their sense of self.[19]

Merry considers that agency is a central component of vulnerability in that vulnerability reduces a person's ability to control their circumstances.[20] Inherent vulnerabilities can make it challenging to exercise agency or control over certain aspects of victims' lives, restricting their ability to undertake activities or goals that would be possible with assistance or home/workplace adjustments. According to Clark Millar, when basic needs are not met, the harm of 'compromised agency' can 'seep into' other aspects of that person's life,[21] such as self-care. In essence vulnerable groups or persons do not lack agency, but their status as 'vulnerable', particularly when compounded with unmet basic needs and structural factors, can inhibit their agency.

Inherent vulnerability deepens our understanding of how harms arising from sexual violence can change a person's life and may create situations that lead to new vulnerabilities.[22] The physical harms of sexual violence can create an inherent

[15] Martha Albertson Fineman, Vulnerability and Inevitable Inequality, *Oslo Law Review* 4(3) (2017) 133–149, p142.

[16] Office of the Special Representative of the Secretary General, Children and Armed Conflict, Working Paper No 1, The Six Grave Violations Against Children During Armed Conflict: The Legal Foundation, updated November 2013, p25.

[17] Kathy Charmaz, Struggling For a Self: Identity Levels of the Chronically Ill, in J Roth, and P Conrad (eds), *The Experience and Management of Chronic Illness*, JAI Press (1987); and Kathy Charmaz, The Body, Identity, and Self: Adapting to Impairment, *Sociological Quarterly* 36(4) (1995) 657–680, pp657–658.

[18] Charmaz, 'The Body, Identity, and Self', n 17, pp657–658. See Chapter 4 on identity.

[19] See Chapter 3.

[20] Sally Engle Merry, The Practice of Human Rights, Tracking Law Between the Global and Local, in M Goodale and Sally Merry (eds), *Cambridge Studies in Law and Society*, CUP (2007) 195–203, p195.

[21] Sarah Clark Millar, *The Ethics of Need: Agency, Dignity and Obligation*, Routledge (2012).

[22] Robert Bluhm, Vulnerability, Health and Illness, *International Journal of Feminist Approaches to Bioethics* 5(2) (2012) 147–161, p148.

vulnerability which can then be exacerbated by other intersecting issues such as nutritional requirements, medical care, or financial support. By way of illustration, the issue of 'vulnerability in pregnancy' offers insights into the broader role of vulnerability concerning reparations and sexual violence. The physiological period of pregnancy can itself be considered a vulnerable state given its potential for pregnancy-related heath complications in both the ante and post-partum period.[23] Domestic and sexual violence during pregnancy (which may or may not have occurred through rape) significantly increases obstetric risks such as pre-term birth and low birthweight.[24]

Males can also have sexual organ-specific inherent vulnerabilities to certain biological harms that may affect their ability to reproduce as well as lead to sexual and urological disorders. For instance, masculine vulnerabilities should include sexual violence that cause major testicular injuries leading to testosterone deficiency—having effects such as reducing libido, infertility, and physical changes like decreased muscle mass.[25] Such consequences may transgress what it means to be a man in some societies and their gender identity,[26] yet many consequences can be amenable to testosterone replacement.[27] Biological harms can become more difficult to conceal in the long term if not treated and can give rise to additional situational vulnerabilities—affecting marriage prospects and reproductive wishes.

The advances in modern medicine can be perceived as reducing further inherent vulnerabilities related to such harms by decreasing uncertainty through better diagnostic capabilities and optimal management of conditions.[28] In this sense, from a medical perspective, secondary harm can be attenuated through alleviation of pain and suffering as well as functional improvement in the case of bodily impairments/chronic conditions. Thus, meeting health needs can reduce inherent vulnerability, promoting victims' agency and flexibility in their life goals. To continue with the example of pregnancy above, Briscoe and colleagues found that when needs are pre-empted in pregnancy, and appropriate support by sensitively trained professionals is offered at an early stage, threats to health are reduced.[29]

[23] There are many pregnancy-specific conditions. Examples include pregnancy-induced hypertensive disorders, hyperemesis gravidarum, and postpartum psychosis. There are also increased non-pregnancy risks such as venous thromboembolism. For more information on pregnancy as a vulnerable state, see Liisa Uusimäki and Karmen Johansson, *The Vulnerability of Pregnancy and the Motherhood Myth: (Re)birthing the Feminine in Academe*, Palgrave (2020) 185–204, p187.

[24] BM Donavan et al, Intimate Partner Violence During Pregnancy and the Risk for Adverse Fetal Outcomes: A Systematic Review and Meta-analysis, *BJOG: An International Journal of Obstetrics and Gynaecology* 123(8) (2016) 1289–1299, pp1291–1295.

[25] Geoff Hackett et al, British Society for Sexual Medicine Guidelines on Adult Testosterone Deficiency, With Statements for UK Practice, *Journal of Sexual Medicine* 14 (2017) 1504–1523.

[26] Philipp Schulz, *Male Survivors of Wartime Sexual Violence, Perspectives from Northern Uganda*, California University Press (2020) p70.

[27] Hackett et al, n.25, pp1514–1517.

[28] Turner, n 8, p113.

[29] Lesley Briscoe, Tina Lavender, and Linda McGowan, A Concept Analysis of Women's Vulnerability During Pregnancy, Birth and the Postnatal Period, *Journal of Advanced Nursing* 72(10) (2016) 2330–2345, p2337.

Similarly, the absence of health and social support entering pregnancy, throughout pregnancy, and postnatally will influence the degree of physical, psychological, and social vulnerability.[30] However, the potential inaccessibility of maternity care during conflict, as well as the lack of sensitivity in subsequent pregnancies to a person's sexual victimization, can have detrimental consequences on wellbeing.[31]

The stress caused by an absence of assistance with bodily and other harms emerged in my fieldwork. Despite a programme for psychosocial and comprehensive medical care for victims of the armed conflict (PAPSIVI) in Colombia,[32] several respondents found that accessing medical and social support for harms was a difficult ordeal:

> Having access to healthcare has not been easy for my harms, the problem gets worse and we have to look for help elsewhere like the Red Cross. It is like placing warm clothing on the worst of diseases, it does not cure it... We have been struggling and swimming against the tide.[33]
>
> Health is terrible here. You will wait months for an appointment. If you want real medical attention, you need private care. The cheapest appointment costs 30,000 pesos which is a day's work and one medication maybe 4 or more days work. However, most of us cannot get a job as the condition of being a victim is a barrier to getting a job."[34]

It is well established that stress further compounds the original harm suffered by victims. As the Chilean National Commission on Truth and Reconciliation noted, 'the permanent stress to which these people [the families of the disappeared] have been subjected has made them more vulnerable'.[35] Victims often spoke of the pressure of managing different stresses including their own health, family responsibilities and relationships, work, engagement in victim organizations, and claiming redress. As one Peruvian healthcare professional who treats and accompanies CRSV victims said:

> If there is no access to basic services like education and health, to good living conditions, there continues to be a set of variables that increase the bad being, that increase the stress.[36]

[30] ibid p2341.

[31] Insensitive obstetric care to victims' past history of sexual violence was a recurrent theme in Colombian interviews: C3 Bogotá, Colombia, September 2018; C11 February 2019; C16 March 2019.

[32] Law 1448 of 2011, Article 135 (rehabilitation), Article 137 (psychosocial care and health programme to victims), and Article 138 (structure, functions and operation of comprehensive psychosocial and healthcare programme).

[33] C15 FG1, Bogotá, Colombia, March 2019.

[34] C15 FG1, Bogotá, Colombia, March 2019.

[35] Part IV, Chapter I: Chile, Report of the Chilean National Commission on Truth and Reconciliation, Proposals for Reparation, in Pablo de Greiff (ed), *The Handbook of Reparations*, OUP (2006) p741.

[36] P7, Lima, Peru, May 2019.

Stigma arising from certain health consequences, as well as complications, adverse reactions to treatment, symptom flare-ups, and disease relapses, may also be a feature of these vulnerable periods. Despite an emphasis in contemporary medical ethics on promoting patient agency and responsibility in health-related decisions, respect for patient autonomy may not always be practised and power imbalances in healthcare relationships can undermine patients' wishes when their inherent vulnerability is enhanced.[37] Victims can also come to further harm due to bias and stigma from medical professionals. Misconceptions regarding persons with disabilities or chronic illnesses may hinder what is possible through medical and social support.[38] Victims may be offered treatments with an unfavourable risk/benefit ratio, confidentiality may be breached, or valid consent may not be obtained.[39] This iatrogenic harm (caused by medical treatment or intervention) is heightened if discrimination exists against victims of sexual violence within healthcare—a form of situational vulnerability detailed further below.

Thus, the degree of inherent vulnerability can be shaped by medical care; while future vulnerability can also be influenced by the extent to which reparative measures support victims.[40] Reparations should be designed and delivered in a way that is sensitive to appropriate care in future medical encounters related to sexual and reproductive health. Positive professional engagement and a trusting and warm relationship between health providers and victims can elevate self-esteem to the extent of being socially empowering.[41] However, attempts to reduce inherent vulnerability by itself may not necessarily be successful and may lead to new harms. Reparative measures can aim to reduce vulnerability, but to do so needs to capture the complexity of victims' lives and intersecting vulnerabilities—including medical, ethical, and spiritual perspectives. This is particularly important when we consider additional situational vulnerabilities that might arise from structural or conflict determinants (eg poverty and ongoing violence). Situational vulnerability is explored further in the following section.

7.2.2 Situational vulnerability

Situational vulnerability is a reference to context-specific vulnerabilities which 'may be caused or exacerbated by the personal, social, political, economic, or

[37] David Armstrong, Actors, Patients & Agency: A Recent History, *Sociology of Health and Illness* 36(2) (2014) 163–174, p172.

[38] Daniels, n 9, p34.

[39] Samia Hurst, Vulnerability in Research and Health Care; Describing the Elephant in the Room? *Bioethics* 22(4) (2008) 191–202, pp189–199.

[40] Briscoe, Lavender, and McGowan, n 29, p2337.

[41] ibid p2337; and Jane E Raymond, 'Creating a Safety Net': Women's Experiences of Antenatal Depression and Their Identification of Helpful Community Support Services During Pregnancy, *Midwifery* 25 (2006) 39–49.

environmental situations of individuals and social groups'.[42] Diverse concepts have been used to describe situational understandings of vulnerability. For example, one similar concept is that of 'structural vulnerability', which has been used by medical anthropologists to understand how the suffering of specific population groups 'is a product of class-based economic exploitation and cultural, gender/sexual, and racialized discrimination'.[43] Bioethics takes a similar stance such that all human beings are ordinarily vulnerable, but appreciates those who are 'especially vulnerable' where their autonomy and integrity are at risk of being abused.[44] Persons unable to access healthcare where this is, or will potentially be, needed (eg being responsible for dependents, rare or pre-existing conditions, distance) are deemed particularly vulnerable within a bioethics framework.[45] Rogers et al describe 'pathogenic vulnerability' as the undermining of a person's autonomy[46] 'generated by morally dysfunctional interpersonal and social relationships characterized by disrespect, prejudice, or abuse, or by socio-political situations characterized by oppression, domination, repression, injustice, persecution, or political violence'.[47]

A well-functioning state that is responsible for safeguarding against gross violations of human rights like widespread sexual violence may not be present during times of conflict and political transition. This resonates with Turner's institutional precariousness which attributes gross violations of human rights with the actions (or inactions) of states and their agents.[48] However, interpersonal relationships in the private sphere can also contribute to pathogenic states of vulnerability and these individuals too are part of the social environment. This wider conception of pathogenic vulnerability is attentive to the sometimes-continuum of sexual violence and its cofactors during both peace and war.[49]

To combat stereotyping of vulnerable groups it is important to note 'that being a member of a vulnerable group does not entail that individual is vulnerable'.[50] In other words, a group may be at higher risk of certain harms, but not everyone within that group is necessarily or equally vulnerable.[51] It is also useful to draw

[42] Mackenzie, Rogers, and Dodds, n 13, p7.

[43] James Quesada, Laurie Kain Hart, and Philippe Bourgois, Structural Vulnerability and Health: Latino Migrant Laborers in the United States, *Medical Anthropology* 30(4) (2011) 339–362, pp339–340.

[44] UNESCO, Universal Declaration on Bioethics and Human Rights (adopted 19 October 2005, published 2006), Article 8 (Respect for human vulnerability and personal integrity).

[45] Barriers to healthcare that lead to vulnerability can be summarized as due to: availability; accessibility; accommodation; affordability; and acceptability. Hurst, n 39, p200.

[46] Mackenzie, Rogers, and Dodds, n 13, p9.

[47] Wendy Rogers, Catriona Mackenzie and Susan Dodds, Why Bioethics Needs a Concept of Vulnerability, *International Journal of Feminist Approaches to Bioethics* 5(2) (2012) 11–38, p25.

[48] Turner, n 8.

[49] The term 'continuum of sexual violence' was coined by Kelly, see Liz Kelly, *Surviving Sexual Violence*, Polity Press (1988); and Malcolm Cowburn, Perceiving the Continuum of Sexual harm and the Need for Varied Responses to Sexual Violence, *International Journal of Offender Therapy and Comparative Criminology* 55(2) (2011) 179–181.

[50] Joseph P DeMarco, Vulnerability: A Needed Moral Safeguard, *American Journal of Bioethics* 4(3) (2004) 82–84, p83.

[51] ibid.

upon vulnerability conceptualization in research and healthcare ethics. A person in a vulnerable group may not actually be harmed (in the physical or typical sense), but they may be affected by oppressive forces that place them at a higher risk of future harm.[52]

Gender discrimination is, of course, a crucial factor shaping situational vulnerability. By way of an example, women can be the main providers of informal low paid work before, during, and post-conflict and so less likely to be the recipients of safe, secure, and formal work.[53] Peterson considers the 'feminisation' of these activities as a reflection of those persons being less valued as well as the structural vulnerability of those who undertake low paid work.[54] The devaluation of the feminine can then foster acceptance of the targeting of women, including sexual violence, as well as 'punishing insufficiently masculine men'.[55] Victims of CRSV face additional situational vulnerabilities after the violence has occurred, which can also impact their physical wellbeing, such as limited health security, inadequate quality of care during pregnancy and childbirth, and delayed access to time-sensitive interventions after sexual violence.[56]

Males too can be rendered vulnerable to sexual violence on the grounds of gendered bodily conceptions that considers the female form as subordinate to the male. The intention can be to destabilize what it means to be a man by recasting the male body as female in sex acts. In the case of male anal rape, the victim's penis plays a subordinate role and the male body is feminized.[57] Marginalized men within armed groups can be targeted for sexual violence.[58] Clark considers phallocentric masculinities (where gender is performed through heteronormative sexual acts) as a source of vulnerability for men.[59] Men and boys who were raped risked being accused of homosexuality, disbelieved, and blamed as active participants due to ingrained heterosexual masculinities.[60]

[52] Tricha Shivas, Contextualizing the Vulnerability Standard, *American Journal of Bioethics* 4(3) (2004) 84–86, p85.

[53] V Spike Peterson, Gendering Insecurities, Informalization, and 'War Economics', in A Mari Tripp, M Marx Ferree, and C Ewig (eds), *Gender, Violence and Human Security: Critical Feminist Perspectives*, New York University Press (2013) 50–78, p55.

[54] ibid p65.

[55] Elizabeth Stites, A Struggle for Rites: Masculinity, Violence and Livelihoods in Karamoja, Uganda, in Mari Tripp, Marx Ferree, and Ewig, n 53, 132–162, pp133 and p137.

[56] Ruth Rubio-Marín and Dorothy Estrada-Tanck, Violence Against Women, Human Security, and Human Rights of Women and Girls Reinforced Obligations in the Context of Structural Vulnerability, in Mari Tripp, Marx Ferree, and Ewig, n 53, p240.

[57] Janine Natalya Clark, The Vulnerability of the Penis: Sexual Violence Against Men in Conflict and Security Frames, *Men and Masculinities* 22(5) (2019) 778–800; and Brendan Gough and Gareth Edwards, The Beer Talking: Four Lads, a Carry Out and the Reproduction of Masculinities, *The Sociological Review* 46(3) (1998) 409–455, p417.

[58] See Sara Meger, Toward a Feminist Political Economy of Wartime Sexual Violence, *International Feminist Journal of Politics* 17(3) (2015) 416–434.

[59] Clark, n 57, p782.

[60] U12, Gulu, Uganda, July 2018.

In a conflict setting, victim vulnerability may be increased because of the risk of repeated violence,[61] depending on the circumstances in which the violence has occurred.[62] Some men (and women) from militarized or combatant backgrounds are assumed to be violent and can become targets of 'revenge' violence by communities,[63] which may include sexual violence. Thus, Enloe encourages us to think about the socialization of gender roles and masculinities within traditional and non-traditional militarized settings including non-state armed groups.[64] In turn, reparations can both consider how masculinities can shape sexual violence perpetration so as to reduce vulnerability to sexual violence, but also how masculinity can function as a vulnerability in itself which marginalizes combatant victims of sexual violence.[65] It is important to recall that masculinities and femininities are socially constructed gender norms that are associated with what it means to be a man or woman respectively.[66] As such, vulnerabilities related to deviations of the status quo must be comprehended by positioning them in relation to the sociocultural context.[67]

Across the three case studies where I conducted fieldwork, I saw evidence that situational vulnerabilities created by discrimination inhibited victims' confidence that their health needs and related vulnerabilities would be taken seriously. This mistrust was produced in part by the harmful attitudes of some healthcare professionals towards victims of sexual violence. Such distrust meant that they were less likely to disclose sexual violence or to seek medical care, for fear of being insensitively questioned about the cause of their harm.[68] One female victim of sexual violence stated:

> You can't just tell the doctor you have been raped by 20 or 30 men. The doctor or the person next to them is going to say, don't you think you had some responsibility? They point at you and say that woman over there has a sexual disease and she is most likely going to infect someone else.[69]

[61] Francesa Ippolito, Vulnerability as a Normative Argument for Accommodating 'Justice' Within AFSJ, *European Law Journal* 25 (2019) 544–560, p547.

[62] ibid p547.

[63] Anne Menzel, Between Ex-Combatantization and Opportunities for Peace: The Double-Edged Qualities of Motorcycle-Taxi Driving in Urban Postwar Sierra Leone, *Africa Today* 58(2) (2011) 97–127.

[64] Cynthia Enloe, Manoeuvrers: The International Politics of Militarizing Women's Lives, University of California Press (2000); and Cynthia Enloe, *Does Khaki Become You? The Militarization of Women's Lives*, Pandora Press London (1983).

[65] Includes marginalization of non-binary and transgender identities.

[66] See Schulz, n 26, pp93–94; or Hannah Wright, *Masculinities, Conflict and Peacebuilding: Perspectives on Men Through a Gender Lens*, Safeworld (2014) p4.

[67] David D Gilmore, *Manhood in the Making: Cultural Concepts of Manhood*, Yale University Press (1990) p50.

[68] P3 FG2, Lima, Peru, May 2019; C3 Bogotá, Colombia, September 2018; C15 FG1, Bogotá, Colombia, March 2019.

[69] C15 FG1, Bogotá, Colombia, March 2019.

Empirical findings from interviews with healthcare professionals supported these claims. One doctor I interviewed referred to victims of sexual violence as 'living a reckless sex life',[70] and another medical coordinator spoke of how they would question women victims on why they go out alone at night.[71]

In Uganda, victims and civil society described instances where male victims of sexual violence were particularly vulnerable after being refused surgical treatment by male doctors for treatment of anal prolapse resulting from rape.[72] The inadequacies of healthcare in sensitively tending to victims goes beyond their preferred gendered health spaces.[73] A study by Médecins Sans Frontiéres (MSF) found that clinics offering integrated medical and psychological care specifically for victims of sexual violence, compared with non-specialized clinics, may facilitate disclosure of sexual violence and are often preferred by victims themselves, particularly men and boys.[74] That said, there is a dearth of research and information on appropriate trauma therapies for male sexual violence compared to female and child sexual abuse, leaving them vulnerable to not receiving tailored, male-centred approaches which could form part of reparations.[75]

7.2.3 Understanding temporal vulnerabilities

Understanding vulnerability through a temporal lens can be helpful in deciding whether to take immediate action, as opposed to a reasonable delay if a harm is unlikely to manifest in the short term or at all.[76] This is apparent with victims of sexual violence who contract HIV, which, without prompt medical management and lifelong antiretroviral therapy, will lead to premature mortality or morbidity. It may be that interim or prioritized reparations are made to victims at high risk

[70] U7, Lira, Uganda, July 2018.

[71] U3, Gulu Uganda, July 2018. These experiences are not limited to the case studies in this thesis. For example, it has also been reported in other reparation programmes, such as the German domestic Nazi persecution compensation procedure of Jewish, Roma, and Sinti victims of forced sterilization, who were blamed for their suffering and denied redress by former Nazi doctors acting as assessors. See Christian Pross, *Paying for the Past: The Struggle Over Reparations for Surviving Victims of the Nazi Terror*, translated by Belinda Cooper, John Hopkins University Press (1998) p158–164.

[72] U12, Gulu, Uganda, July 2018; U10 FG2, Uganda, July 2018.

[73] Heleen Touquet and Ellen Gorris, Out of the Shadows? The Inclusion of Men and Boys in Conceptualisations of Wartime Sexual Violence, *Reproductive Health Matters* 24(47) (2016) 36–46, p38.

[74] Anaïs Broban et al, Assault and Care Characteristics of Victims of Sexual Violence in Eleven Médecins Sans Frontières Programs in Africa, What About Men and Boys? *PLoS ONE* 15(8) (2020) e0299409.

[75] John Thomas and Jonathan Kopel, Male Victims of Sexual Assault: A Review of the Literature, *Behavioural Sciences* 13(4) (2023) 304.

[76] For example, the Human Papilloma Virus may be cleared spontaneously by the body and abnormal cellular activity is not likely to occur in the short term, see Chapter 3.

of further harm proximate in time to the violence,[77] to help mitigate their harm as soon as possible.[78] A clinical care approach to vulnerabilities related to sexual violence holds that healthcare professionals should be alert at all times to persons at risk of sexual violence, particularly in conflict and post-conflict settings.[79] These harms may emerge over time, as victims might also suffer harms as a result of the CRSV without realizing or recognizing them.[80] Across the three case sites, victims told me of harms they did not realize were a result of sexual violence until years afterwards or when they sought help for a particular aggrievance or ailment.[81] This is not to suggest victims were incapable of understanding the links. Rather, in some instances at least, it can be difficult for victims themselves to recognize the medical connections between the original harms and consequences that may manifest at a later date. This was particularly the case with victims of forced sterilization, where consent was not obtained and official information of what had happened to them was obscured.[82]

A medico-legal approach is conscious that victims can be vulnerable to rape myths that place too much weight on physical injuries being present immediately after CRSV, or that physical injuries correlate with the severity of the experience for the victim. This is despite the limitations of forensic medical examinations (FME) and factors such as the rapid healing of many genital injuries, as well as delayed FMEs in conflict/post-conflict settings, if performed at all. Victims can be vulnerable to parties in judicial/legal processes that aim to discredit medical evidence or apply a forensic 'over reach' to available evidence.[83] There is value in considering other ways in which FMEs (generally performed in the acute time period) can lead to a variety of successful outcomes beyond criminal convictions.[84] For instance, there can be avenues for reparative justice that arise later in time, while also striving to minimize the creation of other vulnerabilities, especially if reparations do not materialize.

[77] Lindsey defines vulnerability as 'the precarious living conditions of individuals, households or communities in the face of a threat in the form of an abrupt change in environment'. Charlotte Lindsey, *Women Facing War*, ICRC (2015) p30.

[78] Such as in Sierra Leone—see Mohamad Suma and Cristián Correa, *Report and Proposals for the Implementation of Reparations in Sierra Leone*, ICTJ (2009); and in Tunisia—Article 11, Organic Law on Establishing and Organizing Transitional Justice 2013.

[79] Special Appeal 2019: The ICRC's Response to Sexual Violence, International Committee of the Red Cross, REM 2019/113, p30; Jane Hunt, Rachel Witkin, and Cornelium Katona, Identifying Human Trafficking in Adults, *BMJ* (2020) 371:m4683 31–33, pp31–32; Q&A: The ICRC's Approach to Sexual Violence in Armed Conflict: In Conversation with Peter Maurer, *International Review of the Red Cross* 96(894) (2014) 449–456, p451; and C6, Bogotá, Colombia, September 2018.

[80] Shivas, n 52, p85.

[81] P4, P2 FG1, Lima, Peru, May 2019; C15 FG1, Bogotá, Colombia, March 2019.

[82] P2 FG1 and P3 FG2, Lima, Peru, May 2019.

[83] Stephanie Wright, 'Facts That Are Declared Proven': Sexual Violence, Forensic Medicine, and the Courtroom in early Francoist Spain, *Women's History Review* 32(7) (2023) 939–959.

[84] Emily Tiry, Janine Zweig, and Lily Yu, Beyond Forensic Evidence: Examining Sexual Assault Medical Forensic Exam Mechanisms That Influence Sexual Assault Case Outcomes, *Journal of interpersonal violence* 37(7–8) (2022) NP5693–NP5727.

In some contexts when victims are suspected or identified as having suffered sexual violence or exploitation, local safeguarding protocols are acted upon and individuals are referred to social care and other services where resources allow.[85] However, in conflict settings, professionals may not be skilled to detect such victims, understand cultural cues, or follow up may only be for a short time, leaving victims without vital treatment or socio-economic support.[86] One humanitarian organization in Colombia provides medical support to victims of sexual violence for only six months to ensure they have sufficient service provision across the country and to attend to urgent complaints. To mitigate these limitations, the organization refers patients, and accompanies them, to public health services if this is required and attempts to help local hospitals with anti-retroviral supply with varying degrees of success, particularly in light of some victims' distrust of state institutions or ability to afford to travel to appointments. A lack of a coordinated approach with other institutions can mean that victims, after receiving medical treatment, return to situations that increase their risk of sexual violence occurring again and does not tackle the structural vulnerabilities present pre- and post-conflict that place certain groups at higher risk.

Understanding the temporal dimensions of vulnerability leads to a better appreciation that reparative measures may be required at different points in time.[87] Furthermore, reparations are often designed to address harms that occurred decades before. Understanding temporal vulnerabilities acknowledges that victims may suffer compounded harms in the interim preceding the enactment of reparation schemes. For instance, with victims of forced sterilization in Peru, the provision of reparations over twenty years later meant that opportunities for reproductive rehabilitation were already too late for many.[88] Prioritization can take the form of paying interim relief payments, fast-tracking applications, funding medical rehabilitation, or providing specific forms of payment for those who are vulnerable (eg an increased amount or a lump sum rather than periodic payments).[89] Urgent or interim reparations alongside assistance may attend to immediate vulnerability.

Victims who have escaped the situation of sexual violence are likely to remain vulnerable to further exploitation for a prolonged period of time and therefore need support.[90] By way of an example, one Ugandan victim of sexual slavery told me how a non-governmental organization (NGO) had built a house for her and

[85] Hunt, Witkin, and Katona, n 79, p31.
[86] C2, Bogotá, Colombia, September 2019.
[87] This is apparent with protocols around being gender-sensitive and trauma-informed in engagements with victims.
[88] Sunneva Gilmore and Luke Moffett, Redressing Forced Sterilisation: The Role of the Medical Profession, *British Journal of Obstetrics and Gynaecology* 127 (2020) 923–926, p924.
[89] Such as in Nepal; section 16, Agreement between the Federal Republic of Germany and the State of Israel 1952; and section 24(1), Victims' Payment Regulations 2020.
[90] Hunt, Witkin, and Katona, n 79.

her children, but her brothers and clan came to seize it soon after, forcing them to leave, and she now lived in a poor area rife with criminality.[91] Reparations can be designed to consider dispositional vulnerability through guarantees of non-recurrence; focusing on the relationship between generations ensuring those yet to exist do not endure similar violence. Thompson frames this as 'intergenerational dependency' relying less on the experience of suffering and more on the harms that transcend a lifetime.[92] Consequences can span and morph through generations, such as for children born out of rape,[93] or children born post-conflict who were raised by traumatized parents, who can suffer various harms via several pathways.[94]

Inter or transgenerational vulnerability over time also considers the value of reparations that look to the past. For instance, the identity and good name of deceased victims (and possibly that of their family) may be morally harmed, such as through victim-blaming in cases of sexual violence (eg the 'Comfort Women'), or physical harms, namely post-mortem sexual mutilation. Family members and partners may seek to recover their loved ones remains and dispose of them in a dignified way (as per the deceased's wishes) after being sexually enslaved and killed. While some vulnerabilities appear less urgent in the occurrent state, they can have implications for the next generation, such as the disadvantages victims of sexual violence encounter, including raising their children, maternity risks, and socio-economic hardship. Furthermore, the care and remembrance of the dead can set a precedent for future generations as well as act as a form of resistance to stigma and negative stereotypes surrounding victims of sexual violence.

7.2.4 Problematizing vulnerability and recognizing resilience

As this section has sought to demonstrate, it is important to consider how both inherent and situational vulnerabilities coalesce and interact when redressing the harms victims of sexual violence experience. However, it is also important to note that the notion of vulnerability can be misused, patronizing, and even perpetuate the stigma already encountered by victims of sexual violence if it is framed in such a way as to suggest that they are being 'judged' for failing to withstand trauma.[95]

[91] U4 FG1, Gulu, Uganda, July 2018.

[92] Janna Thompson, Being in Time: Ethics and Temporal Vulnerability, in C Mackenzie, W Rogers, and S Dodds (eds), *Vulnerability: New Essays in Ethics and Feminist Philosophy*, 162–180.

[93] Joanne Neenan, *Closing the Protection Gap for Children Born of War: Addressing Stigmatisation and the Intergenerational Impact of Sexual Violence in Conflict*, Centre for Women, Peace and Security for UK Foreign and Commonwealth Office, 2017.

[94] Monsterrat Fargas-Malet and Karola Dillenburger, Intergenerational Transmission of Conflict-Related Trauma in Northern Ireland: A Behaviour Analytic Approach, *Journal of Aggression, Maltreatment & Trauma* 25(4) (2016) 436–454.

[95] See Brown, n 7; and Fineman, n 15, p19.

Some victims of sexual violence may feel a degree of shame in acknowledging their own vulnerability, feelings which may be exacerbated by negative reactions by others to such admissions,[96] which may in turn further damage a victim's self-esteem.[97] Self-denigration may then further reduce victims' resilience or capacity to adapt.[98]

Freedman considers how the humanitarian field's notion of vulnerability is generally reconstructed along gendered and racialized lines.[99] Similarly, Baines found that transnational campaigns that advocate for gender equality depict refugee women as particularly vulnerable.[100] Women and children are often collectively labelled as vulnerable, fuelling the false dichotomy that women and children are more at risk of being victimized whereas men are viewed as perpetrators or protectors. In essence, decisions can make others vulnerable through a discretionary act that imposes or assumes vulnerability.[101] Some feminist commentators are particularly wary of applying the notion of vulnerability to sexual violence.[102] Specifically, they express concerns that vulnerability is tied to notions of weak, passive femininity.[103] For some, this is a strong theme in historical narratives portraying women, girls, and sexual minorities as the main victims of sexual violence at the hands of 'aggressive' men during conflicts.[104] In some such accounts, victimization is attached to a particular kind of sexualized vulnerability that considers the female body inferior in strength, sexually stimulating and, in extremis, another 'battleground'.[105] Again this association of women's bodies with warfare fits into the simplistic narrative of 'rape as a weapon of war', which eclipses other forms of sexual violence and reifies victimhood.

[96] Sandra Walklate, Reframing Criminal Victimization: Finding a Place For Vulnerability and Resilience, *Theoretical Criminology* 15(2) (2011) 179–194, p190.

[97] Brigette Piquard, From Symbolic Violence to Symbolic Reparation. Strengthening Resilience and Reparation in Conflict-Affected Areas through Place-(re)making. Examples From the West Bank and Colombia, *DEARQ: Journal of Architecture* 18(1) (2016) 68–79, p70.

[98] ibid p70.

[99] Jane Freedman, The Uses and Abuses of 'Vulnerability' in EU Asylum and Refugee Protection: Protecting Women or Reducing Autonomy? *Papeles del CEIC: International Journal on Collective Identity Research* (1) (2019) 1–15.

[100] Erin K Baines, *Vulnerable Bodies: Gender, the UN and the Global Refugee Crisis*, Routledge (2004) p1.

[101] For more on 'discretionary vulnerability', see Mianna Lotz, Vulnerability and Resilience: A Critical Nexus, *Theoretical Medicine and Bioethics* 37(1) (2016) 45–59.

[102] Erin Cuniff Gilson, Vulnerability and Victimization: Rethinking Key Concepts in Feminist Discourses on Sexual Violence, *Signs: Journal of Women in Culture and Society* 42(1) (2016) 71–98, p71; Ann Murphy, *Violence and the Philosophical Imaginary*, State University of New York (2012) p23.

[103] Cunniff Gilson, n 102, p75.

[104] Marysia Zalewski, 'Well, What is the Feminist Perspective on Bosnia?' *International Affairs* 17(2) (1995) 339–356, p352.

[105] Women's Bodies as a Battleground: Sexual Violence Against Women and Girls During the War in the Democratic Republic of Congo, South Kivu (1996–2003), Réseau des Femmes pour un Développement Associatif, Réseau des Femmes pour la Défense des Droits et la Paix and International Alert (2005) p46.

Reparation programmes need to be mindful of the risk of reifying particular notions of vulnerable categories that are often gendered,[106] and that may undermine the resilience and self-repair strategies of victims as well as risking the exclusion of other groups. Reparations which perpetuate the victim as the weaker individual dependent on the provider as their 'saviour' should be avoided.[107] Victims of sexual violence related to conflict are typically perceived as vulnerable and can be excluded during the design stage.[108] Conceptions of reductive vulnerability and invulnerability shape sexual victimization, therefore reparations should be cognizant of challenging beliefs around gender norms.

One way of combatting a disempowering approach to vulnerability is to consider it alongside the concept of resilience, an interdisciplinary term that has largely become concerned with the interactions between individuals and their socio-economic environment.[109] Indeed, resilience can be a driving factor in the campaigning work of victims and survivors, their families, and their supporters, in the pursuit of reparations and justice campaigns.[110] Within health studies, there is a particular focus on 'resilient organizations' to explore the work of some victims groups (and humanitarian organizations) which have sustained services and support for victims of sexual violence, often in the face of opposition from states, armed groups, and other powerful actors and institutions.[111]

Feminist perspectives in criminology have encouraged an experiential view of resilience where sexual violence is overcome on a continuous basis through various strategies, rather been seen as a singular event that can be fixed.[112] A process-orientated resilience offers a mediating place for reparations to build capacities that counteract vulnerabilities contributing towards harm.[113] Reparations are among the mediating factors that assist in producing positive resilient outcomes when adversity occurs.[114] There is also a gendered dimension to resilience and coping,

[106] Charli Carpenter, 'Women, Children and Other Vulnerable Groups': Gender, Strategic Frames and the Protection of Civilians as a Transnational Issue, *International Studies Quarterly* 49(2) (2005) 295–334.

[107] For an example of the importance of interrogating the narrative of a dependent individual or group in need of the medical provider, see Joachim Boldt, The Concept of Vulnerability in Medical Ethics and Philosophy, *Philosophy, Ethics and Humanities in Medicine* 14(6) (2019), doi.org/10.1186/s13010-019-0075-6.

[108] P2 FG1; P6, Lima Peru, May 2019.

[109] Clark, n 57; and Michael Ungar, 'Resilience Across Cultures', *British Journal of Social Work* 38(2) (2008) 218–235, p225.

[110] Luke Moffett, *Reparations and Conflict: Seeking Balance after War*, OUP (2022).

[111] For more on resilient healthcare (RHC), see J Anderson et al, Defining Adaptive Capacity in Healthcare: A New Framework for Researching Resilient Performance, *Applied Ergonomics* (2020), http://doi.org/10.1016/j.apergo.2020.103111.

[112] Jan Jordan, *Serial Survivors: Women's Narrative of Surviving Rape*, Federation Press (2007); and Fineman, n 15, p187.

[113] For more on the role of mediators in the face of adversity, see Adrian Van Breda, A Critical Review of Resilience Theory and Its Relevance for Social Work, *Social Work/Maatskaplike Werk* 54(1) (2018) 1-18, doi:10.15270/54-1-611.

[114] ibid.

where girls and women whose partners, children, or parents are killed take on increased care-giving roles for remaining family members as a way of processing their trauma.[115] However, those responsible for looking after direct or primary victims can often suffer secondary traumatic stress from being worn-down or overwhelmed by their efforts to cope with the changed socio-economic situation.[116]

Resilience is linked to vulnerability in a number of ways. Walklate suggests that there are complex interconnections between vulnerability, resilience, and victimization 'all of which have inherent, structural and experiential dimensions'.[117] Other authors use vulnerability and resilience interchangeably with (level of) capacity as the common denominator. For example, Ippolito refers to vulnerability over resilience as the 'means used to cope' or withstand and recover from harm in the face of a traumatic or discriminatory event.[118] Resilience is not necessarily the binary opposite of vulnerability, nor is being resilient equated with invulnerability. Rather, resilience is increasingly being understood as both an individual and a social condition that encourages the ability to defy adversity.[119]

Of course, determinations on who is considered resilient or capable of resilience and what are considered acceptable displays of resilience are also socially constructed.[120] An elderly female victim of sexual violence may be considered 'weak' or unable to cope, whereas a young male victim may be thought of as more able to bounce back.[121] Of course, the resilience or not of male victims is often directly affected by societal notions of masculinity and what it means to be a man.[122] Ideas of individual resilience needs to be understood within the specific socio-cultural context in which harms occur. With regards to reparations, resilience helps to see a more lived experience of victims navigating structural dynamics (their social, economic, and cultural environment) as well as their efforts of self-repair and coping with intersecting vulnerabilities in the face of the violations they have suffered.

[115] Jelke Boesten and Polly Wilding, Transformative Gender Justice: Setting an Agenda, *Women's Studies International Forum* 51 (2015) 75–80. This was a sentiment shared by some interviewees, such as COL03, Bogotá, September 2018.

[116] Charles R Figley and Rolf J Kleber, Beyond the 'Victim': Secondary Traumatic Stress, in Rolf J Kleber, Charles R Figley and BPR Gersons (eds), *Beyond Trauma: Cultural and Societal Dynamics*, Plenum (1995) 75–98, p93.

[117] Sandra Walklate, Reframing Criminal Victimization: Finding a Place For Vulnerability and Resilience, *Theoretical Criminology* 15(2) (2011) 179–194, p188; and Ingrid Schoon, *Risk and Resilience: Adaptations in Changing Times*, CUP (2006) p24.

[118] Francesa Ippolito, Vulnerability as a Normative Argument for Accommodating 'Justice' Within the AFSJ, *European Law Journal* 25 (2019) 544–560, p544.

[119] Walklate, n 117, p185; and Schoon, n 117, p17.

[120] Walklate, n 117, p186.

[121] Nils Christie, Ideal Victim, in E Fattah (ed), *From Crime Policy to Victim Policy*, Palgrave (1983) 17–30.

[122] U10 FG2 and U12, Lira, Uganda, July 2018.

7.3 Vulnerability, Resilience, and Reparations

7.3.1 Reparations as a source of vulnerability

Reparations can be responsive to vulnerability as they are a means of recognizing the violations of the 'powerful against the powerless', a 'concept for the have-nots', and is 'tilted toward the bottom'.[123] The absence of reparations can result in the continuation of existing vulnerabilities and the creation of new ones. For example, the UN Committee Against Torture found that the absence of a proper national reparations scheme in Bosnia unnecessarily subjected victims of wartime sexual violence to a violation of their rights due to lengthy proceedings to bring court claims.[124] Indeed, even once they are established, reparation institutions can be precarious, as they are vulnerable to political will and annual budget redesign, or take years to implement making victims too vulnerable to their uncertain dynamics.[125]

However, the process of obtaining reparations can itself create new situations of vulnerability and harm. This resonates with research in victimology, which shows that the effects of legal proceedings on victims can expose them to secondary victimization that is 'partly systemic' in such proceedings and reflects institutional culture in 'fostering insensitive attitudes to victims'.[126] In a similar vein, the bureaucratic operation of reparation programmes sometimes lead to the unnecessary and repeated questioning of victims to ensure they fulfil a particular criteria.[127] Reparation processes that require detailed or repeated recounting of traumatic events can heighten psychological distress in persons with PTSD.[128] Legal categorizations can also cause frictions. Wiebelhaus-Brahm notes that reparations can cause tensions between victims and those who are equally marginalized and vulnerable.[129] Indeed, in Uganda, Peru, and Colombia, respondents spoke about community frictions with other marginalized members of their villages between

[123] Mari Matsuda, Looking to the Bottom: Critical Legal Studies and Reparations, *Harvard Civil Rights-Civil Liberties Law Review* 22(2) (1987) 323–400, 393–394.

[124] Concluding observations VI periodic Report of Bosnia, Committee Against Torture, CAT/C/BIH/CO/6, 22 December 2017.

[125] C8, Bogotá, Colombia, September 2018.

[126] Lorraine Wolhuter, Neil Olley, and David Denham, *Victimology: Victimisation and Victims' Rights*, Routledge (2008) pp47–48.

[127] Denis Martinez and Luisa Gomez, A Promise to be Fulfilled: Reparations for Victims of the Armed Conflict in Guatemala, Reparations, Responsibility and Victimhood in Transitional Societies, RRV (2019) p.23; and Actoras de Cambio (ECAP and UNAMG), Recommendation to PNR; and Sunneva Gilmore, Julie Guillerot, and Clara Sandoval, Beyond Silence and Stigma: Crafting a Gender-Sensitive Approach for Victims of Sexual Violence in Domestic Reparation Programmes (2020) (Project Report, Reparations, Responsibility and Victimhood in Transitional Societies, Queen's University Belfast), p40.

[128] Anna E Jaffe et al, Does It Hurt To Ask? A Meta-Analysis of Participant Reactions to Trauma Research, *Clinical Psychology Review* 40 (2015) 40–56.

[129] Eric Wiebelhaus-Brahm, After Shocks: Exploring the Relationships Between Transitional Justice and Resilience in Post-Conflict Societies, *Justice Mosaics*, ICTJ (2017) 140–165, p156.

those who fitted into legal categories and those who did not. As one doctor commented when engaging with the Trust Fund for Victims of the ICC, when victims are only eligible for assistance or reparations for harm they have suffered after its commencement on 1 July 2002, or for the charges for which Dominic Ongwen was convicted,

> it really pains them. When we do go to the villages they say why are you leaving me, I suffered just like those other people. But we have to follow the Rome Statute of the ICC.[130]

Reparation processes can also increase the vulnerability of those responsible for assisting in reparation claims or implementing reparations, such as registering victims, providing healthcare, or helping design of a museum. Local NGOs that partner in delivering rehabilitation may not be included in the larger decisions regarding reparations and implementation.[131] It may be dangerous for local organizations to receive donations for the rehabilitation of victims of sexual violence or particular gender identities, and organizations themselves may become stigmatized and targeted for helping victims. For instance, in Colombia, one victim group spoke about women attending health facilities in rural areas being targeted for killings due to sexual violence they suffered at the hands of paramilitaries.[132]

Depending on the level of engagement, those responsible for providing reparations may also be vulnerable to vicarious trauma by over-identifying with victims or encouraging silence to protect both provider and recipient.[133] Throughout the three case sites, healthcare professionals felt unprepared clinically and emotionally. One gynaecologist, who is a director of a Colombian medical centre specializing in sexual and reproductive healthcare said: 'The biggest problem for doctors was that when a woman said she was a victim of sexual violence, they didn't know how to protect or interact with her . . . it's difficult to talk about it. For doctors, and for people.'[134] This underscores the need for reparation processes to create space in which to listen to vulnerability, as explored in the following section.

[130] U6, Lira, Uganda, July 2018.

[131] Heideman found the exclusion of local NGOs in decisions affecting human security post-conflict created new vulnerabilities, see Laura J Heideman, The Vulnerable Protecting the Vulnerable: NGOs and Human Security in the Aftermath of War, in Mari Tripp, Marx Ferree, and Ewig, n 53, 214–237.

[132] C15 FG1, Bogotá, Colombia, March 2019. See also Deborah Zalesne, Making Rights a Reality: Access To Health Care for Afro-Colombian Survivors of Conflict-Related Sexual Violence, *Colombia Human Rights Law Review* 51 (2019) 670–724, p693.

[133] Christian Pross, Burnout, Vicarious Traumatization and its Prevention, *Torture* 16(1) (2006) 1–9; and Yael Danieli, Massive Trauma and the Healing Role of Reparative Justice: an Update, in Ferstman and Goetz (eds), *Reparations for Victims of Genocide, War Crimes and Crimes against Humanity*, Second Revised Edition (2020), p38–85

[134] C8, Bogotá, Colombia, September 2018.

7.3.2 Listening to vulnerability

Without experiencing harm and suffering it is difficult to know what it is like.[135] Therefore, if vulnerability in reparation discourse is to have normative significance it should draw directly from the voice of the victims (if they wish to express it) to ensure the intricacies of the lived reality inform responses (eg barriers to applying for reparations). This will assist in disrupting perceptions that victims who are inherently vulnerable on account of their gender or harm lack agency and should be shielded from articulating their ideas and concerns. However, victims may be silenced by their vulnerability or marginalization. Schulz's work in Uganda underscores this challenge, especially around masculine cultural norms and the aversion to appear vulnerable in a patriarchal society.[136] Agrawal and Hurst encourage the labelling of vulnerable subjects to ensure they are identified and not disadvantaged via lost opportunities.[137] At the same time, vulnerability and victimhood can be instrumentalized by victims and other actors for social gains as well as advocating for reparation.[138] Thus, the ways in which victims exercise their agency while occupying epitomized vulnerability categories should dismantle associations of weakness. Responses aimed at 'protecting' the vulnerable can isolate them from genuinely participating in the design and request of reparations. While retraumatization is a real risk, victims' autonomy should not be compromised at the expense of adapting trauma-sensitive methods of engaging them in reparations.

Gilson considers that the untapped positive potential of vulnerability lies in its ability to create empathy and appreciate multifaceted experiences of being 'especially' vulnerable.[139] Vulnerability lends itself to enhanced gender-sensitivity by foregrounding how gender and sex create differential experiences as well as those that intersect with factors such as ethnicity, socio-economics, and disability. Applying a similar approach of vulnerability to reparation not only attends to the complexities of harms as a precursor to designing reparations but also provokes a discussion about the precipitating structural, cultural, and social factors that led to the violation. As structural vulnerabilities can be a barrier to enjoying the right to reparation, then transforming previous structures of discrimination is necessary.[140]

[135] Trudy Govier, *Victims and Victimhood*, Broadview Press (2015) p83

[136] Schulz, n 26, p93.

[137] Manish Agrawal, Voluntariness in Clinical Research at the End of Life, *Journal of Pain Symptom Management* 25(4) (2003) S25–S32; and Hurst, n 39, 191–202.

[138] Valerie Meredith, Victim Identity and Respect for Human Dignity: A Terminological Analysis, *International Review of the Red Cross* 91(874) (2009) 259–277, p261.

[139] Erinn C Gilson, *The Ethics of Vulnerability. A Feminist Analysis of Social Life and Practice*, Routledge (2016) pp8–9.

[140] Ruth Rubio-Marín and Dorothy Estrada-Tanck, Violence Against Women, Human Security, and Human Rights of Women and Girls: Reinforced Obligations in the Context of Structural Vulnerability, in Mari Tripp, Marz Ferree, and Ewig (n 53) 238–259, p254.

Agrawal and Hurst's perspective on the ethics of vulnerability in health research resonates with the treatment of categorized vulnerable groups in the design and implementation of reparations.[141] They consider 'labelling the inclusion of vulnerable subjects as unethical is incorrect' as it potentially creates disadvantages through missed opportunities to participate.[142] It may even systemically exclude certain victims to the detriment of not obtaining useful knowledge to inform reparations. Instead, they propose greater safeguards. However, victims of sexual violence may be faced with a vulnerability–victimhood paradox where they are considered 'too vulnerable' to be consulted. As Arendt points out, the sentiment of pity can be 'cold and abstract' as it is committed to an ideal that maintains a 'sentimental distance', and has a 'vested interest in the existence of the unhappy . . . and the suffering of others'.[143] In recovery, victims continue to be faced with the social pressure of 'overcoming' their harms. A number of victims I interviewed took issue with this characterization of their recovery. Others, it appeared to me, embraced the narrative of overcoming vulnerability, striving to make their own 'success story' of having overcome the odds.[144]

The concerns raised by critics of vulnerability's usefulness calls for a change in its narrow conceptualization, while preserving its practical capacity to avoid further harm and provide organization against a backdrop of widespread suffering. The principle of vulnerability can be refined and legitimized further in three ways. First, by crafting group-orientated vulnerability only where there are clear and acceptable reasons relevant to the context. Second, vulnerability can act as a reminder of the capacity of individuals or groups to cope or informally repair their harm and to what extent this has been beneficial. Third, vulnerability can emphasize the structural conditions that need modifying through non-repetition as reparation or as a succinct set of reforms. These can be complemented by framing reparations as rehabilitation directly responding to vulnerability. This is explored in the following section.

7.3.3 Rehabilitation and vulnerability

The significance of rehabilitation to reparation has yet to be fully explored. Rehabilitation as a specific form of reparation has only featured in a few human rights treaties and is similarly under-developed as a notion in medicine.[145] There has been some development of expertise in relation to the rehabilitation of torture

[141] Agrawal, n 137; and Hurst n 39, p195.
[142] Hurst, n 39, p195.
[143] Hannah Arendt, *On Revolution*, Penguin (2006) p85.
[144] See Chapter 4 regarding identity; and interviews C3, Victim of CRSV, Colombia, September 2018; C15 FG1, Colombia, March 2019; U13 Victim of CRSV, Uganda, July 2018.
[145] UN Committee on Economic, Social and Cultural Rights, General Comment No 14, para 59.

survivors, but a disconnect remains between the disciplines of medicine and law in this area.[146]

As argued elsewhere in this book, I would contend that *restitutio integrum* it not achievable for most victims,[147] but the rehabilitative aims of restored function and an acceptable quality of life may be more modestly feasible. Medical rehabilitation may play a role in this. This rehabilitation–vulnerability nexus problematizes the pursuit of fixing individuals, while appreciating that as human beings they will be vulnerable to biological injury and social stigma, and provides them some of the care, support, and tools to manage such dispositional harms. Vulnerability is the way in which we are differently affected by injury and so can shed light on how to develop new abilities and capacities to remedy such harm.[148] One Ugandan doctor articulated the value of rehabilitation in pursuit of a level of health that enabled persons to fulfil their aims as:

> fixing one health problem needs to be appreciated more, it comes back to human resource, you cannot lead a country where everyone is sick. If people are healthy, they will do farming, trade, army - so health is at the core and it is the beginning of justice. Let someone who has suffered have good health and the rest will come.[149]

Rehabilitation at the individual level must take into account factors that support its success. Medicine has been instrumental to the development and dissemination of trauma-informed care (TIC), with the research on Adverse Childhood Experiences helping to catalyse approaches.[150] TIC aims to minimize retraumatization for victims when engaging with professionals. It also aims to prevent secondary traumatization to caregivers and family members of victims.[151] This approach has increasingly influenced care practices in response to sexual violence,[152] including conflict-related sexual violence.[153] However, its connection to rehabilitation and reparation remains under-explored. While various TIC models exist,[154] approaches that are sensitive to gender, cultural context, and intersecting forms of

[146] Nimisha Patel, Conceptualising Rehabilitation as Reparation For Torture Survivors: A Clinical Perspective, *International Journal of Human Rights* 23(9) (2019) 1546–1568, pp1546–1547.

[147] Brandon Hamber, Repairing the Irreparable: Dealing With the Double-Blinds of Making Reparations for Crimes of the Past, *Ethnicity & Health* 5(3/4) (2000) 215–226.

[148] Cuniff Gilson, n 102, p77.

[149] U6, Lira, Uganda, July 2018.

[150] Gordon JG Asmundson and Tracie O Afifi (eds) *Adverse Childhood Experiences: Using Evidence to Advance Research, Practice, Policy, and Prevention*, Academic Press (2020) pp26–28.

[151] ibid pp370–372

[152] Sarah Nathan and Meghan Ferrara, An Innovative Trauma-Informed Curriculum for Sexual Assault Care, *Journal of Nursing Education* 59(6) (2020) 336–340.

[153] RM Olson et al, Assessing Knowledge and Acceptability of a Trauma-Informed Training Model to Strengthen Response to Conflict and Gender-Based Violence in the Democratic Republic of Congo, *Violence and Victims* 37(6) (2022) 739–767.

[154] For an overview of common trauma-informed approaches, see Catrin Wallace, An Overview of Trauma-Informed Approaches, CASCADE, Cardiff University (TIA), July 2020.

discrimination are especially important for addressing CRSV. Though further research is needed, current work on integrating shame-sensitivity into TIC may offer valuable insights into addressing the specific experiences of shame among CRSV victims especially where it becomes embedded in their sense of self.[155]

Research on the effects of non-TIC approaches and environments suggests there may be a risk of exacerbating distress symptoms and could present a barrier to rehabilitation.[156] Where there is a lack of understanding on traumatogenic sequelae then ineffective treatment may be offered or individuals may disengage with healthcare.[157] This can leave them vulnerable to long-term health consequences of CRSV, as discussed in Chapter 3. The lack of TIC in other reparation processes, such as applying for compensation, may disincentivize victims from coming forward. Therefore, connectivity between reparation forms and the potential for positive rehabilitative outcomes could be limited by the absence of TIC.

Free or subsidized public healthcare may already operate on a vulnerability model,[158] however there has been a fragmented approach as to how medical rehabilitation as reparations can complement other healthcare being delivered by public or private actors.[159] Therefore, greater attention is necessary on how reparations can 'fit' within a healthcare system, potentially dealing with a broad spectrum of worsened health outcomes. According to a medical coordinator at a Ugandan regional hospital specializing in war injuries, regarding the widespread health impacts, 'the war is over, the guns are silent and people are back but there is a time bomb of health. There are many diseases in the community not attended to and the worst is HIV.'[160] Yet, victims interviewed described how they were unable to access free long-term or specialist medical care despite comprehensive medical care forming part of reparations in Colombia and Peru.[161] The reasons given included: inadequate healthcare infrastructure; absence of referral pathways; unaffordable quality care; stigma within health institutions; and distrust of medics.[162] This is felt not only by patients, but also medical staff themselves who may have fled conflict-affected areas and were unable to return to work. As one Ugandan doctor said,

[155] Luna Dolezal and Matthew Gibson, Beyond a Trauma-Informed Approach and Towards Shame-Sensitive Practice, *Humanities and Social Sciences Communication*, 9(1) (2022) 214 https://doi.org/10.1057/s41599-022-01227-z.

[156] Asmundson and Afifi, n 150, pp374–376.

[157] Kirsten Havig, The Health Care Experiences of Adult Survivors of Child Sexual Abuse: A Systematic Review of Evidence on Sensitive Practice, *Trauma, Violence & Abuse* 9(1) (2008) 19–33.

[158] Graeme Laurie, Shawn Harmon, and Edward Dove, *Law and Medical Ethics*, 11th Edition, OUP (2019) p147.

[159] See Gilmore, ICC-01/04-02/06-2623-Anx2-Red2, pp80–81.

[160] U7, July 2018, Lira, Uganda.

[161] PAPSIVI in Colombia and the comprehensive reparations programme (PIR) in Peru.

[162] C3, Bogotá, Colombia, September 2018; C4, Bogotá, Colombia, September 2018; C15 FG1, Bogotá, Colombia, March 2019; P2 FG1, Lima, Peru, May 2019; U12, Gulu, Uganda, July 2018.

> The health personnel ran away to greener pastures and for safety of their lives. Even up to now, some time after the war with all the health facilities and infrastructure being brought back into place, the health workers still fear to stay 10 km away from the town because psychologically they are not safe. They build permanent houses for staff, but no one is sleeping inside them. They go and work in their motorcycle and they go away back on them. So that is another thing that the infrastructure is being restored but the heart of working and serving the community is not there. There is that fear, they still remember how the bombs were flying, houses burnt, or neighbour killed, and you escaped narrowly. There is a lot still to be done.[163]

Medical rehabilitation alone is unlikely to lead to improved health outcomes as it fails to address the social, political, and cultural context within which suffering such as rape occurs.[164] Bourgois and colleagues argue that social determinants of health can 'sabotage the health of the patient' despite clinical care efforts.[165] In other words, victims of sexual violence may be embedded in networks of inequitable power relationships post-conflict that directly impede achieving 'good health'. As social and political participation can be linked to health outcomes, stigma risks excluding victims from social participation, and opportunities for repair may be even more hindered.[166] In addition and as explored above, some marginalized groups can face situational vulnerabilities which increase their risk of health harms. These can include systemic difficulties such as accessing water, healthcare, and sanitation. Inevitably, this raises tensions within reparations programmes regarding how to balance the inherent vulnerabilities being experienced by specific victims with the broader situational vulnerabilities experienced by the harmed community.[167]

Reparations can sometimes be tasked with addressing overwhelming structural and systemic issues of discrimination which are the root cause of prevalent harms and poor health outcomes. Fully recognizing structural vulnerabilities to sexual violence and barriers to repair could help justify the mobilization of resources both within and outside medical care to promote access and long-term health.[168] While the range of harms may overwhelm reparation programmes,

[163] U6, Lira, Uganda, July 2018.

[164] For more information on how social relationships lead to structural violence and suffering, see Paul Farmer, *Pathologies of Power: Health, Human Rights and the New War on the Poor*, University of California Press (2005) pxiv.

[165] Philippe Bourgois et al, Structural Vulnerability: Operationalizing the Concept to Address Health Disparities in Clinical Care, *Academic Medicine* 92(3) (2017) 299–307.

[166] Furthermore, Turner draws attention to 'a well established argument in political economy that social and political participation in society is closely associated with health outcomes'—n 8, p10.

[167] Judith Bueno de Mesquita, Gen Sander, and Paul Hunt, Rehabilitation and the Right to Health in Times of Transition: Are Administrative Reparations Programmes Doing Enough to Redress Violations of the Right to Health?, *International Human Rights Law Review* 5(2) (2016) 169–193, p188.

[168] Bourgois et al, n 165.

separating transitional justice from development may neglect the specific aspects of care needed for victims emerging from conflict. For example, this includes the demands for improved sexual and reproductive healthcare services for victims and survivors of sexual violence, mental health and trauma services, or investment in rural healthcare (particularly where they have been attacked or neglected). As a minimum, state-funded reparations may be able to complement the reconstruction of healthcare systems post-conflict, help identify some of the most vulnerable in need of urgent and specialized rehabilitation, and support a long-term strategy for health infrastructure.

7.3.4 Resilience, informal repair, and self-repair

For the purpose of reparations, resilience can be considered as the process whereby capacity to adapt successfully in the face of adversity is strengthened.[169] Fineman recognizes that resilience can be accrued by giving 'an individual . . . the means and ability to recover from harm, setbacks and the misfortunes that affect our lives'.[170] Being resilient is the outcome of the resilience process and can materialize in a variety of ways.[171] A resilient outcome may be positive health-related phenomena for a person or population, academic accomplishments, or greater self-esteem. Some reparation measures have become empowerment projects emulating a sense that victims are in control of their own recovery.[172] However, resilience is at risk of becoming an empty term if it is not accompanied by other measures aimed at restoring the health of the person after adversity.[173] Resilience should not be equated with the ultimate aim of reparations, as doing so places too much emphasis on making victims productive or reduces the process to a box-ticking exercise.[174]

Resilience can be used politically to undermine rights to reparation if there is too much emphasis placed on the individual capacity to adapt. Resilience's place within reparations can be manipulated to suit the aims of powerful actors and place the repair responsibility on the victim rather than the state or perpetrator. Resilience can be used as a means to 'responsibilize' victims into coping with the harms of CRSV and even preventing its reoccurrence which speaks to neoliberal agendas that reduces state responsibility.[175] Clark highlights the social ecologies

[169] Ann S Masten, Pathways to Integrated Resilience Science, *Psychological Inquiry* 26 (2015) 187–196.
[170] Fineman, n 15, p146.
[171] Van Breda, n 113, p4.
[172] Rachel Killean and Luke Moffett, What's in a Name? 'Reparations' at the Extraordinary Chambers in the Courts of Cambodia, *Melbourne Journal of International Law* 21(1) (2020) 115–143.
[173] Van Breda, n 113, p2.
[174] See Max Counter, Producing Victimhood: Landmines, Reparations, and Law in Colombia, *Antipode* 50(1) (2018) 122–141.
[175] Alison Howell, Resilience as Enhancement: Governmentality and Political Economy Beyond 'Responsibilisation', *Politics* 35(1) (2015) 67–71.

of resilience in CRSV by focusing on the dynamic connectivities individuals have with their social and physical environments.[176] This aligns partly with post-traumatic growth conceptualizations that appreciate how changes in relationships, including spirituality, can amount to positive growth. Unfortunately, Clark does not give space to the meaning of vulnerability and its relationship to resilience, nor to self-relationships. Progressive interpretations of resilience acknowledge that it can exist on multiple levels which are interconnected.[177]

Despite the great subtlety in the literature on resilience over the years in capturing the intersection of individual and structural variables,[178] there remains a strong sense in the field that victims of sexual violence are expected to 'overcome' their harm particularly where the 'correct' social conditions are in place.[179] Some victims who receive social support from donated funds and are accepted into families become the focus of 'a good news story' in the media which fits the narrative of the resilient victim. As one medical professional told me, 'a journalist will come and interview her about gender-based violence and war victims, there is 1 in 100 of these success stories, but that is the one they focus on'.[180]

It can be useful to look beyond official reparative processes to consider informal and self-repair as means to understand vulnerability and resilience.[181] Informal repair intends to distinguish those assistance or community-based measures aimed at acknowledging or alleviating victims or affected communities' suffering from reparations. Self-repair is distinguished from informal repair in that the former comes from within those who suffer, whereas the latter requires external involvement and support for civil initiatives not provided by the state. These distinctions are intended to better discern the agency of victims and affected communities, the limitations of such measures, and the tensions between them and reparations. Self-repair can also be seen as a process through official and unofficial channels for victims to find their own resolution of the past. In the case countries, victims and affected communities have developed their own processes to recover, inform, acknowledge, and memorialize the harm they have suffered and to some extent shame the state for failing to act or resist its approach to dealing with the past, such

[176] Janine Natalya Clark, *Resilience, Conflict-Related Sexual Violence and Transitional Justice: A Social-Ecological Framing.* Routledge, (2023), p30, pp58–59.

[177] Christophe Béné et al, Resilience: New Utopia or New Tyranny? Reflection About the Potentials and Limits of the Concept of Resilience in Relation to Vulnerability Reduction Programmes, *IDS Working Papers* 404 (2012) 1–61.; Nicola McKinley et al, Resilience in Medical Doctors: A Systematic Review, *Postgraduate Medical Journal* 95(1121) (2019) 140–147.

[178] Bourgois et al, n 153; and Nicole L Johnson and MaryBeth Grove, Why Us? Toward an Understanding of Bisexual Women's Vulnerability for and Negative Consequences of Sexual Violence, *Journal of Bisexuality* 17(4) (2017) 435–450.

[179] See Maria José dos Reis, Maria Helena Baena de Moraes Lopes, and Maria José Duarte Osis, 'It's Much Worse Than Dying': The Experiences of Female Victims of Sexual Violence, *Journal of Clinical Nursing* 26 (2016) 2353–2361.

[180] U7, Lira, Uganda, July 2018.

[181] See Sunneva Gilmore and Luke Moffett, Finding a Way to Live with the Past: Self-Repair, Informal Repair and Reparations in Transitional Justice, *Journal of Law and Society* 48(3) (2021) 455–480.

as annual memorial prayers at massacre sites, memorial quilts, or self-supporting victim groups. For some victims, being able to speak to a friend, family member, or counsellor about their suffering helped to repair the emotional loss. One Ugandan victim said that at times it was easier to 'open up' and speak about common challenges with victims of similar violations, such as sexual violence.[182] However, not everyone has this social support, and many instead face further suffering and isolation.[183]

However, the creation of support networks can be powerful in their impact. A focus group with Colombian CRSV victims reflected on their experience of reparations. They had received compensation and were offered psychological support, but they found that coming together as a women's network had helped them the most. As the victims remarked:

> The network that has been very helpful, the program we are participating in has been a great companion, we have grown, our self-esteem is slightly better, we feel important, we don't feel guilty for something that shouldn't have happened to us, something that money can't take back, nobody can take it away. Because the trace is there, the mark is there, the pain, I have nothing left to say, I have no words to explain what this feels like.

Second speaker:

> For me, reparation is fixing, it is like a little cup has been broken, and what has happened is that they have put glue in the edges, but the damage is still there.... All of us, we live in vulnerable conditions. The State should guarantee decent living conditions, but for us this hasn't happened. Many women got an apartment, they told them here, *this is your apartment*. But right afterwards, they put next to her a man from the paramilitary groups, a man from the FARC. So this is a terrible social problem.

Third speaker:

> Some even have their own perpetrator as a neighbour. My perpetrator lives in the same condo. That is not going to repair us. That doesn't repair our dignity, it improves our living conditions, but this process has been one step ahead, two steps back.

[182] UG05, Gulu, Uganda, July 2018.

[183] Simon Robins, Towards Victim-Centred Transitional Justice: Understanding the Needs of Families of the Disappeared in Postconflict Nepal, *International Journal of Transitional Justice* 5(1) (2011) 75–98, pp88–89.

Fourth speaker:

> Well, for me, reparation arrived very late, because only after 15 years they asked me if I needed a psychologist, asking what happened to me . . . and I had to be in silence, all of the suffering, hushed, because you don't want to tell this to anyone, because nobody in my family knew, not my children, no one, I was repressed, I fell into depression and anxiety, I still live like this, I still do.

Religion or spirituality can also be a form of informal repair, in that a victim is no longer socially isolated, but has their suffering acknowledged by the community, even if it is not by a responsible actor. In Uganda, medical practitioners who offered to pray with a victim added a further level of care and compassion, as the doctors or nurses were acting in spiritual solidarity with them.[184] Informal repair can also include traditional medicine or 'home remedies' that victims used to treat suffering, as well as massages to deal with chronic pain, due to the high cost or distance to hospitals.[185] This can fit into indigenous or tribal groups' cosmovision and their understanding of being connected to the land and nature, and the need to maintain equilibrium, with time not being linear but rather circular in their experience of suffering. Moreover, it also speaks to a more collective understanding of repairing harm and identity practised by indigenous groups, rather than simply focusing on individual consequences. As such, informal repair can be a means through which victims emphasize collective action and empowerment while resisting state narratives on what resilience and self-sufficiency post-CRSV looks like.

Strong, resilient victims are not simply the way forward; coping mechanisms can sometimes last only for a time. Self-repair is about finding ways or forms for victims to reconcile themselves with their past suffering. This may work for some victims and survivors, or only for a limited time without external support, but the range of vulnerabilities posed by age, disability, further traumatizing events, and psychological trauma can present challenges. That said, when reparations are implemented, they have to be appreciated for their longevity and sustainability in the life of the victim, which may involve dependency on the state. Vulnerability and suffering can be effectively instrumentalized by victims to morally motivate and shame society to redress their harms,[186] but it can also be used by the state to normalize service provision to them as dependents. Seeing victims only as powerless and vulnerable obscures their potential for resilience and their capacity to exercise 'agency, resistance and defiance'.[187]

[184] U6, Lira, Uganda, July 2018.

[185] C7, Bogotá, Colombia, September 2018.

[186] VM Meredith, Victim Identity and Respect for Human Dignity: A Terminological Analysis', *International Review of the Red Cross* 91(874) (2009) 259–277, pp261–262.

[187] Eilish Rooney and Fionnuala Ní Aoláin, Transitional Justice from the Margins: Intersections of Identities, Power and Human Rights, *International Journal of Transitional Justice* 12(1) (2018) 1–8, p3; and C Lindsey, *Women Facing War*, ICRC (2015) 28–30.

At the same time, the responsiveness of the state to vulnerable individuals and groups may risk stifling them from building community and individual resilience, by being subjected to the political whims of the state supporting them.[188] While dependency is often stigmatized or seen as something negative in conservative political discourses, it is 'inherent in the human condition'.[189] There is a clear role for the state to be more than just responsive, but actively involved the in the provision of services and support to minimize dependence.[190] Independence is achieved by providing basic resources to a person enabling them to make choices unconstrained by inequalities.[191] It is apparent that in the case of victims of CRSV in Colombia this is a complex process that requires navigating difficult social and interpersonal terrains, within families and between victims and their victimizers. At the same time, victim groups can play a key role in supporting victims to not only claim redress, but to have a sense of belonging and solidarity with other similarly situated individuals. This broader appreciation of repair, being both self and informal, can complement, not substitute, reparations.

In a similar vein, reparations need to appreciate the vulnerability in resilience, especially when reparations may materialize many years after the injuries were sustained. For instance, severity-based compensation models can be a way of distributing finite resources to those inherently vulnerable due to severe disability, including from CRSV. It may be interpreted that victims are penalized if they do not exhibit symptoms of a certain severity, and the scheme fails to compensate those who successfully self-manage or attenuate their disability over time. This can be particularly problematic for psychological harm, where resilience—understood as adaptive coping—can paradoxically lead to under-recognition of enduring distress. Thus, the 'resilient' victim may be revictimized or dismissed for having coped or relied on self-repair or informal repair strategies. Medicalized definitions of harm prioritize quantifiable criteria, yet many victims—especially of CRSV—lack permanent physical injuries (see Chapter 3) or have never sought formal psychological care, especially when treatment options were limited at the time. Victims may be doubly disadvantaged by severity-based models, owing to stigma that suppresses evidence of CRSV and shame surrounding mental health. More recently, some may refuse assessment out of fear of retraumatization or mistrust of mainstream medicine and state institutions. A contextualized approach ensures that lack of medico-legal documentation is not a barrier to reparation, and that victims' chosen paths to personal redress are respected while the social and

188 Fineman, n 15, p134.

189 Martha Fineman, Cracking the Foundational Myths: Independence, Autonomy, and Self-Sufficiency, *American University Journal of Gender Social Policy and Law* 8 (2000) 13–29, p18.

190 ibid p26.

191 ibid pp25–26.

moral harm is acknowledged, perhaps through supplementary criteria (eg quality of life).[192]

A medico-legal approach can help in understanding the wide array of trauma responses that can inhibit a person from receiving reparation for harm. Drawing on psychodynamic psychotherapy,[193] a person may adopt defence mechanisms—such as avoidance, denial, or dissociation—to protect themselves from further harm caused by CRSV trauma. These defences then become barriers to applying for reparations: avoidance may manifest as refusal to undergo a psychological assessment; denial can obscure the link between CRSV and subsequent mental health impacts; and dissociation may disrupt coherent testimony. In cases where victims have a psychological diagnosis as a result of CRSV and there is concern that it may impair their capacity to make informed financial decisions, appropriate safeguards and supported decision-making mechanisms should be implemented.[194] There is a risk that recipients of large financial reparations may become vulnerable to exploitation, financial mismanagement, or further distress. Therefore, reparations could be more cognizant of the impacts of trauma and consider how the option for complementing therapies could be integrated into reparation schemes alongside the role of other actors (eg healthcare professionals) not traditionally involved in transitional justice.

7.4 Conclusion

There is added value in substantively incorporating vulnerability into reparations. On a normative and practical level vulnerability provides a framework to tackle challenges of delivering reparations for CRSV, and helps to better appreciate victims' needs and struggles in benefiting from such measures. Vulnerability can gain greater traction in reparations by being sensitive to the situation harm occurs and evolves in, the potential for secondary harm, and the ways in which vulnerability can be misused—infusing victims with further notions of passivity and powerlessness. Reparations need to set aside the labelling problem with vulnerability that sensationalizes the suffering of some groups to the detriment of others. It can also be a mistake for reparations to prioritize traditional categories of vulnerability, missing other pressing needs individuals encounter.[195] This has been brought

[192] While forensic examinations were possible during the Troubles, structures to facilitate a holistic trauma-informed, multi-sector approach—such as the Northern Ireland Sexual Assault Referral Centre—only opened in 2013.

[193] Jonathan Shedler, The Efficacy of Psychodynamic Psychotherapy, *The American psychologist* 65(2) (2010) 98–109.

[194] Eilionoir Flynn and Anna Arstein-Kerslake, Legislating Personhood: Realising the Right to Support in Exercising Legal Capacity, *International Journal of Law in Context* 10(1) (2014) 81–104.

[195] Justin Oakley, Diagnosing True Virtue? Remote Scenarios, Warranted Virtue Attributions, and Virtuous Medical Practice, *Theoretical Medicine and Bioethics Philosophy of Medical Research and Practice* 37(1) (2016) 85–96.

into sharp effect in humanitarian efforts focused on women and girls, over a more complex contextually relevant set of masculine and feminine vulnerabilities that contribute to the commission of sexual violence or exacerbate its resultant harms. Discretionary categorization may risk reifying groups as vulnerable and exposing them to new risks.[196] Therefore, it may be important for reparations to challenge the acceptability of vulnerable labelling if greater protections or repair mechanisms are not provided.[197] Imposing vulnerability also risks overlooking victims' resilience understood as their capacities to positively cope and the innovative ways victims informally repair on their own or through grassroots work. Women in particular who have suffered conflict-related sexual violence have formed organizations in Colombia to support each other, resist such threats, and provide improved medical rehabilitation.[198] That said, victims may pursue dangerous pathways to cope with harms and meet their basic needs, such as unregulated sex work to feed their dependents. This calls for a structural vulnerability lens to be integrated into how victims are left to contend with their situation before reparations are granted.

While vulnerability can be overwhelmingly broad and complex, categorizing it in inherent and situational sources in the present and future are useful for its application to reparations for CRSV. Drawing on health philosophy and rehabilitation/ethics, reparations may aim for a restored equilibrium between a person's abilities as a result of the harm incurred (if any impairment) and the opportunity to pursue personal goals.[199] Vulnerability reveals how it can be more difficult to fulfil the right to reparation for some individuals over others. This may be due to the severity of current harms they face as a result of sexual violence, or embedded cultural beliefs (like patriarchal) that shape future harms victims are at risk of, or practical barriers to participation in reparations. I argue that disregarding vulnerability's theoretical and practical application may mean reparations lose a 'moral safeguard'.[200] However, reparations must have an end point, and responses arising from vulnerability should centre on fostering resilience, anticipating future needs, and addressing wider structural determinants of vulnerability through a mixture of actions. Under this premise, reparation preserves and encourages the agency where possible of persons considered vulnerable to particular harms, rather than denying them genuine participation in the name of protection. The violation legitimizes the right to reparation, and vulnerability in its broad and diverse form can enrich the ways in which harm is captured, understood, and responded to.

[196] Christina Zarowsky, Slim Haddad, and Vinh-Kim Nguyen, Beyond 'Vulnerable Groups': Contexts and Dynamics of Vulnerability, *Global Health Promotion* 20(Supp 1) (2013) 3–9, p5.

[197] For more on the problem of accepted 'vulnerabilization', see Mianna Lotz, Vulnerability and Resilience: A Critical Nexus, *Theoretical Medicine and Bioethics Philosophy of Medical Research and Practice* 37(1) (2016) 45–59, pp45–46.

[198] Maitane Arnoso Martínez et al, *Universitas Psychologica* 16(3) (2017) 1–12.

[199] The ability to carry out a desired goal rather than being successful at it is arguably as meaningful for the person. See Bluhm, n 22, p160.

[200] DeMarco, n 50, p83.

On a final note, vulnerability can reveal the positive dimensions of reparations being interconnected and interdependent to other assistance and development measures. Reparations' relationship with other social and transitional justice mechanisms redressing harm requires consideration of what is feasible and possible within a given context. As discussed, victims and their allies create new pathways of coping while waiting for formal repair if this is desired. This draws on the relational nature of vulnerability, where harms and responsibilities are shaped by social relationships, and a variety of actors can feel responsible to respond—such as through informal repair or self-coping.[201] Reparations are innately strained by the breadth of harms they seek to redress, but vulnerability encourages a framework in which to understand the complexities of harm and inform the ways we respond. When not conceptualized in a narrow or reductive fashion, vulnerability challenges assumptions around sexual victimization that can be productive to achieving modest transformative aims. A vulnerability approach to reparations is a demanding one but gives attention to how harms are playing out in the lives of victims. This may lead to different, greater, and/or prompt efforts to satisfy a level of repair that takes into account the health of the victim. It may not be possible or desirable to return victims to their baseline prior to the violence, which can be made clearer through a vulnerability lens, but it equally considers what is necessary to strive for equity and reduce harms.

[201] Goodin, n 7, pxi.

8

Conclusion - From Fracture to Function: Golden Seams of Redress

Conflict-related sexual violence remains a pervasive part of conflicts around the world. Despite progress in the evolution of reparations to tackle such violence a more nuanced approach is needed to redress the multifaceted harms. This book has drawn upon fieldwork across three diverse sites as well as academic literature to provide a more comprehensive framework for remedying conflict-related sexual violence (CRSV). Given the serious physical, psychological, cultural, and social consequences of sexual violence for victims and their families, I have argued that the responsibility to ensure that reparations—designed to help repair some of those consequences—are fit for purpose lies with healthcare practitioners, lawyers, civil society actors, and reparation officials alike. Given its pervasiveness in conflicted and authoritarian contexts, CRSV is likely to remain a priority policy area for the international community, donors, and transitional justice practitioners for the foreseeable future.

To recap, the book drew upon elements of the scholarship from transitional justice, restorative justice, and medicine as key fields which have helped shape reparations-related research. Transitional justice and reparations are framed around how such measures can assist in addressing the rights and needs of victim, whereas restorative justice also includes a focus on the responsibility of those who have committed harms (both state and non-state actors) to make amends to those they have harmed. As I argued in Chapter 2, there has been relatively little analysis of the intersection of medicine and these fields, which represents a significant gap in the literature. I argued, in particular, that the intersection of transitional justice, restorative justice, and medicine can shed important light on the ethics of care, the continuity of treatment and support in the absence of justice, and on how to ensure that victims receive more holistic, and long-term treatment. Taking a medico-legal approach to CRSV also addresses the importance of health and quality of life as valuable outcomes, which requires a deeper understanding of the harm caused by such violations and measures to rehabilitate them. However, I also argued that efforts to 'repair' victims are not enough. Reparations must be accompanied by attention to transform the social, political, and cultural contexts which produced such CRSV in the first place.

In Chapter 3 I critically examined the range and pervasiveness of harms that can result from CRSV for victims, their families, and communities. I also explored the

Redressing Rape in War. Sunneva Gilmore, Oxford University Press.
DOI: 10.1093/9780198919735.003.0008

particular impact of stigma and highlighted how it impinges on victims' identities in their social life with family, friends, and communities and the imaginative ways in which some have navigated such harm and stigma. Some of these resilience-related themes were expanded in Chapters 4 and 7, which explored identity and vulnerability, respectively. This chapter underscored that physical injuries from sexual violence may not be present, highlighting the complexities of forensic assessments and challenging assumptions on resultant harm. It explored the role of forensic medicine for conflict-related sexual violence, demonstrating how medico-legal documentation supports claims-making for reparations and can help identify the specific needs of affected groups. It addressed both the evidentiary and reparative dimensions that shape responses to CRSV. In essence, I argued that reparations have not fully engaged with the lived bodily harms of sexual violence, which can be complex and overlap with other forms of violence as well as conflict-related or structural harms. I then sought to address this oversight by systematically analysing harms through a medical lens which captured the variety of physical, psychological, and social harms that can arise from sexual violence. I then argued that the complexity of these harms underlined the limitations of a 'one-size fits all' approach to reparations for victims of CRSV. I further contended that having a deeper understanding of victims' harm helps to highlight the challenges faced by victims of CRSV, including their relationship with their own body, as well as societal norms of ableism, sexual relationships, and innocence.

In Chapter 4, I focused upon the complex intersection between identity and CRSV for those who have suffered such sexual violence, those who work with them as transitional justice practitioners, and those who treat them as health-care practitioners. I examined the meaning of the term 'victim', both in terms of its connotations of passivity and silence, and as a basis for legal and political claims-making. I then tracked how the term 'survivor' has emerged as a counter to the negative associations of victim across the sites of my fieldwork and the particular meaning of survival as the basis for reparations after CRSV. I also interrogated the political and sociological term 'patient' and the explicit and implicit power-relations it connotes, not least regarding patient–doctor interactions. I argued that while considering those who have suffered CRSV as patients has value in encouraging a more comprehensive understanding of their harm, it is also a politically loaded term. I concluded that reparation practices need to be more cognizant of the implications of internally and externally prescribed identities of persons who have suffered CRSV. This specifically entails considering how identity, harms, and opportunities for reparations can be created or missed depending on the use of certain identities, such as victim, survivor, and/or patient. By better understanding and catering to multifaceted identities of individuals affected by CRSV, I argued that efforts to provide reparations for such violations can be enhanced, including improving gender and sexual sensitivity and confronting unaddressed taboos.

Chapters 5 and 6 set out the historical development of reparations for CRSV along with current principles and practice which underpin their delivery. I charted the legal developments in the reparations field before regional human rights courts and domestic reparation programmes and the ways in which the law has been driven by the activism of victims, feminists, and broader civil society groups. I argued that this has been particularly manifest in the articulation of clear legal principles on the rights of women and girls harmed as a result of sexual violence (evidenced through the Nairobi Declaration) and the evolution of a broader vision of change through transformative reparations. I also argued that while such increased gender awareness in the legal sphere is of course to be welcomed, this transformative approach to reparations is the most effective route to challenging the political, social, and cultural causes of such abuses in the first place. A gender-sensitive and transformative approach to reparations for CRSV may be a way to overcome or mitigate the social and political stigmatization of victims through education and public acknowledgement, which (as Chapter 7 further develops) requires coordinated efforts beyond reparations.

In Chapter 6 I expanded on these themes. While traditionally the focus of most reparation measures has been on compensation, more recent scholarship has concentrated on a more ambitious understanding of reparations as measures of satisfaction and guarantees of non-repetition. I argued in particular that the notion of rehabilitation should be given more attention as the basis for a more holistic approach to healthcare for victims of CRSV in societies emerging from conflict. Having highlighted the knowledge gaps in transitional justice regarding the nature of sexual violence and its relationship to harm on the human body, I argued that the notion of rehabilitation offers a route to recognizing the role of reparations in improving victims' quality of physical and psychological health and their capacity to fulfil their potential as citizens in their respective societies. I explore the mismatch between regional court-ordered reparations and domestic reparation programmes on rehabilitation which makes it difficult to establish a standard of healthcare and rehabilitation in post-conflict societies that can meet this broader understanding of reparations. In this chapter, I also contended that rehabilitation requires a shift in vision towards seeing victims as not simply vulnerable but functional, and rehabilitation as part of the process of helping victims move away from their suffering.

In Chapter 7 I examined the intersection between reparations and vulnerability. Amongst the issues I explored were the ways that healthcare practitioners can themselves cause further harm to victims of sexual violence, and even be complicit in violations, for example by performing forced sterilization as in Peru or collaborating with armed groups around forced contraception. I cautioned that reparation processes can be potential sites of vulnerability for victims of CRSV and for those assisting in reparation claims and implementation, thus calling for greater safeguards and for reparations to pay heed to potential vulnerability. I also contended that the notion of vulnerability can shed light on victims' lived experience in terms of the passage of time as well as the ways in which victims can exercise agency and resilience despite their circumstances and suffering. Moreover, acknowledging vulnerability and promoting resilience are, I suggested, an appropriate framework for developing more attuned reparations programmes to remedy the harm of CRSV.

8.1 Moving Forward

It bears repeating that, in many instances, the implementation of reparations for sexual violence does not fully meet the needs of victims of CRSV. This was clear to me when conducting my fieldwork across the three case studies. For example, victims in Uganda continue to struggle just for legal identity for children born of war. In Colombia, despite the ambition of the reparations programme in general, the roll out of healthcare benefits as reparations to rural victims remains painfully slow. In Peru, victims of CRSV continue to be embroiled in seemingly interminable litigation against former President Fujimori and the Peruvian state for its forced sterilization programme.[1] As these case studies illustrate, comprehensively delivering on the promise of reparations for victims of conflict-related violence requires a broad engagement, ownership, and political will from the state, civil society, and broader society. In reality, in many post-conflict societies, victims of sexual violence continue to be silenced, scorned, and stigmatized as a result of engrained misogynistic cultures. While we need to be careful about overselling the transformative potential of reparations per se, I would argue that properly attuned reparations for victims of CRSV can make a significant difference in the lives of those victims.

There is a clear linkage between different types of identity adapted by individuals affected by CRSV to survive the experience and as a basis for claims-making with regards to reparations and service provision. Of course, identities are not static and may change over time or be used concurrently by individuals affected by CRSV depending on their audience or the particular self-image of victims at a certain time. Awareness of the complex ways in which victims respond to CRSV has important implications for stigma and transformative processes. For example, reparations programmes are often premised on the need for victims to 'speak up' and make a claim. However, in some contexts, speaking up may expose victims to risks including social and communal stigma. As a social, cultural, and moral experience,

[1] In October 2024, the UN Committee on the Elimination of Discrimination against Women found that such a policy amounted to crimes against humanity and recommended Peru to implement full reparations for such victims. See *María Elena Carbajal Cepeda et al. v Peru*, CEDAW/C/89/D/170/2021, 4 October 2024.

stigma impacts the lives of victims, their families and communities and it can inhibit victims from coming forward to seek healthcare or reparations. A greater awareness of the effects of stigma on victims of CRSV amongst health professionals is key to the ethic of care which must underpin the delivery of reparations to address such violations. It is not enough to simply place a purple armband on victims of CRSV to distinguish them as requiring extra care. Rather, it requires specific training, protocols, and monitoring of healthcare professionals to navigate the effects of stigma during conflict and in its aftermath, and to ensure victims of CRSV have adequate treatment to mitigate the worst consequences of sexual violence.

There is a clear role for a medico-legal approach to transitional justice and specifically to reparations for conflict-related sexual violence. A medico-legal approach brings three benefits in approaching transitional justice and reparations. First, such an approach appreciates that a wider group of actors play a key role in supporting and providing care to victims, but can also cause further harm, whether through direct involvement in violations, such as forced sterilization, complicity, such as supplying armed groups in the carrying out of forced contraception, or secondary victimization in treating victims unfavourably. Healthcare practitioners need to be critically reflexive in both appreciating the public position of trust they can often enjoy, and the need to maintain neutrality and ensure adherence to medical best practice and ethics so as not to contribute to the continuation of suffering. Second, the intersection of repair across medicine and law with regards to reparations brings together a useful synergy in the measure of rehabilitation that, through a medico-legal approach, can more fully appreciate the continuity of care, improve quality of life in a comprehensive and sustained way, and focus on outcomes and goals in achieving some sort of normality and dignified quality of life. This rests on understanding the harm, what loss has occurred, and what this means for moving forward with repair. Third, a medico-legal approach in appreciating the victim as a patient, as well as incorporating vulnerability, takes a more holistic view to repairing victims harm that is not limited to the instance of claiming reparations, but takes a more long-term approach to recovery and well-being.

In relation to operationalizing a medico-legal approach with regards to the implementation of reparations programmes there are three key takeaways. First, medical personnel should be trained in identifying, documenting, and treating sexual violence, including training on discrimination, stigma, and unconscious bias. As discussed, healthcare practitioners can often be the first person a victim of sexual violence comes into contact with, and their interaction can shape the extent to which the victim can avail themselves of repair. Second, efforts should be made to incorporate healthcare practitioners into the design and delivery of reparations. This can include being involved in steering committees, specialist working groups to shed light on the harm, educational development and training, to even developing specific protocols in the treatment of victims of conflict-related sexual violence that can be integrated into public and private healthcare settings. Third, healthcare practitioners can be important allies to victims beyond the provision of treatment and support, offering solidarity for social and spiritual wellbeing that often transcends the legal and political concerns of traditional transitional justice mechanisms.

Reparations need to be framed in ways that see those harmed by sexual violence as more than just victims. They are also agents with multiple and intersecting identities and potential. Seeing victims as individuals, their identity, and bodies, can better help craft appropriate reparations. Understanding the harm and the continuing conditions victims live with can better tailor reparations to have a meaningful impact in ameliorating and remedying the continuing consequences of sexual violence. Reparations should of course include measures designed to repair the harms done as much as possible, but also to help create the circumstances where their potential agency can be maximized. Ultimately reparations are just one part of the puzzle in responding to conflict-related sexual violence, which also requires a range of measures including prosecutions, truth recovery, guarantees of non-repetition, transformation of structural violence, and repair of the relational and social harm caused that reparations by themselves are unable to fully grapple with. As such, reparations can modestly serve to vindicate victims' experiences as wrongful, support their path to recovery, and dispel the cloud of stigma that lingers around such violations.

Index

For the benefit of digital users, indexed terms that span two pages (e.g., 52–53) may, on occasion, appear on only one of those pages.